SCHOLASTIC

GO MATHS

Ruchi Mehta

Course Book

Level 6

Cover design by Kavita C. Dikshit

Published by Scholastic India Pvt. Ltd.
A subsidiary of Scholastic Inc., New York, 10012 (USA)
Publishers since 1920, with international operations in Canada, Australia, New Zealand, the United Kingdom, India, and Hong Kong.

For information regarding permission, write to:
Scholastic India Pvt. Ltd.
A-27, Ground Floor, Bharti Sigma Centre
Infocity-1, Sector 34, Gurgaon (Haryana) - 122001
Email: education@scholastic.co.in

Typeset by: Access to Solutions

Series editor: Sonia Kapoor

First edition: 2010
Reprinted: 2011 (thrice), 2012 (twice), 2013 (twice), 2014 (sixth time), 2015 (twice), 2016 (thrice), 2017 (thrice), 2018 (twice), 2019 (thrice), 2020, 2021, 2022, 2023, 2024, 2025, 2026

ISBN-13 978-81-8477-494-8
Printed in India

Contents

Introduction

Go Maths is a graded series of middle school mathematics course books that have been authored by a highly respected and experienced mathematics educator. The series conforms to the NCERT syllabus and the books are provided with tools for Continuous and Comprehensive Evaluation (CCE). The objective of these books is to move away from the rote method of learning and associate the knowledge gained with everyday life experiences.

These books are designed to help students learn a wide range of mathematical concepts including the number system, algebra, geometry, mensuration, data handling and much more. Each topic has a set of challenging and imaginative activities.

The *Go Maths* series is comprehensive and rigorous. It has been created based on the following beliefs:

Learning through involvement

Students learn through involvement and substantive communication between teachers and students, as well as between students and students. This helps students internalise and acquire new skills

Learning through interaction

Students build their mathematical understanding by interacting with the world around them through a range of engaging learning experiences using real-life contexts to explore mathematical ideas. Quality teaching and learning is required for students to develop a rich conceptual understanding of mathematical ideas.

Learning through thinking critically

Learning should be as much 'minds on' as it is 'hands on'. Students should be encouraged to think critically.

Learning through practice

Skills should be practiced after they have developed from deep conceptual understanding.

Some of the unique features of this series are:

- Mathematical concepts introduced in a simple and concise manner and aid in developing sharp calculation skills and clear concepts.
- Summary **Highlights** at the end of each chapter and **Rewind** after every two chapters to recapitulate and reinforce concepts and formulae.
- Several practice exercises, **Test Yourself** and a **Model question paper** to assess mathematical proficiency with a focus on confidence, speed and accuracy.
- Enrichment material and **HOTS** questions for curious minds and fast finishers.
- **Maths Lab Activity** to strengthen basic mathematical concepts.
- **Alert**, a section emphasising the important points, and brainteasers/jokes in every chapter.

The *Go Maths* series provides an innovative and interactive approach to learning mathematics. The emphasis on critical thinking ensures that students learn concepts and basic operations with great thoroughness and clarity.

Ruchi Mehta is a post graduate in mathematics with thirty-five years of teaching experience. She started her career at St Joseph's College, Allahabad and has taught at Mount Saint Mary's, New Delhi, for thirty-one years. Post retirement, she is a visiting faculty at DPS, Gurgaon and Mount Saint Mary's, New Delhi.

Knowing our Numbers

CHAPTER 1

Let us recall the magic of the digits 0, 1, 2, 3, 4, 5, 6, 7, 8 and 9. There are just ten digits but we can make wonders using them.

When you learn counting, you begin with one-digit numbers. The next step is counting two-digit numbers that begin at 10 and end at 99. By this stage you must be familiar with numbers having five digits. Let us look at the pattern followed by the smallest and largest numbers made of different number of digits.

Table 1.1

Digits	Smallest Number	Largest Number
One-digit numbers	1	9
Two-digit numbers	10	99
Three-digit numbers	100	999
Four-digit numbers	1,000	9,999
Five-digit numbers	10,000	99,999

Can you see the pattern followed by the smallest numbers of different digits? It is one followed by zeroes. The pattern followed by the largest numbers is even simpler. The largest digit has all the nines.

The total numbers that can be counted beginning with the smallest and ending with the largest numbers would be the difference between the two numbers followed by adding 1 to it.

These numbers can be written in groups of ones, tens, hundreds, thousands and ten thousands. By placing appropriate commas, it becomes easy to read and write numbers.

Example 1: 2,468 Two thousand four hundred and sixty-eight.

Example 2: 32,468 Thirty-two thousand four hundred and sixty-eight.

Ascending and Descending Numbers

Ascending means to go up. The arrangement of numbers from the smallest number to the largest number is called the ascending order.

Example:

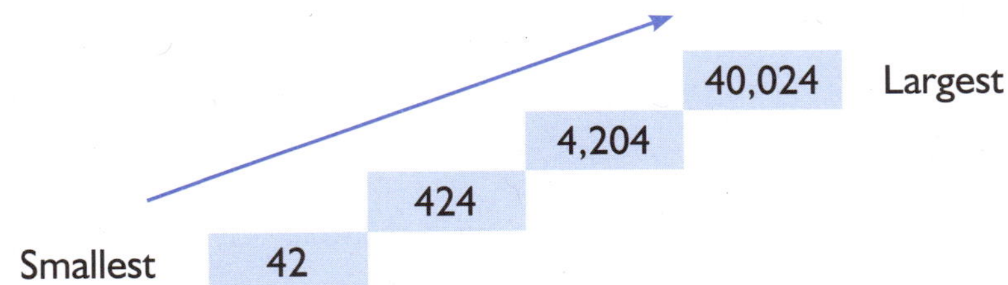

Descending means to come down.

The arrangement of numbers from the largest number to the smallest number is called the descending order.

Example:

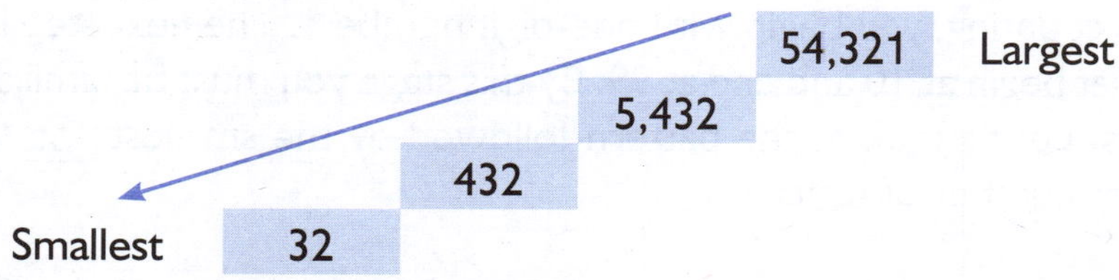

Place Value and Face Value

Usually, the location or place of a home, a school or a park is fixed. In the same way, the place for a number is fixed when we write it. Each number has two values: face value and place value.

The **face value** of a digit is the value of the digit itself. It *never* changes.

The **place value** of a digit defines its place or position in a number.

Let us clarify the concepts using the following example. Consider the number 1,42,680.

1,42,680

The place value ( ) of the number 4 is ten thousand, and the place value ( ) of the number 6 is hundred.

The face value of 4 is 4 and the face value of 6 is 6.

While the place value of a digit can change depending on its position or place in a number, its face value remains constant.

Expanded Form

When a number is written as the sum of the place values of all the digits of the number, then the number is said to be in its expanded form.

Example 1: 4,582 = 4,000 + 500 + 80 + 2

Example 2: 45,827 = 40,000 + 5,000 + 800 + 20 + 7

Example 3: 4,58,279 = 4,00,000 + 50,000 + 8,000 + 200 + 70 + 9

Successor

The number that comes just *after* a given number is called its successor.

It is easy to write this number. Just add 1 to the given number and you get its successor.

Example 1: The successor of 2,468 is 2,469.

$2{,}468 + 1 = 2{,}469$

Example 2: The successor of 40,243 is 40,244.

$40{,}243 + 1 = 40{,}244$

Predecessor

The number that comes just *before* a given number is called its predecessor.

It is easy to write this number also. Just subtract 1 from the given number and you get its predecessor.

Example 1: The predecessor of 2,465 is 2,464.

$2{,}465 - 1 = 2{,}464$

Example 2: The predecessor of 24,658 is 24,657.

$24{,}658 - 1 = 24{,}657$

Practice Exercise 1.1

1. Write the smallest five-digit numbers with the given digits, using each digit only once.

   a. 4, 9, 8, 7, 2 b. 1, 3, 5, 9, 7 c. 6, 8, 3, 4, 2

2. Write the largest five-digit numbers with the given digits, using each digit only once.

   a. 1, 3, 5, 9, 7 b. 4, 9, 8, 7, 2 c. 6, 8, 3, 4, 2

3. Write the successor of each of the following numbers.

   a. 24,781 b. 52,789 c. 98,700

4. Write the predecessor of each of the following numbers.

   a. 98,700 b. 24,781 c. 52,789

5. Write the following numbers in ascending order.

   62,345 24,789 22,199 98,912 56,482

6. Write the following numbers in descending order.

   12,345   23,451   54,321   45,123   31,245

7. Write the following numbers in the expanded form.

   a. 96,720   b. 81,945   c. 65,483

8. Write the following expanded forms in the standard form.

   a. 80,000 + 7,000 + 500 + 40 + 2

   b. 10,000 + 5,000 + 600 + 30 + 9

   c. 60,000 + 9,000 + 300 + 20 +7

9. Write the place value and face value of the underlined digits in the following numbers.

   a. 48,713   place value ____________

   face value ____________

   b. 47,192   place value ____________

   face value ____________

   c. 78,963   place value ____________

   face value ____________

10. Answer the following questions in the space provided.

    a. Which is the largest one-digit number? ____________

    b. Which is the smallest two-digit number? ____________

    c. Which is the smallest three-digit number? ____________

    d. Which is the largest four-digit number? ____________

    e. Which is the smallest five-digit number? ____________

    f. Add the five numbers that you have obtained. ____________

    g. Write the addendum answer in words. ____________

    ____

Larger Numbers

The smallest five-digit number is 10,000 and the largest is 99,999. Now, if we add 1 to the largest five-digit number, we get its successor, which is a six-digit number.

$$\begin{array}{r} 99999 \\ +1 \\ \hline 1,00,000 \\ \hline \end{array}$$

This is the smallest six-digit number. It is one lakh.

The largest six-digit number is 9,99,999.

If we add 1 to it, we will get the smallest seven-digit number.

$$\begin{array}{r} 9,99,999 \\ +1 \\ \hline 10,00,000 \\ \hline \end{array}$$

This is the smallest seven-digit number. It is ten lakh.

The largest seven-digit number is 99,99,999.

If we add 1 to it, we get the smallest eight-digit number.

$$\begin{array}{r} 99,99,999 \\ +1 \\ \hline 1,00,00,000 \\ \hline \end{array}$$

This is the smallest eight-digit number. It is one crore.

The table below provides a list of the smallest and largest five-, six-, seven- and eight-digit numbers.

Table 1.2

Digits	Smallest Number	Largest Number
5	10,000	99,999
6	1,00,000	9,99,999
7	10,00,000	99,99,999
8	1,00,00,000	9,99,99,999

Indian and International Systems of Numbers

There are two systems of writing numbers:

1. The Indian system of numbers.
2. The International system of numbers.

The Indian System of Numbers

The Indian system of numbers is also called the Hindu-Arabic system. In this system, we have the first period (comma) after three places from the right, the second period (comma) after the next two places, the third period again after the next two places and so on.

First period	hundreds	☐☐☐
Second period	thousands	☐☐
Third period	lakhs	☐☐
Fourth period	crores	☐☐

To write and read large numbers, we put a comma after every period.

Example: Consider the number 98,24,653.

This can be read as ninety-eight lakh twenty-four thousand six hundred and fifty-three.

Table 1.3 Indian System of Numbers Place Value Chart

Crores		Lakhs		Thousands		Ones		
Ten Crores (TC)	Crores (C)	Ten Lakhs (TL)	Lakh (L)	Ten Thousands (T Th)	Thousands (Th)	Hundreds (H)	Tens (T)	Ones (O)
10,00,00,000	1,00,00,000	10,00,000	1,00,000	10,000	1,000	100	10	1
Nine digits	Eight digits	Seven digits	Six digits	Five digits	Four digits	Three digits	Two digits	One digit

The International System of Numbers

In the International system of numbers, we have the first period after three places from the right, the second period again after three places, and the third period also after three places. Hence, all the periods comprise three place values.

First period	hundreds	☐☐☐
Second period	thousands	☐☐☐
Third period	millions	☐☐☐
Fourth period	billions	☐☐☐

Example: Consider the number 9,824,653.

This will be read as nine million eight hundred and twenty-four thousand six hundred and fifty-three.

Table 1.4 **International System of Numbers Place Value Chart**

Millions			Thousands			Ones		
Hundred Millions HM	Ten Millions TM	Millions M	Hundred Thousands HTh	Ten Thousands T Th	Thousands Th	Hundreds H	Tens T	Ones (O)
100,000,000	10,000,000	1,000,000	100,000	10,000	1000	100	10	1
Nine digits	Eight digits	Seven digits	Six digits	Five digits	Four digits	Three digits	Two digits	One digit

Comparing the two systems of numeration, we can conclude:

One lakh = Hundred thousand = 100000 (six digits)

Ten lakhs = One million = 1000000 (seven digits)

One Crore = Ten million = 10000000 (eight digits)

Ten Crores = Hundred million = 100000000 (nine digits)

Formation of Numbers

We can write and form amazing numbers with just ten digits. It is very easy and interesting to do so. Let us learn to form numbers.

Writing the smallest number given a set of digits

Suppose we are given seven different digits and asked to use each digit only once to write the smallest number, we write the digits in ascending order.

Suppose we are given the numbers, 9, 8, 1, 2, 4, 6 and 7. The smallest seven-digit number that can be written with the given digits will be 12,46,789.

Writing the largest number given a set of digits

Suppose we are asked to write the largest number possible given a set of digits, we need to write the digits in descending order. For example, if we are given the digits 9, 8, 1, 2, 4, 6 and 7, then the largest number comprising these digits will be 98,76,421.

Comparison of Numbers

Two numbers can be compared by checking on the number of digits. The number with more digits is clearly bigger. If the number of digits in two numbers is the same, then the place value of the digits is compared.

Example 1: To compare the two numbers: 423 and 523.

Both are three-digit numbers and hence we check the place value. Here, 423 is less than 523 (since 400 is less than 500).

Example 2: 5,431 and 5,429

The number of digits in both the numbers is the same, hence we compare the place value of the digits starting from the left. The first two digits are the same in both the numbers, so we compare the third digit. The third digit, 3, is greater than 2, therefore 5,431 is greater than 5,429.

The following boxes consist of more solved examples.

201 > 21	210 > 209	4,219 > 4,209
4,225 < 4,227	57,731 = 57,731	57,635 > 57,631

Rounding off Numbers

Numbers can be rounded off to the nearest tens, hundreds, thousands or other place value. Numbers can be rounded off beyond that too.

First, we begin step by step and learn rounding off to the nearest tens.

Step 1 Rounding off to the nearest tens (10) place.

We look at the digit in the ones place. All digits in the ones place that are 5 or greater than 5 are rounded off to 10. All digits in the ones place that are less than 5 are rounded off to 0. Keeping this in mind, we observe the following solved examples:

Example 1: $\underline{7}$ is rounded off to 10

Example 2: $\underline{4}$ is rounded off to 0

Example 3: 2$\underline{2}$ is rounded off to 20

Example 4: 2$\underline{8}$ is rounded off to 30

Example 5: 41$\underline{2}$ is rounded off to 410

Example 6: 47$\underline{8}$ is rounded off to 480

Example 7: 1,09$\underline{1}$ is rounded off to 1,090

Example 8: 1,88$\underline{7}$ is rounded off to 1,890

Example 9: 14,32$\underline{1}$ is rounded off to 14,320

Example 10: 14,32$\underline{7}$ is rounded off to 14,330

Step 2 Rounding off to the nearest hundreds (100) place.

We look at the digits in the tens place. The numbers between 1–49 are rounded off to the lower number which is 0. While numbers between 50–99 are rounded off to the higher number which is 100.

Example 1: 345 is rounded off to 300

Example 2: 379 is rounded off to 400

Example 3: 9,128 is rounded off to 9,100

Example 4: 9,267 is rounded off to 9,300

Example 5: 54,088 is rounded off to 54,100

Example 6: 54,025 is rounded off to 54,000

Step 3 Rounding off to the nearest thousands (1,000) place.

We look for the digits in the hundreds place.

The numbers between 1–499 are rounded off to the lower number which is 0. While the numbers between 500–999 are rounded off to the higher number which is 1,000.

Example 1: 5,473 is rounded off to 5,000

Example 2: 5,783 is rounded off to 6,000

Example 3: 7,618 is rounded off to 8,000

Example 4: 5,187 is rounded off to 5,000

Step 4 Rounding off to the nearest ten thousands (10,000) place.

We look for the digits in the thousands place.

The numbers between 1–4,999 are rounded off to the lower number which is 0. While the numbers between 5,000–9,999 are rounded off to the higher number which is 10,000.

Example 1: 18,785 is rounded off to 20,000

Example 2: 73,568 is rounded off to 70,000

Step 5 Rounding off to the nearest lakhs (1,00,000) place.

We look for the digits in the ten thousands place.

The numbers between 1–49,999 are rounded off to the lower number which is 0. While the numbers between 50,000–99,999 are rounded off to the higher number which is 1,00,000.

Example 1: 5,60,712 is rounded off to 6,00,000

Example 2: 5,14,329 is rounded off to 5,00,000

Solved examples:

Rounding off to the nearest		explanation
10	17	is rounded off to 20
	429	is rounded off to 430
	4,134	is rounded off to 4,130
100	617	is rounded off to 600
	5,693	is rounded off to 5,700
	78,152	is rounded off to 78,200
1,000	5,618	is rounded off to 6,000
	7,139	is rounded off to 7,000
10,000	78,765	is rounded off to 80,000
	91,345	is rounded off to 90,000
1,00,000	7,86,432	is rounded off to 8,00,000
	6,14,789	is rounded off to 6,00,000

Estimation

Estimation plays a vital role in our daily lives. A family estimates the expenditure for the month; a child estimates the expenditure of his pocket money; a company head makes an estimate of the profit; an event organiser estimates the number of spectators for a show and so on.

Estimation is an *approximate value*, not the exact value. Hence, we use the property of rounding off for estimating cost, profit, expenditure, etc.

While studying the following examples, we will learn how *estimating* the sum and difference of two or more numbers is achieved by rounding off.

Example 1: Find the sum of 77 and 777 by rounding off to the nearest tens and hundreds.

77 will be rounded off to 80

777 will be rounded off to 800

Their sum will be $80 + 800 = 880$

By actual addition, their sum would be:

$$\begin{array}{r} 77 \\ +777 \\ \hline 854 \\ \hline \end{array}$$

Thus, the estimated and actual sums are 880 and 854, respectively.

Example 2: Find the sum of the following numbers by rounding off to the nearest hundreds place.

2,213 and 6,792.

	Estimated	Actual
2,213 =	2,200	2,213
6,792 =	+6,800	+6,792
	9,000	9,005

Example 3: Find the difference of the following numbers by rounding off to the nearest hundreds place.

8,865 and 2,360

	Estimated	Actual
8,865 =	8,900	8,865
2,360 =	−2,400	−2,360
	6,500	6,505

Example 4: Find the estimated product of the following numbers by rounding them off to the nearest tens or hundreds place.

a. $527 \times 85 = 500 \times 90 = 45{,}000$

b. $616 \times 234 = 600 \times 200 = 1{,}20{,}000$

c. $491 \times 421 = 500 \times 400 = 2{,}00{,}000$

Example 5: Find the estimated quotient of the following numbers by rounding them off to the nearest thousands place.

a. $2{,}698 \div 61 = \frac{3{,}000}{60} = 50$

b. $2{,}362 \div 21 = \frac{2{,}000}{20} = 100$

c. $5{,}555 \div 11 = \frac{6{,}000}{10} = 600$

Practice Exercise 1.2

1. Round off the following numbers to the nearest thousand.

a. 2,932 b. 3,846 c. 7,915 d. 8,134 e. 6,271

2. Round off the following numbers to the nearest ten thousand.

a. 89,231 b. 1,73,246 c. 6,86,865 d. 71,234 e. 2,41,289

3. Round off the following numbers to the nearest lakh.

a. 1,65,263 b. 3,71,234 c. 8,12,345 d. 36,39,152 e. 45,78,214

4. Estimate the sum of the following numbers by rounding them off to the indicated place. Also find the actual sum.

a. 78 + 2,135 to the nearest tens place.

b. 157 + 5,234 to the nearest hundreds place.

c. 6,732 + 7,140 to the nearest thousands place.

d. 54,631 + 87,421 to the nearest ten thousands place.

e. 1,63,926 + 8,73,426 to the nearest lakhs place.

5. Estimate the difference between the following numbers by rounding off to the indicated place and find the actual difference.

a. 86 and 121 to the nearest tens place.

b. 175 and 673 to the nearest hundreds place.

c. 6,732 and 9,140 to the nearest thousands place.

d. 55,631 and 87,421 to the nearest ten thousands place.

e. 1,63,926 and 8,73,426 to the nearest lakhs place.

6. Estimate the product of the following numbers by rounding off.

a. 25 × 73 b. 491 × 421 c. 659 × 34 d. 97 × 472 e. 2,698 × 61

7. Estimate the quotient of the following numbers by rounding off.

a. 64 ÷ 28 b. 2,697 ÷ 61 c. 4,426 ÷ 358 d. 5,555 ÷ 11 e. 4,040 ÷ 20

8. Roli has ₹13,563 as savings in one bank account and ₹26,587 in another account. She has to pay off a loan of ₹40,000. By the method of estimation, find out whether she will be able to pay off her loan.

9. Mr Narula owns a pastry shop. He has baked 568 pastries for the day. He sells about 38 pastries in an hour. How many pastries will be left after 12 hours of sale? Give the answer by rounding off to the nearest hundred.

10. A school principal decides to distribute ice creams on Foundation Day. There are 42 ice creams in a carton. How many cartons does the principal need to order if there are 987 students in the school?

Roman Numerals

Roman numerals are part of the ancient Roman number system that remains in use today. The Indian and the international systems of numeration are based on the ten-digits 0–9. The Roman system of numeration is based on seven basic symbols.

These seven symbols are I, V, X, L, C, D, M.

I $\leftrightarrow$ 1	X $\leftrightarrow$ 10	C $\leftrightarrow$ 100	M $\leftrightarrow$ 1,000
V $\leftrightarrow$ 5	L $\leftrightarrow$ 50	D $\leftrightarrow$ 500	

Today Roman numerals are used for listing items, on watch and clock faces, chapter numbers, copyright dates and to denote film listing.

Rules for Writing Numbers Using Roman Numerals

Rule 1 If a symbol of a *smaller value* is written on the *right* of a symbol of *greater value*, its value is *added* to the symbol of the *greater value*.

Examples: (i) VII = 5 + 1 + 1 = 7 (ii) XI = 10 + 1 = 11

(iii) CL = 100 + 50 = 150

Rule 2 If a symbol of a *smaller value* is written on the *left* of a symbol of *greater value*, its value is subtracted from the symbol of the *greater value*.

Examples: (i) IV = 5 − 1 = 4 (ii) IX = 10 − 1 = 9

Rule 3 The symbols I, X, C and M can be repeated but not more than three times.

Example: III = 3 but 4 is written as IV = 5 − 1= 4

XXX = 30 but 40 = XL

Rule 4 The symbols V, L and D are not repeated.

The symbols V, L and D are not written to the left of higher value symbols. This implies that V, L and D are used for addition only; they are not subtracted.

Rule 5 The symbol I can be subtracted from V and X only.

Example: 49 cannot be written as IL

It is written as XLIX = 40 + 9 = 49

Rule 6 The symbol X can be subtracted from L, C and M but not from D.

Example: 490 cannot be written as XD

It is written as CD × C = (500 − 100) + (100 − 10)

= 400 + 90 = 490

Rule 7 The symbol C can be subtracted from D and M.

Example: CD = 500 − 100 = 400

CM = 1000 − 100 = 900

Rule 8 If a symbol of smaller value comes in between two symbols of larger values, then its value is subtracted from the value of the symbol immediately following it.

Example: XXIV = 10 + 10 + 5 − 1 = 25 − 1 = 24

(I is subtracted from 5 and not added to 10.)

Example 1: Write the following numbers in Roman numerals.

a. 57 = 50 + 5 + 2 = LVII

b. 89 = 50 + 10 + 10 + 10 + 9 = LXXXIX

c. 125 = 100 + 10 + 10 + 5 = CXXV

Example 2: Write the following Roman numerals in Arabic numbers.

a. LXII = 50 + 10 + 2 = 62

b. DCXXXVI = 500 + 100 + 10 + 10 + 10 + 5 + 1 = 636

c. CDXXVII = (500 − 100) + 10 + 10 + 5 + 2 = 427

Practice Exercise 1.3

1. Write the following numbers in Roman numerals.

   a. 45 b. 69 c. 99 d. 80 e. 75

2. Write the following Roman numerals as Arabic numbers.

   a. LXXII b. XLIX c. CCXLIX d. MDCLIV e. XCVIII

3. Classify the following as meaningful or meaningless. If meaningful, write them in Hindu-Arabic numerals.

   a. IXX b. IVC c. LIL d. XLIV e. CCLXIV

4. Put the correct symbol >, < or = in the blank boxes.

   a. XL ☐ LV b. XLIX ☐ LXXI c. XLIV ☐ LXIV

   d. XL ☐ XC e. XCVIII ☐ LXIII

5. Find the sum of the following Roman numerals and give the answer in both Roman numerals and Arabic numbers.

   a. LX + XC b. DC + XLIX c. XCIV + XL

   d. XXXVI + IX e. CLIX + CD

Highlights

- The place value of any digit depends on its position in the number.
- The face value of any digit is the digit itself, regardless of its position in the number.
- Two or more numbers can be compared by comparing the number of digits. If the number of digits are the same, then the digits in the highest place of each of the numbers are compared, and then the next highest place and so on.
- In the Indian system of numeration, the first three places from the right make the ones period, the next two places make the thousands period and the next two places make the lakhs period and so on.
- In the international system of numeration, the first three places from the right make the ones period, the next three places make the thousands period and the next three places make the millions period and so on.
- Estimation can be done by rounding off numbers to the nearest tens, hundreds, thousands and so on. To get an estimated product or quotient, we have to round off numbers nearest to the greatest place.
- The seven basic symbols in the Roman numeration system are I (1), V (5), X (10), L (50), C (100), D (500) and M (1,000).

Higher Order Thinking Skills

HOTS

1. Write the smallest and the largest seven-digit numbers using the following digits if repetition of digits is allowed.

   a. 7, 9, 5, 4, 3 b. 2, 4, 0, 6, 8

2. A national daily prints 2,13,000 copies from Monday to Saturday and 3,12,000 copies on Sunday. If each copy has 24 pages, how many pages are printed in a week?

3. Using the digits 7, 2, 6 and 5, form a number which when rounded off to the nearest hundred and nearest thousand is 6,500 and 7,000, respectively.

Calculator Trick (Unlucky 13)

Here is a trick that will really leave your friends surprised. The following set of calculations will always result in the same answer—13.

Material required: A calculator

Method: Ask your friend to do the trick while you direct him/her.

		Example
Step 1	Enter any number (it should be less than an eight-digit number).	75
Step 2	Double that number.	150
Step 3	Add 15 to that number.	165
Step 4	Triple the result.	495
Step 5	Add 33 to the total that you get.	528
Step 6	Divide the answer by 6.	88
Step 7	Subtract the original number from this.	88–75

The answer will be 13!!

Maths Lab Activity

"Kaun Banega Crorepati"

Objective: To use number cards to compare numbers.

Material required: A chart

Procedure: Cut a 10 cm × 10 cm piece of chart paper for each student in class. On each card print any digit from 0–9. Draw the chart given below such that each cell is about 10 cm × 10 cm.

1. Divide the class into groups of nine. Each group selects one person to be their leader. The groups are named A, B, C, etc.

2. Each student chooses a digit card without looking at the number printed on it.

3. Each student in each group now needs to fix his/her number card on the chart in any blank space on the chart in the row assigned to his/her team.

4. Once every student has fixed his/her number on the chart, the leader of each group reads out the number formed.

	1	2	3	4	5	6	7	8	9
A									
B									
C									
D									
E									

5. The group with the largest nine-digit number is the winner.

   This is the crorepati group.

CHAPTER 2

Playing with Numbers

We will learn a lot of new terms other than addition, subtraction, multiplication and division in this chapter. What are they called? Yes, the fundamental or basic operations on numbers!

We will now perform the basic operations on numbers as a game of mixed operations for combining numbers. When we play any game, we follow a certain set of rules. So also when we combine numbers using the basic operations in a mixed manner, we follow certain rules.

The rules are simple.

The operations are performed from left to right in a fixed order which is, DMAS.

D – division

M – multiplication

A – addition

S – subtraction

Example: Consider the following numerical expression:

$$9 + 6 \div 2 \times 9 - 3 + 1$$

Step 1 $9 + \underbrace{6 \div 2} \times 9 - 3 + 1$ (division)

Step 2 $= 9 + \underbrace{3 \times 9} - 3 + 1$ (multiplication)

Step 3 $= \underbrace{9 + 27} - 3 + 1$ (addition)

Step 4 $= 37 - 3$ (subtraction)

$= 34$ We finally arrive at the answer when all the steps are carried out.

For simpler understanding, grouping of numbers is done using brackets. The different types of brackets that are used are:

1. ___ bar bracket or vinculum
2. ( ) common brackets or parentheses
3. { } curly brackets or braces
4. [ ] box brackets or square brackets

While simplifying an expression, the brackets are removed in the order given above.

Example: Consider the following numerical expression:

$$215 - [1{,}320 \div (12 \times 11) + 7 - \{5 - \overline{7 - 5}\}]$$

Step 1 $215 - [1{,}320 \div (12 \times 11) + 7 - \{5 - \overline{7 - 5}\}]$
Solving the bar bracket: $7 - 5 = 2$

Step 2 $= 215 - [1{,}320 \div (12 \times 11) + 7 - \{5 - 2\}]$
Solving the common bracket: $12 \times 11 = 132$

Step 3 $= 215 - [1{,}320 \div 132 + 7 - \{5 - 2\}]$
Solving the curly bracket: $5 - 2 = 3$

Step 4 $= 215 - [1{,}320 \div 132 + 7 - 3]$
Solving within the box bracket: $1{,}320 \div 132 = 10$.

Step 5 $= 215 - [10 + 7 - 3]$
Performing addition and then subtraction within the bracket: $10 + 7 = 17 - 3 = 14$
$= 215 - [17 - 3]$ solving box bracket

Step 6 $= 215 - 14$
$= 201$ Finally, we arrive at the answer.

The Operation 'of'

The meaning of 'of' in a numerical expression is multiplication.

Example: Half **of** 8 means $\frac{1}{2} \times 8 = 4$.

One-third **of** 27 means $\frac{1}{3} \times 27 = 9$.

The operation brackets, 'of' and fundamental operations constitute BODMAS, the rule for simplifying a given numerical expression.

BODMAS can be learnt as a word, where

B for brackets [in the order —, ( ), { }, [ ]]

O for 'of' means multiplication

D for division

M for multiplication

A for addition

S for subtraction

Example 1: $65 - [36 - \{15 - (2 - \overline{5 - 3})\}]$

By solving the bar bracket, we get	$65 - [36 - \{15 - (2 - 2)\}]$
By solving the common bracket, we get	$65 - [36 - \{15 - 0\}]$
By solving the curly bracket, we get	$65 - [36 - 15]$
By performing subtraction within the box bracket	$65 - [21]$
By solving the box bracket, we get	$65 - 21 = 44$, which is the final answer.

Example 2: $16 + [7 + \{(3 + 7) - \overline{5 - 3}\}]$

By solving the bar bracket, we get	$= 16 + [7 + \{(3 + 7) - 2\}]$
By solving the common bracket, we get	$= 16 + [7 + \{10 - 2\}]$
By solving the curly bracket, we get	$= 16 + [7 + 8]$
By performing addition within the box bracket, we get	$= 16 + 15$
By solving the box bracket, we get	$= 31$, which is the final answer.

Practice Exercise 2.1

Simplify the following numerical expressions.

1.a. $25 + 14 - 27$ b. $848 + 597 - 635 \times 2$

2.a. $40 \times 10 \div 5 + 20 - 27$ b. $-37 + 96 \div 16 \times 7$

3.a. $2 \div \overline{6 - 5}$ b. $9 - [9 - \{9 - (9 - \overline{9 - 9})\}]$

4.a. $30 - 5 \times 2$ of $3 + (19 - 3) \div 8$ b. $15 \div 3 \times 2 + 4 \times 20 \div 2$ of 5

5.a. $72 - 12 \div 3$ of $2 + 2\,(18 - 6) \div 4$ b. $(9 + 12) \div 7 + 36 \div 2$ of 3

6.a. $96 \div [18 - \{63 \div 7 - (18 - 5 \text{ of } 3)\}]$ b. $75 \div [20 - \{42 \div 6 - (20 - 3 \text{ of } 6)\}]$

7.a. $11 \div \{1 + (5 - 3) \times 5\}$ b. $15 - 3\{4 - (7 - 3)\} + 3\,(5 + 2 - 1)$

8.a. $18\,[59 - \{7 \times 8\,(11 - 2 \times 5)\}]$ b. $70 - \{73 - 2\,(6 \text{ of } 6 - 4)\}$

9.a. $(14 - 7) \times \{8 + (3 + \overline{7 - 1})\}$ b. $27 - [18 \div \{16 + (5 - \overline{4 - 1})\}]$

10.a. 81 of $[59 - \{7 \times 8 + (13 - 2 \text{ of } 5)\}]$ b. 81 of $[60 - \{8 \times 7 - (13 - 5 \text{ of } 2)\}]$

Factors And Multiples

In this section, we will study in detail the concept of **highest common factor** (HCF) and **least common multiple** (LCM).

Factors

A number which divides a given number exactly, with no remainder, is called a factor of the given number.

Example 1:

Factors of 15

$15 = 1 \times 15$

$15 = 3 \times 5$

$15 = 5 \times 3$

Here, 1, 3, 5 and 15 are factors of 15 since

1, 3, 5 and 15 divide 15 exactly with the remainder being 0.

Example 2:

Factors of 22

$22 = 1 \times 22$

$22 = 2 \times 11$

The factors of 22 are 1, 2, 11 and 22 since

1, 2, 11 and 22 divide 22 exactly with the remainder being 0.

We observe:

1. 1 is a factor of every number.
2. Any number is a factor of itself.
3. The factors of a number will be less than or equal to the given number.
4. If the number is divided by any of the factors, the remainder is 0.
5. The factors of a given number are finite (that is, they can be counted).

Multiples

A multiple of a natural number is a number formed by multiplying it by another natural number.

Example 1:

Let us consider the number 7. The multiples of 7 would be:

$7 \times 1 = 7$
$7 \times 2 = 14$
$7 \times 3 = 21$

7, 14, 21 … are multiples of 7.

Example 2:

Consider the number 10. The multiples of 10 would be:

$10 \times 1 = 10$

$10 \times 2 = 20$

$10 \times 3 = 30$

10, 20, 30 … are multiples of 10.

We observe:

1. Every number is a multiple of itself.
2. Every number is a multiple of the number 1.
3. All multiples of a number are either equal to or greater than the given number.
4. The multiples of a given number are infinite (that is, they are unlimited; they cannot be counted).

Alert!

$3 \times 5 = 15$

3 and 5 are factors of 15.
15 is a multiple of 3 and 5.

Types of Numbers

Even Numbers

A number which is a multiple of 2 is called an even number.

Example: 2, 4, 6, 8, 10, 12 …

Question: How will you make seven even?

Answer: By taking the 's' away.

Odd Numbers

A number which is not a multiple of 2 is called an odd number.

Example: 1, 3, 5, 7, 9, 11 …

Prime Numbers

Numbers that have only two factors, 1 and the number itself, are called prime numbers.

Example 1: 2 The factors of 2 are 1 and 2.

Example 2: 3 The factors of 3 are 1 and 3.

Example 3: 5 The factors of 5 are 1 and 5.

Example 4: 7 The factors of 7 are 1 and 7.

Example 5: 11 The factors of 11 are 1 and 11.

Alert!

The only even prime number is 2. All other prime numbers are odd numbers.

Composite Numbers

Numbers that have more than two factors are called composite numbers.

Example 1: 4 The factors of 4 are 1, 2, 4

Example 2: 6 The factors of 6 are 1, 2, 3, 6

Example 3: 10 The factors of 10 are 1, 2, 5, 10

Example 4: 14 The factors of 14 are 1, 2, 7, 14

Example 5: 28 The factors of 28 are 1, 2, 7, 14, 28

Unique Number

The number 1 is called a unique number. It is neither a prime number nor a composite number. It is a factor of every number. Every number is a multiple of 1.

Twin Primes

Two prime numbers having a difference of 2 are called twin prime numbers.

Example 1: 3 and 5

Example 2: 5 and 7

Example 3: 11 and 13

Co-Prime Numbers

Two numbers that have no common factors other than 1 are called co-primes.

Example 1: 2 and 3

Example 2: 3 and 4

Example 3: 5 and 6

Example 4: 6 and 7

Example 5: 8 and 9

Perfect Number

A number which is equal to the sum of its factor other than itself is called a perfect number.

Example 1: Consider the number 6.
The factors of 6 are 1, 2, 3, 6.
The sum of the factors (other than 6) is $1 + 2 + 3 = 6$.

Example 2: Consider the number 28.
The factors of 28 are 1, 2, 4, 7, 14, 28.
The sum of the factors (other than 28) is $1 + 2 + 4 + 7 + 14 = 28$.

To find prime numbers from 1 to 100, we use the "Sieve of Eratosthenes", a method devised by the Greek mathematician Eratosthenes.

Step 1 Write the numbers 1 to 100 in rows and columns as shown on page 29.

Step 2 As 1 is a unique number (neither prime nor composite), cross it out.

Step 3 Since 2 is the first prime number and an even number, circle it and cross out all multiples of 2.

Step 4 Since 3 is the second prime number and an odd number, circle it and cross out all multiples of 3.

Step 5 Since 5 is the next prime number, circle it and cross out all multiples of 5.

Step 6 Continue the process till all the numbers are circled or crossed out.

~~1~~	(2)	(3)	~~4~~	(5)	~~6~~	(7)	~~8~~	~~9~~	~~10~~
(11)	~~12~~	(13)	~~14~~	~~15~~	~~16~~	(17)	~~18~~	(19)	~~20~~
~~21~~	~~22~~	(23)	~~24~~	~~25~~	~~26~~	~~27~~	~~28~~	(29)	~~30~~
(31)	~~32~~	~~33~~	~~34~~	~~35~~	~~36~~	(37)	~~38~~	~~39~~	~~40~~
(41)	~~42~~	(43)	~~44~~	~~45~~	~~46~~	(47)	~~48~~	~~49~~	~~50~~
~~51~~	~~52~~	(53)	~~54~~	~~55~~	~~56~~	~~57~~	~~58~~	(59)	~~60~~
(61)	~~62~~	~~63~~	~~64~~	~~65~~	~~66~~	(67)	~~68~~	~~69~~	~~70~~
(71)	~~72~~	(73)	~~74~~	~~75~~	~~76~~	~~77~~	~~78~~	(79)	~~80~~
~~81~~	~~82~~	(83)	~~84~~	~~85~~	~~86~~	~~87~~	~~88~~	(89)	~~90~~
~~91~~	~~92~~	~~93~~	~~94~~	~~95~~	~~96~~	(97)	~~98~~	~~99~~	~~100~~

All the numbers that are circled are the prime numbers between 1 and 100.

Thus, the prime numbers between 1 to 100 are 2, 3, 5, 7, 11, 13, 17, 19, 23, 29, 31, 37, 41, 43, 47, 53, 59, 61, 67, 71, 73, 79, 83, 89 and 97.

There are twenty-five prime numbers between 1 and 100.

Practice Exercise 2.2

1. Write all the possible factors of the following numbers.

   a. 35 b. 64 c. 120 d. 17 e. 729

2. Write the first five multiples of the following numbers.

   a. 7 b. 11 c. 13 d. 20 e. 25

3. Answer the following questions.

   a. List the even prime numbers between 1 and 20.

   b. List the odd prime numbers between 30 and 50.

   c. List the prime numbers between 70 and 100.

   d. List the prime numbers between 100 and 150.

   e. List the composite numbers between 50 and 70.

4. Identify which of the following pairs are co-primes and which are twin primes.

   a. 5 and 7 b. 11 and 13 c. 15 and 17 d. 41 and 43 e. 49 and 51

5. Write seven consecutive composite numbers between two prime numbers from 1 to 100.

6. Express each of the following numbers as the sum of two or more primes.

   a. 32 b. 56 c. 63 d. 130 e. 80

7. Write down a number which is a multiple of both the numbers.

   a. 7 and 5 b. 11 and 13 c. 3 and 19 d. 2 and 17 e. 23 and 7

8. Are 23 and 92 co-prime numbers? If not, why?

9. Which of the following numbers has 15 as a factor?

   a. 115 b. 225 c. 15,625 d. 51,015 e. 16,215.

10. Which of the following statements are true?

    a. All even numbers, except 2, are composite numbers.

    b. No composite number is an odd number.

    c. The number 2 is the smallest prime number.

    d. There is no largest prime number.

    e. Every number is either a prime number or a composite number.

    f. Two consecutive numbers cannot be prime numbers.

    g. A number and its successor are always co-prime numbers.

    h. If two numbers are co-prime numbers, at least one of these must be a prime number.

    i. The sum of two prime numbers cannot be a prime number.

    j. The product of two prime numbers is a prime number.

Tests for Divisibility

A number is said to be divisible by another number if the remainder is 0. This can be done by actual division. There are certain tests that can be performed on numbers without actually dividing them to check whether a number is divisible by a certain number or not.

1. Divisibility by 2 ★★

A number is divisible by 2 if the digit in the units place is 0, 2, 4, 6 or 8.

Examples: $4\underline{2}$, $19\underline{4}$, $25\underline{6}$, $37\underline{8}$, $40\underline{0}$

2. Divisibility by 3 ★★★

A number is divisible by 3 if the sum of its digits is divisible by 3.

Examples: 75, 126, 204, 351, 465

Example 1:	75	$7 + 5 = 12$	The sum of the digits of all the numbers are all multiples of 3, hence they will be divisible by 3.
Example 2:	126	$1 + 2 + 6 = 9$	
Example 3:	204	$2 + 0 + 4 = 6$	
Example 4:	351	$3 + 5 + 1 = 9$	
Example 5:	465	$4 + 6 + 5 = 15$	

3. Divisibility by 4 ★★★★

A number is divisible by 4 if the number formed by the last two digits is divisible by 4 or a multiple of 4.

Examples: 148, 256, 980, 1,024, 7,816

The last two digits in the numbers above that are underlined are multiples of 4, hence they are divisible by 4. Thus, all the numbers listed above are divisible by 4.

4. Divisibility by 5 ★★★★★

A number is divisible by 5 if the digit in the units place is either 0 or 5.

Examples: 55, 160, 265, 300, 985

All the numbers given above are divisible by 5.

5. Divisibility by 6 ★★★★★★

A number is divisible by 6 if it is divisible by both 2 3.

Examples: 36, 714, 510, 648, 108

Since all the numbers are even, they are all divisible by 2. To check for divisibility by 3, we have to add the digits and the addendum should be divisible by 3.

Example 1:	36	$3 + 6 = 9$	It is divisible by 3.
Example 2:	714	$7 + 1 + 4 = 12$	It is divisible by 3.
Example 3:	510	$5 + 1 + 0 = 6$	It is divisible by 3.
Example 4:	648	$6 + 4 + 8 = 18$	It is divisible by 3.
Example 5:	108	$1 + 0 + 8 = 9$	It is divisible by 3.

Since all the numbers are divisible by 2 as well as 3, they are all divisible by 6.

6. Divisibility by 7 ★★★★★★★

A number is divisible by 7 if the difference between twice the last digit and the number formed by the other digits is either 0 or a multiple of 7.

Examples: 84, 714, 847, 1,666, 2,975

Example 1:	84	8 − (4 × 2) = 8 − 8 = 0	It is divisible by 7.
Example 2:	714	71 − (4 × 2) = 71 − 8 = 63	It is divisible by 7.
Example 3:	847	84 − (7 × 2) = 84 − 14 = 70	It is divisible by 7.
Example 4:	1,666	166 − (6 × 2) = 166 − 12 = 154	It is divisible by 7.
Example 5:	2,975	297 − (5 × 2) = 297 − 10 = 287	It is divisible by 7.

7. Divisibility by 8 ★★★★★★★★

A number is divisible by 8 if the number formed by its last three digits is divisible by 8.

Examples: 3,024, 4,192, 56,712, 2,13,456, 6,16,640

Example 1:	3,024	024 is divisible by 8
Example 2:	4,192	192 is divisible by 8
Example 3:	56,712	712 is divisible by 8
Example 4:	2,13,456	456 is divisible by 8
Example 5:	6,16,640	640 is divisible by 8

Therefore, all the numbers listed here are divisible by 8.

8. Divisibility by 9 ★★★★★★★★★

A number is divisible by 9 if the sum of its digits is divisible by 9.

Examples: 63, 126, 3267, 7659, 18000

Example 1:	63 = 6 + 3 = 9	It is divisible by 9.
Example 2:	126 = 1 + 2 + 6 = 9	It is divisible by 9.
Example 3:	3,267 = 3 + 2 + 6 + 7 = 18	It is divisible by 9.
Example 4:	7,659 = 7 + 6 + 5 + 9 = 27	It is divisible by 9.
Example 5:	18,000 = 1 + 8 + 0 + 0 + 0 = 9	It is divisible by 9.

9. Divisibility by 10 ★★★★★★★★★★

A number is divisible by 10 if the digit in the units place is zero.

Examples: 90, 1,080, 75,060, 23,450, 16,380

10. Divisibility by 11 ★★★★★★★★★★★

A number is divisible by 11 if the difference of the digits in the odd and even places is either 0 or a multiple of 11.

Examples: 121, 2,442, 98,725, 28,457, 61,908

Example 1:	121	$(1 + 1) - 2 = 2 - 2 = 0$	It is divisible by 11.
Example 2:	2,442	$(2 + 4) - (4 + 2) = 6 - 6 = 0$	It is divisible by 11.
Example 3:	98,725	$(9 + 7 + 5) - (8 + 2) = 21 - 10 = 11$	It is divisible by 11.
Example 4:	28,457	$(2 + 4 + 7) - (8 + 5) = 13 - 13 = 0$	It is divisible by 11.
Example 5:	61,908	$(6 + 9 + 8) - (1 + 0) = 23 - 1 = 22$	It is divisible by 11.

Practice Exercise 2.3

1. Test the divisibility of the following numbers by 2.

   a. 492 b. 683 c. 7,876 d. 1,120 e. 2,467

2. Test the divisibility of the following numbers by 3.

   a. 417 b. 8,146 c. 5,190 d. 98,117 e. 1,34,712

3. Test the divisibility of the following numbers by 4.

   a. 31,672 b. 560 c. 3,807 d. 9,865 e. 8,73,248

4. Test the divisibility of the following numbers by 5.

   a. 3,140 b. 1,560 c. 12,345 d. 24,685 e. 55,557

5. Test the divisibility of the following numbers by 6.

   a. 18,198 b. 13,467 c. 34,542 d. 3,21,003 e. 3,00,630

6. Test the divisibility of the following numbers by 7.

   a. 364 b. 1,505 c. 3,199 d. 7,021 e. 4,507

7. Test the divisibility of the following numbers by 8.

   a. 1,728 b. 47,780 c. 63,904 d. 1,36,979 e. 17,90,184

8. Test the divisibility of the following numbers by 9.

   a. 3,159 b. 7,218 c. 7,878 d. 1,34,755 e. 4,57,893

9. Test the divisibility of the following numbers by 10.

   a. 10,010 b. 1,00,005 c. 21,420 d. 89,760 e. 64,64,645

10. Test the divisibility of the following numbers by 11.

    a. 7,69,483 b. 3,581 c. 17,864 d. 20,916 e. 4,598

Prime Factorisation

Prime factorisation means to write a composite number as a product of its prime factors.

Prime factorisation of a composite number can be done in two ways:

1. Factor tree method.
2. Division method.

Factor Tree Method

Example 1: Find the prime factors of 30.

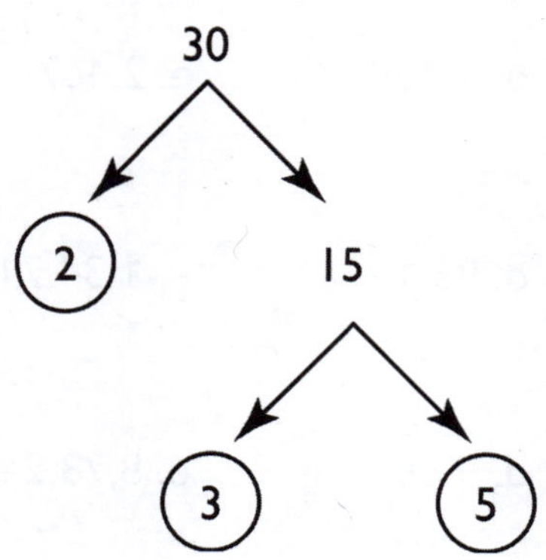

Hence, the prime factors of 30 are $2 \times 3 \times 5$.

Example 2: Find the prime factors of 56.

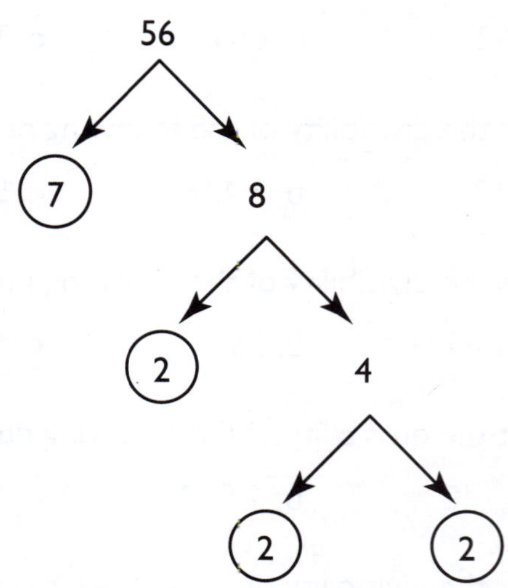

Hence, the prime factors of 56 are $7 \times 2 \times 2 \times 2$.

The factor tree method is practical for finding prime factors of small numbers.

Division Method

Example 1: Find the prime factors of 216.

2	216
2	108
2	54
3	27
3	9
3	3
	1

The prime factors of 216 are $2 \times 2 \times 2 \times 3 \times 3 \times 3$.

Example 2: Find the prime factors of 375.

5	375
5	75
5	15
3	3
	1

The prime factors of 375 are $5 \times 5 \times 5 \times 3$.

With the basic knowledge of prime factorisation, we will now study two important concepts of factors and multiples:

1. Highest common factor (HCF).
2. Least common multiple (LCM).

Highest Common Factor (HCF)

The largest common factor between two or more numbers is called the highest common factor.

It is also called the greatest common divisor (GCD).

The highest common factor can be found by two methods:

1. Prime factorisation method.
2. Long division method.

Finding the HCF by the Prime Factorisation Method

Step 1 Find the prime factors of the given numbers.

Step 2 Write the prime factors of the given numbers found in Step 1. Cricle or underline the common factors.

Step 3 List the common factors found in Step 2.

Step 4 Find the product of the factors found in Step 3. This is the highest common factor (HCF) of the given numbers.

Example 1: Find the HCF of 36 and 60 by the prime factorisation method.

Step 1

2	36
2	18
3	9
3	3
	1

2	60
2	30
3	15
5	5
	1

Step 2 $36 = \textcircled{2} \times \textcircled{2} \times \textcircled{3} \times 3$

$60 = \textcircled{2} \times \textcircled{2} \times \textcircled{3} \times 5$

Step 3 The common factors of 36 and 60 are 2, 2, 3.

Step 4 The product of the common factors of 36 and 60 is $= 2 \times 2 \times 3 = 12$

Therefore, HCF = 12.

Example 2: Find the HCF of 42, 63 and 105.

Step 1

2	42
3	21
7	7
	1

3	63
3	21
7	7
	1

3	105
5	35
7	7
	1

Step 2 $42 = 2 \times \textcircled{3} \times \textcircled{7}$

$63 = \textcircled{3} \times 3 \times \textcircled{7}$

$105 = \textcircled{3} \times 5 \times \textcircled{7}$

Step 3 The common factors of 42, 63 and 105 are 3 and 7.

Step 4 The product of the common factors of 42, 63 and 105 is $3 \times 7 = 21$.

Therefore, HCF = 21.

Finding the HCF by the Long Division Method

Step 1 Divide the greater number by the smaller number.

Step 2 Take the remainder as the divisor and the divisor as the dividend.

Step 3 Continue the procedure till you get 0 as the remainder.

Step 4 The last divisor will be the HCF of the given numbers.

Example 1: Find the HCF of 144 and 372 by the long division method.

The number 372 is greater and 144 is smaller.

Hence, divide 372 by 144.

```
144 )372( 2
    -288
    ----
      84 )144( 1
          -84
          ---
           60 )84(1
               -60
               ---
                24 )60(2
                    -48
                    ---
                     12)24(2
                        24
                        --
                        xx
```

The last divisor is 12. Hence, HCF of 144 and 372 is 12.

Example 2: Find the HCF of 75, 225 and 675 by the long division method.

We first find the HCF of 75 and 225 by the steps given.

The greater number is 225 and the smaller number 75.

Hence, divide 225 by 75.

```
75 )225( 3
   -225
   ----
    xxx
```

The HCF of 75 and 225 is 75.

We will now find the HCF of 75 and 675 by the long division method.

```
75)675(9
   675
   ---
   xxx
```

The HCF of 75 and 675 is 75.

Hence, the HCF of the three given numbers is 75.

Example 3: Find the greatest number which divides 245 and 1,029 leaving a remainder of 5 in each case.

The remainder is 5 in each case when 245 and 1029 are divided by the common number.

Thus, $245 - 5 = 240$ and
$1{,}029 - 5 = 1{,}024$ will be exactly divisible by the common number.

The common number will be the HCF of the two numbers.

The greater number is 1,024, and the smaller number is 240.

Hence, divide 1,024 by 240.

```
240)1,024(4
     -960
       64 )240(3
          -192
            48 )64(1
               -48
                16)48(3
                   48
                   xx
```

The HCF of 240 and 1,024 is 16.

So, the required number is 16.

Practice Exercise 2.4

1. Write the prime factors of the following numbers.

   a. 49 b. 216 c. 312 d. 1024 e. 8000

2. Complete the factor tree using prime numbers.

   a.

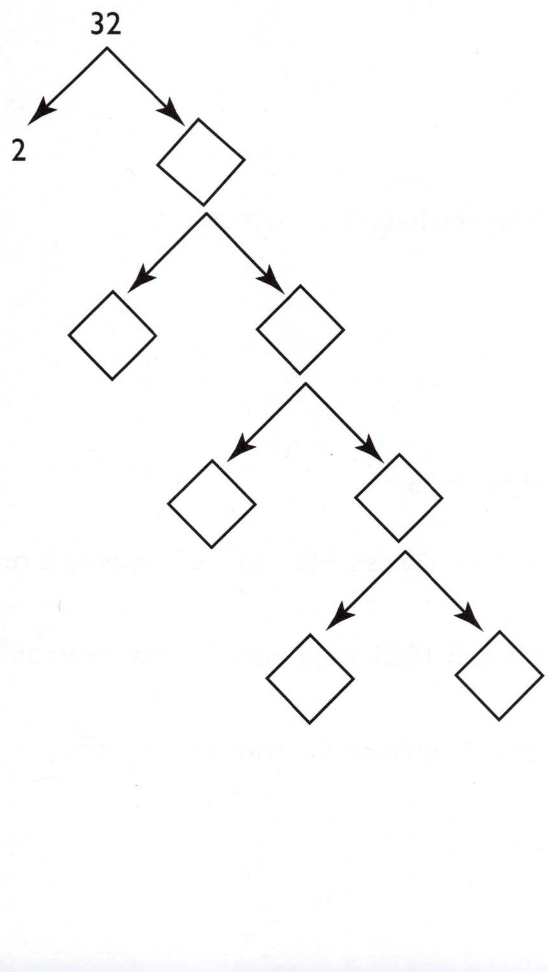

   b.

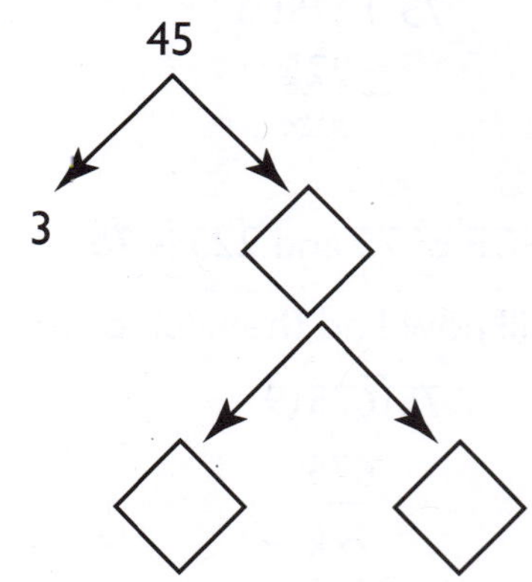

c.

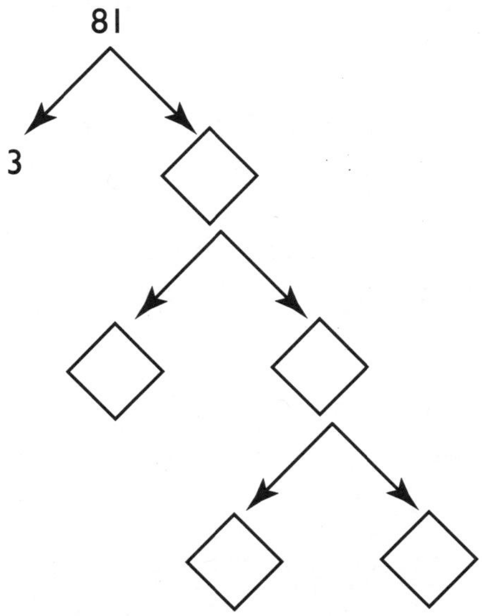

d.

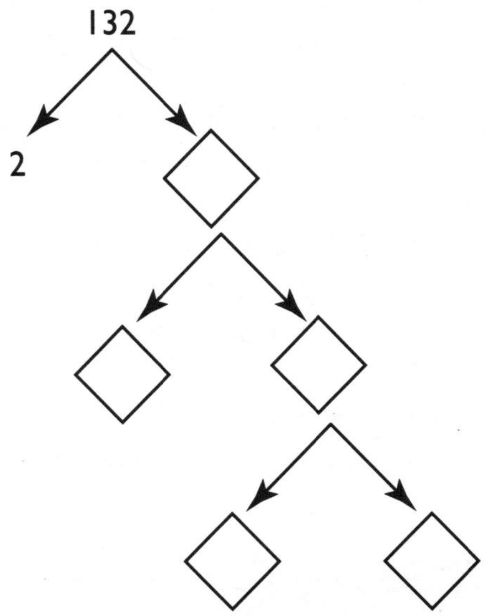

e.

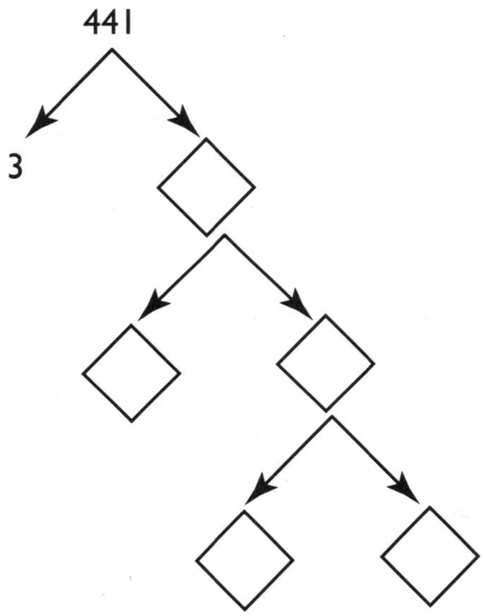

3. Find the HCF of the following numbers using the prime factorisation method.

a. 27, 81 b. 18, 117 c. 250, 450

d. 256, 1,024 e. 180, 270, 630

4. Find the HCF of the following using the long division method.

a. 144, 372 b. 575, 920 c. 891, 1377

d. 830, 790, 650 e. 2,241, 8,217, 747

5. Find the greatest number that divides 43 and 61 leaving a remainder of 1 in each case.

6. Find the largest number that divides 246 and 1,030 leaving a remainder of 6 in each case.

7. Find the largest number that divides 1,385 and 1,457 leaving remainders of 5 and 2, respectively.

8. Find the greatest number that divides 131, 160 and 223 leaving remainders of 7, 5 and 6, respectively.

9. Two tankers contain 960 litres and 1,024 litres of petrol, respectively. Find the capacity of the container that can measure the petrol in either tanker an exact number of times.

10. The length of two rods is 7 m 50 cm and 10 m 50 cm, respectively. Find the length of the longest tape that can measure these lengths exactly.

Least Common Multiple (LCM)

The least common multiple (LCM) of two or more numbers is a number that is a common multiple of the numbers and is the smallest among all common multiples.

It is also called the lowest common multiple.

The least common multiple can be found by two methods:

1. The prime factorisation method.
2. The common division method.

Finding the LCM by the Prime Factorisation Method

Step 1 Write the prime factors of the given numbers.

Step 2 Count the maximum number of times each factor appears and then multiply them.

Step 3 The product of these factors is the LCM.

Example 1: Find the LCM of 36, 72, 96 by the prime factorisation method.

$$\begin{array}{r|l} 2 & 36 \\ \hline 2 & 18 \\ \hline 3 & 9 \\ \hline 3 & 3 \\ \hline & 1 \end{array} \qquad \begin{array}{r|l} 2 & 72 \\ \hline 2 & 36 \\ \hline 2 & 18 \\ \hline 3 & 9 \\ \hline 3 & 3 \\ \hline & 1 \end{array} \qquad \begin{array}{r|l} 2 & 96 \\ \hline 2 & 48 \\ \hline 2 & 24 \\ \hline 2 & 12 \\ \hline 2 & 6 \\ \hline 3 & 3 \\ \hline & 1 \end{array}$$

The prime factors of 36 are $2 \times 2 \times 3 \times 3$.

The prime factors of 72 are $2 \times 2 \times 2 \times 3 \times 3$

The prime factors of 96 are $2 \times 2 \times 2 \times 2 \times 2 \times 3$

Here, the number 2 appears 5 times, the number 3 appears twice.

Therefore, LCM $= 2 \times 2 \times 2 \times 2 \times 2 \times 3 \times 3 \boxed{= 32 \times 9 = 288}$.

Example 2: Find the LCM of 25, 75 and 100 by the prime factorisation method.

5	25
5	5
	1

3	75
5	25
5	5
	1

2	100
2	50
5	25
5	5
	1

Question: Can you help me find the lowest common multiple (LCM)?

Answer: Don't tell me they still haven't found it. My dad said they were finding it when he was in school.

The prime factors of 25 are 5×5

The prime factors of 75 are $3 \times 5 \times 5$

The prime factors of 100 are $2 \times 2 \times 5 \times 5$

Here, the number 2 appears twice, the number 3 appears once and the number 5 appears twice.

Therefore, LCM of 25, 75 and 100 $= 2 \times 2 \times 3 \times 5 \times 5 = 300$.

Finding the LCM by the Common Division Method

Step 1 Arrange the numbers in a row separated by commas.

Step 2 Choose the smallest prime number that divides at least one of the given numbers.

Step 3 Divide the numbers by the number chosen in Step 2 and carry forward the undivided numbers.

Step 4 Repeat the process till the number left in the last row is 1.

Step 5 Multiply all the prime divisors to get the LCM.

Example 1: Find the LCM of 72, 90 and 108 by the common division method.

2	72, 90, 108
2	36, 45, 54
2	18, 45, 27
3	9, 45, 27
3	3, 15, 9
3	1, 5, 3
5	1, 5, 1
	1, 1, 1

The LCM of 72, 90 and 108 $= 2 \times 2 \times 2 \times 3 \times 3 \times 3 \times 5 = 1{,}080$.

Example 2: Find the LCM of 220, 440 and 660 by the long division method.

2	220, 440, 660
2	110, 220, 330
2	55, 110, 165
5	55, 55, 165
11	11, 11, 3
3	1, 1, 3
	1, 1, 1

The LCM of 220, 440 and 660 $= 2 \times 2 \times 2 \times 5 \times 11 \times 3 = 1{,}320$.

Example 3: Find the smallest number which when divided by 20, 25 and 40 leaves a remainder 5 in each case.

The smallest (least) number which is exactly divisible by 20, 25 and 40 is the LCM of these numbers. We first find the LCM of 20, 25 and 40.

2	20, 25, 40
2	10, 25, 20
2	5, 25, 10
5	5, 25, 5
5	1, 5, 1
	1, 1, 1

LCM of 20, 25 and 40 $= 2 \times 2 \times 2 \times 5 \times 5 = 200$

But, the required number should leave a remainder of 5 in each case.

Thus, the required number is 5 more than the LCM of the given numbers.

$\therefore$ Required number $= 200 + 5 = 205$.

The Relationship Between Two Numbers and their HCF and LCM

The product of the LCM and HCF of two natural numbers is equal to the product of the given natural numbers.

Thus, the product of the HCF and LCM of two given numbers = product of the two given numbers.

Example:

Let us consider the numbers 48 and 60.

The prime factors of 48 are (2) × (2) × 2 × 2 × (3)

The prime factors of 60 are (2) × (2) × (3) × 5

The HCF of 48 and 60 $= 2 \times 2 \times 3 = 12$

The LCM of 48 and 60 $= 2 \times 2 \times 2 \times 2 \times 3 \times 5 = 240$

The product of HCF $\times$ LCM $= 12 \times 240 = 2{,}880$

The product of the given numbers $= 48 \times 60 = 2{,}880$

Therefore, the product of the HCF $\times$ LCM $=$ the product of the numbers.

From the above equation we can say that

$$\text{HCF} = \frac{\text{Product of the numbers}}{\text{LCM}}$$

$$\text{LCM} = \frac{\text{Product of the numbers}}{\text{HCF}}$$

Practice Exercise 2.5

1. Find the LCM of the following numbers by the prime factorisation method.

   a. 18, 66 b. 24, 117 c. 60, 105, 165

   d. 140, 180, 220 e. 36, 72, 96, 108

2. Find the LCM of the following numbers by the common division method.

   a. 48, 64 b. 96, 128, 240 c. 180, 360, 144

   d. 9, 15, 21 e. 19, 57, 36

3. Find the HCF and LCM of the following pairs of numbers. Show that the product of the HCF and LCM is the same as the product of the given pair of numbers.

   a. 21, 27 b. 13, 52 c. 225, 625 d. 120, 350 e. 135, 162

4. The LCM of two numbers is 370 and the HCF is 1. If one of the numbers is 37, find the other number. What type of numbers are these?

5. The product of two numbers is 15,870 and their HCF is 23. Find their LCM.

6. The product of two numbers is 800 and their LCM is 400. Find their HCF.

7. Find the smallest number which when divided by 35, 56 and 105 leaves a remainder of 5 in each case.

8. Four bells ring at intervals of 8, 10, 12 and 15 minutes, respectively. At what time will they again ring simultaneously, if they rang together at 6 am?

9. Find the smallest four-digit number that is exactly divisible by 32, 36, 40 and 45.

10. Find the greatest six-digit number that is exactly divisible by 15, 18, and 24.

Highlights

- A number that divides a given number exactly is called a factor of the given number.
- 1 is a factor of every number.
- Every number is a factor of itself.
- Each number has a finite number of factors.
- A multiple of a number is exactly divisible by that number.
- Every number is a multiple of itself.
- A number can have an infinite number of multiples.
- A number that has only two factors, 1 and the number itself, are called prime numbers.
- 2 is the only even prime number.
- 1 is neither a prime number nor a composite number. It is unique.
- A number is divisible by:

  (i) 2, if the digit in the ones place is 0, 2, 4, 6, or 8.
  (ii) 3, if the sum of the digits of the number is divisible by 3.
  (iii) 4, if the number formed by the digits in its tens and units place is divisible by 4.
  (iv) 5, if the digit in the ones place is 0 or 5.
  (v) 6, if it is divisible by 2 and 3.
  (vi) 8, if the number formed by the digits in its hundreds, tens and units place is divisible by 8.
  (vii) 9, if the sum of its digits is divisible by 9.
  (viii) 10, if the digit in the units place is 0.
  (ix) 11, if the difference of the sum of the digits in the odd places and the sum of the digits in the even places is either 0 or divisible by 11.

- The HCF of two or more numbers is the largest number that divides all the given numbers.
- The LCM of two or more numbers is the smallest number which is divisible by all the given numbers.
- The product of HCF and LCM of two numbers equals their product.
- The HCF of any two prime or co-prime numbers is equal to 1.

Highlights

- The LCM of any two prime or co-prime numbers is equal to their product.
- The HCF of two numbers is always less than or equal to the smaller number.
- The LCM of two numbers is always greater than or equal to the bigger number.
- The HCF of two numbers is a factor of their LCM.
- If a number is a factor of two numbers, it is also a factor of their sum and their difference.
- If two prime numbers are factors of a third number, then their product is also a factor of the third number.

Higher Order Thinking Skills

HOTS

1. Can two numbers have 16 as their HCF and 204 as their LCM? Give the reason.
2. Replace ★ in 27★20 with the smallest number such that it becomes divisible by 2, 3, 5, 7 and 9.
3. If three planets complete a revolution around the sun once every 200, 250 and 300 days, respectively, when do they all come together again?

Sieve of Eratosthenes

Objective: To play with numbers and learn about prime numbers and composite numbers.

Material required: A thermocol board 25 cm × 25 cm in dimension, black sketch pen and two other coloured sketch pens of your choice

Procedure:

1. Make a table of 10 rows and 10 columns.
2. Write the numbers 1 to 10 in Row 1 and 11 to 20 in Row 2 and so on.
3. Circle all the prime numbers in a colour of your choice.
4. Cross out all the other numbers with another coloured sketch pen.
5. Answer the following simple questions and see how fast you can answer them.
   a. How many prime numbers are there between 1 and 100?
   b. Which column has the maximum number of prime numbers? Which digit is in the units place in this column?
   c. Which columns have no prime numbers? Can you guess why? Ask your teacher if you are not sure of the answer.
   d. Which two columns have only one prime number each?
   e. Which is the only even prime number?

Eratosthenes was a Greek mathematician who lived in the third century BC. He discovered the method of finding prime numbers by sieving all the numbers that are not prime. This method that is used to retain prime numbers is known as the "Sieve of Eratosthenes". This method is used to obtain all prime numbers less than 100.

1. Write the predecessor and successor of the following numbers.

   a. 24,689 b. 10,00,000

2. Write the following numbers in their expanded form.

   a. 84,53,765 b. 5,00,10,809

3. Rewrite the following numbers in the Indian system and the international system of numbers using appropriate commas (,). Also, write the place value of the underlined digits in both the systems.

   a. 2219939 b. 9891285375

4. a. Estimate the sum of the following numbers to the nearest thousand.

   31,750 + 47,807 + 12,397

   b. Estimate the difference of the following numbers to the nearest thousand.

   31,750 − 12,397

5. Compare the following Roman numerals using ($>$, $<$, $=$) after converting them into Arabic numerals.

   a. DCCXLVI - DLXXXVII

   b. CMLXIV - CMXLIX

6. Simplify the following numerical expressions.

   a. $60 - [48 - \{63 \div 3 - (12 - 9 \div 3)\}]$

   b. $99 \div [17 - \{15 - 3(8 - 5)\}]$

7. Find the HCF and the LCM of the following numbers and verify that the product of the numbers = HCF × LCM

   a. 270, 450 b. 120, 350

8. Find the largest number that will divide 398, 436 and 542 leaving behind remainders of 7, 11 and 15, respectively.

9. In the morning, three people, A, B and C start walking together. Their steps measure 80 cm, 90 cm and 100 cm, respectively. What is the minimum distance each should walk so that all can cover the distance in complete steps?

10. A rectangular courtyard is 20 m 16 cm long and 15 m 60 cm broad. It is to be paved with square stones of the same size. Find the least possible number of stones that would be required.

CHAPTER 3 Whole Numbers

Numbers are used for counting.

Things can be counted with the help of numbers. These numbers are called natural numbers. Natural numbers are 1, 2, 3, 4 and so on. They are unlimited.

1. Elephants

2. Camels

3. Bears

4. Apples

5. Oranges

6. Bananas

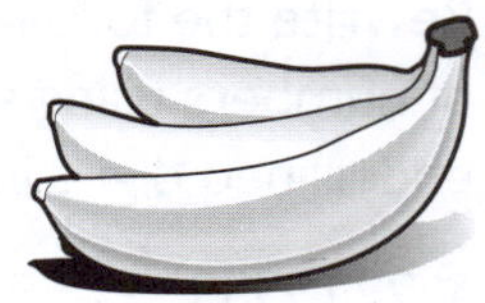

7. Kites

8. Pencils

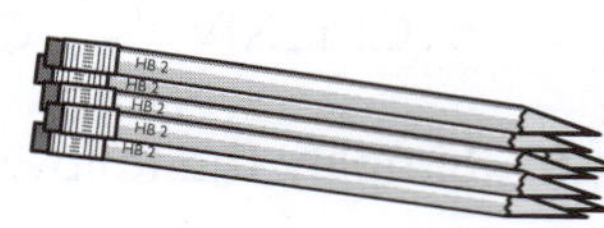

9. Umbrellas

10. Chocolates

These are some of the things that can be counted with numbers.

When we add any two natural numbers, we get a third number, which is also a natural number.

Example 1:

$$\underset{\text{(natural number)}}{\underset{\downarrow}{100}} + \underset{\text{(natural number)}}{\underset{\downarrow}{50}} = \underset{\text{(natural number)}}{\underset{\downarrow}{150}}$$

Example 2:

20	+	20	=	40
(natural number)	+	(natural number)	=	(natural number)

Now, let us see what happens when we subtract two natural numbers.

Example 1:

100	−	50	=	50
(natural number)	−	(natural number)	=	(natural number)

Example 2:

20	−	20	=	0
(natural number)	−	(natural number)	=	zero

0 is not a counting number. It is not a natural number.

When we add 0 to any natural number, we get a new set of numbers called whole numbers. This set of whole numbers is denoted by W and is written as W = {0, 1, 2, 3, 4 ...}

Thus, natural numbers or N = {1, 2, 3, 4, 5 ...}

and whole numbers or W = {0, 1, 2, 3, 4, 5 ...}.

The smallest natural number is 1.

The smallest whole number is 0.

The fundamental or basic operations on natural numbers can be performed on whole numbers as well. Whole numbers, however, have some additional properties as well.

Properties of Whole Numbers

Properties of Addition

(a) Closure Property

The sum of two whole numbers is always a whole number. This is called the closure property. If a and b are two whole numbers, then a + b = c is also a whole number. When the sum of two whole numbers is also a whole number, we say that the closure property is satisfied for addition.

Example:

15	+	17	=	32
whole number	+	whole number	=	whole number

(b) Commutative Property

The sum of two whole numbers remains the same, even if the order of the numbers is changed. This property is called the commutative property. If a and b are two whole numbers, then $a + b = b + a$.

Example:

$$15 + 17 = 17 + 15$$
$$32 = 32$$

We say that the addition of two whole numbers is commutative.

(c) Associative Property

The sum of three whole numbers remains the same even if the grouping is changed. This property is called the associative property. If a, b and c are three whole numbers, then $(a + b) + c = a + (b + c)$

Example:

$$(2 + 3) + 5 = 2 + (3 + 5)$$
$$5 + 5 = 2 + 8$$
$$10 = 10$$

We say that the addition of three whole numbers is associative.

(d) Identity Element

If 0 is added to any whole number, the sum is the number itself. Therefore, the number 0 is called the additive identity as it does not change the value of the number when the addition operation is performed on the number. Thus, $a + 0 = 0 + a = a$.

Example:

$$7 + 0 = 0 + 7 = 7$$

Properties of Subtraction

(a) Closure Property

The difference of two whole numbers is not always a whole number. If a and b are two whole numbers then, if

i) $a > b$ — $a - b$ is a whole number

ii) $a = b$ — $a - b = 0$, which is a whole number

iii) $a < b$ — $a - b$ is not a whole number

Hence, the closure property of subtraction does not hold good for the subtraction of whole numbers.

Example: Consider the two numbers 12 and 5.

Here $12 - 5 = 7$ is a whole number

but $5 - 12 = -7$, which is not a whole number.

(b) Commutative Property

The subtraction of two whole numbers is not commutative. If a and b are two whole numbers, then $a - b$ is not equal to $b - a$.

$$a - b \neq b - a$$

Hence, the commutative property of subtraction does not hold good for the subtraction of two whole numbers.

Example:
$$12 - 5 \neq 5 - 12$$
$$7 \neq -7$$

(c) Associative Property

The subtraction of three whole numbers is not associative. If a, b and c are three whole numbers, then $(a - b) - c \neq a - (b - c)$.

Hence, the associative property does not hold good for the subtraction of whole numbers.

Example:
$$(40 - 25) - 10 \neq 40 - (25 - 10)$$
$$15 - 10 \neq 40 - 15$$
$$5 \neq 25$$

(d) Property of 0

If we subtract 0 from any whole number, the result remains the number itself.

Example: $7 - 0 = 7$

Properties of Multiplication

(a) Closure Property

The product of two whole numbers is always a whole number. If a and b are two whole numbers, then $a \times b = c$ is also a whole number.

Thus, we say that the closure property is satisfied for multiplication.

Example:

5	$\times$	7	=	35
whole number		whole number		whole number

(b) Commutative Property

The product of two whole numbers remains unchanged even if the order of the whole numbers is changed. This is called the commutative property of multiplication. If a and b are two whole numbers, then $a \times b = b \times a$.

Example: $5 \times 7 = 7 \times 5$

$$35 = 35$$

Thus, we say that multiplication of two whole numbers is commutative.

(c) Associative Property

The product of three numbers remains unchanged even if the grouping is changed. This is the associative property of multiplication. If a, b and c are three whole numbers, then $(a \times b) \times c = a \times (b \times c)$.

Thus, we say that the multiplication of three numbers is associative.

Example: $(7 \times 5) \times 2 = 7 \times (5 \times 2)$

$$35 \times 2 = 7 \times 10$$

$$70 = 70$$

(d) Identity Element

If the number 1 is multiplied with any whole number, the product is the number itself. Let a be a whole number, then $a \times 1 = 1 \times a = a$.

Thus, the number '1' is called the multiplicative identity.

Example: $75 \times 1 = 1 \times 75 = 75$

(e) Multiplicative Property of 0

Any whole number multiplied by 0 gives the product as 0. If a is any whole number, then $a \times 0 = 0 \times a = 0$.

Example: $8 \times 0 = 0 \times 8 = 0$

Properties of Division

(a) Closure Property

The division of whole numbers does not always result in a whole number. If a and b are whole numbers, then $a \div b$ is *not* always a whole number. Hence, the closure property does not hold good for the division of whole numbers.

Example: $15 \div 5 = 3$, which is a whole number

However, $15 \div 7 = \frac{15}{7}$, which is *not* a whole number.

(b) Commutative Property

The division of whole numbers is not commutative. If a and b are two whole numbers, then $a \div b \neq b \div a$. Thus, the commutative property for the division of two whole numbers does not hold good.

Example:

$$15 \div 5 \neq 5 \div 15$$

$$\frac{15}{5} \neq \frac{5}{15}$$

$$3 \neq \frac{1}{3}$$

(c) Associative Property

The division of three whole numbers is not associative. If a, b and c are three whole numbers, then $(a \div b) \div c \neq a \div (b \div c)$. Hence, the associative property does not hold good for the division of whole numbers.

Example:

$$(15 \div 3) \div 5 \neq 15 \div (3 \div 5)$$

$$\left(\frac{15}{3}\right) \div 5 \neq 15 \div \left(\frac{3}{5}\right)$$

$$5 \div 5 \neq 15 \div \frac{3}{5}$$

$$\frac{5}{5} \neq 15 \times \frac{5}{3}$$

$$1 \neq 25$$

(d) Property of 0

If a is a whole number then $0 \div a = 0$ but $a \div 0$ is undefined.

Example: Here, $\frac{0}{7} = 0$ but $\frac{7}{0}$ is undefined.

Distributive Property

Distributive property is a property of multiplication.

(a) Multiplication distributes over addition. If a, b and c are three whole numbers, then $a(b + c) = ab + ac$.

We are distributing or breaking b and c into two parts and multiplying each of them with a.

(b) Multiplication distributes over subtraction. If a, b and c are three whole numbers, then $a(b - c) = ab - ac$, if $b > c$.

We are distributing or breaking b and c into two parts and multiplying each of them with a.

Patterns in Numbers

Let us observe patterns involving numbers.

First, we will try to arrange numbers in the following shapes:

a. line b. triangle c. rectangle d. square

a. Line:

We can write the number 2 as • •
3 as • • •
4 as • • • •

Thus, every number can be arranged in a line.

b. Triangle:

Not every number can be arranged as a triangle. A triangle has three vertices. Hence, the first number that can be arranged in the shape of a triangle shape is the number 3.

We can arrange 3 as 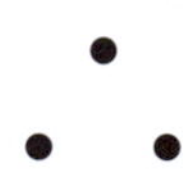

Now, when 3 is added to 3, we get 6.

We can arrange 6 as: 

When 4 is added to 6, we get 10.

We can arrange 10 as: 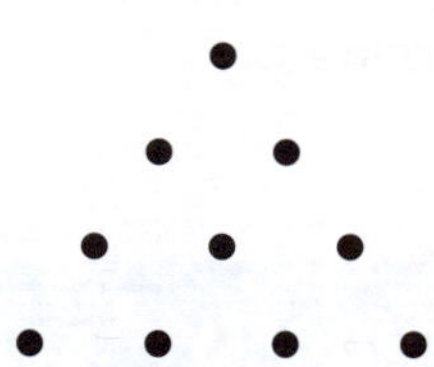

When 5 is added to 10, we get 15.

We can arrange 15 as: 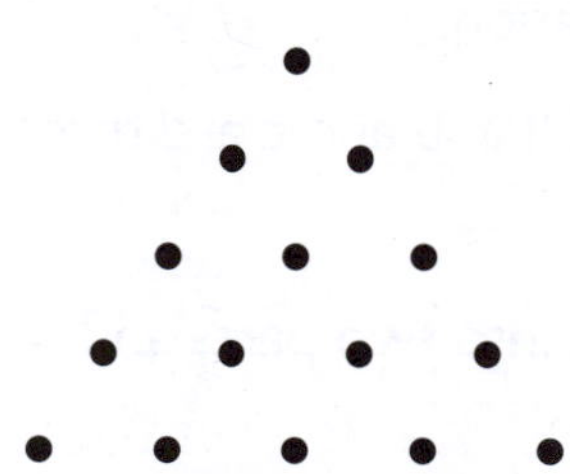

When 6 is added to 15, we get 21.

Try and form the pattern yourself.

Wasn't that fun? Now, continue with the patterns and enjoy! In more senior classes you will learn about Pascal's triangle, which provides some very interesting patterns of numbers.

c. Rectangle:

All even numbers that are greater than two can be arranged in the shape of a rectangle. In a rectangle, the horizontal lines are called rows and the vertical lines are called columns. By convention, in any rectangular pattern the number of rows are fewer than the number of columns.

The number 6 can be arranged as:

There are 2 rows and 3 columns in this pattern.

The number 8 can be arranged as:

There are 2 rows and 4 columns in this pattern.

d. Square:

When the rows and the columns are the same or equal, we get the pattern of a square. All numbers that are arranged in a square pattern are called square numbers.

Examples:

$2 \times 2 = 4$

$3 \times 3 = 9$

$4 \times 4 = 16$

$5 \times 5 = 25$

You can draw $6 \times 6 = 36$ on your own.

Let us observe some other interesting patterns in natural numbers.

a.

$$\underline{1} \times 8 + \underline{1} = 9$$
$$1\underline{2} \times 8 + \underline{2} = 98$$
$$12\underline{3} \times 8 + \underline{3} = 987$$
$$1{,}23\underline{4} \times 8 + \underline{4} = 9{,}876$$
$$12{,}34\underline{5} \times 8 + \underline{5} = 98{,}765$$
$$1{,}23{,}45\underline{6} \times 8 + \underline{6} = 9{,}87{,}654$$

and so on.

b. $\underline{1} \times 9 + \underline{2} = 11$

$1\underline{2} \times 9 + \underline{3} = 111$

$12\underline{3} \times 9 + \underline{4} = 1{,}111$

$1{,}23\underline{4} \times 9 + \underline{5} = 11{,}111$

$12{,}34\underline{5} \times 9 + \underline{6} = 1{,}11{,}111$

$1{,}23{,}45\underline{6} \times 9 + \underline{7} = 11{,}11{,}111$

and so on.

c. $9 \times 9 + 7 = 88$

$98 \times 9 + 6 = 888$

$987 \times 9 + 5 = 8{,}888$

$9{,}876 \times 9 + 4 = 88{,}888$

$98{,}765 \times 9 + 3 = 8{,}88{,}888$

$9{,}87{,}654 \times 9 + 2 = 88{,}88{,}888$

and so on.

d. $(11)^2 = 121$

$(111)^2 = 12{,}321$

$(1{,}111)^2 = 12{,}34{,}321$

$(11{,}111)^2 = 12{,}34{,}54{,}321$

and so on.

e. $1 = \frac{1 \times 2}{2}$

$1 + 2 = \frac{2 \times 3}{2}$

$1 + 2 + 3 = \frac{3 \times 4}{2}$

$1 + 2 + 3 + 4 = \frac{4 \times 5}{2}$

$1 + 2 + 3 + 4 + 5 = \frac{5 \times 6}{2}$

and so on.

Practice Exercise 3.1

1. Which property do the following represent?

a. $17 + 18 = 18 + 17$

b. $(20 + 22) + 24 = 20 + (22 + 24)$

c. $25 + 0 = 25 = 0 + 25$

d. $(15 \times 17) \times 16 = 15 \times (17 \times 16)$

e. $25 \times 22 = 22 \times 25$

f. $41 \times 1 = 41 = 1 \times 41$

g. $9 \times (8 + 7) = 9 \times 8 + 9 \times 7$

h. $5 \times 20 = 100 = 20 \times 5$

i. $100 + 101 = 201 = 101 + 100$

j. $16 + (8 \times 7) = 16 + 8 \times 16 + 7$

2. Find the product of the following.

   a. $2 \times 127 \times 50$ b. $1{,}234 \times 4 \times 25$ c. $40 \times 625 \times 25$

   d. $125 \times 426 \times 8$ e. $5 \times 650 \times 10$

3. Solve the following using the distributive property of multiplication over addition.

   a. $20 \times 7 + 12 \times 7$ b. $16 \times 12 + 16 \times 8$ c. $25 \times 7 + 8 \times 25$

   d. $6{,}725 \times 99 + 6{,}725$ e. $42 \times 860 + 860 \times 58$

4. Solve the following using the distributive property of multiplication over addition.

   a. 642×110 b. 857×102 c. 46×506

   d. $112 \times 1{,}004$ e. $678 \times 10{,}001$

5. Radha secured 96 marks in mathematics and 69 marks in social studies in the final examination, whereas Sudha secured 69 marks in social studies and 96 marks in mathematics. Who secured better marks in the combined subjects? Which property is applicable to find the sum?

6. There are two bookshops in a shopping arcade. Shop A sold 245 copies of the latest *Harry Potter* book per day and Shop B sold 305 copies of the same per day. Find the total number of books sold by Shop A and Shop B in 10 days. Name the property of whole numbers used for finding the answer.

7. The population of a village is 84,975. One out of every 11 persons is educated in the village. Find the number of educated and uneducated people in the village.

8. Determine the product of the greatest number of four digits and the smallest number of three digits. Also find the product of the smallest number of four digits and the greatest number of three digits. Find the difference between the two products.

9. New tables and chairs are required for a class of 50 students. A table costs ₹180 and a chair ₹220. Use the distributive property of multiplication over addition to find the total cost of the tables and chairs.

10. Study the following patterns and write the next two steps for each pattern.

a. $1 + 2 + 3 + 4 + 5 + 6 + 7 + 8 + 9 + 10 = 55$

$11 + 12 + 13 + 14 + 15 + 16 + 17 + 18 + 19 + 20 = 155$

$21 + 22 + 23 + 24 + 25 + 26 + 27 + 28 + 29 + 30 = 255$

$31 + 32 + 33 + 34 + 35 + 36 + 37 + 38 + 39 + 40 = 355$

__ __ __ __ __ __ __ __ __ __ ___

__ __ __ __ __ __ __ __ __ __ ___

b. $(1 \times 2) + (2 \times 3) = \frac{2 \times 3 \times 4}{3}$

$(1 \times 2) + (2 \times 3) + (3 \times 4) = \frac{3 \times 4 \times 5}{3}$

$(1 \times 2) + (2 \times 3) + (3 \times 4) + (4 \times 5) = \frac{4 \times 5 \times 6}{3}$

____

____

c. $1 + 3 = 4 = 2 \times 2$

$1 + 3 + 5 = 9 = 3 \times 3$

$1 + 3 + 5 + 7 = 16 = 4 \times 4$

__________ __ _____

__________ __ _____

d.

1

$1 + 1$

$1 + 2 + 1$

$1 + 3 + 3 + 1$

$1 + 4 + 6 + 4 + 1$

____

____

Highlights

- The numbers 1, 2, 3, 4, 5 … are called natural numbers.
- All natural numbers together with 0 are called whole numbers.
- Every natural number is a whole number whereas 0 is a whole number that is not a natural number.
- The smallest natural number is 1. The smallest whole number is 0.
- Addition and multiplication of whole numbers always gives a whole number. The closure property holds true for the addition and multiplication of whole numbers.
- Subtraction and division do not satisfy the closure property of whole numbers.
- Addition and multiplication satisfy the commutative property of whole numbers. Thus, $a + b = b + a$ and $a \times b = b \times a$

  where a and b are any two whole numbers.
- Subtraction and division do not satisfy the commutative property of whole numbers.
- Addition and multiplication satisfy the associative property of whole numbers. Thus, $(a + b) + c = a + (b + c)$ and $(a \times b) \times c = a \times (b \times c)$

  where a, b and c are any three whole numbers.
- Subtraction and division do not satisfy the associative property of whole numbers.
- For whole numbers, the additive identity is 0 and the multiplicative identity is 1.
- If we multiply 0 with any whole number, the answer is always 0.
- If we divide 0 by any whole number, the answer is always 0.
- Division by 0 is not defined.
- When any whole number (other than 0) is divided by itself, the quotient is always 1.
- Multiplication is distributive over addition for whole numbers.
- For division of whole numbers, the relationship—

  dividend = (divisor × quotient) + remainder—holds true.
- Numbers can be arranged in simple elementary shapes, which makes it easy to understand their properties.
- Being aware of patterns in numbers helps to make mental calculations.

Higher Order Thinking Skills

HOTS

1. Find the smallest whole number that can be added to 750 so that the resulting number is divisible by 13.

2. Find the smallest whole number that must be subtracted from 13,666 to get a number exactly divisible by 78.

3. Using the distributive property of whole numbers, find the product of $12{,}345 \times 6{,}789 - 12{,}345 \times 5{,}789$.

Cool trick with a dice.

The opposite sides of a dice always add up to 7. You can use this fact and become a magician. Your friends will be amazed when you tell them what number is on the opposite side of the dice without looking. They will think you have X-ray vision.

Magic with Numbers

Objective: To arrange numbers in a pattern for demonstrating an elementary shape.

Material required: Sheet of chart paper, colourful small round bindis or dots made with sketch pens

Procedure:

1. To show a triangle you need three dots.

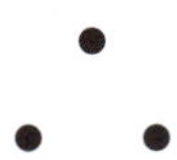

2. When you add 3 to the initial 3 dots, you get 3 + 3 = 6 dots.
3. So you make a pattern with 6 dots.

4. Now, if you add 4 to 6, you get 6 + 4 = 10.
5. Now, the next triangle that can be formed will be with $10 + \underline{5} = 15$
6. You can make varied designs and show your friends the magic of numbers.

$$\begin{array}{c} 3 \\ 3 + \underline{3} = 6 \\ 6 + \underline{4} = 10 \\ 10 + \underline{5} = 15 \\ 15 + \underline{6} = 21 \\ 21 + \underline{7} = 28 \end{array}$$

7. You can also show perfect squares by making patterns as follows.

$1 \times 1 = 1$
(1 dot)

$2 \times 2 = 4$
(4 dots)

$3 \times 3 = 9$
(9 dots)

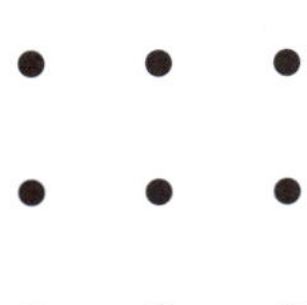

$4 \times 4 = 16$
(16 dots)

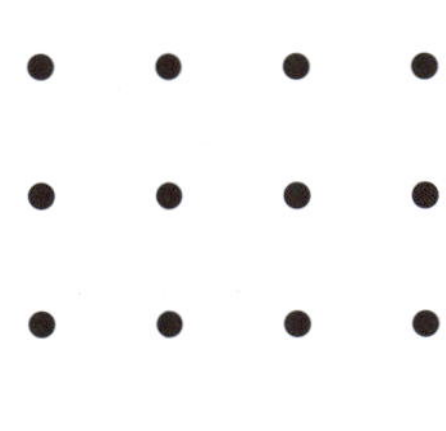

CHAPTER 4

Negative Numbers and Integers

By now you must have a clear understanding of natural and whole numbers. In this chapter we will discuss negative numbers and integers.

When a smaller whole number is subtracted from a larger whole number, the answer obtained is also a whole number.

For example, consider there are 5 birds sitting on a tree. They hear a loud noise and all of them fly away. Now there are *no* birds on the tree or, there are 0 birds on the tree.

Now, let us examine what happens when a bigger whole number is subtracted from a smaller whole number.

For example, if you are asked to subtract 25 from 15, what would the answer be?

Here, $15 - 25 = -10$.

A negative (or minus) sign in front of a number symbolises that it is a negative number.

Before we proceed further, let us look at this example and understand the number system.

We have $25 - 15 = 10$, which is a whole number and a natural number.

We see $25 - 25 = 0$, which is a whole number but not a natural number.

Finally, $15 - 25 = -10$, which is neither a whole number nor a natural number.

We can say that negative numbers are the opposite of positive numbers.

Just as in the English language, the opposite of hot is cold and the opposite of day is night, similarly in the number system, the opposite of $+7$ is -7 and the opposite of $+100$ is -100.

All the numbers with a positive (+ve) sign are called positive numbers. While all the numbers with a negative (−ve) sign are called negative numbers. Zero is neither positive nor negative.

A set of numbers that includes all positive numbers, negative numbers and 0 are called integers. We can denote the set by I or Z.

Thus, $+1$, $+2$, $+3$ are positive integers,

while -1, -2, -3 are negative integers.

As the set of whole numbers is unlimited, the positive integers as well as the negative integers are also unlimited.

Let us compare natural numbers, whole numbers and integers with the help of a number line.

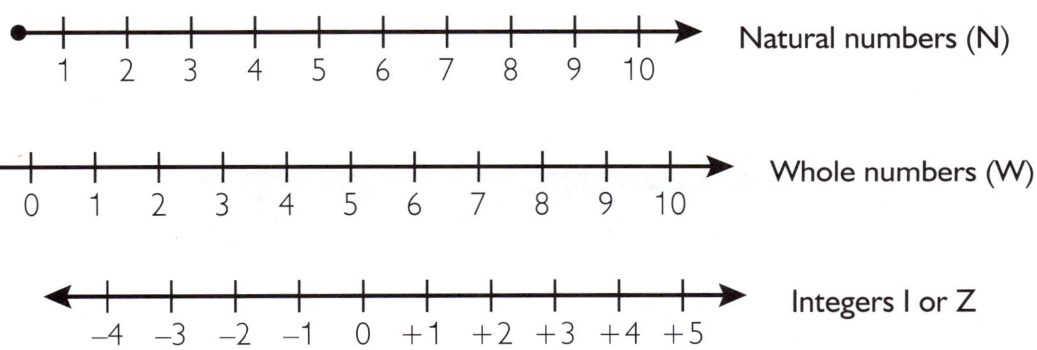

On the number line, the positive integers on the right of 0 go on increasing and the negative integers on the left of 0 go on decreasing.

A number on the right of any number is always greater. Thus $+4 > +3$, and $-3 > -4$.

Examples:

Indicate each of the conditions mentioned below by using integers.

a. 13° above zero	$+13°$
b. A deposit of ₹350 in the bank	+₹350
c. A withdrawal of ₹250 from the bank.	−₹250
d. Lose by 10 runs	−10 runs
e. 5% increase in marks	+5%

Negative of a Negative Integer

As per the number line, we can deduce:

1. +1 is the smallest positive integer
2. −1 is the largest negative integer
3. 0 is less than every positive integer
4. 0 is greater than every negative integer

Absolute Value of an Integer

The absolute value of an integer is its numerical value irrespective of the sign in front of it. The absolute value is denoted by $| \, |$. It is always positive.

$|8| = 8$ $\qquad |-8| = 8$

$-|8| = -8$ $\qquad -|-8| = -8$

Practice Exercise 4.1

1. Write the opposites of the following.

   a. +234 b. increase in marks c. 70 km to the east

   d. 10°C below 0°C e. 5 years hence

2. Use + or − sign to represent the following.

   a. ₹500 profit b. 20 years ago c. 10 steps into the basement

   d. 600 m above sea level e. 5 kg decrease in weight

3. Write the opposites of the following.

   a. −10 b. +200 c. +120 d. −21 e. 0

4. Find the values of the following.

   a. $|-10|$ b. $26 - |6|$ c. $|12 - 10|$ d. $|9 + 11|$ e. $-|-100|$

5. Mark the following integers on the number line.

a. -10 b. 12 c. -4 d. 0 e. 8

6. Replace $\triangle$ in each of the following by $>$ or $<$ so that the statement is correct.

a. $0 \triangle 15$ b. $-10 \triangle -15$ c. $-20 \triangle -15$ d. $15 \triangle 20$ e. $15 \triangle -20$

7. Write all the integers that fall between each of the two sets of numbers given here.

a. -3 and 2 b. 0 and 5 c. -4 and 4 d. -7 and -4 e. -1 and 1

8. Arrange the integers in ascending order.

a. $-4, -7, 2, 0, -3$

b. $3, 9, -2, -4, 1$

c. $-7, -17, -27, 7, 17$

d. $6, -7, 8, -9, 10$

e. $-11, 24, -29, -101, 50$

9. Arrange the integers in descending order.

a. $-8, 11, 14, 0, -7$ b. $15, -12, -6, -5, 8$ c. $6, -4, 0, -3, 1$

d. $7, -8, 8, 3, -9$ e. $-200, -150, 10, 20, -50$

10. Where will we reach on the number line if we move:

a. 5 numbers to the right of l.

b. 5 numbers to the left of 0.

c. 5 numbers to the left of -1.

d. 5 numbers to the right of 3.

e. 5 numbers to the left of -4.

Operations on Integers

We can perform four fundamental operations on integers—addition, subtraction, multiplication and division.

Addition of Integers

We will study different cases with the help of a number line.

Case 1. Integers with the same sign. Add 7 and 2.

a. Both the integers are positive.

Let us represent 7 + 2 on the number line. We move 7 steps to the right of 0, we again move 2 steps to the right of 7 and reach 9.

$\therefore \quad 7 + 2 = 9$ or

$|7| + |2| = 9$

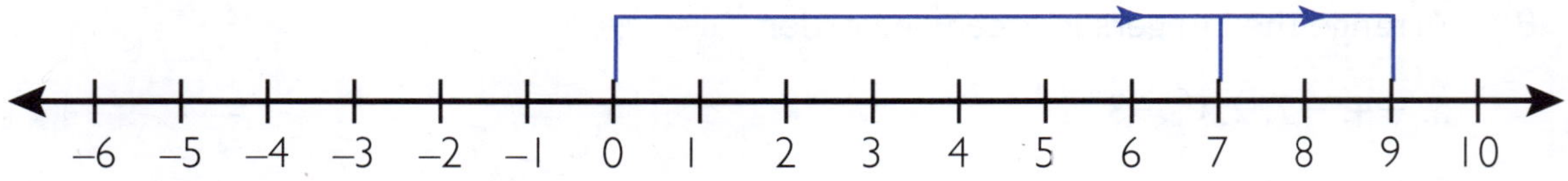

b. Both the integers are negative. Add −3 and −4.

Let us represent −3 plus −4 on the number line.

We move 3 steps to the left of 0 and then again 4 steps to the left of −3 to reach −7.

$\therefore \quad -3 - 4 = -7$

$|-3| + |-4| = -7$

$-[-3 + -4] = -7$

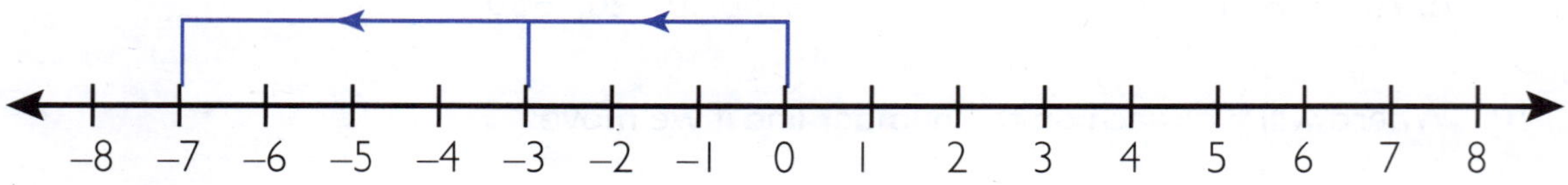

Case 2. Integers with opposite signs. Add +3 and −7.
One integer is positive and one is negative.

Let us represent +3 − 7 on the number line. We start from 0 and move 3 steps towards its right and reach 3, then move 7 steps to the left to represent the negative integer 7 and reach −4.

$3 - 7 = -4$

$|3| - |-7| = 3 - 7 = -4$

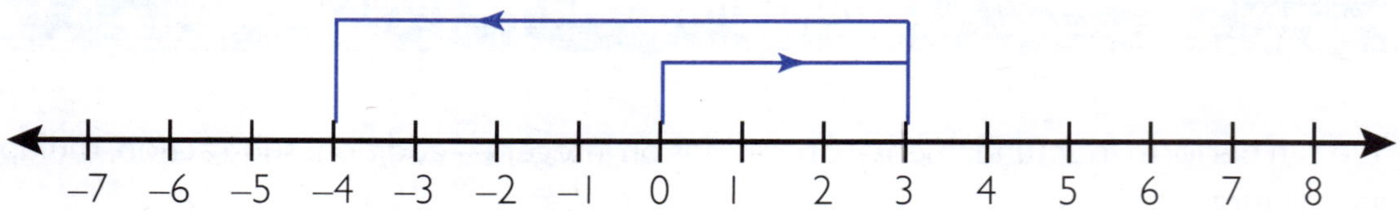

Additive Inverse

If two integers have the same absolute value but have opposite signs, their sum is 0. Each is called the additive inverse of the other.

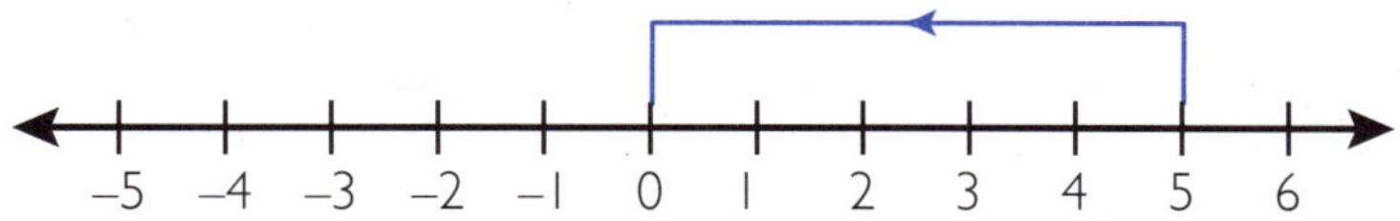

The additive inverse of $+5$ is -5 as $(+5) + (-5) = 0$.

Example 1: Subtract 12 from -5.

$12 + (-5) = 7$

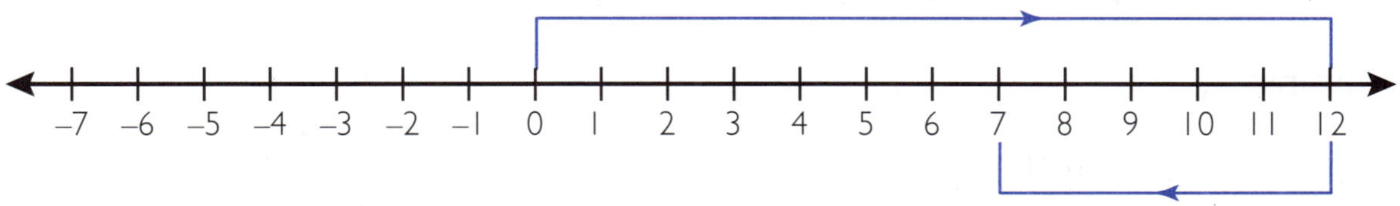

First, move 12 steps to the right from 0 and then 5 steps to the left of 12. The answer will be 7.

Example 2: Subtract -7 from -12.

$(-12) - (-7) = (-12) + 7 = -5$

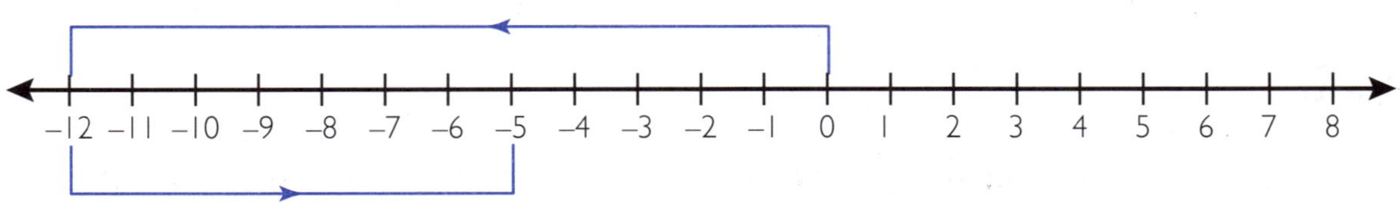

First, move 12 steps to the left of 0 and then 7 steps to the right of -12. We reach -5.

Example 3: Subtract 7 from -12.

$(-12) - (7) = (-12) + (-7) = -19$

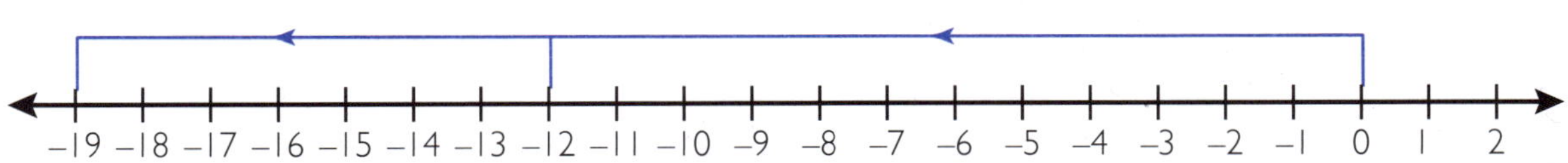

First, move 12 steps to the left of 0 and then again 7 steps to the left of -12. We reach -19.

Subtraction of Integers

In subtraction, we change the sign of the integer that is to be subtracted and then add to the first integer. Subtraction is also called negative addition.

Example 1:

Subtract 5 from 12

$(12) - 5 = 12 + (-5) = 7$

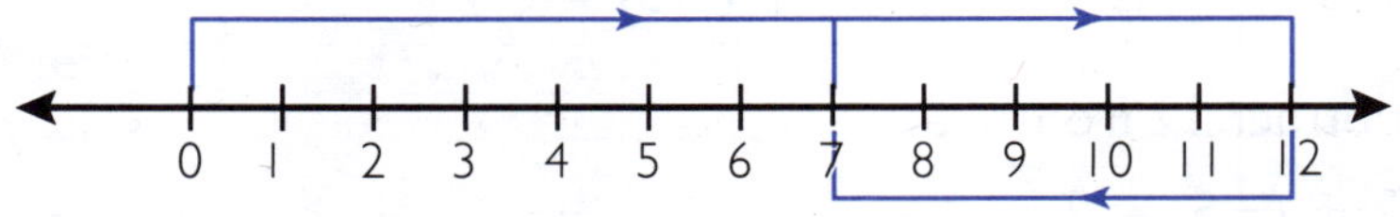

First, move 12 steps on the right of 0 and then 5 steps to the left of 12 to reach 7.

Example 2:

Subtract (-7) from 10

$10 - (-7) = 10 + 7 = 17$

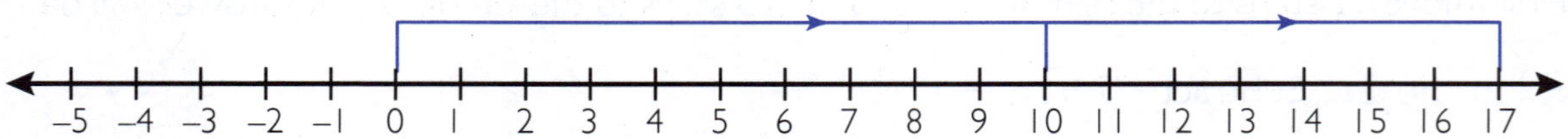

First, move 10 steps on the right of 0 and then another 7 steps to the right of 10, to reach 17.

Alert!

1. The sum of two integers with the same sign is the difference of their absolute values with the same sign.

   $(+10) + (+7) = +17$

   $(-10) + (-7) = -17$

2. The sum of two integers with opposite signs is the sum of their absolute values with the sign of the greater number.

   $(+10) + (-7) = +3$

   $(-10) + (+7) = -3$

Alert!

In subtraction, the sign of the integer that is to be subtracted is changed and then that integer is added to the first integer.

The negative of a negative integer becomes a positive.

Multiplication of Integers

Case 1. Multiplication of integers with the same sign

When two integers have the same sign, their product is the product of their absolute values with a positive sign.

Example 1: $(+7) \times (+8) = +56$ or 56

Example 2: $(-7) \times (-8) = +56$ or 56

Case 2. Multiplication of integers with opposite signs

When two integers have the opposite sign, their product is the product of their absolute values with a negative sign.

Example 1: $(+10) \times (-8) = -80$

Example 2: $(-10) \times (+8) = -80$

Alert!

plus × plus = plus	$(+) \times (+) = +$
minus × minus = plus	$(-) \times (-) = +$
plus × minus = minus	$(+) \times (-) = -$
minus × plus = minus	$(-) \times (+) = -$

Division of Integers

Case 1. Division of integers with the same sign

Division of integers with the same sign is the division of their absolute values with a positive sign. If both integers have the same sign, then the quotient will be positive.

Example 1: $(+18) \div (+6) = +3$ or 3

Example 2: $(-18) \div (-6) = +3$ or 3

Case 2. Division of integers with opposite signs

Division of integers with the opposite sign is the division of their absolute values with a negative sign. If both integers have opposite signs, the quotient will have a negative sign.

Example 1: $(+18) \div (-3) = -6$

Example 2: $(-18) \div (+3) = -6$

Alert!

(plus) ÷ (plus) = plus	$(+) \div (+) = +$
(minus) ÷ (minus) = plus	$(-) \div (-) = +$
(plus) ÷ (minus) = minus	$(+) \div (-) = -$
(minus) ÷ (plus) = minus	$(-) \div (+) = -$

Practice Exercise 4.2

1. Represent the following numbers on a number line.

   a. 4 more than (-6) b. 2 less than 6 c. $2 + 3 + (-5)$

   d. $(-8) + (+8)$ e. $0 + (10) + (-10)$

2. Find the successor of each of the following.

   a. 256 b. (-256) c. -1 d. 89 e. (-89)

3. Find the predecessor of each of the following.

   a. 0 b. 42 c. (-42) d. 90 e. (-90)

4. Add the following integers.

   a. $78, -15$ b. $48, 38$ c. $-32, 68$

   d. $-42, -35$ e. $36, 32, -34$

5. Subtract the following integers.

   a. 64 from 46 b. -28 from -42 c. -18 from 27

   d. -45 from 0 e. 53 from (-58)

6. Multiply the following integers.

a. $(-18) \times (-3)$ b. $(24) \times (6)$ c. $52 \times (-5)$

d. $(-48) \times 7$ e. $(-92) \times (-1)$

7. Divide the following integers.

a. $(-64) \div (-8)$ b. $84 \div 7$ c) $(-55) \div 5$

d. $2010 \div (-10)$ e. $(-462) \div (-11)$

8. Fill in the blanks.

a. $250 \quad + \quad \boxed{} \quad = -2$

b. $-18 \quad - \quad \boxed{} \quad = +2$

c. $-41 \quad + \quad \boxed{} \quad = +4$

d. $85 \quad \times \quad \boxed{} \quad = -85$

e. $(-78) \quad \div \quad \boxed{} \quad = 78$

9. In a set of 30 multiple choice questions, 5 (five) marks are awarded for each correct answer, -3 (minus three) marks for every wrong answer and 0 (zero) for any question left unattempted. Raju gets 9 answers correct, 15 answers wrong and leaves 6 questions unattempted. How much did Raju score?

10. What should be added to the sum of -25 and 20 to make it equal to the sum of -19 and 18?

A child in the class was being scolded by his teacher.

Teacher: All the problems that you have solved are wrong. I should call your mother and tell her that.

Child: Yes, you should. Because she has solved all of them.

Highlights

- The numbers −5, −4, −3, −2, −1, 0, 1, 2, 3, 4, 5 ... are called integers.
- 1, 2, 3, 4, 5, ... are positive integers, while −1, −2, −3, −4, −5... are negative integers.
- Zero (0) is an integer but it is neither positive nor negative.
- The absolute value of an integer is the numerical value of the integer without any regard to its sign.
- The sum of two negative integers is a negative integer having the absolute value equal to the sum of the absolute values of the given integers.
- To find the sum of a positive integer and a negative integer, we find the difference of their absolute values and assign to it the sign of the integer having a greater absolute value.
- To subtract an integer 'b' from an integer 'a', we change the sign of 'b' and add it to 'a'.
- The product of two integers with the same sign is positive.
- The product of two integers with opposite signs is negative.
- Two integers that when added give 0 are called the additive inverse of each other.

Higher Order Thinking Skills

HOTS

1. At 9 pm, the temperature at a place was 3°C. It fell by 4°C after six hours and remained constant for two hours. Find the temperature at 4 am.

2. Which integer is equal to its additive inverse? What is the difference between the smallest positive integer and the largest negative integer?

3. If the number of fives in $5 + (-5) + (5) + (-5) + 5 + (-5) + \ldots.$ is 251, then the sum is zero. Is this statement true or false? Why?

Understanding Integers

Objective: To develop the concept of addition of integers.

Material required: Coloured glazed paper (red and green), glue / fevicol and a chart paper

Procedure:

1. The students must work in pairs. Each pair should have red and green paper where red represents negative integers and green represents positive integers.
2. Cut small squares of 1 inch $\times$ 1 inch from the glazed paper.
3. The teacher will give the class some problems to solve.
4. The students begin the game. For example,

   the teacher writes $5 + (-3)$ on the board.

   One student out of the pair puts 5 green squares on the chart paper.

   The other student puts 3 red squares on the chart paper.

G	G	G	G	G
R	R	R		

Now the students have to cancel the equal number of green and red squares. After this, the total number of green squares remaining would be the answer. In this case it is $+2$.

If the sum given by the teacher is $(-3) + (-4)$, then only one student will put the red squares and count them.

This way the activity proceeds for all the students. You can use various colours as pairs such as blue–yellow, black–red, orange–yellow, green–yellow and so on to make the activity colourful.

The pair of students who complete all the questions first will be the winners.

CHAPTERS 3–4 Rewind

1. Simplify $272 \times 42 + 272 \times 50 + 272 \times 8$, by using the distributive property of multiplication.

2. Simplify $31170 \times 641 - 31170 \times 541$, by using the distributive property of multiplication.

3. Find the products by rearranging the numbers.

   a. $1500 \times 6 \times 25 \times 40$

   b. $125 \times 8 \times 750 \times 20$

4. Arrange the following numbers using dots.

   a. 12 as a rectangular pattern.

   b. 25 as a square pattern.

   c. 28 as a triangular pattern.

5. Find the sum of the following numbers by suitable rearrangement.

   a. $829 + 106 + 244 + 121$

   b. $222 + 333 + 667 + 778$

6. Find the value of: $53 + (-42) - (-29) + (-11)$

7. Find the value of: $(-1001) - (-450) + (-750)$

8. A shopkeeper makes a profit of ₹20 by selling a pair of shoes and loses ₹15 on selling a pair of socks. Find his profit or loss if he sells 3 pairs of shoes and 4 pairs of socks.

9. Raman has to reach the temple by climbing steps. He climbs 65 steps and then comes down 30 steps to drink water. He then climbs 70 steps. He drops his bag and comes down 3 steps. After climbing 6 steps he reaches the temple. Find out the total numbers of steps to the temple.

10. Subtract the sum of -1360 and 1258 from the sum of 1245 and -1425.

CHAPTER 5
Fractions

A number that compares part of an object or a set with the whole is called a fraction. The quotient of two whole numbers a and b is written as a ÷ b. It means a divided by b. It can also be written as $\frac{a}{b}$. Here, $\frac{a}{b}$ is called a fraction, where a is the numerator of the fraction and b is the denominator.

Fraction as a Part of the Whole

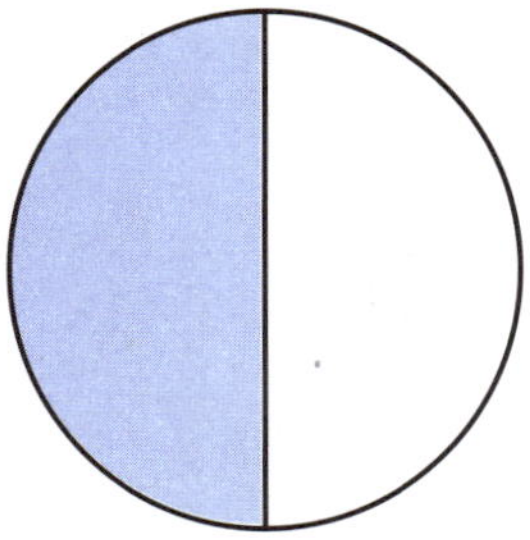

One circle divided into 2 parts.

1 part is blue
1 part is white } together the 2 parts make one circle

There are two equal parts of the circle. Each part is written as $\frac{1}{2}$, which means 1 out of 2 equal parts.

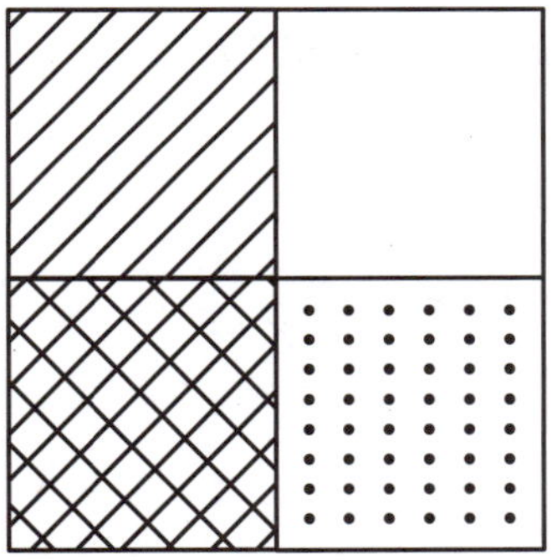

One square divided into 4 parts.

1 part is striped
1 part is dotted
1 part is blank
1 part is checked } together the 4 parts make one square

There are four equal parts of the square. Each part is written as $\frac{1}{4}$, which means 1 out of 4 equal parts.

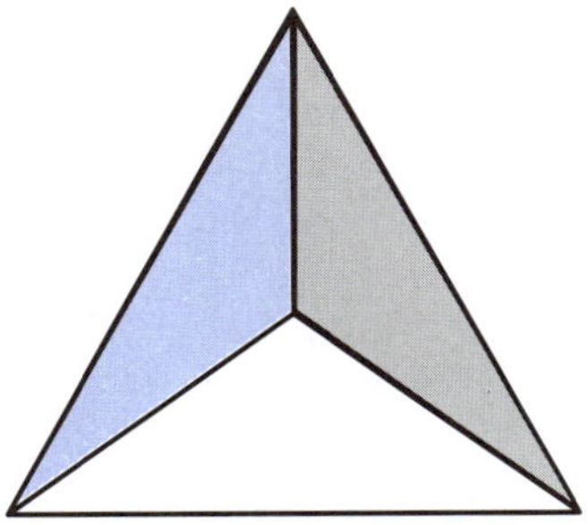

One triangle divided into 3 parts

1 part is blue
1 part is grey
1 part is white } together the 3 parts make one triangle

There are 3 equal parts of the triangle. Each part is written as $\frac{1}{3}$, which means one out of 3 equal parts.

In all the three cases mentioned above,

$\frac{1}{2}, \frac{1}{3}, \frac{1}{4}$ are the fractions of a whole.

Fraction as a Part of a Collection

Example 1: There are one dozen pencils in a box.

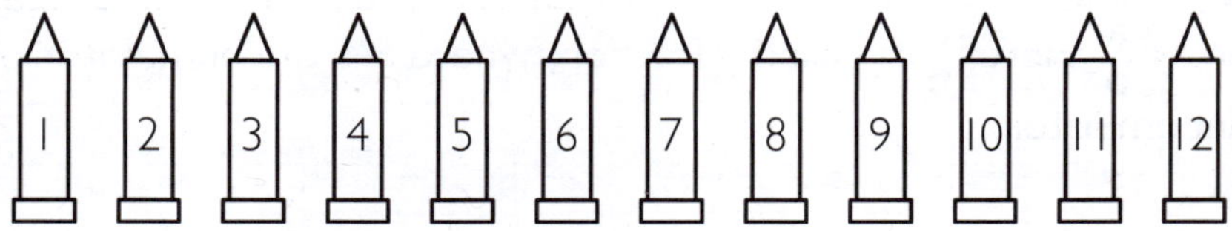

Sonu and Monu want to take equal number of pencils each. So their mother divides the pencils into two parts.

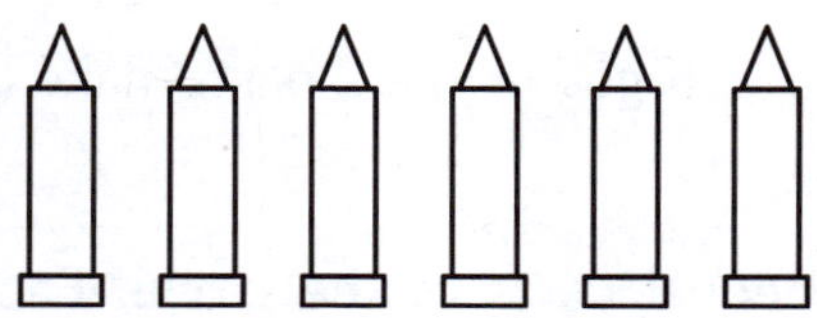

Sonu gets 6 pencils out of 12

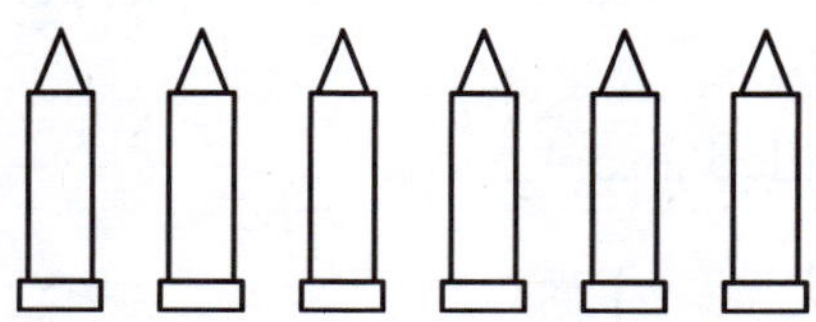

Monu gets 6 pencils out of 12

Each part is $\frac{1}{2}$ of 12. This can be represented as $= \frac{1}{2} \times 12 = 6$.

Example 2: Ashish won a chocolate bar in a competition. The bar had eight equal pieces that were demarcated.

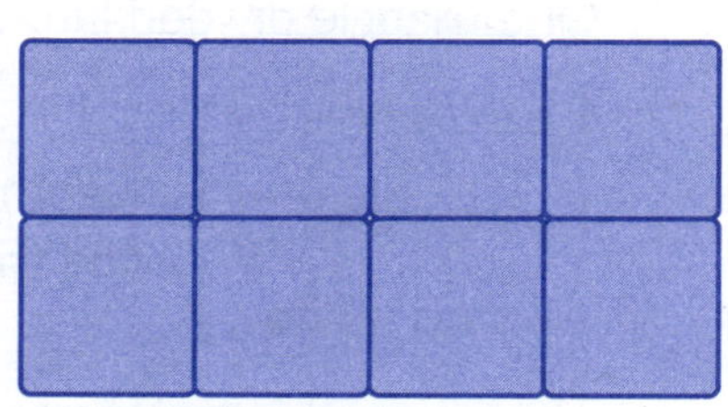

Ashish wants to share the chocolate with three of his friends. The bar of chocolate needs to be shared between 4 people: Ashish + three of his friends.

Each person will get $\frac{1}{4}$ of 8. This can be represented as $\frac{1}{4} \times 8 = 2$ pieces.

Example 3: There are 30 apples to be kept equally in 3 baskets. Each basket will have $30 \div 3 = 10$ apples.

These 10 apples are $\frac{10}{30}$ of the 30 apples.

A fraction represents a part of a collection. The numerator is the number of parts we have and the denominator is the total number of parts in the collection.

Types of Fractions

Like Fractions

Fractions having the same denominators are called like fractions.

Example: $\frac{1}{5}, \frac{2}{5}, \frac{3}{5}, \frac{4}{5}$ are like fractions

Unlike Fractions

Fractions having different denominators are called unlike fractions.

Example: $\frac{2}{5}, \frac{3}{7}, \frac{4}{9}, \frac{5}{8}$ are unlike fractions

Unit Fractions

Fractions having a numerator of 1 are called unit fractions.

Example: $\frac{1}{3}, \frac{1}{4}, \frac{1}{5}$ are unit fractions

Proper Fractions

Fraction whose numerator is less than its denominator is called a proper fraction.

Example: $\frac{2}{3}, \frac{4}{5}, \frac{7}{10}$ are proper fractions

Improper Fractions

A fraction whose numerator is greater than or equal to its denominator is called an improper fraction.

Example: $\frac{9}{8}, \frac{7}{5}, \frac{6}{6}$ are improper fractions

Mixed Fractions

A fraction that is a combination of a whole number and a proper fraction is called a mixed fraction. All improper fractions can be written in the form of mixed fractions and vice versa.

Example: $3\frac{1}{4}$ 3 is the whole number and $\frac{1}{4}$ is the proper fraction

$5\frac{2}{3}$ 5 is the whole number and $\frac{2}{3}$ is the proper fraction

$10\frac{1}{2}$ 10 is the whole number and $\frac{1}{2}$ is the proper fraction

Conversion of Improper Fractions to Mixed Fractions

To convert an improper fraction to a mixed fraction, divide the numerator by the denominator. The quotient obtained is the whole number. Write the remainder as the numerator and the divisor as the denominator.

Example: Consider an improper fraction, $\frac{13}{5}$.

$$5\overline{)13}\ \text{quotient } 2,\quad 13 - 10 = 3$$

Quotient = 2
Reminder = 3
Divisor = 5

The mixed fraction is $2\frac{3}{5}$.

Conversion of Mixed Fractions to Improper Fractions

To convert a mixed fraction to an improper fraction, multiply the whole number by the denominator. Add the numerator to the product. This addition gives the numerator of the improper fraction. The denominator remains the same.

Example: Consider a mixed fractions, $3\frac{1}{4}$

$$\frac{4 \times 3 + 1}{4} = \frac{12 + 1}{4} = \frac{13}{4}$$

The improper fraction is $\frac{13}{4}$.

Alert!

1. To change an improper fraction into a mixed fraction the formula is
   $= \text{quotient}\ \frac{\text{remainder}}{\text{divisor}}$
2. To change a mixed fraction to an improper fraction the formula is
   $= \frac{\text{whole number} \times \text{denominator} + \text{remainder}}{\text{denominator}}$

Practice Exercise 5.1

1. Write how many parts of the whole are shaded in each of the following shapes.

a. 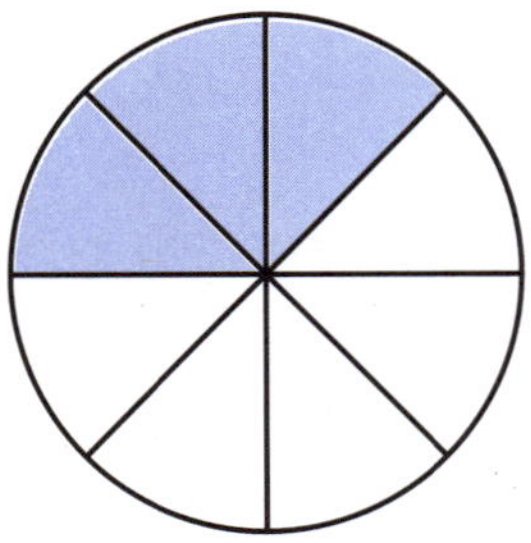

b. 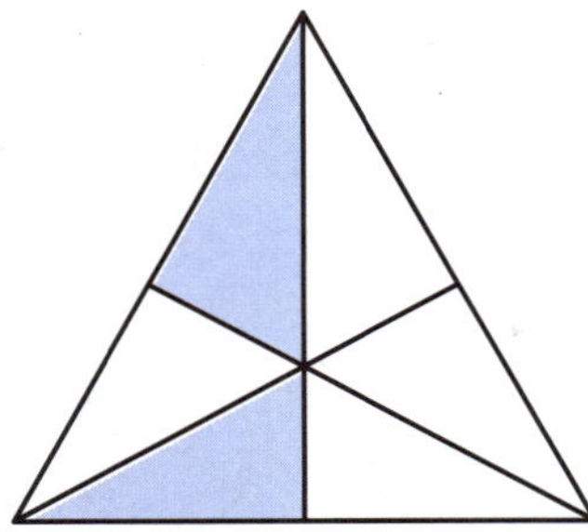

c. 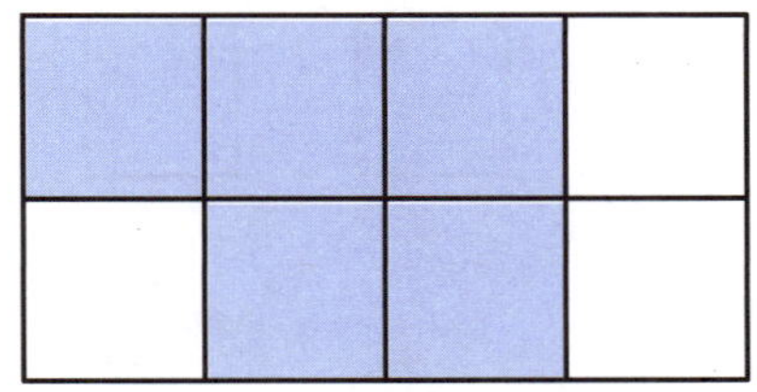

d. 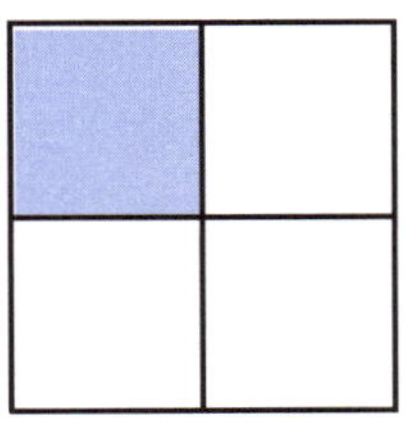

e. 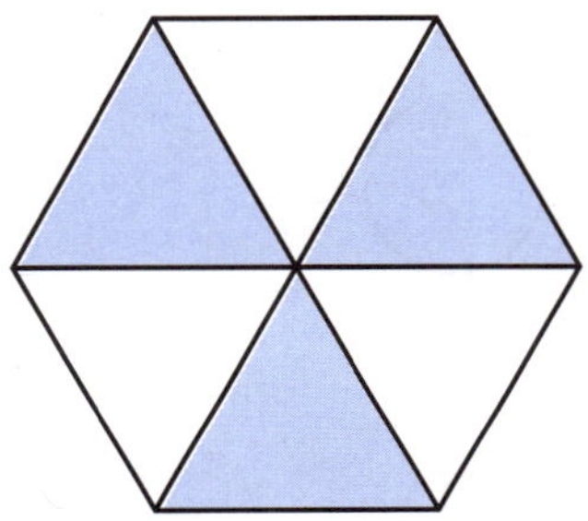

2. Name the fraction represented by the shaded parts in the following collections.

a. 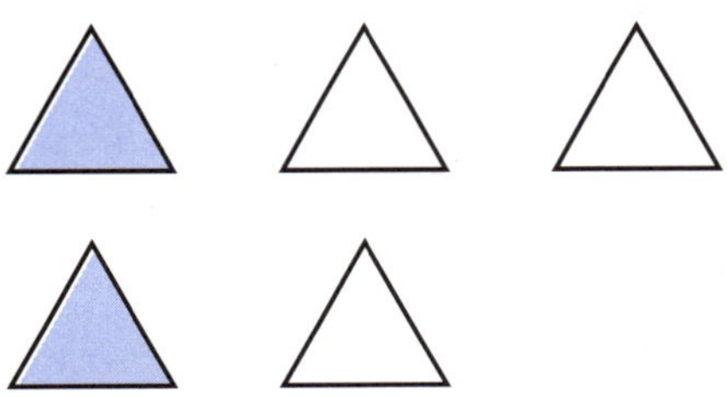

b. 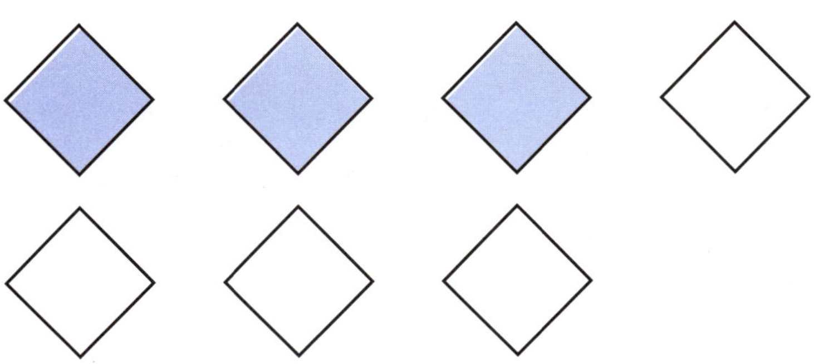

c. 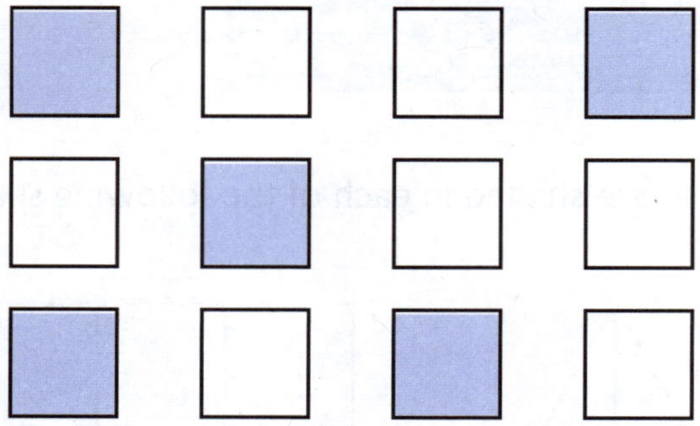

d. 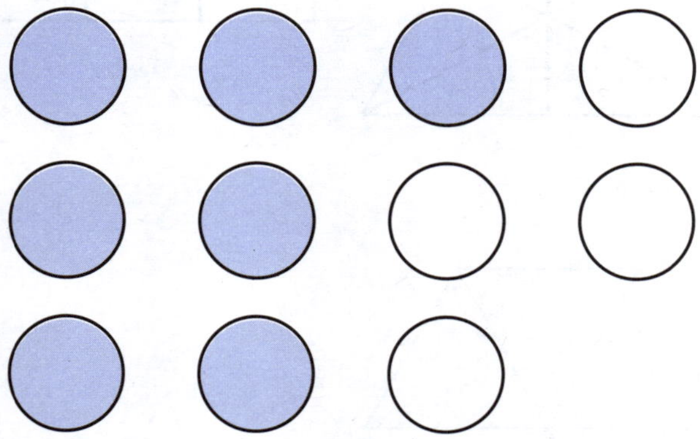

e. 

3. Write the numerator and denominator of each fraction.

a. $\frac{7}{8}$ b. $\frac{11}{13}$ c. $\frac{5}{17}$ d. $\frac{31}{60}$ e. $\frac{19}{39}$

4. Express the following as fractions.

a. Three-thirteenths b. Two-fifths c. One-third

d. Seven-ninths e. Five-eighths

5. Write the fraction for each of the following statements.

a. Nine out of 42 students are absent from the class.

b. Deepa answered 8 questions out of 15 in a mathematics test.

c. Anita spent ₹17 out of ₹25 her mother gave her.

d. Seven plants out of 20 died in a garden due to heat.

e. Meeta had three pieces of cake out of a box containing 16 pieces.

6. Pick out the proper fractions.

a. $\frac{7}{8}$ b. $\frac{9}{8}$ c. $\frac{5}{5}$ d. $\frac{3}{4}$ e. $\frac{6}{5}$

7. Convert the following improper fractions into mixed fractions.

a. $\frac{7}{3}$ b. $\frac{11}{5}$ c. $\frac{25}{6}$ d. $\frac{16}{7}$ e. $\frac{31}{8}$

8. Convert the following mixed fractions into improper fractions.

a. $2\frac{1}{5}$ b. $1\frac{1}{7}$ c. $3\frac{4}{11}$ d. $9\frac{1}{2}$ e. $2\frac{1}{3}$

9. Pick out the like fractions.

a. $\frac{1}{7}$ b. $\frac{3}{7}$ c. $\frac{7}{9}$ d. $\frac{7}{15}$ e. $\frac{4}{7}$

10. Represent the following fractions as a rectangle with shaded parts.

a. $\frac{1}{3}$ b. $\frac{3}{5}$ c. $\frac{4}{7}$ d. $\frac{7}{10}$ e. $\frac{9}{16}$

Equivalent Fractions

Look at the following figures:

(1) (2) (3) (4)

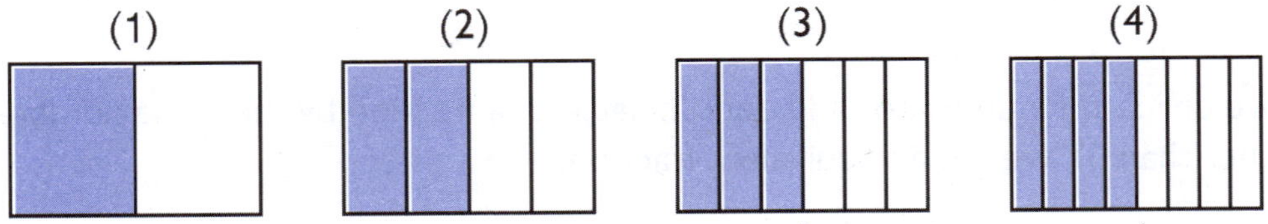

$\frac{1}{2}$ $\frac{2}{4}$ $\frac{3}{6}$ $\frac{4}{8}$

Madhuri has four loaves of bread. She wants to use them for cooking different recipes. She needs only half a loaf of bread for each recipe but the loaves have been cut in 2 slices, 4 slices, 6 slices and 8 slices, respectively, so she takes

$\frac{1}{2}$ from loaf (1). 1 part of 2 equal parts

$\frac{2}{4}$ from loaf (2). 2 parts of 4 equal parts

$\frac{3}{6}$ from loaf (3). 3 parts of 6 equal parts

$\frac{4}{8}$ from loaf (4). 4 parts of 8 equal parts

In each figure, only half the figure is shaded. So $\frac{1}{2}, \frac{2}{4}, \frac{3}{6}, \frac{4}{8}$ represent the same part of the whole.

Therefore, $\frac{1}{2} = \frac{2}{4} = \frac{3}{6} = \frac{4}{8}$

$\frac{1}{2}, \frac{2}{4}, \frac{3}{6}, \frac{4}{8}$ are called equivalent fractions.

Two or more fractions that represent the same part of a whole are called equivalent fractions. Each fraction is said to be equivalent to all the others.

Properties of Equivalent Fractions

1. If we multiply the numerator and denominator of a fraction by the same number (other than 0), we get an equivalent fraction.

   Example 1: $\frac{1}{2} \times \frac{2}{2} = \frac{2}{4}$

   Example 2: $\frac{1}{2} \times \frac{3}{3} = \frac{3}{6}$

   Example 3: $\frac{1}{2} \times \frac{4}{4} = \frac{4}{8}$

   We have just seen above that

   $$\frac{1}{2} = \frac{2}{4} = \frac{3}{6} = \frac{4}{8}$$

2. If we divide the numerator and denominator of a fraction by the same number (other than 0), we get an equivalent fraction.

   Example 1: $\frac{2}{4} \div \frac{2}{2} = \frac{1}{2}$

   Example 2: $\frac{3}{6} \div \frac{2}{2} = \frac{1}{2}$

   Example 3: $\frac{4}{8} \div \frac{2}{2} = \frac{1}{2}$

3. If two fractions are equivalent, then the equation would be:

Numerator of the first × Denominator of the second

= Denominator of the first × Numerator of the second

Thus if $\frac{a}{b} = \frac{c}{d}$ then $ad = bc$

Again if $\frac{3}{6} = \frac{4}{8}$ then $3 \times 8 = 6 \times 4$

Here, $24 = 24$

This property is used to check if the fractions are equivalent.

Simplest Form of a Fraction

A fraction is said to be in the simplest form or in its lowest term if the HCF of the numerator and denominator is equal to one.

Method to Reduce a Fraction to its Simplest Form

To reduce a fraction to its simplest form, we take the following steps.

Step 1 Find the HCF of the numerator and denominator.

Step 2 Divide its numerator and denominator by their HCF.

Step 3 If we divide the numerator and denominator of a fraction by the same number, we get an equivalent fraction. (Property 2)

Example: $\frac{90}{162}$

HCF of 90 and 162 = 18

When the numerator and denominator of the fraction are divided by their HCF, we get,

$$\frac{90 \div 18}{162 \div 18} = \frac{5}{9}$$

So, $\frac{5}{9}$ is the lowest form of the given fraction because the common factor of 5 and 9 is 1.

Comparison of Fractions

Fractions with the Same Numerator

Let us consider the following examples:

Example 1: 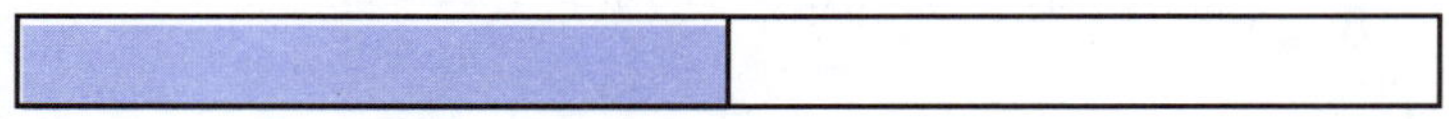 $\frac{1}{2}$

Example 2:  $\frac{1}{3}$

Example 3: 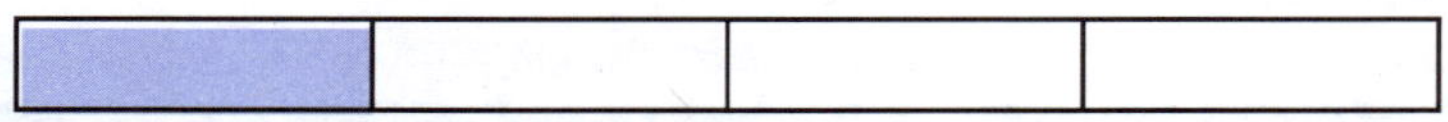 $\frac{1}{4}$

Example 4: 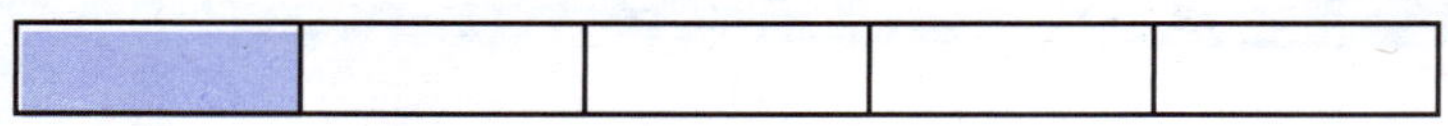 $\frac{1}{5}$

The shaded portion in Example 1 is more than the shaded portion in Example 2, which is more than the shaded portion in Example 3, which is more than the shaded portion in Example 4.

Hence, we can conclude that $\frac{1}{2} > \frac{1}{3} > \frac{1}{4} > \frac{1}{5}$

If two fractions have the same numerator, then the fraction which has the smaller denominator represents the greater fraction.

Fractions with the Same Denominator

Let us consider the following examples:

Example 1: 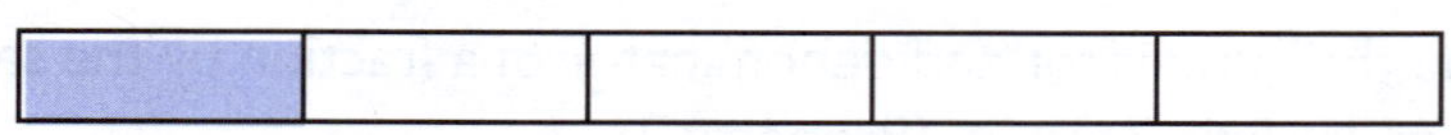 $\frac{1}{5}$

Example 2: 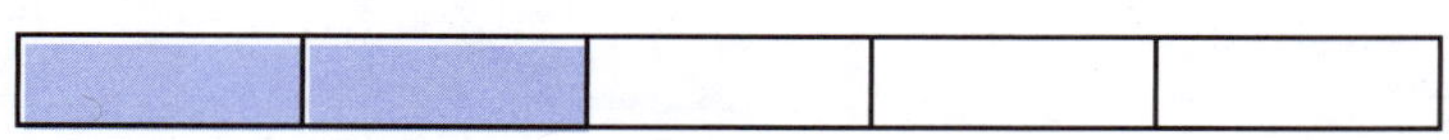 $\frac{2}{5}$

Example 3:  $\frac{3}{5}$

Example 4:  $\frac{4}{5}$

The shaded portion in Example 1 is less than the shaded portion in Example 2, which is less than the shaded portion in Example 3, which is less than the shaded portion in Example 4.

Hence, we conclude $\frac{1}{5} < \frac{2}{5} < \frac{3}{5} < \frac{4}{5}$

If two fractions have the same denominator, then the fraction that has the greater numerator represents the greater fraction.

Fractions with Different Numerators and Different Denominators

To make two or more fractions into like fractions, that is, to make their denominators the same, we find the LCM of the denominators. We then multiply the numerators and denominator of each fraction with a number such that the new denominator is the same as the LCM of all the fractions. This needs to be done for all fractions. Once all fractions have the same denominator, they can be compared.

Example 1: Arrange $\frac{2}{3}, \frac{3}{4}, \frac{4}{5}, \frac{5}{6}$ in descending order. To arrange the fractions $\frac{2}{3}, \frac{3}{4}, \frac{4}{5}, \frac{5}{6}$ in descending order,

we find the LCM of 3, 4, 5, 6, which is 60. Now the given fractions can be written as:

$$\frac{2}{3} \times \frac{20}{20} = \frac{40}{60}$$

$$\frac{3}{4} \times \frac{15}{15} = \frac{45}{60}$$

$$\frac{4}{5} \times \frac{12}{12} = \frac{48}{60}$$

$$\frac{5}{6} \times \frac{10}{10} = \frac{50}{60}$$

The denominators are all the same (i.e. 60). If the denominators are same, then the fraction which has the greater numerator is the greater fraction.

$$\text{Thus, } \frac{50}{60} > \frac{48}{60} > \frac{45}{60} > \frac{40}{60}$$

$$\text{or } \frac{5}{6} > \frac{4}{5} > \frac{3}{4} > \frac{2}{3}$$

Example 2: Arrange $\frac{1}{6}, \frac{5}{12}, \frac{2}{3}, \frac{5}{18}$ in ascending order. If we have to arrange the $\frac{1}{6}, \frac{5}{12}, \frac{2}{3}, \frac{5}{18}$ in ascending order,

we find the LCM of 6, 12, 3, 18, which is 36. Now the given fractions can be written as:

$$\frac{1}{6} \times \frac{6}{6} = \frac{6}{36}$$

$$\frac{5}{12} \times \frac{3}{3} = \frac{15}{36}$$

$$\frac{2}{3} \times \frac{12}{12} = \frac{24}{36}$$

$$\frac{5}{18} \times \frac{2}{2} = \frac{10}{36}$$

The denominators are all the same (i.e., 36).

Here, the largest fraction is the one with the greater numerator.

$$\text{Thus,} \quad \frac{24}{36} > \frac{15}{36} > \frac{10}{36} > \frac{6}{36}$$

$$\text{or} \quad \frac{2}{3} > \frac{5}{12} > \frac{5}{18} > \frac{1}{6}$$

But, we have to write the fractions in the ascending order, that is, from the smallest to the largest. So the order will be $\frac{1}{6}, \frac{5}{18}, \frac{5}{12}, \frac{2}{3}$.

Practice Exercise 5.2

1. State whether the following pairs of fractions are equivalent or not.

   a. $\frac{3}{7}, \frac{6}{7}$ b. $\frac{1}{5}, \frac{3}{15}$ c. $\frac{3}{7}, \frac{9}{21}$ d. $\frac{14}{28}, \frac{15}{30}$ e. $\frac{8}{9}, \frac{7}{8}$

2. Write five equivalent fractions of the following.

   a. $\frac{2}{9}$ b. $\frac{3}{7}$ c. $\frac{4}{11}$ d. $\frac{4}{5}$ e. $\frac{5}{8}$

3. Convert the following fractions into their simplest form (or lowest terms).

   a. $\frac{32}{36}$ b. $\frac{13}{43}$ c. $\frac{36}{63}$ d. $\frac{55}{125}$ e. $\frac{70}{84}$

4. Fill in the blanks.

   a. $\frac{1}{3} = \frac{\square}{48}$ b. $\frac{4}{5} = \frac{60}{\square}$ c. $\frac{13}{18} = \frac{\square}{144}$

   d. $\frac{6}{11} = \frac{24}{\square}$ e. $\frac{2}{3} = \frac{\square}{9} = \frac{12}{\square} = \frac{16}{\square} = \frac{\square}{27}$

5. Put the appropriate symbol $>$, $=$ or $<$, to compare the following fractions.

   a. $\frac{2}{5} \square \frac{2}{3}$ b. $\frac{3}{5} \square \frac{4}{5}$ c. $\frac{7}{10} \square \frac{21}{30}$ d. $\frac{3}{8} \square \frac{2}{5}$ e. $\frac{4}{5} \square \frac{3}{4}$

6. Arrange the following fractions in ascending order.

   a. $\frac{1}{6}, \frac{5}{12}, \frac{2}{3}$ b. $\frac{5}{18}, \frac{11}{8}, \frac{7}{12}$ c. $\frac{3}{5}, \frac{5}{6}, \frac{7}{10}$

   d. $\frac{5}{12}, \frac{7}{12}, \frac{3}{12}$ e. $\frac{4}{15}, \frac{11}{15}, \frac{7}{15}, \frac{2}{15}$

7. Arrange the following fractions in descending order.

   a. $\frac{2}{3}, \frac{5}{3}, \frac{1}{3}$ b. $\frac{1}{4}, \frac{5}{6}, \frac{7}{12}$ c. $\frac{3}{7}, \frac{3}{11}, \frac{3}{13}$ d. $\frac{1}{4}, \frac{7}{8}, \frac{1}{16}$ e. $\frac{2}{3}, \frac{4}{9}, \frac{5}{6}, \frac{11}{12}$

8. In a science examination, Anita secured 7 out of 10 for her project work, 18 out of 25 in the practicals and 85 out of 100 in the theory paper. Find out in which part of the examination did she perform the best.

9. Nidhi read $\frac{1}{5}$th of a book on Friday, $\frac{2}{3}$rd of the book on Saturday and $\frac{2}{15}$th of the book on Sunday. Find out on which day she read the most pages.

10. All three sections of Class VI have an equal number of students. The number of absentees on a rainy day in sections A, B and C were $\frac{1}{12}$, $\frac{3}{10}$ and $\frac{1}{5}$, respectively. Find out which section had the maximum attendance on that particular day.

Operations on Fractions

Fractions can be added or subtracted. Let us consider the two cases: addition and subtraction of like fractions, addition and subtraction of unlike fractions.

Addition and Subtraction of Like Fractions

For adding and subtracting like fractions, we follow these steps.

Step 1 Since the fractions are "like", that is, the denominators are the same, we add or subtract the numerators.

Step 2 Reduce the fraction to its lowest term.

Step 3 If the result is an improper fraction, convert it into a mixed fraction.

Example 1: Find the sum of $\frac{4}{9} + \frac{1}{9}$

We have $\frac{4}{9} + \frac{1}{9} = \frac{4+1}{9} = \frac{5}{9}$

Example 2: Find the sum of $3\frac{1}{5}$ and $6\frac{2}{5}$

We have $3\frac{1}{5} + 6\frac{2}{5}$

First convert these mixed fractions into improper fractions.

Thus, $3\frac{1}{5} + 6\frac{2}{5}$ will be $= \frac{16}{5} + \frac{32}{5}$

$= \frac{48}{5} = 9\frac{3}{5}$

Example 3: Subtract $\frac{6}{15}$ from $\frac{13}{15}$

$$= \frac{13}{15} - \frac{6}{15} = \frac{7}{15}$$

Example 4: Subtract $1\frac{1}{3}$ from $5\frac{2}{3}$

First convert the mixed fractions into improper fractions.

Thus, $5\frac{2}{3} - 1\frac{1}{3}$ will be

$$= \frac{17}{3} - \frac{4}{3}$$

$$= \frac{13}{3} = 4\frac{1}{3}$$

Addition and Subtraction of Unlike Fractions

For adding and subtracting unlike fractions, we follow these steps.

1. Find the LCM of the denominators of the given fractions.
2. Convert unlike fractions into like fractions by making the LCM the denominator.
3. Add or subtract the like fractions.

Example 1: Add $\frac{2}{3}$ and $\frac{3}{5}$

Find the LCM of 3 and 5, which is 15.

We have $\frac{2}{3} \times \frac{5}{5} = \frac{10}{15}$ $\qquad$ $\frac{3}{5} \times \frac{3}{3} = \frac{9}{15}$

Thus, $\frac{10}{15} + \frac{9}{15} = \frac{19}{15} = 1\frac{4}{15}$

Example 2: Add $2\frac{3}{4}$ and $4\frac{1}{8}$

First convert the mixed fractions into improper fractions and then add them.

$$\frac{11}{4} + \frac{33}{8}$$

Find the LCM of 4 and 8 which is 8.

$\frac{11}{4} \times \frac{2}{2} = \frac{22}{8}$ $\qquad$ $\frac{33}{8} \times \frac{1}{1} = \frac{33}{8}$

$$\frac{22}{8} + \frac{33}{8} = \frac{55}{8} = 6\frac{7}{8}$$

Practice Exercise 5.3

1. Add the following fractions and reduce them to the lowest terms.

   a. $\frac{5}{12} + \frac{3}{12}$ b. $\frac{3}{11} + \frac{5}{11} + \frac{1}{11}$ c. $\frac{3}{7} + \frac{2}{5} + \frac{1}{10}$

   d. $1\frac{5}{8} + 2\frac{3}{4} + 3\frac{1}{12}$ e. $2 + 3\frac{1}{2} + 4\frac{1}{3} + 5\frac{1}{4}$

2. Subtract the following fractions and reduce them to the lowest terms.

   a. $\frac{8}{15} - \frac{4}{15}$ b. $\frac{11}{25} - \frac{9}{25}$ c. $5\frac{2}{3} - 3\frac{1}{3}$ d. $3\frac{3}{5} - 1\frac{1}{15}$ e. $7\frac{1}{6} - 4\frac{1}{18}$

3. Simplify the following and reduce them to the lowest terms.

   a. $\frac{4}{5} + \frac{2}{5} - \frac{3}{5}$ b. $\frac{11}{21} - \frac{4}{21} + \frac{6}{21}$ c. $3\frac{1}{2} + 2\frac{4}{5} - 1\frac{1}{2}$

   d. $\frac{21}{10} + \frac{201}{100} - \frac{431}{200}$ e. $4\frac{3}{35} + 2\frac{5}{7} - 1\frac{1}{5}$

4. Tapur and Tupur wanted to gift a shawl to their mother. Tapur knitted $\frac{3}{5}$th of the shawl and Tupur $\frac{1}{5}$th. Is the shawl complete? If not, how much of the knitting is yet to be done for the gift to be ready?

5. Seema and Reena go for jogging. Seema jogs for $2\frac{1}{5}$ km and Reena $2\frac{1}{7}$ km. Who jogs more and by how much?

6. Mini bought 5 litres of oil. She used $3\frac{3}{5}$ litres of oil for cooking during the month. How much oil is left at the end of the month?

7. Vinita bought $5\frac{1}{2}$ kg of guavas, $3\frac{3}{4}$ kg of apples and $4\frac{1}{4}$ kg of oranges. Find the total weight of the fruits bought by her.

8. Neeta bought curtain material for her house. She bought $7\frac{1}{2}$ m for the living room, $5\frac{3}{4}$ m for the study and $10\frac{1}{4}$ m for the bedrooms. How much curtain cloth did she buy in all?

9. Mukul returns from school at 2 pm. He goes to bed at 10 pm. He has 8 hours to spend out of which $1\frac{1}{2}$ hours are spent playing outdoors, $3\frac{1}{4}$ hours studying and $1\frac{1}{3}$ hours on the computer. The remaining time he spends with his parents. How much time does he spend with his parents?

10. Rohit spends $\frac{2}{3}$rd of his salary on rations, $\frac{1}{5}$th of it on transport and $\frac{1}{10}$th of it on rent. What part of his salary does he spend in all? What part of his salary is left as savings?

Highlights

- A fraction is a number representing a part of the whole. The whole may be a single object or a collection of objects.
- A fraction is denoted by $\frac{a}{b}$, where a and b are natural numbers. Here, "a" is called the numerator and "b" is called the denominator.
- If the numerator is smaller than the denominator, then the fraction is called a proper fraction.
- If the numerator is larger than the denominator, then the fraction is called an improper fraction.
- A combination of a natural number and a proper fraction is called a mixed fraction. Mixed fractions can be converted into improper fractions and vice versa.
- Two fractions are said to be equivalent if they represent the same quantity, that is, if they have equal value.
- To find an equivalent fraction of a given fraction, the numerator and the denominator of the given fraction are either multiplied or divided by the same natural number.
- A fraction is said to be in its lowest terms if the numerator and the denominator do not have any common factor except 1.
- Fractions that have 1 as the numerator are called unit fractions.
- Fractions with the same denominator are called like fractions and fractions with different denominators are called unlike fractions.
- Two fractions having different numerators and denominators are compared by making the denominators same.
- To add or subtract unlike fractions, we convert them into like fractions by finding suitable equivalent fractions for them.

Remove two lines from the figure below to get two squares.

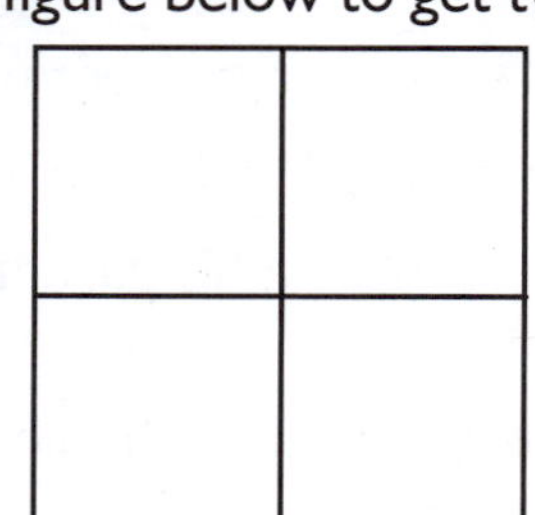

Answer for Brainteaser on page 94

Higher Order Thinking Skills

HOTS

1. Find the difference between the greatest and the smallest fractions from the following.

$$3\frac{3}{5}, 2\frac{4}{7}, \frac{19}{6}, \frac{18}{8}$$

2. Atul jogged $\frac{2}{5}$ of $\frac{1}{2}$ of $\frac{2}{3}$ of 9 km in the morning.

   How many metres did he jog?

3. Shade $\frac{7}{16}$ of the given figure.

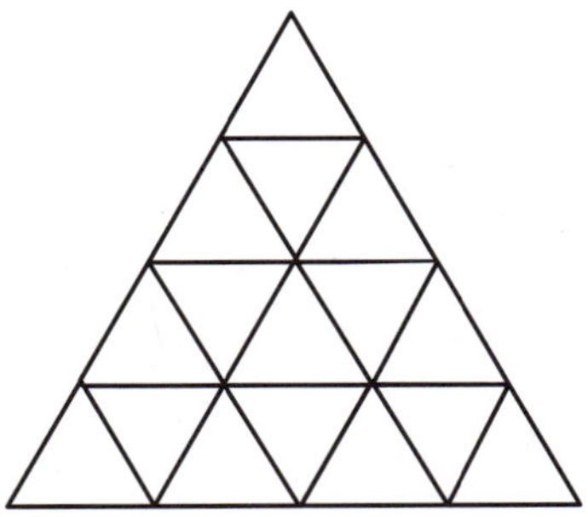

Maths Lab Activity

Fraction Wall

Objective: To create a fraction wall.

Material required: Coloured pencils

Procedure: A fraction wall has been created as an example. Two blank walls are provided for you to fill in the missing fractions.

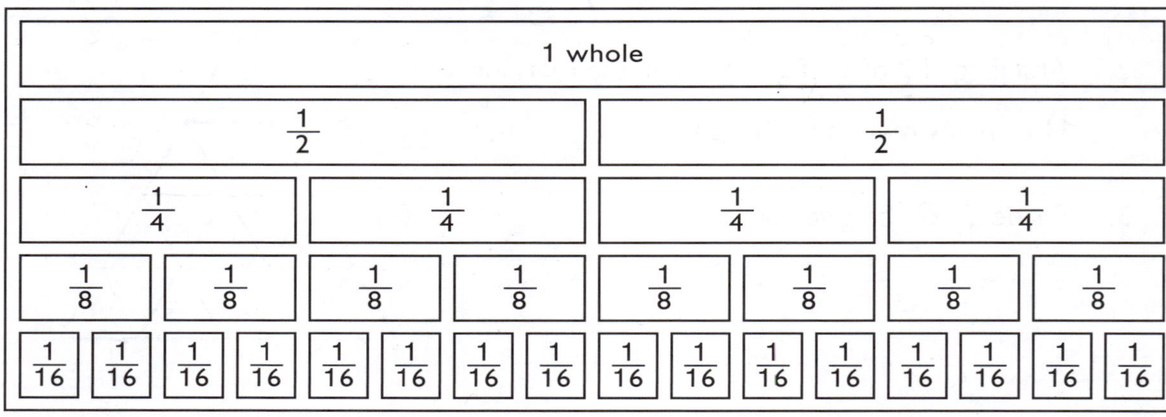

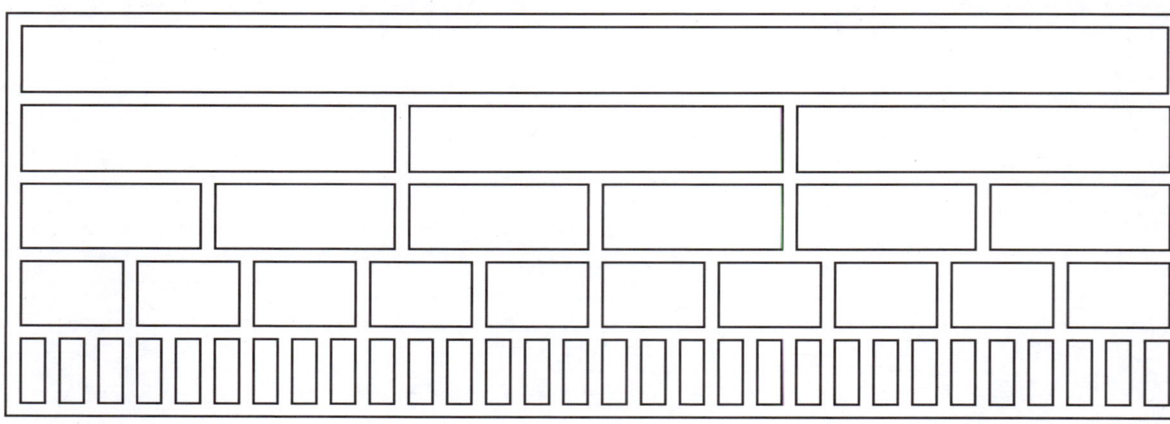

Test Yourself

Unit I

1. Write the predecessors and successors of the following numbers.

   a. 63,980   b. 85,000   c. 86,541

2. Round off the following numbers as indicated:

   a. 67,235 (to the nearest hundred)

   b. 78,923 (to the nearest thousand)

   c. 7,59,825 (to the nearest ten thousand)

3. Write the following in Roman numerals.

   a. 75   b. 689   c. 1699

4. Find the largest five-digit number divisible by 18, 24 and 32.

5. Check the divisibility of the following numbers as indicated.

   a. 63,863 (by 3)   b. 7,59,825 (by 9)   c. 1,13,011 (by 11)

6. Three containers contain 450 litres, 360 litres and 240 litres of milk, respectively. Find the maximum capacity of a container that can measure the milk from all the containers an exact number of times.

7. Simplify the following numerical expressions.

   a. $18 + [40 - \{12 + 12 \div 3 \times 4\}]$

   b. $75 \div [20 - \{42 \div 6 - (20 - 3 \text{ of } 6)\}]$

   c. $20 - \{6 + 4 - (6 + 3 - \overline{3-5})\}]$

8. Find the number that when divided by 45 gives the quotient 27 and remainder 39.

9. A cooperative housing society constructed 532 flats. If the cost of construction of each flat is ₹19,78,600, what is the total cost of all the flats?

10. For the Commonwealth Games, 1 lakh spectators are expected to come in from abroad. These include 45,028 men and 35,762 women. The rest of the foreign visitors are children. Find out how many children are expected.

11. Arrange the following integers as indicated.

    a. −4, 5, −26, 0, −99 (in ascending order)

    b. 15, 0, −75, −18, 90 (in descending order)

    c. 23, −23, 45, −71, 27 (in ascending order)

Test Yourself

12. Find the values of the following.

    a. $(-42) + (-66) - 18$ b. $32 - (-65) + 25$ c. $-(-69) + 22 + (-71)$

13. Complete the following multiplication table.

X	−5	−4	−3	−2	−1	0	1	2	3	4	5	6
−4												−24
−3												
−2												
−1												
0												
1												
2												
3												
4												

14. Find the value of:

    $2\frac{1}{4} + 1\frac{1}{2} - \frac{5}{8}$

15. Find the value of:

    $10\frac{1}{3} - \frac{11}{12} - 5\frac{1}{4}$

16. Find the value of:

    $1\frac{1}{2} - 2\frac{1}{4} + 5\frac{3}{6}$

17. Arrange the following in ascending order.

    a. $\frac{3}{4}, \frac{2}{3}, \frac{11}{15}, \frac{28}{30}$ b. $\frac{2}{6}, \frac{5}{8}, \frac{1}{4}, \frac{11}{12}$ c. $\frac{3}{4}, \frac{5}{8}, \frac{8}{9}, \frac{2}{3}$

18. Samir had 14 bars of chocolates. He bought 4 more. He gave $\frac{1}{6}$ of the chocolates to his sister and $\frac{1}{3}$ of the chocolates to his younger brother. How many chocolates were left with Samir?

19. The HCF and LCM of two numbers are 16 and 672, respectively. If one of the numbers is 112, find the other.

20. Rita had $1\frac{2}{3}$ m of ribbon. She gave $\frac{3}{11}$ m of the ribbon to her friend Gita. What length of ribbon is left with Rita now?

Answer for Brainteaser on page 90

Decimals

CHAPTER
6

We will now study a special type of fraction where the denominator is either 10 or powers of 10. These are decimal numbers or decimal fractions. Further, instead of writing this fraction in the form of numerator and denominator, we use a "*dot*" or point called the decimal. The word deci means based on 10. The number before the decimal point is the whole part and the number after the decimal point is called the fractional part.

Fractions as Decimals

1. One-tenth $\left(\frac{1}{10}\right)$

You are familiar with fractions.

Look at the figure given below:

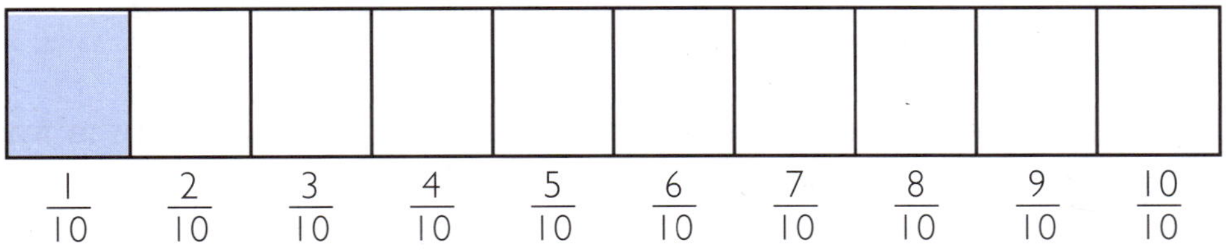

Here, one whole has been divided into 10 equal parts. The shaded portion represents $\frac{1}{10}$ of the whole. It is also called one-tenth.

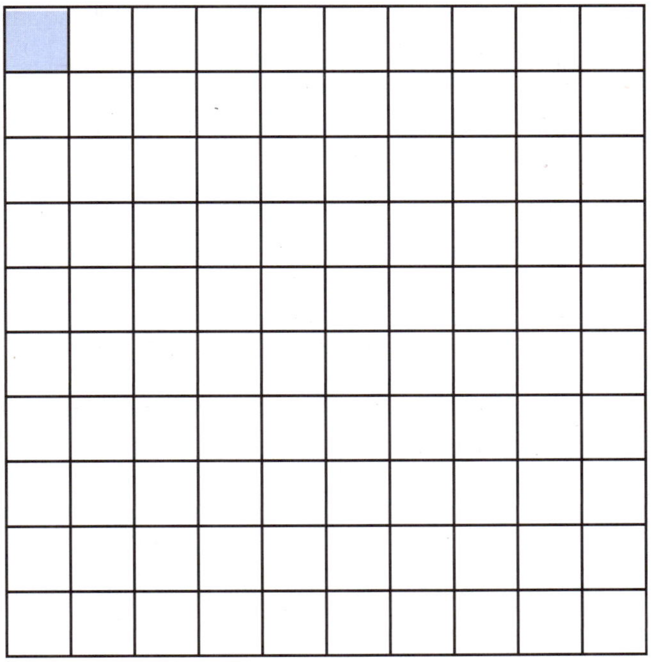

Let us write it in another form.

$$\frac{1}{10} = 0.1$$

The dot or point is called a decimal point.

2. One-hundredth $\left(\frac{1}{100}\right)$

Here, we have divided 1 big square (1 whole) into 100 small squares. Each small square is one-hundredth of the big square.

The shaded portion represents $\frac{1}{100}$ of the whole. It is called one-hundredth.

Now, let us write this fraction in another form.

$$\frac{1}{100} = 0.01$$

We read it as zero point zero one.

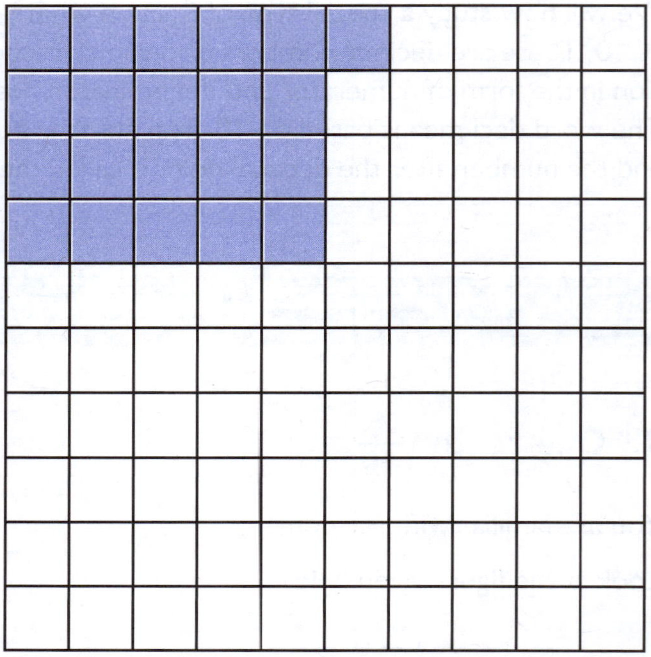

Look at this square. It has been divided into 100 small squares. The shaded portion represents $\frac{21}{100}$.

It represents 21 hundredth parts.

In the decimal fraction form this can be written as 0.21.

Now, let us consider the fraction $\frac{438}{100}$.

To express this improper fraction in the decimal form, we first convert it to a mixed fraction. So:

$$\frac{438}{100} = 4\frac{38}{100}$$

Now, this is expressed in the decimal form as 4.38.

That is, the whole number is written on the left of the decimal point and the fraction is expressed in the decimal form to the right of the decimal point.

3. One-thousandth $\left(\frac{1}{1,000}\right)$

Here we divide one whole square into 1,000 equal small squares. Each small square is one-thousandth of the big square. It is written as $\frac{1}{1,000}$ in the fraction form.

Again, $\frac{1}{1,000}$ as a decimal fraction is expressed as 0.001.

We read it as zero point zero zero one.

$$\text{Hence,} \quad \frac{4}{1,000} = 0.004$$

$$\text{or,} \quad \frac{54}{1,000} = 0.054$$

If we have an improper fraction, we will first convert it into a mixed fraction and then change the proper fraction into a decimal fraction.

$$\text{Thus,} \quad \frac{4,387}{1,000} = 4\frac{387}{1,000} = 4.387$$

The whole number 4 is to the left of the decimal point and 387 parts of a thousand are on the right of the decimal point.

Table 6.1 **Chart to Depict Decimal Fractions**

Part	Fraction	Decimal Fraction	Position of the Decimal Point
One-tenth	$\frac{1}{10} = \frac{1}{10}$	0.1	1 place from the extreme right number.
One-hundredth	$\frac{1}{100} = \frac{1}{10 \times 10}$	0.01	2 places from the extreme right number.
One-thousandth	$\frac{1}{1,000} = \frac{1}{10 \times 10 \times 10}$	0.001	3 places from the extreme right number.
One-ten thousandth	$\frac{1}{10,000} = \frac{1}{10 \times 10 \times 10 \times 10}$	0.0001	4 places from the extreme right number.
One-hundred thousandth	$\frac{1}{1,00,000} = \frac{1}{10 \times 10 \times 10 \times 10 \times 10}$	0.00001	5 places from the extreme right number.

Alert!

If there is no whole number part in a decimal number, then we should always write a 0 on the left side of the point.

Decimals in Expanded Form

Consider the number 72.63.

This can be written in the expanded form as

$$72.63 = 70 + 2 + \frac{6}{10} + \frac{3}{100}$$

70 ↓ 7 tens; 2 ↓ 2 ones; $\frac{6}{10}$ ↓ 6 tenths; $\frac{3}{100}$ ↓ 3 hundredths

Now, consider the number 742.375.

742.375 will be used as seven hundred and forty-two point three seven five (not three hundred and seventy-five).

We read the whole part as a complete number and the decimal part as "point" and then read the number that follows the decimal point digit wise. Hence, 72.63 will be read as seventy-two point six three (not sixty-three).

The two examples can also be shown in the tabular form.

Table 6.2 **Place Value Table**

Number	Thousands 1,000	Hundreds 100	Tens 10	Ones 1	Decimal Point •	Tenth $\frac{1}{10}$	Hundredth $\frac{1}{100}$	Thousandth $\frac{1}{1,000}$
72.63			7	2	•	6	3	
742.375		7	4	2	•	3	7	5

Equivalent Decimals

Decimals are a special type of fractions. Just as there are equivalent fractions, there are equivalent decimals too.

Consider, $0.2 = \frac{2}{10} = \frac{1}{5}$ as $\frac{1}{5} \times \frac{2}{2} = \frac{2}{10}$

Now $0.20 = \frac{20}{100} = \frac{1}{5}$ as $\frac{1}{5} \times \frac{20}{20} = \frac{20}{100}$

and $0.200 = \frac{200}{1000} = \frac{1}{5}$ as $\frac{1}{5} \times \frac{200}{200} = \frac{200}{1000}$

Thus, 0.2, 0.20 and 0.200 are equivalent decimals.

Practice Exercise 6.1

1. Write the following fractions in their decimal form.

   a. $\frac{6}{10}$ b. $\frac{9}{100}$ c. $\frac{52}{100}$ d. $\frac{57}{1000}$ e. $\frac{245}{1000}$

2. Write the following in the decimal form.

   a. Fifteen-hundredths

   b. Seven-tenths

   c. Forty-five-thousandths

   d. Eight and eight thousandth

   e. Two hundred twenty-two and two hunderdth

3. Write the following in decimal form.

   a. $\frac{3}{10}$ b. $\frac{11}{100}$ c. $\frac{2036}{10}$ d. $\frac{14703}{100}$ e. $\frac{500005}{100}$

4. Fill in the blanks.

   a. $8.53 = 8 + \frac{5}{\square} + \frac{3}{\square}$

   b. $29.175 = 29 + \frac{1}{\square} + \frac{7}{\square} + \frac{5}{\square}$

   c. $81.81 = \square + \frac{8}{\square} + \frac{1}{\square}$

   d. $93.628 = 93 + \frac{\square}{10} + \frac{2}{\square} + \frac{8}{\square}$

   e. $66.666 = \square + \frac{6}{\square} + \frac{6}{\square} + \frac{6}{\square}$

5. Write in the expanded form.

   a. 5.83 b. 62.37 c. 125.4 d. 12.543 e. 326.543

6. Write in the short form.

   a. 0.8 + 0.08 + 0.008

   b. 3 + 0.1 + 0.02 + 0.003

   c. 51 + 0.02 + 0.003

   d. 100 + 10 + 1 + 0.1 + 0.01 + 0.001

   e. 900 + 80 + 9 + 0.5 + 0.009

7. Complete the given sequences by writing the next three decimal numbers.

   a. 2.1, 2.2, 2.3, ______, ______, ______.

   b. 7.123, 7.124, 7.125, ______, ______, ______.

   c. 15.8, 15.9, 16.0, ______, ______, ______.

   d. 20.01, 20.02, 20.03, ______, ______, ______.

   e. 152.1, 152.2, 152.3, ______, ______, ______.

8. Write three equivalent decimals for each of the following.

   a. 0.5 b. 3.6 c. 20.7 d. 62.35 e. 146.9

9. Write each of the following fractions as decimals by converting the denominators into multiples of 10.

   a. $\frac{1}{2}$ b. $\frac{3}{5}$ c. $\frac{17}{20}$ d. $\frac{4}{25}$ e. $\frac{29}{500}$

10. Use a graph paper to illustrate the following decimal fractions.

   a. $\frac{7}{10}$ b. $\frac{3}{10}$ c. $\frac{21}{100}$ d. $\frac{47}{100}$ e. $\frac{3}{100}$

Like and Unlike Decimals

Like Decimals

Decimals with the same number of decimal places are called like decimals. It means that the number of digits after the decimal point are the same.

Example 1: One decimal place: 2.5, 10.6, 215.9

Example 2: Two decimal places: 2.51, 10.62, 215.97

Unlike Decimals

Decimals having different number of decimal places are called unlike decimals.

Example: 2.5, 10.62, 245.356

Converting Unlike Decimals into Like Decimals

We can convert unlike decimals into like decimals by adding zeroes after the last digit to the right of the decimal point.

Example: Consider three unlike decimal fractions

2.7	3.45	6.237
one decimal place	two decimal places	three decimal places

We would want to convert the decimals into three places of decimals since that is the maximum.

Then	2.7 = 2.700	(3 places of decimals) (two zeroes added)
	3.45 = 3.450	(3 places of decimals) (one zero added)
	6.237 = 6.237	(3 places of decimals)

Alert!

Zeroes can be added after the last digit to the right of the decimal point of any decimal number without changing its value.

Comparing Decimals

To compare decimals, we take the following steps.

Step 1 Convert unlike decimals into like decimals.

Step 2 Compare the whole numbers. The decimal fraction with the greater whole number is greater.

Step 3 If the whole numbers are equal, check for the digit in the tenth place, that is, the first place of decimal to the right of the point. The number with the greater digit in the tenth place will be greater.

Step 4 If the tenth place is the same, then we look for the digit in the hundredth place, that is, the second place of decimal to the right of the point. The number with the greater digit in the hundredth place will be greater. If the digit in the hundredth place is also the same, we check the next place and so on.

Examples:

a. Which number is greater, 10.<u>5</u>1 or 10.<u>8</u>1?

The whole number is same so we check the digit in the tenth place 8 > 5.

Hence, 10.81 > 10.51.

b. Which number is greater, 2.56<u>3</u> or 2.561?

The whole number is same, while the tenth place and the hundredth place are also the same. Then we check the thousandth place. The digit 3 is greater than the digit 1.

Hence, 2.563 > 2.561.

Conversion of a Decimal into a Fraction

To change a decimal into a fraction, we take the following steps:

Step 1 Write the given number without the decimal point in the numerator.

Step 2 Write 1 in the denominator followed by as many zeros as the number of decimal places in the given number.

Step 3 Reduce the fraction into the lowest form. If it is a proper fraction, then it is the required answer. If it is an improper fraction, convert it into a mixed fraction.

Example 1:

Convert 2.5 into a fraction.

Write the numerator as 25.

Write the denominator as 10 (because there is only one number after the decimal point).

The fraction is $= \frac{25}{10}$

When we reduce it to its lowest form we get $\frac{5}{2}$

This is an improper fraction, so we convert it into a mixed fraction.

$$2\frac{1}{2} \qquad \text{Quotient} \cdot \left[\frac{\text{Remainder}}{\text{Divisor}}\right]$$

Example 2:

Convert 1.<u>35</u> into a fraction.

The numerator will be written as 135.

The denominator will be written as 100 (since there will be two numbers after the decimal point).

The fraction is $\frac{135}{100}$

When we reduce it to its lowest form, we get $\frac{27}{20}$

This is an improper fraction, so we convert it into a mixed fraction,

$$1\frac{7}{20} \qquad \text{Quotient} \cdot \left[\frac{\text{Remainder}}{\text{Divisor}}\right]$$

Example 3:

Convert 4.127 into a fraction.

The numerator will be written as 4,127.

The denominator will be written as 1,000. (Since there are three digits after the decimal point)

The fraction is $\frac{4{,}127}{1{,}000} = 4\frac{127}{1{,}000}$.

When we have to write an improper fraction as a decimal fraction, we change it into a mixed number and then place the point.

Example:

$$\frac{21}{10} = 2\frac{1}{10} = 2.1$$

$$\frac{43}{10} = 4\frac{3}{10} = 4.3$$

The whole number remains the same while only the proper fraction is changed to a decimal.

The number is divided into two parts. One part is to the left of the decimal point and the other to the right of the decimal point. The left part denotes the whole number and the right denotes the proper fraction, which is written in the form of a decimal.

Hence, 0.1 is read as zero point one.

Alert!

1. We always read the zero (or any number) before the point and then read the decimal.
2. Decimal fractions can be simply called decimals.

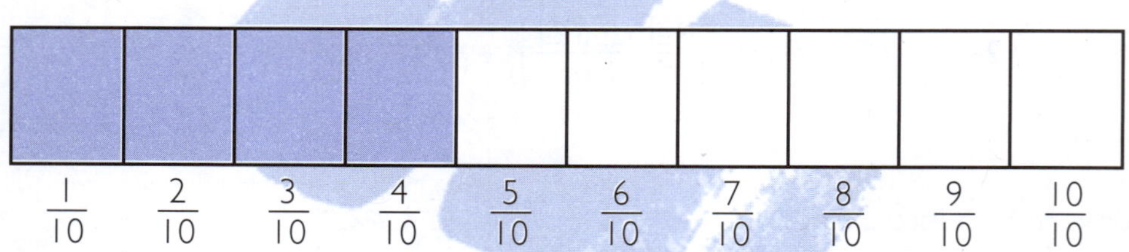

The shaded portion in this figure represents the fraction $\frac{4}{10}$ or four-tenths.

Expressed as a decimal fraction, it will be written as 0.4.

We read 0.4 as zero point four.

Conversion of a Fraction into a Decimal

To change a fraction into a decimal, we take the following steps:

Step 1 First, change the given fraction into an equivalent fraction with the denominator as 10, 100, 1,000, etc.

Step 2 Count the number of zeros in the denominator after 1. Put the decimal in the numerator. Start from the extreme right and move the decimal point to the left and add an equal number of zeros.

Example 1: $\frac{3}{5} = \frac{3 \times 20}{5 \times 20} = \frac{60}{100} = 0.60$

Example 2: $5\frac{1}{4} = \frac{21}{4} \times \frac{25}{25} = \frac{525}{100} = 5.25$

We can also convert a fraction into its decimal form using the long division method.

Practice Exercise 6.2

1. Compare the following decimal fractions by using $>$, $=$ or $<$ symbols.

   a. 0.3 ☐ 3.0 b. 72.9 ☐ 7.29 c. 8.88 ☐ 8.880

   d. 70.7 ☐ 70.08 e. 6.359 ☐ 6.4

2. Convert the following unlike decimals into like decimals.

   a. 1.2, 2.15, 5.631 b. 0.8, 10.81, 10.801 c. 6.35, 6.53, 6.5, 6.513

   d. 9.01, 9.001, 9.1, 9.10 e. 49.9, 4.99, 0.499

3. Arrange the following decimals in ascending order.

   a. 0.05, 0.15, 5.115, 5.005 b. 7.39, 7.19, 17.309, 17.390

   c. 10.0, 10.01, 10.1, 10.105 d. 55.5, 5.55, 0.555, 5550

   e. 14.2, 14.25, 14.27, 1.427

4. Arrange the following decimals in descending order.

   a. 4.23, 4.2, 42.3, 0.423, 42.0 b. 0.19, 0.21, 1.21, 1.91, 0.03

   c. 55.6, 6.56, 66.5, 666.5, 0.665 d. 89.1, 89.2, 89.02, 89.03, 89.01

   e. 19.91, 1.999, 199.1, 1991

5. Convert the following decimals into fractions.

a. 1.9 b. 0.27 c. 333.3 d. 87.003 e. 4.125

6. Convert the following fractions into decimals.

a. $\frac{17}{10}$ b. $\frac{157}{10}$ c. $\frac{257}{100}$ d. $\frac{2,468}{100}$ e. $\frac{2,219}{1,000}$

7. Convert the following fractions into decimals by changing the denominator into 10 or multiples of 10.

a. $\frac{4}{5}$ b. $\frac{9}{4}$ c. $\frac{9}{125}$ d. $\frac{209}{500}$ e. $\frac{43}{50}$

8. Convert the following fractions into decimals by the long division method.

a. $9\frac{3}{5}$ b. $2\frac{3}{50}$ c. $13\frac{3}{8}$ d. $70\frac{1}{4}$ e. $7\frac{4}{25}$

9. Write any three decimals less than each of the following.

a. 0.65 b. 0.789 c. 0.9 d. 4.1 e. 12.11

10. Write any three decimals more than each of the following.

a. 4.6 b. 82.3 c. 987.1 d. 19.4 e. 0.001

Addition and Subtraction of Decimals

For the addition and subtraction of decimals, we take the following steps.

Step 1 Convert all decimals into like decimals.

Step 2 Arrange the numbers in columns so that the digits are aligned according to their place values. The decimal points will, hence, be placed one directly below the other.

Step 3 Add and subtract the digits as we do for whole numbers.

Step 4 Put the decimal in the sum or difference directly under the decimal point of all the decimals.

The decimal point in the answer should be placed directly below the preceding decimal points.

Example 1: Add 3.2, 47.26 and 3.832

First convert the decimals into like decimals, and then arrange them columnwise.

$$\begin{array}{rcr} 3.2 & \rightarrow & 3.200 \\ 47.26 & \rightarrow & 47.260 \\ 3.832 & \rightarrow & +\ 3.832 \\ \hline & & \boxed{54.292} \end{array}$$

Example 2: Subtract 42.375 from 6.7

First convert the decimals into like decimals and then arrange them columnwise.

$$\begin{array}{lcr} 42.375 & \rightarrow & 42.375 \\ 6.7 & \rightarrow & -\ 6.700 \\ \hline & & \boxed{35.675} \end{array}$$

Alert!

1. Ensure that unlike decimals are converted into like decimals.
2. The decimal point should be in one column or line.

Practice Exercise 6.3

1. Add the following decimals.

   a. 6.78, 23.5 and 42.8 b. 0.009, 9.9 and 99.09 c. 41.5, 5.62, 9.638

   d. 100.5, 10.5, 1.005 e. 12.8, 12.71, 12.395

2. Subtract the following decimals.

   a. 12.65 from 29.860 b. 21.11 from 211.111 c. 437.5 from 563.895

   d. 108.032 from 868.8 e. 46.532 from 50.1

3. Simplify the following.

   a. 7.86 – 6.23 + 11.2 b. 18.369 + 2.1 – 4.6 c. 25 + 15.261 – 28.02

   d. 145.09 – 45.91 + 7.683 e. 13.31 + 133.1 – 33.111

4. What should be added to 61.55 to get 100?
5. What should be added to 24.67 to get the greatest two-digit number?
6. Subtract the sum of 0.0018 and 997.35 from 1000.1.
7. Radhika spent ₹46.38 on soap, ₹52.15 on shampoo and ₹195.62 on medicines. How much money will she get back if she gave the shopkeeper a ₹500 note?
8. The temperature in Delhi over the weekend was 39.2°C and in Mumbai was 18.3°C. Which city was hotter during the weekend and by how much?

9. The tallest girl in the class is 155.6 cm tall and the shortest girl is 149.8 cm tall. What is the difference between their heights?

10. An oil tanker has a capacity of 750 litres. Three containers of 100.75 litres, 250.35 litres and 325.15 litres are filled with the oil from the oil tanker. How much oil is left in the tanker?

Highlights

- Fractions with denominators 10, 100, 1,000, etc. (that is, multiples of 10) are known as decimal fractions or decimals.
- Decimal fractions have a whole number part and a decimal part separated by a point (or dot) called the decimal point.
- The number of digits in the decimal part is called the number of places of the decimal.
- Numbers with the same number of decimal places are called like decimals, while those with different number of decimal places are called unlike decimals.
- Unlike decimals can be converted into like decimals by adding zeros after the last digit to the right of the decimal point.
- Zeros added to make unlike decimals into like decimals have no value.

Higher Order Thinking Skills

HOTS

1. Ranbir purchased 15.500 kg of rice, 26.750 kg of flour and 3.250 kg of sugar. Did he carry 50 kg of weight or less? If less, by how much was it less?

2. Write in decimal form—four hundred twenty-two hundredths.

3. Express $\frac{1}{10,000}$ as a decimal quantity.

Maths Lab Activity

Colouring Decimal Numbers

Objective: To create decimal numbers.

Material Required: Coloured pencils

Method: In the tables below, create the target decimal numbers by colouring two boxes with the same colour. The first one is done for you.

Table 1

0.1	0.2	0.3	0.4	0.5	0.6	0.7	0.8	0.9
1	2	3	4	5	6	7	8	9

Target numbers:

1. 7.1
2. 6.9
3. 2.5
4. 9.7
5. 4.4
6. 8.2

Table 2

0.01	0.02	0.03	0.04	0.05	0.06	0.07	0.08	0.09
0.1	0.2	0.3	0.4	0.5	0.6	0.7	0.8	0.9
1	2	3	4	5	6	7	8	9

Target numbers:

1. 7.97
2. 3.46
3. 9.19
4. 1.84
5. 5.51
6. 2.23

Table 3

0.001	0.002	0.003	0.004	0.005	0.006	0.007	0.008	0.009
0.01	0.02	0.03	0.04	0.05	0.06	0.07	0.08	0.09
0.1	0.2	0.3	0.4	0.5	0.6	0.7	0.8	0.9
1	2	3	4	5	6	7	8	9

Target numbers:

1. 2.222
2. 7.898
3. 1.363
4. 8.616
5. 6.787
6. 5.971

CHAPTERS 5–6

Rewind

1. Write a fraction with numerator (N) and denominator (D) as given below.

   a. N = 3, D = 5 b. N = 5, D = 9 c. N = 13, D = 7
   d. N = 15, D = 4 e. N = 7, D = 11

   Classify each of them as proper or improper fractions.

2. Write an equivalent fraction with denominator (D) for each of the following.

   a. $\frac{3}{5}$ (D = 15) b. $\frac{3}{11}$ (D = 55) c. $\frac{3}{8}$ (D = 48)
   d. $\frac{7}{9}$ (D = 108) e. $\frac{4}{13}$ (D = 52)

3. Find the value of the following and give the answer as directed.

   a. $\frac{7}{9} + \frac{11}{12}$ (answer in the lowest form)
   b. $\frac{32}{3} + 4\frac{1}{6}$ (answer as a mixed fraction)
   c. $\frac{13}{14} - \frac{15}{21}$ (answer in the lowest form)
   d. $10\frac{3}{7} - 4\frac{1}{4}$ (answer as a mixed fraction)
   e. $10\frac{1}{2} - 5\frac{1}{4} - 1\frac{1}{2}$ (answer as a mixed fraction)

4. Convert the following into decimals.

   a. $\frac{2}{100}$ b. $\frac{6}{1000}$ c. $\frac{49}{10}$ d. $\frac{4}{25}$ e. $\frac{31}{100}$

5. Convert the following into fractions.

   a. 0.5 b. 0.9 c. 0.35 d. 0.03 e. 0.97

6. Add or subtract these numbers as directed.

   a. 16.533 + 13.325 b. 10.999 − 9.101 c. 39.535 + 12.565

7. Sonu got ₹100 from his grandmother. He bought a pen for ₹5.50, a notebook for ₹16.75 and a geometry box for ₹25.25. How much money is left with Sonu?

8. Manpreet filled 20 litres of petrol in his car in the morning. During the day he used $16\frac{4}{5}$ litres of petrol. How much petrol was left in the tank in the evening?

9. Arrange the fractions $\frac{3}{5}, \frac{4}{7}, \frac{19}{35}$ in ascending order and find the difference between the largest and the smallest fraction.

10. Abha drove her scooty for various errands during the day. Find the total distance travelled by her if she drove 2.85 km, 3.15 km, 6.72 km, 4.53 km and 7.00 km.

Basic Geometrical Concepts

CHAPTER 7

The word geometry is derived from the Greek word "geometron". "Geo" means earth and "metron" means to measure. So the meaning of "geometry" in ancent times was the "measurement of earth" or land. Geometry deals with figures, points and lines.

In this chapter, we will learn the basic concepts of geometry. These concepts will help us to study the different shapes and figures used in geometry. We begin with the study of basic elements.

Point

A point gives an idea of a location and is marked as a dot. It has no length, breadth or thickness. It has just a position and only its location can be determined. A full stop is a dot and that is the simplest example of a point.

A point is denoted by a capital letter like A, B, C, etc.

For example.

. P (This is point P.)

Line

A line is a collection of points that can be extended endlessly on both sides. It has length only. It does not have breadth or thickness.

A line is denoted by the symbol $\longleftrightarrow$

We can denote a line in two ways:

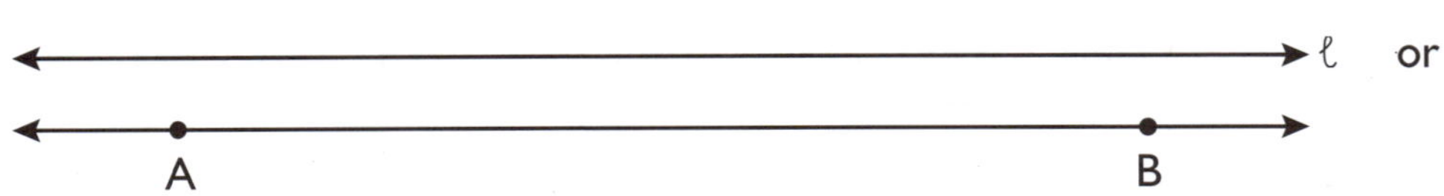

A line is either named by the small letters like ℓ, m, n, etc., or we can represent two points on the line — A and B and write the line as $\overleftrightarrow{AB}$. The two arrows depict that the line is endless on both sides.

Line Segment

A line segment is a part of a line that is bounded by two *distinct* end points. It has a definite length but no breadth or thickness.

In the example above, the line segment is the length between the two points A and B.

It is denoted by $\overline{AB}$ or $\overline{BA}$.

Ray

A ray is also a part of a line. It has only one end point and can be extended endlessly in the other direction. A ray has no breadth or thickness.

A ray is denoted by $\overrightarrow{AB}$.

It shows that the path of the ray is from a fixed point A to B.

When we consider a ray of light from the sun to the earth, A is a fixed point on the sun and B is any point on earth.

Table 7.1 Comparison Between a Line, Line Segment and Ray

	Line	Line Segment	Ray
1.	A line has no definite length.	A line segment has a definite length.	A ray has no definite length.
2.	A line has no end point.	A line segment has two end points.	A ray has one end point.
3.	A line has no thickness.	A line segment has no thickness.	A ray has no thickness.
4.	The line AB is represented by $\overleftrightarrow{AB}$.	The line segment AB is represented by $\overline{AB}$.	The ray AB is represented by $\overrightarrow{AB}$.

Plane

A plane is a flat and smooth surface that extends indefinitely in all directions. It has length and breadth but no thickness.

Example: The top of a table, the page of a book, the surface of a blackboard are all planes.

A plane can be denoted by taking three or more points on it that do not lie on the same line.

Examples:

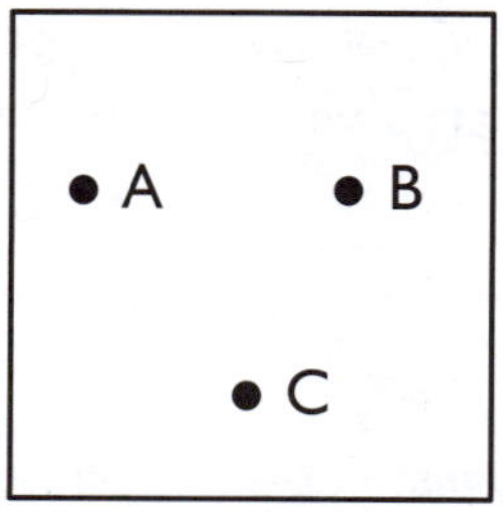

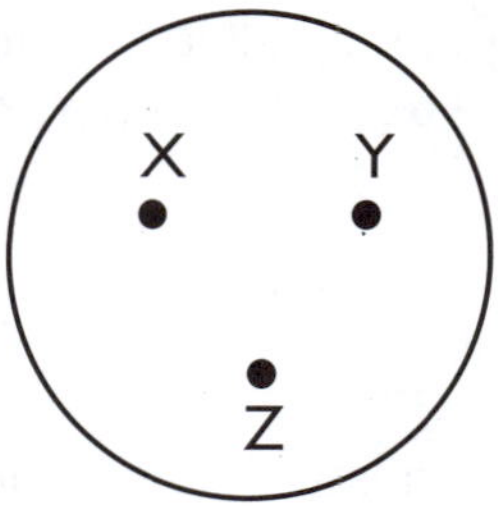

Incidence Properties of Points, Lines and Planes

The relationship between a point and a line on a plane is called the incidence property. It states that:

1. Infinite number of lines can be drawn passing through a given fixed point on a plane.

   Example: Lines ℓ_1, ℓ_2, ℓ_3, … all pass through a given point A.

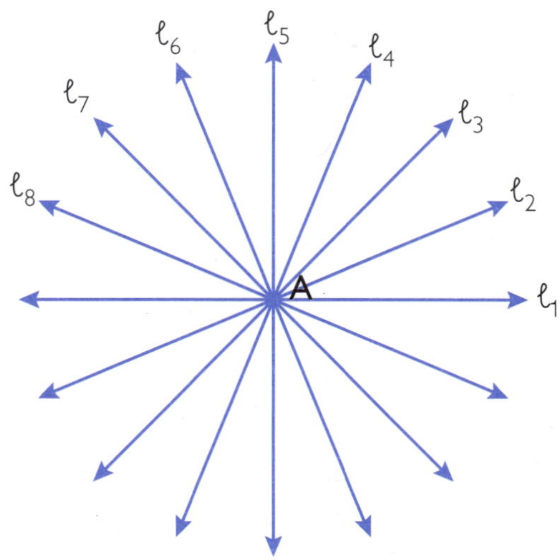

2. One and only one line can be drawn passing through two given points in a plane.

Collinear Points

Three or more points are said to be *collinear* if they lie on the same line on a plane. If the line is drawn with two given points and a third point does not lie on the line then the three points are said to be non-collinear.

Example:

The three points A, B and C in the figure above are collinear.

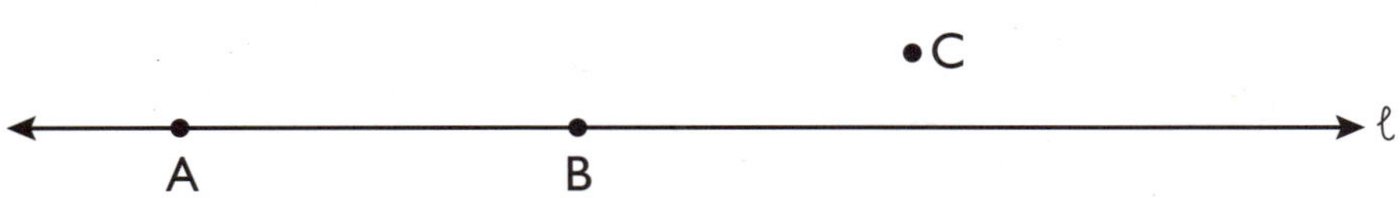

The three points A, B and C in the figure above are non-collinear as C does not lie on the line "ℓ".

Closed and Open Figures

Closed Figures

Figures in which the initial and the end points coincide with each other are called closed figures.

Example 1:

Example 2:

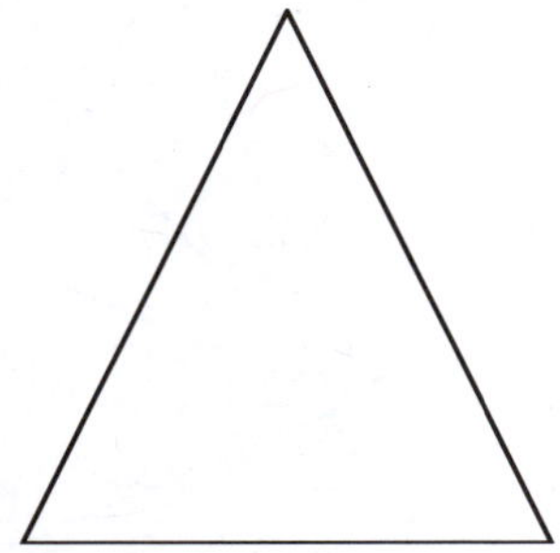

Example 3:

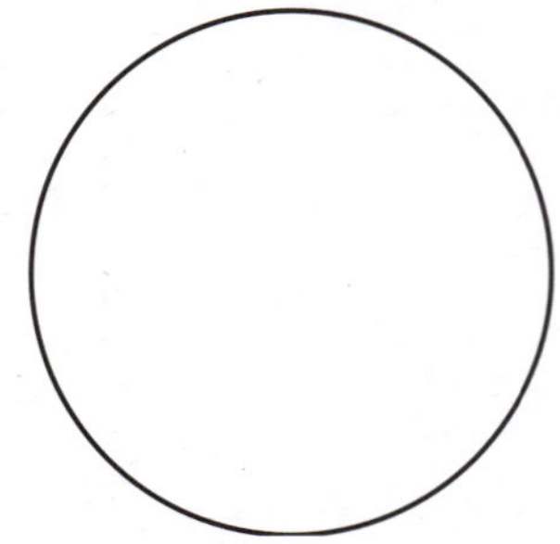

Open Figures

Figures that have different initial and end points are called open figures.

Example1:

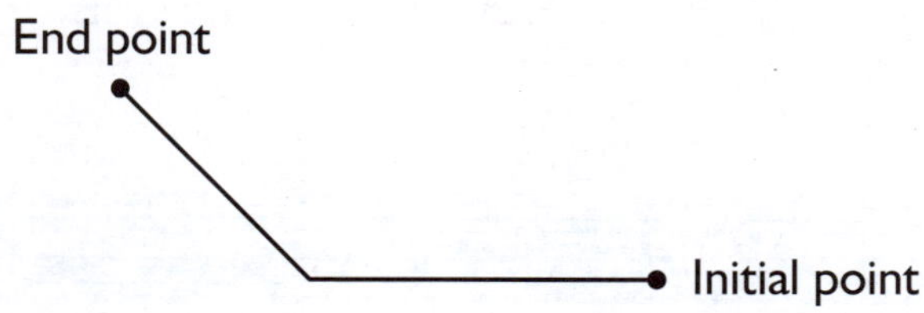

Example 2:

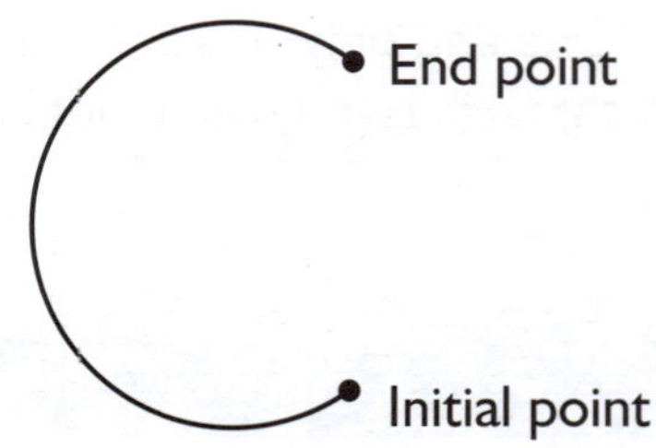

Simple and Complex Closed Figures

Closed figures are called simple if there are no points where the boundary crosses itself.

Example 1:

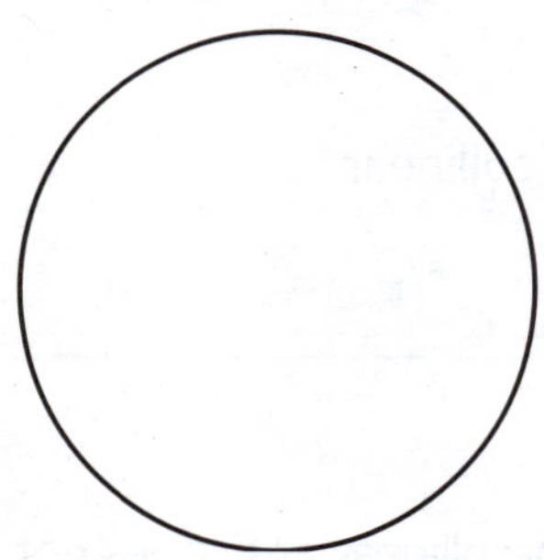

Example 2:

Closed figures are called complex if there are points where the boundary crosses itself.

Example 1:

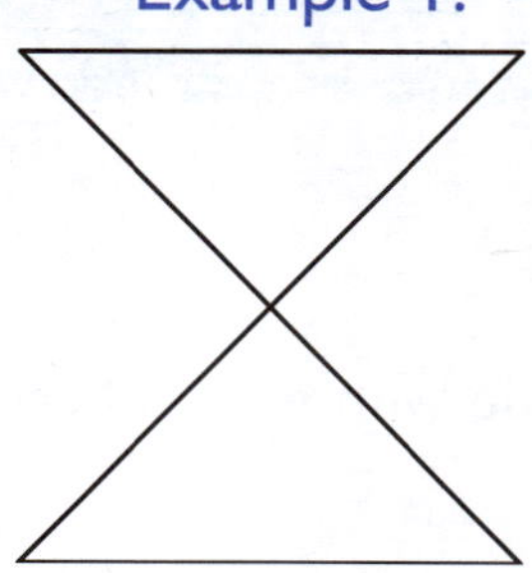

Example 2:

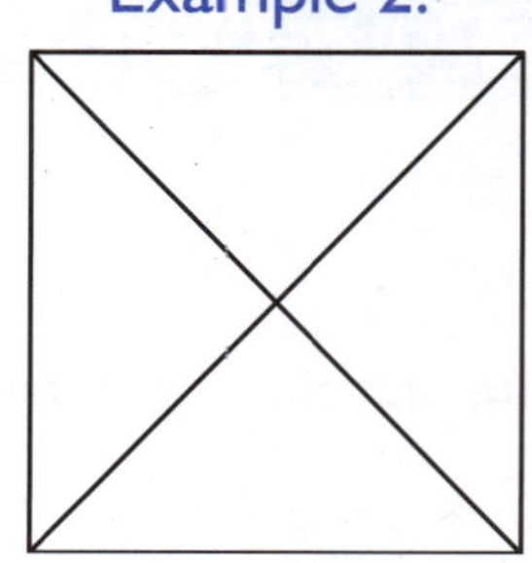

Interior and Exterior of Closed Figures

The figures shown below are examples of closed figures.

Example 1:

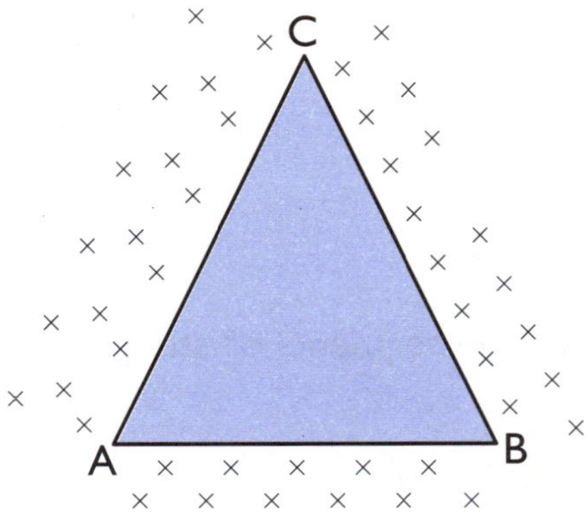

Example 2:

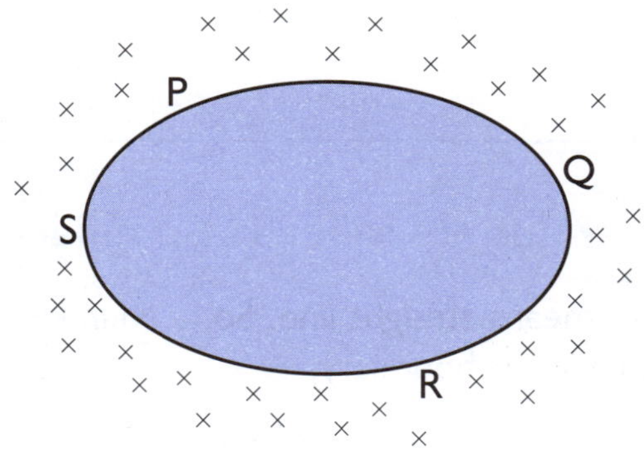

In the two examples, the shaded portion represents the interior region, the points A, B, C and P, Q, R, S represent the boundaries of the closed figures and "*x*" represents the exterior of the closed figures.

The exterior of a closed figure is unlimited. It can extend indefinitely in all directions.

Polygon

A polygon is a rectilinear figure bounded by three or more sides. It is a *closed* curve made up of line segments only. The minimum number of line segments needed to make a polygon are *three* (3).

If all the *sides* and all the *angles* of a polygon are equal, it is called a regular polygon. If the sides and angles of a polygon are unequal then it is called an irregular polygon.

The table below shows the shapes of different regular and irregular polygons.

Table 7.2 Shapes of Polygons

Number of Sides	Name	Regular	Irregular
3	Triangle		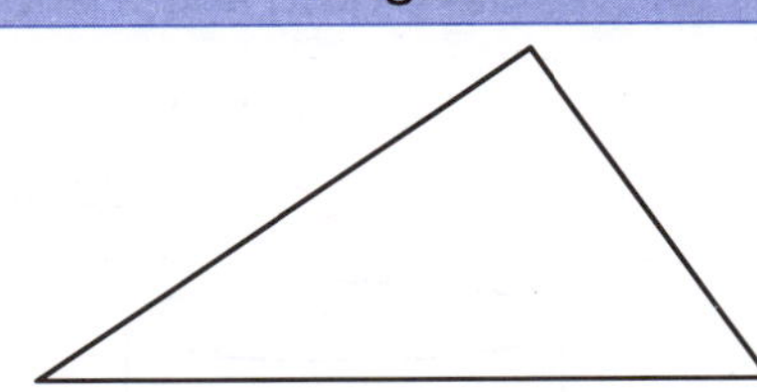
4	Quadrilateral		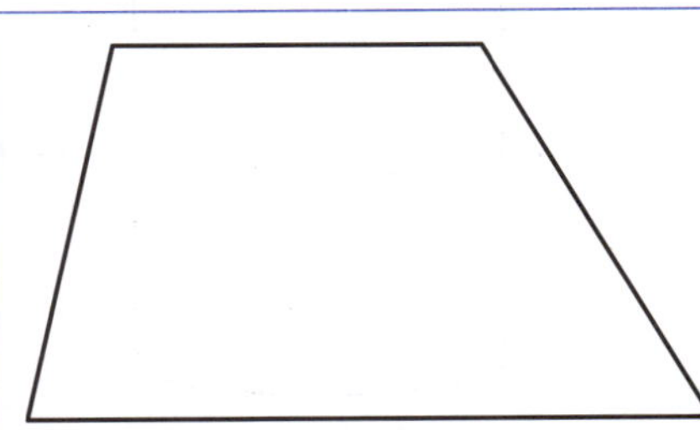

5	Pentagon	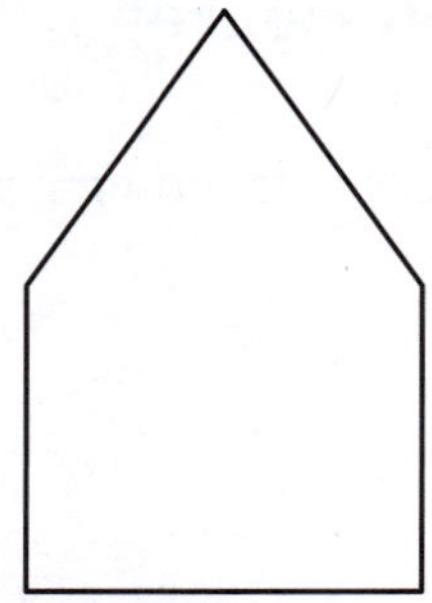	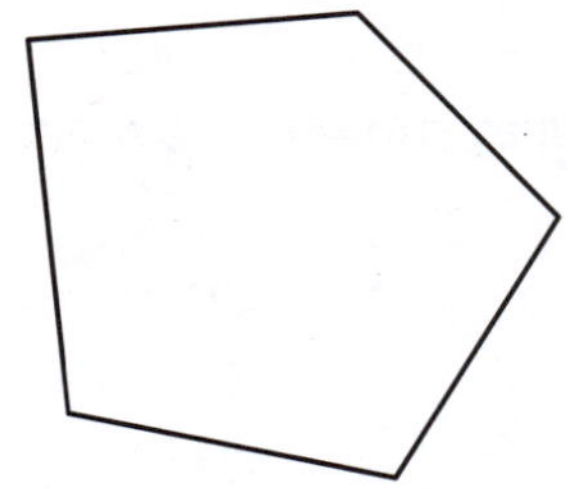

Linear and Curvilinear Boundaries

Linear means straight line. So, a *boundary* containing only line segments or straight lines is called a linear boundary.

Example 1:

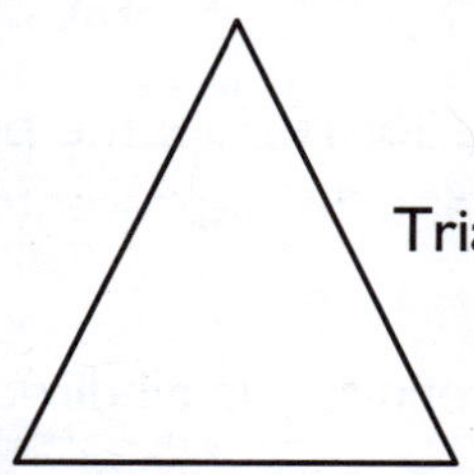

Triangle

Example 2:

Square

Curvilinear means a curved line. So, a boundary containing only curved lines is called a curvilinear boundary.

Example 1:

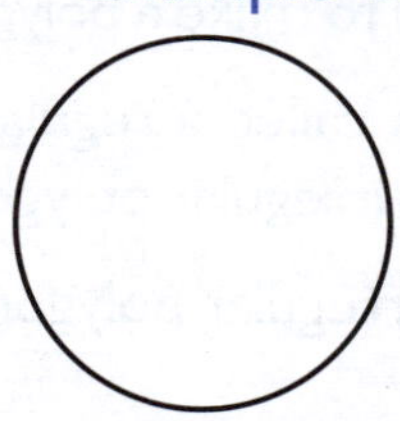

Circle

Example 2:

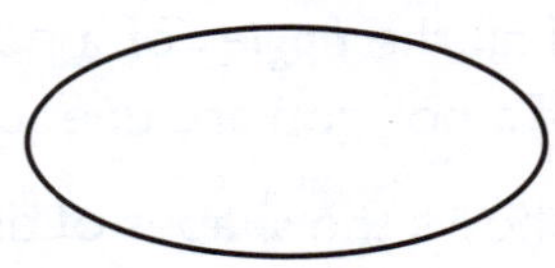

Ellipse

Some shapes have both linear and curvilinear boundaries.

Example 1:

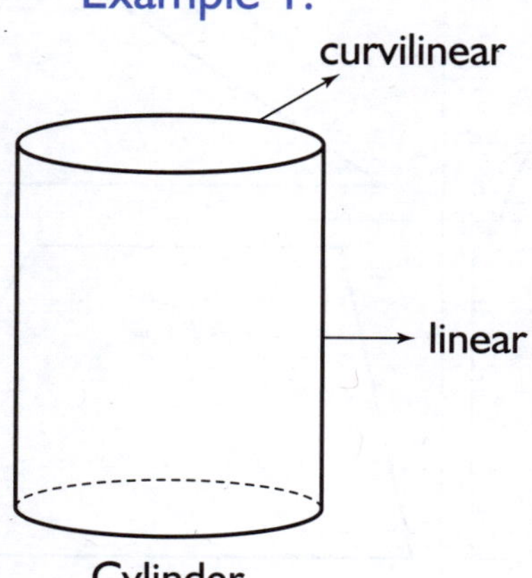

Cylinder

Example 2:

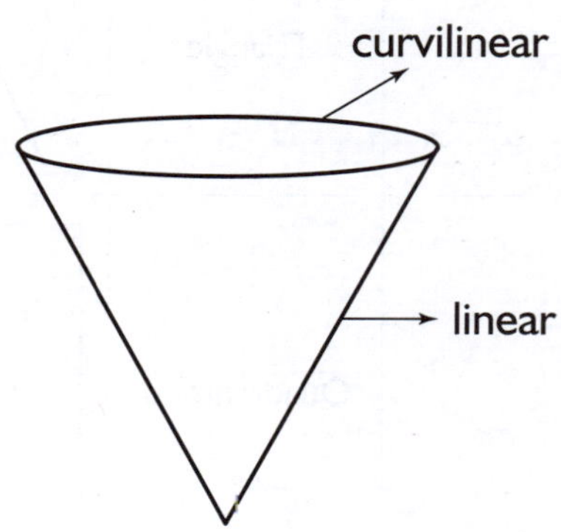

Cone

Practice Exercise 7.1

1. In the given figure, identify and write the following.

   a. 3 points. b. 3 line segments. c. 2 rays. d. 1 line.

2. In the given figure, identify and write the following.

   a. One point not on the rays. b. Two rays.

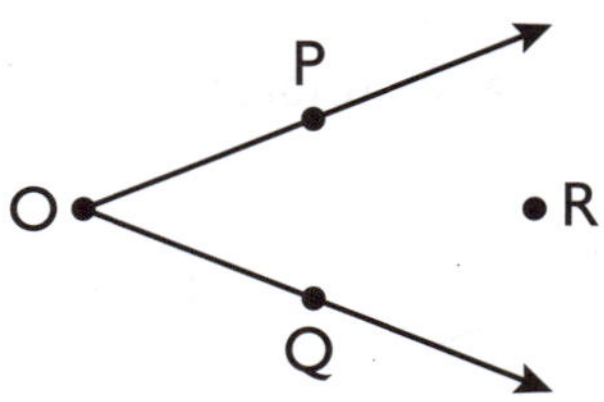

3. In the given figure, identify and write the following.

   a. One line.

   b. Four rays.

   c. Two line segments.

   d. Three points on the line.

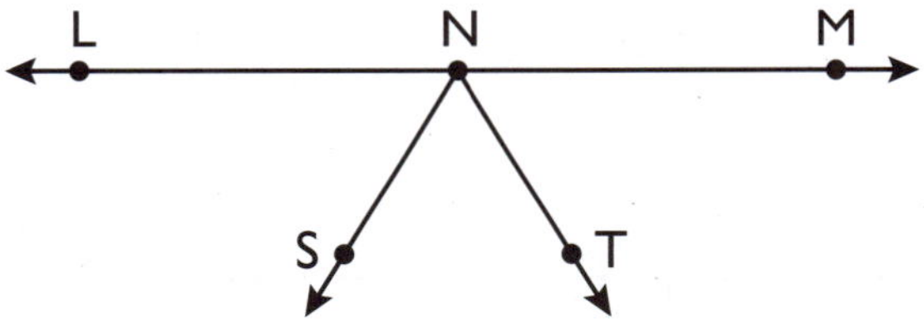

4. Name the points that are:

   a. in the interior of the closed figure.

   b. in the exterior of the closed figure.

   c. on the boundary of the closed figure.

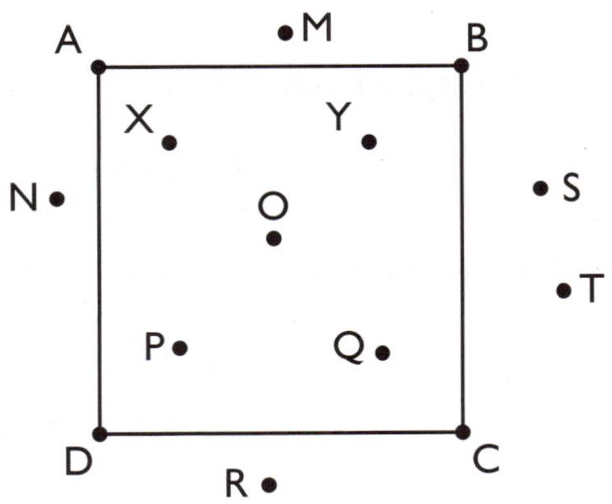

5. Draw and name the following polygons.

a. Polygon with three sides.

b. Polygon with five sides.

c. Polygon with seven sides.

6. Answer the following.

a. How many lines can you draw passing through two points?

b. How many lines can you draw through a single point?

c. Three points, A, B and C, are collinear. Depict this statement through an appropriate figure.

7. Identify the linear and curvilinear boundaries of the following figures.

a. 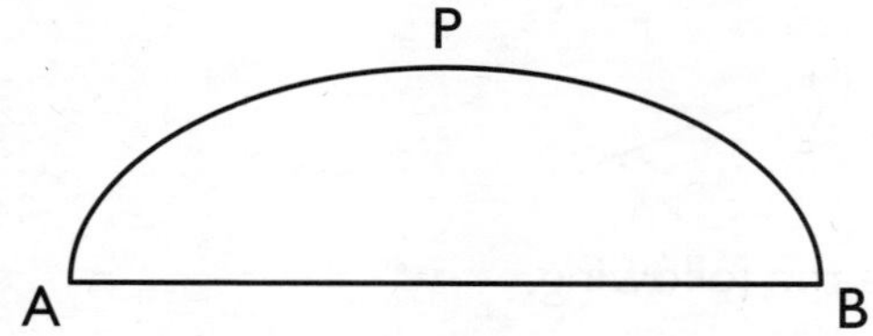

b. 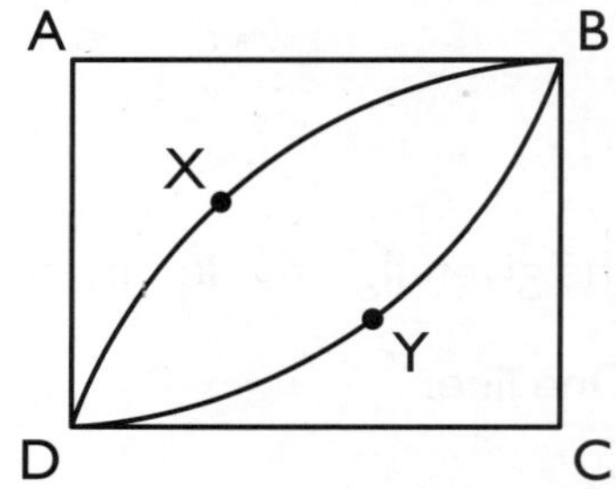

c. 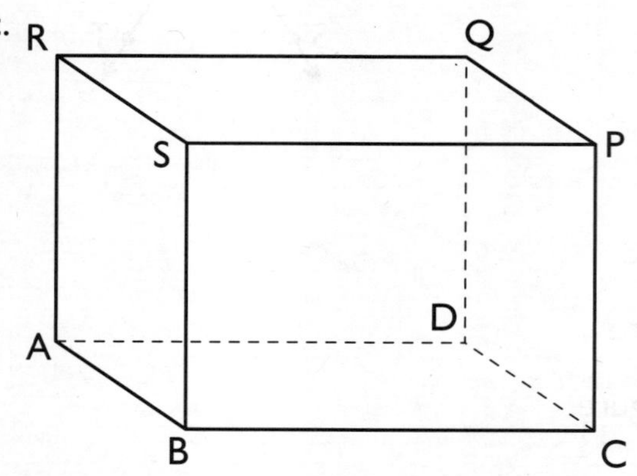

d. 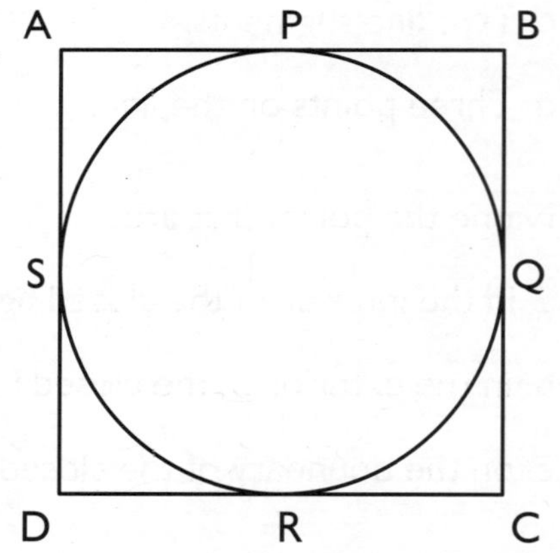

8. Draw two figures each to depict the following.

a. A closed figure.

b. An open figure.

9. Give one example from daily life to depict the following.

a. Plane surface.

b. Curved surface.

c. Linear boundary.

d. Curved boundary.

e. Partly linear and partly curved boundary.

10. Classify the following as a line, line segment or ray.

a. $\overline{PQ}$ b. $\overrightarrow{PQ}$ c. $\overleftrightarrow{AB}$ d. $\overline{QP}$ e. $\overrightarrow{RS}$

Angles

An angle is a figure formed when two rays have the same initial point (starting point). The common initial point is called the vertex of the angle, while the two rays are called the arms or sides of the angle.

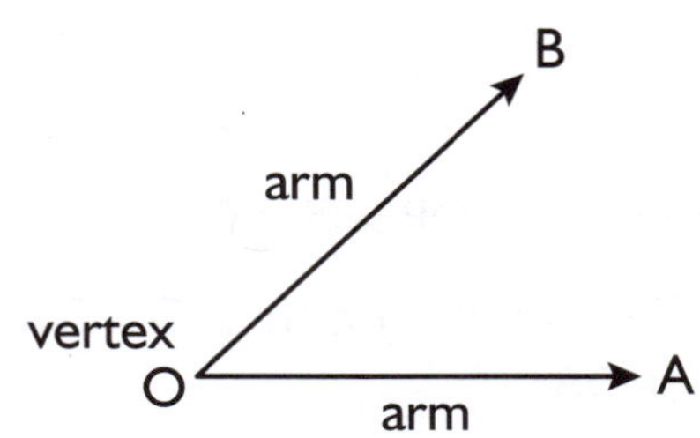

The two rays are $\overrightarrow{OA}$ and $\overrightarrow{OB}$. The common initial point is O. The rays $\overrightarrow{OA}$ and $\overrightarrow{OB}$ are called the arms or sides of the angle and the common point is called the vertex of the angle. Looking at the shape of the angle, the symbol used to represent it is $\angle$.

Naming an Angle

Consider the figure ABC, which has an angle 1.

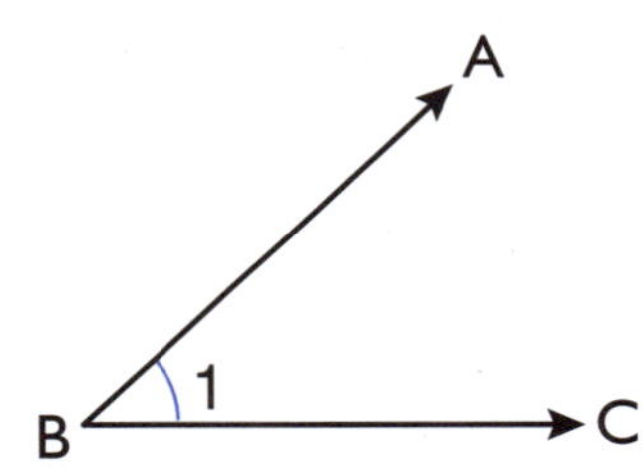

By using the symbol $\angle$, an angle can be named in three ways.

1. $\angle 1$ (By assigning a number)
2. $\angle B$ (By the vertex of the angle)
3. $\angle ABC$ (By the two rays or arms with the vertex in the middle)

The Exterior and Interior of an Angle

Just as we have an exterior, interior and boundary of any closed figure, we can also have the same for the angle (an open figure) as well.

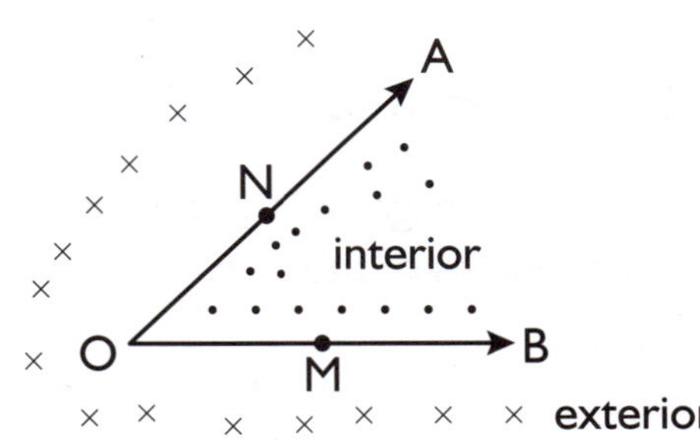

Adjacent Angles

Two angles in a plane are said to be adjacent, if:

1. they have a common vertex
2. they have a common arm
3. the other two non-common arms are on the opposite sides of the common arm.

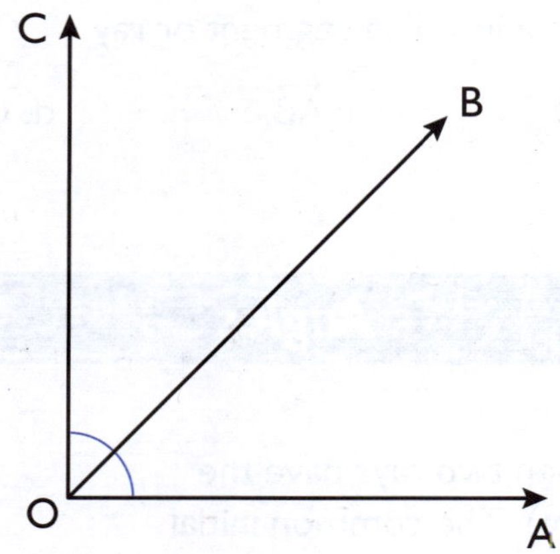

Here ∠AOB and ∠BOC are adjacent angles. The common vertex is O.

The common arm is OB. The non-common arms are $\overrightarrow{OA}$ and $\overrightarrow{OC}$ on the opposite sides of $\overrightarrow{OB}$.

Linear Pair

If the sum of ∠AOB and ∠BOC is 180°, then we say that the two adjacent angles form a linear pair.

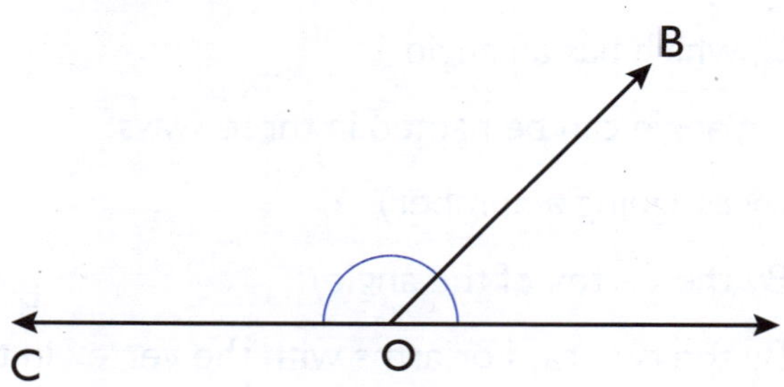

Magnitude of an Angle

The size or magnitude of an angle depends on the distance between the two arms and not on the lengths of the arms.

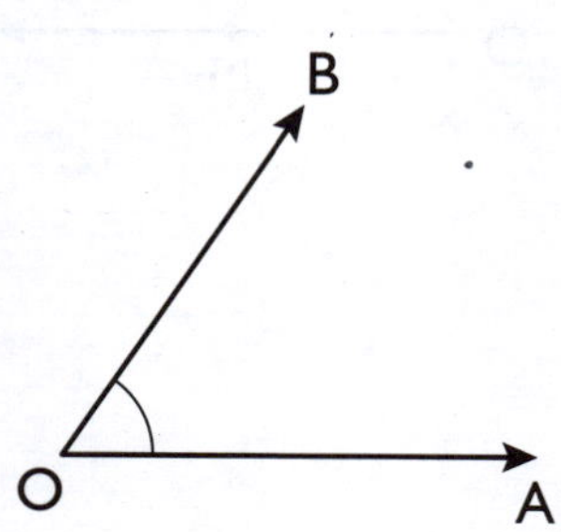

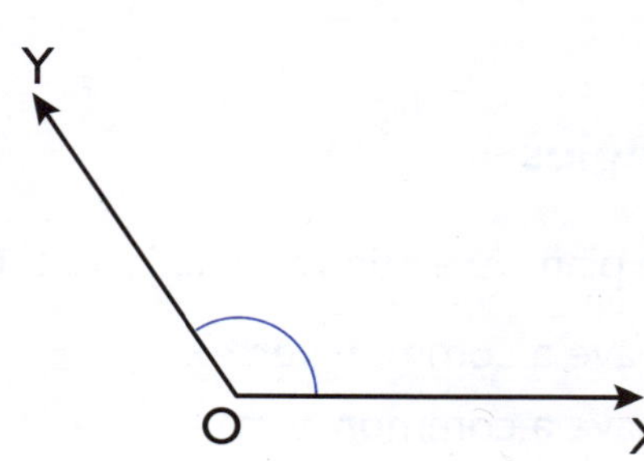

The magnitudes of ∠AOB and ∠XOY are different as the distance between the arms are different.

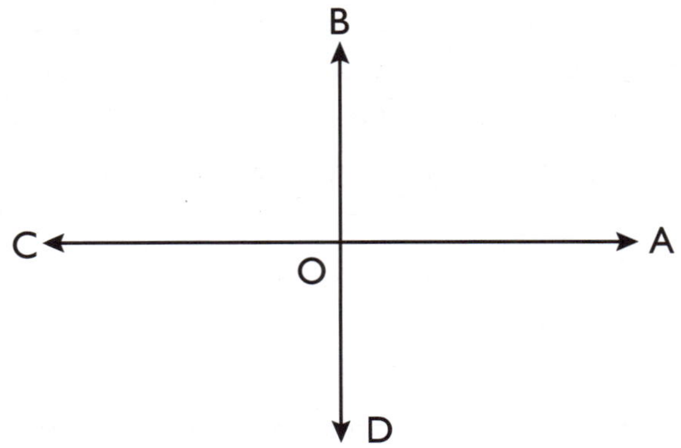

Look at the figure above and imagine the ray $\overrightarrow{OA}$ to revolve and reach $\overrightarrow{OB}$. The magnitude of the angle traced is 90°. If it revolves further and reaches $\overrightarrow{OC}$, the angle traced is 180°. In position D, the ray becomes $\overrightarrow{OD}$ and the angle is 270°. Finally, when it reaches point A again, the angle is 360°. So in one complete rotation, the angle traced is 360°.

We can compare this to the hands of a watch or the placement of the four directions east, west, north and south.

The magnitude of an angle is measured in degrees.

1. A measure of 90° is called a right angle.
2. A measure of 180° is called a straight angle.
3. An angle less than 90° is called an acute angle.
4. An angle more than 90° and less than 180° is called an obtuse angle.
5. An angle more than 180° and less than 360° is called a reflex angle.
6. An angle whose degree measure is 360° is called a complete angle.
7. An angle whose measure is 0° is called a zero angle.

Triangles

A closed figure bounded by three line segments is called a triangle.

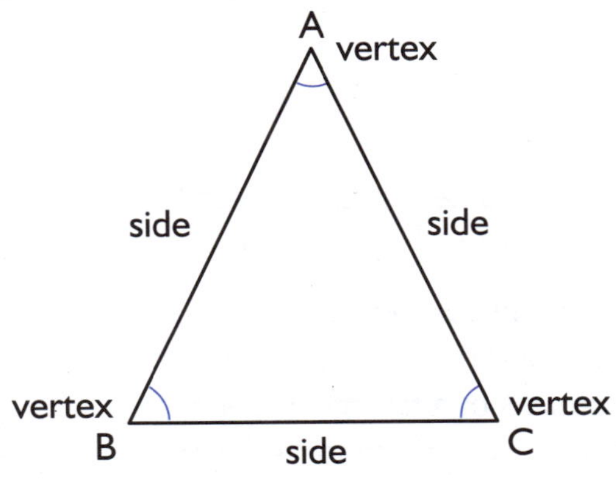

ABC is a closed figure. It is a three-sided polygon where A, B and C are called the vertices of the triangle. $\overline{AB}$, $\overline{BC}$ and $\overline{CA}$ are the three sides of the triangle and ∠A, ∠B and ∠C are the three angles of the triangle. Sum of the three angles of a triangle is always equal to 180°.

The side BC is called the base of the triangle. The angle opposite the base is called the vertical angle.

Altitude of a Triangle

The perpendicular drawn from the vertex of a triangle to its opposite side is called an altitude. Since there are 3 vertices, 3 perpendiculars can be drawn. Hence, a triangle has three altitudes.

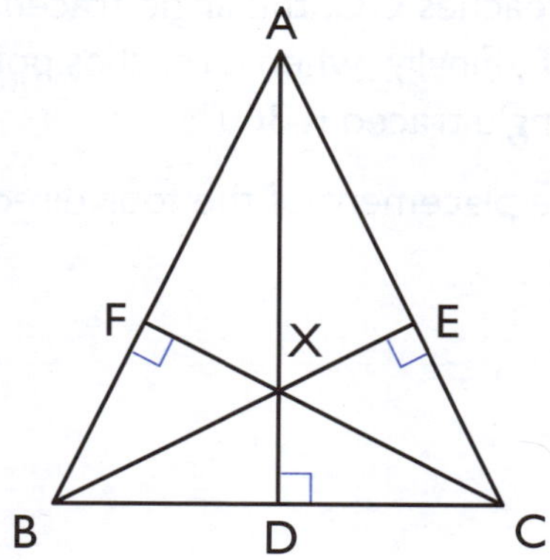

Question: Why was the obtuse angle upset?

Answer: Because he was never right!!

In the above figure, ABC is a triangle.

AD is the perpendicular from point A on BC.

BE is the perpendicular from point B on AC.

CF is the perpendicular from point C on AB.

The three altitudes meet at the point X.

That point of meeting or concurrence is called the orthocentre of the triangle.

Median of a Triangle

The line joining the midpoint of a side of a triangle and its opposite vertex is called the median of the triangle.

Here X, Y and Z are the midpoints of the sides of QR, RP and PQ, respectively. PX, QY and RZ are the medians of the triangle PQR. The medians of a triangle meet at a point. That point of meeting or concurrence is called the centroid of the triangle.

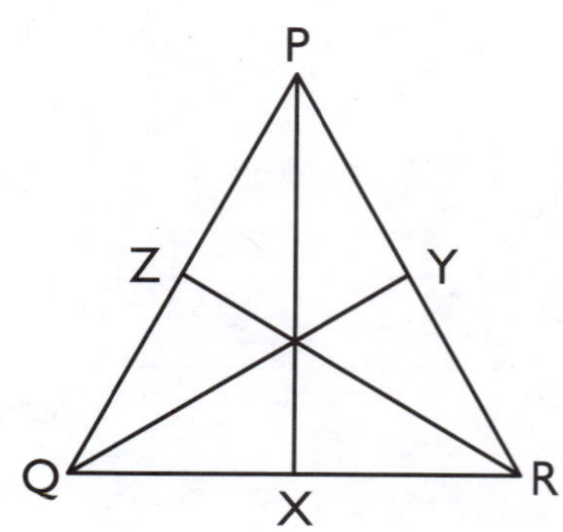

Practice Exercise 7.2

1. Name the vertex and arms of the following angles.

a.

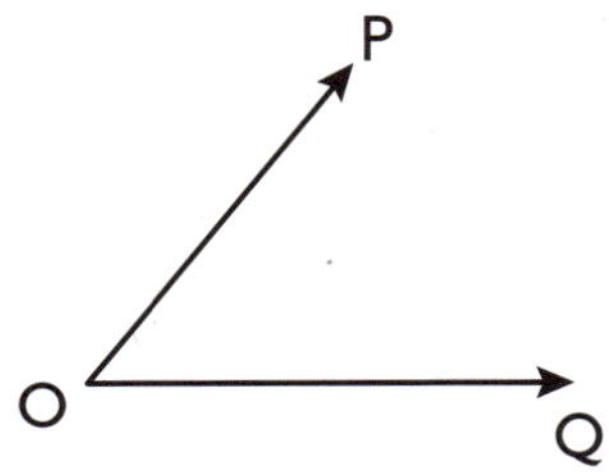

b.

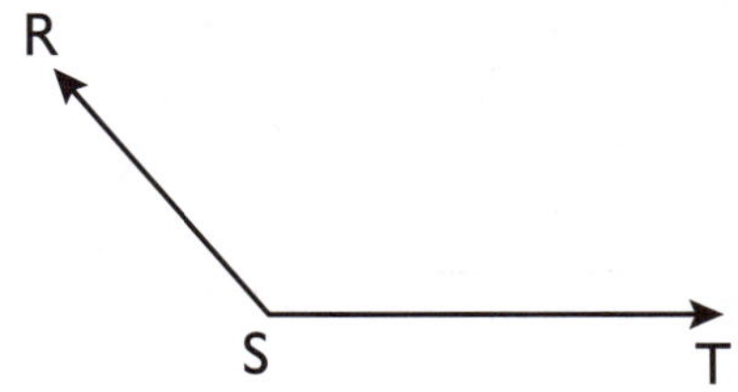

c.

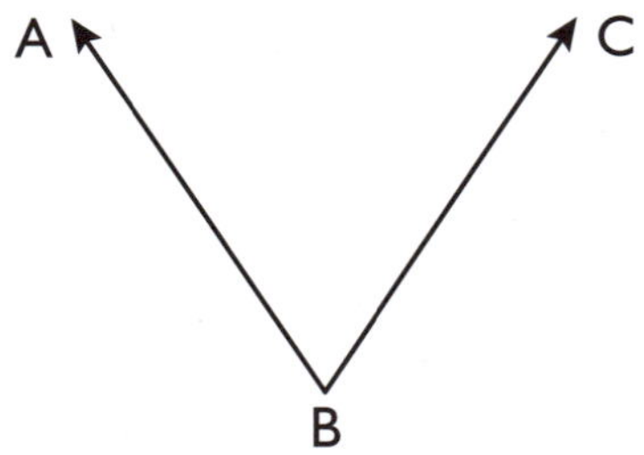

2. Write the adjacent angles in the following figures.

a.

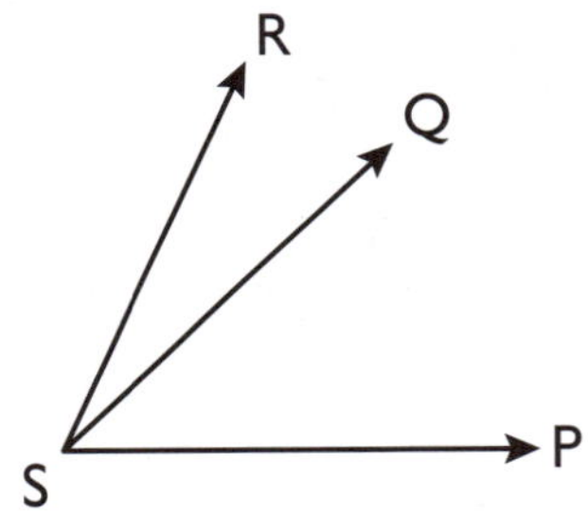

b.

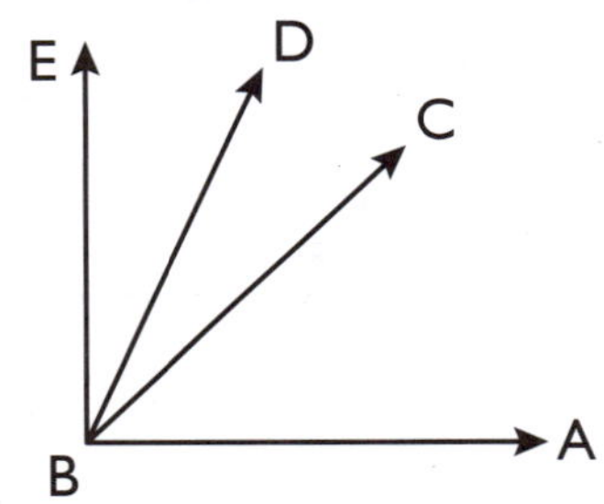

c.

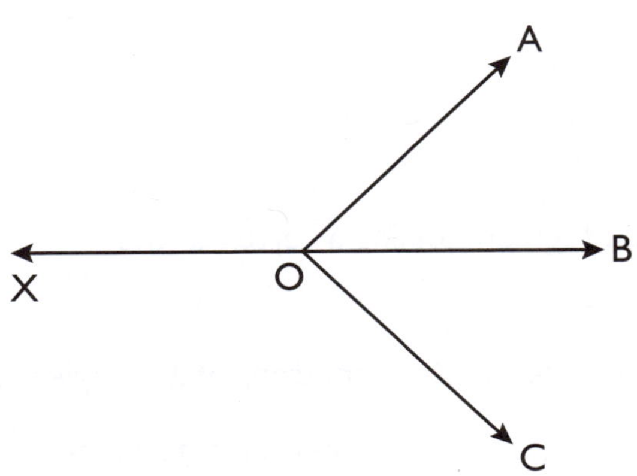

3.

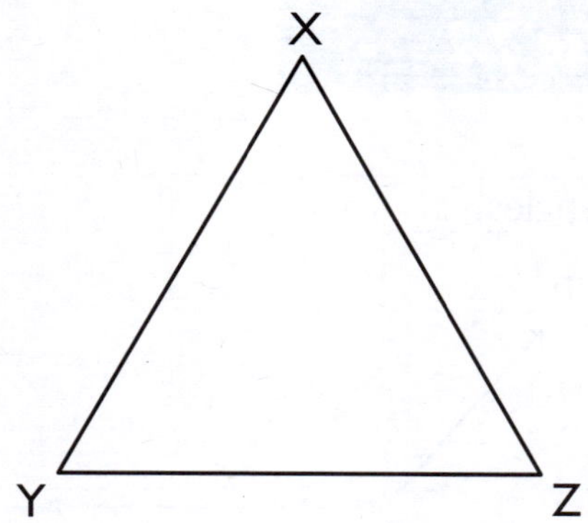

Study the triangle given above.

a. List the three vertices of the triangle.

b. List the three arms or sides of the triangle.

c. List the three angles of the triangle.

4. Draw separate figures to represent ∠CED, ∠ABC, ∠POQ, ∠MON and ∠XYZ.

5. PQ and PR are any two rays. Do they always form an angle? Why?

6. In the figure given below, name all the eight angles.

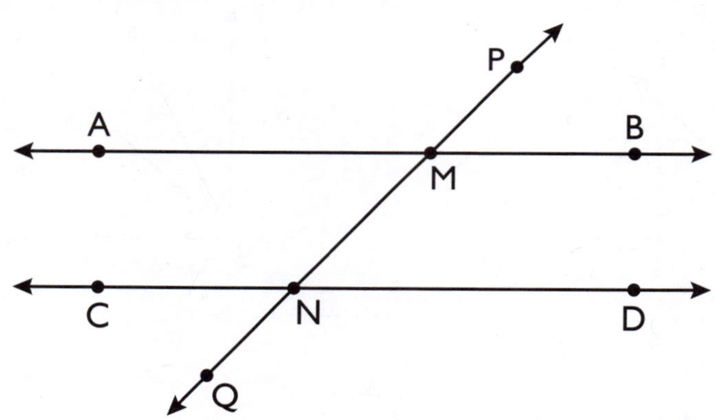

7. Fill in the blanks.

a. A median of a triangle is the line segment joining a vertex to the ______________ of the opposite side.

b. ______________ is the point where the three medians of a triangle meet.

c. An altitude of a triangle is the ______________ drawn from a vertex to the opposite side.

d. An angle greater than 0° and less than 90° is called an ______________ angle.

e. An angle that measures 90° is called a ______________ angle.

f. A straight angle measures ______________.

8. In the figure given below, name the following.

   a. All pairs of parallel lines.

   b. All pairs of intersecting lines.

   c. Lines whose point of intersection is B.

   d. Lines whose point of intersection is D.

   e. Name the triangles seen in the figure.

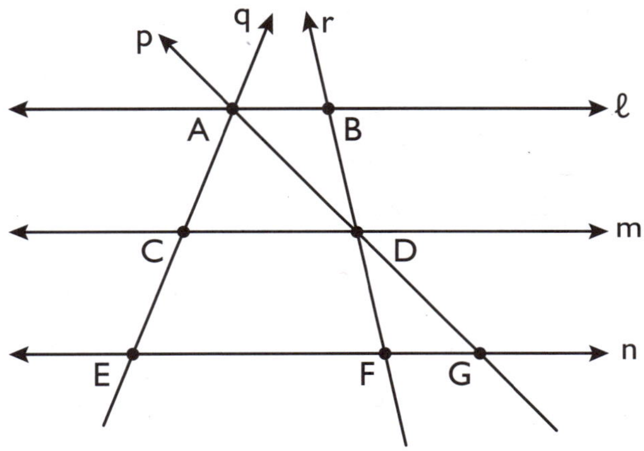

9. In the given figure, ∠AOB and ∠BOC form a linear pair. If ∠AOB is 60°, find ∠BOC

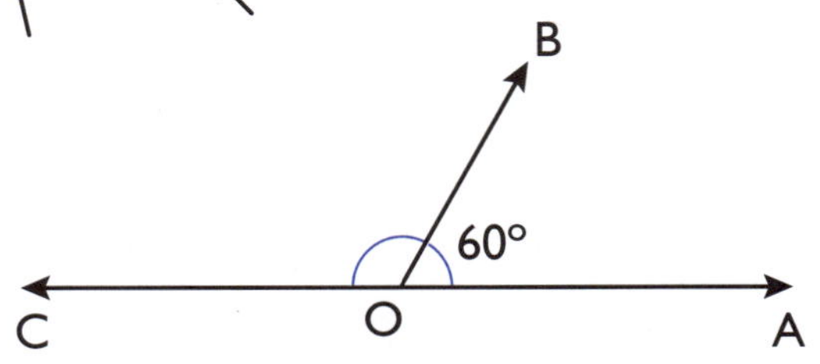

10. In the given triangle PQR, if ∠PQR is 30° and ∠PRQ is 90°, find ∠QPR.

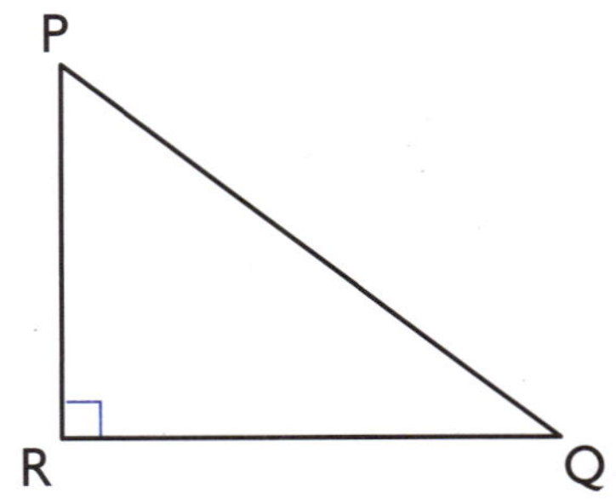

Quadrilateral

A quadrilateral is a four-sided polygon.

"Quad" means four, "lateral" means straight line. So quadrilateral means a closed figure bounded by four line segments.

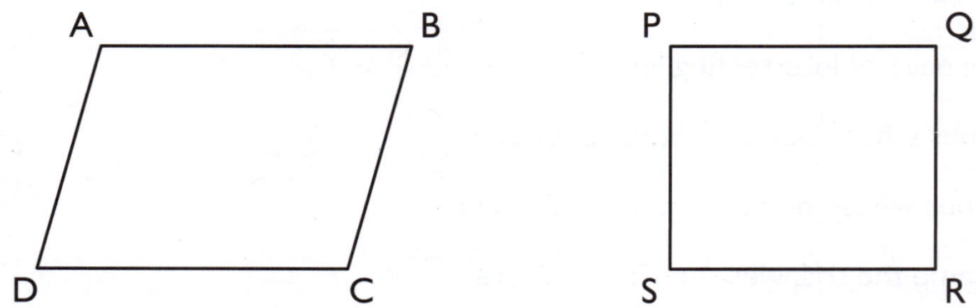

The figures ABCD and PQRS given above are quadrilaterals.

A quadrilateral is named in a *cyclic* order. We can begin from any corner and then go around in a cyclic order.

Sides, Vertices and Angles of a Quadrilateral

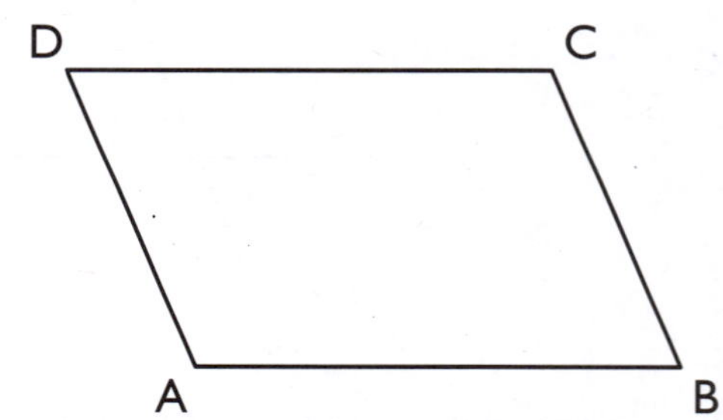

A quadrilateral has four sides, four vertices and four angles.

Consider the quadrilateral ABCD.

The four sides are AB, BC, CD and DA.

They can also be written as BA, AD, DC and CB.

The four vertices are the four corner points, where any two sides or a pair of sides meet.

AB and BC meet at B.

BC and CD meet at C.

CD and DA meet at D.

DA and AB meet at A.

So, the four vertices of the quadrilateral are A, B, C and D.

The four angles of the quadrilateral are:

$\angle DAB$	or	$\angle A$
$\angle ABC$	or	$\angle B$
$\angle BCD$	or	$\angle C$
$\angle CDA$	or	$\angle D$

Diagonals of a Quadrilateral

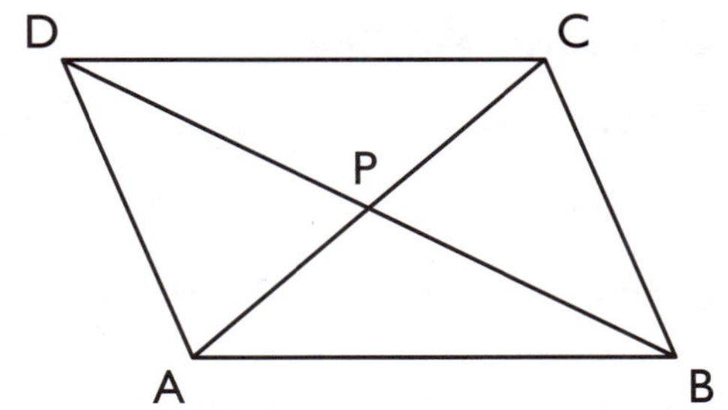

A quadrilateral has *two* diagonals. The line segments joining the opposite vertices of a quadrilateral are called its diagonals. The two diagonals meet or intersect at a point. If we name the point of intersection, we observe that four triangles are formed.

In the quadrilateral ABCD, the line segment joining the opposite vertices A and C is the diagonal AC and the line segment joining the opposite vertices B and D is the diagonal BD.

Alert!

A quadrilateral has four sides.

A quadrilateral has four vertices.

A quadrilateral has four angles.

A quadrilateral has two diagonals.

Adjacent Sides of a Quadrilateral

The sides AB and AD of the quadrilateral ABCD are called adjacent sides. Similarly, AB and BC, BC and CD and CD and DA are adjacent sides.

The adjacent sides have a common point, which is the vertex of the quadrilateral.

Opposite Sides of a Quadrilateral

AB and CD are the opposite sides of a quadrilateral.

BC and DA are the opposite sides of a quadrilateral.

There are two pairs of opposite sides.

The opposite sides have no common point.

Adjacent Angles

The two angles of a quadrilateral that have a common arm are called adjacent angles.

$\angle A$ and $\angle B$
$\angle B$ and $\angle C$
$\angle C$ and $\angle D$
$\angle D$ and $\angle A$

} Pairs of adjacent angles

Opposite Angles

The two angles of a quadrilateral that have no common arm are called opposite angles.

$\angle$A and $\angle$C are opposite angles.

$\angle$B and $\angle$D are opposite angles.

Interior and Exterior of a Quadrilateral

Just as the triangle divides a plane into three regions so also a quadrilateral.

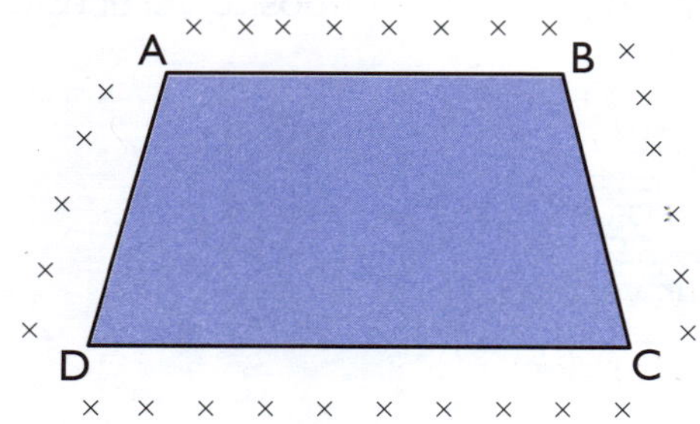

In the given quadrilateral ABCD, the shaded region is the interior region and the four bounding lines are the boundary of the quadrilateral. Any point on the lines are said to be on the quadrilateral. The region outside the boundary is the exterior region of the quadrilateral.

Thus, shaded region	$\longrightarrow$	interior of the quadrilateral.
x x x x x x x	$\longrightarrow$	exterior of the quadrilateral.
AB, BC, CD, DA	$\longrightarrow$	the line segments that form the quadrilateral.

Types of Quadrilaterals

Quadrilaterals can be classified into two types on the basis of the measures of the angles:

1. Convex quadrilaterals.
2. Concave quadrilaterals.

Convex Quadrilateral

A quadrilateral is said to be a convex quadrilateral if the measure of each of its angles is less than 180°.

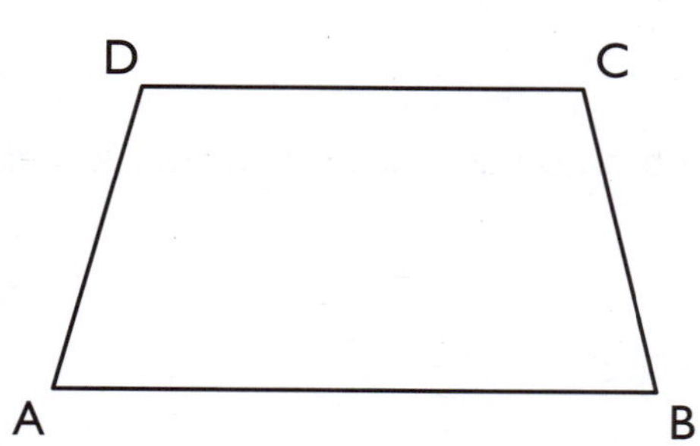

a.

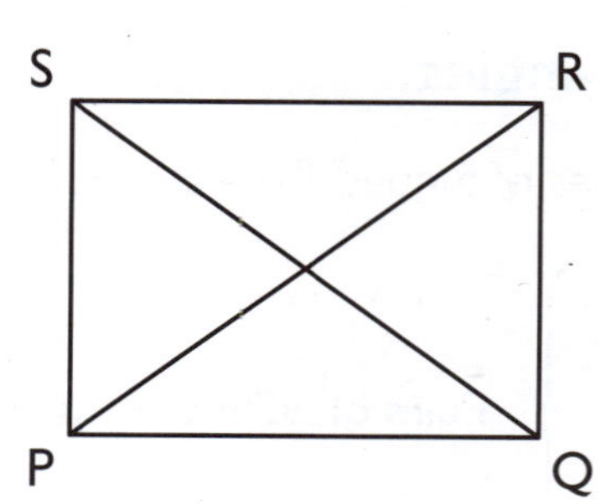

b.

In the above figures, (a) and (b), quadrilaterals ABCD and PQRS are convex quadrilaterals.

Some important features of a convex quadrilateral are:

1. the line containing any side of the convex quadrilateral has the remaining vertices on the same side of it.
2. the diagonals of a convex quadrilateral lie within the quadrilateral region.

Concave Quadrilateral

If the measure of any angle of a quadrilateral is more than 180°, the quadrilateral is said to be a concave quadrilateral.

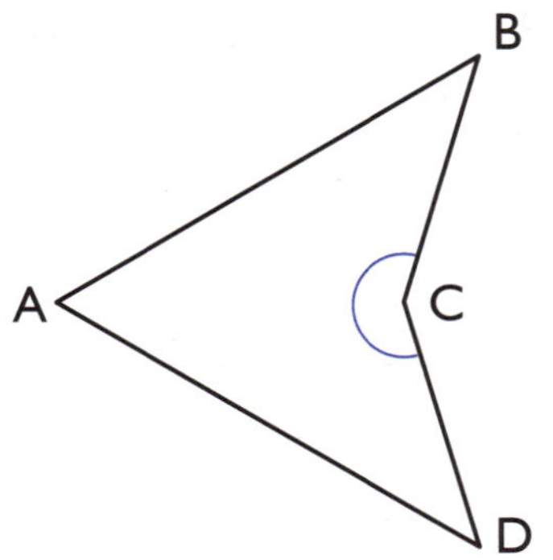

a.
∠BCD is greater than 180°

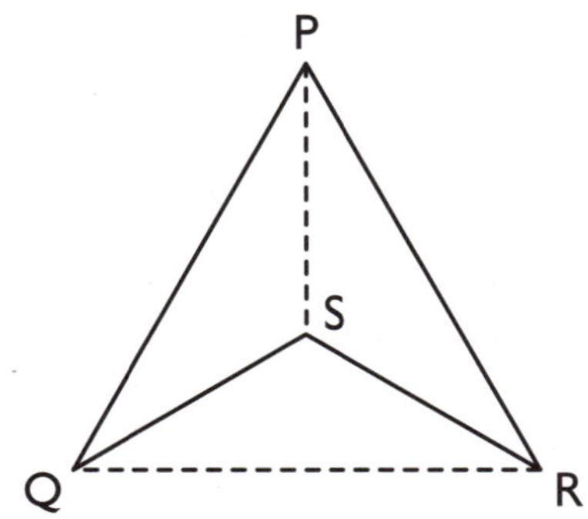

b.
The dotted lines are the diagonals of the quadrilateral

The diagonals of a concave quadrilateral lie outside the quadrilateral.

Alert!

When the word quadrilateral is used, it generally means a convex quadrilateral.

Angle Sum Property of a Quadrilateral

The sum of all the angles of a quadrilateral is 360°.

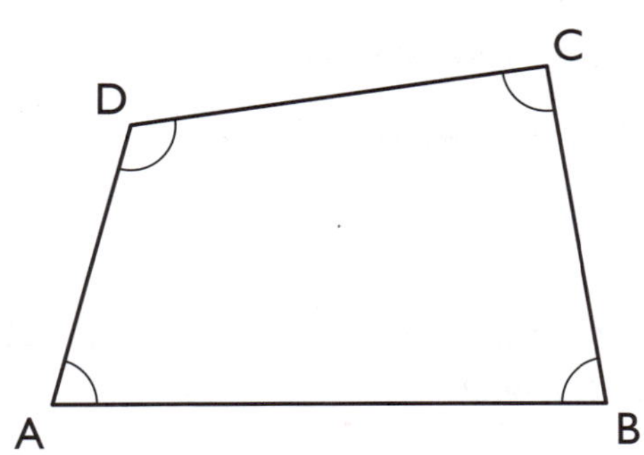

ABCD is a given quarilateral.

The sum of the interior angles of the quadrilateral is equal to 360°.

$$\angle A + \angle B + \angle C + \angle D = 360^\circ$$

Practice Exercise 7.3

1. Name the sides, vertices and angles of the given quadrilaterals.

a. 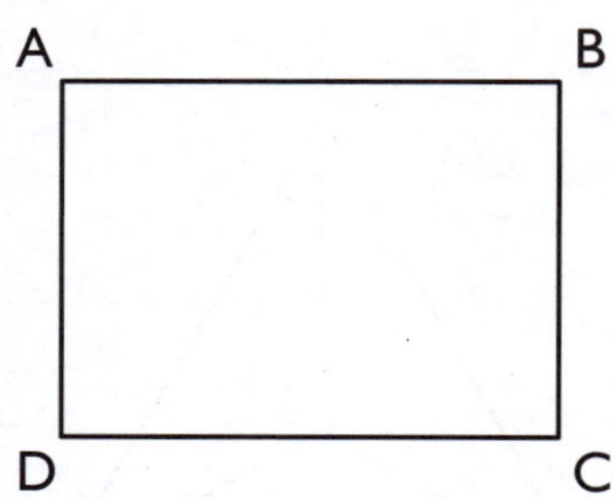

b. 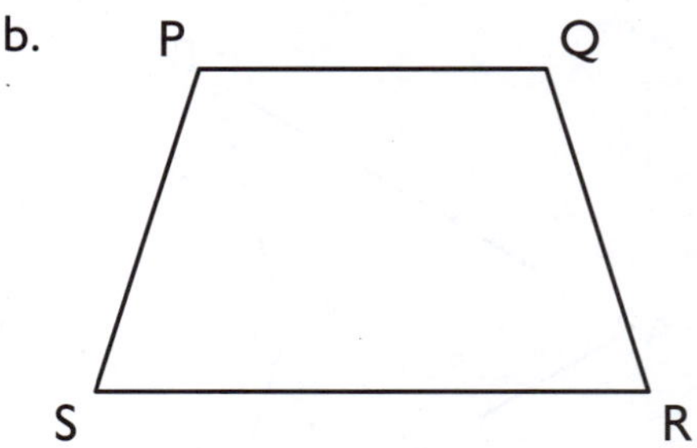

c. 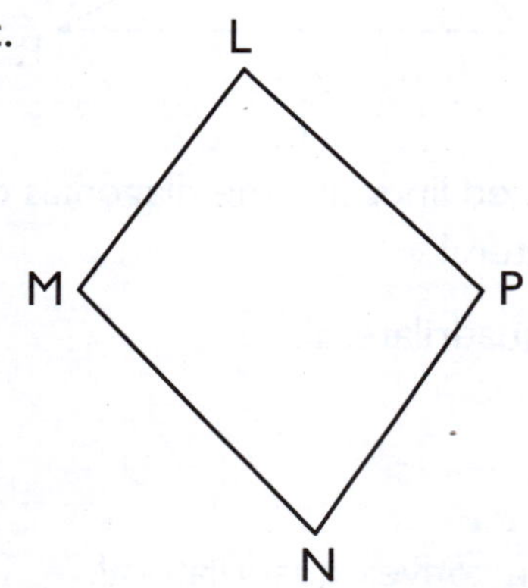

2. Draw a quadrilateral. Name it AXYB.

   Draw its diagonals and name them.

3. In the given figure, list the points that lie

   a. in the interior of the quadrilateral PQRS.

   b. in the exterior of the quadrilateral PQRS.

   c. on the boundary of the quadrilateral PQRS.

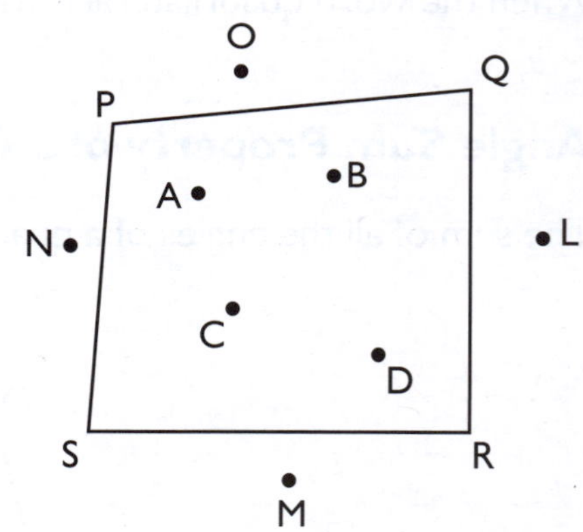

4. Three angles of a quadrilateral measure 120°, 60° and 100°, respectively. Find the measure of the fourth angle.

5. Draw two quadrilaterals to show the difference between a convex and a concave quadrilateral.

6. Study the figure on the right and answer the questions that follow.

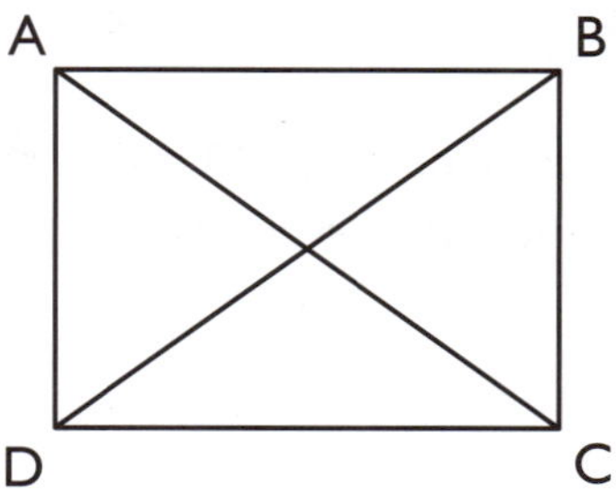

a. Name the quadrilateral in two different ways.

b. Name the vertices of the quadrilateral.

c. List the adjacent sides of the quadrilateral.

d. Name the opposite sides of the quadrilateral.

e. Name the diagonals of the quadrilateral.

7. Study the figure on the right and answer the questions that follow.

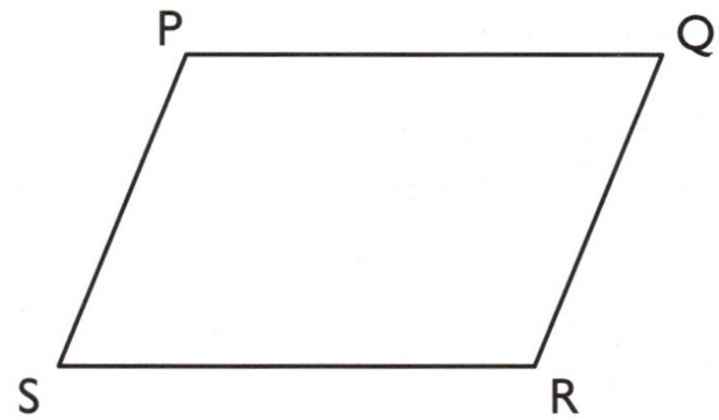

a. List the interior angles of the quadrilateral.

b. List the adjacent angles of the quadrilateral.

c. List the opposite angles of the quadrilateral.

8. All four angles of a quadrilateral measure the same. What is the measure of each angle?

9. In the figure given on the right, find the measure of $\angle BCD$.

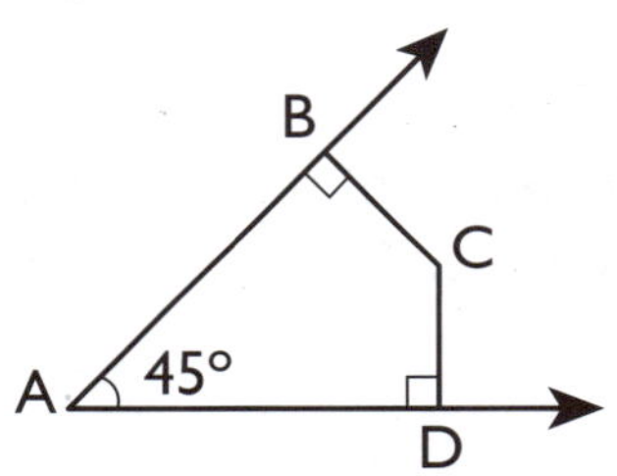

10. Is it possible to draw a quadrilateral with angles 90°, 90°, 180° and 270°?

If yes, draw the figure.

If no, give the reason for your answer.

Circles

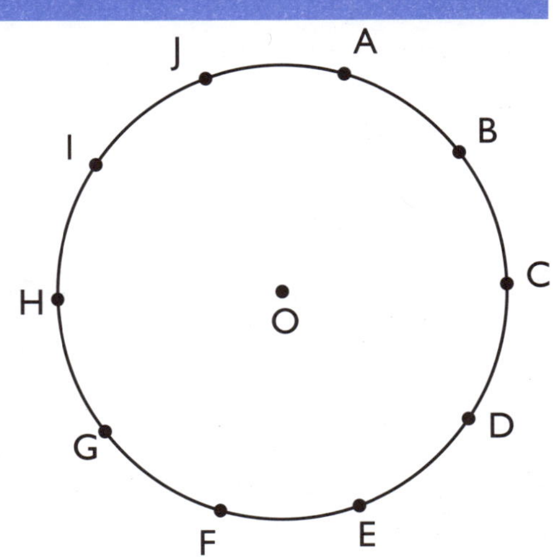

A circle is a closed figure that has a curvilinear boundary. A circle has a round shape. A coin, a bangle, a ring are all circular in shape.

A circle is a collection of points that are always equidistant from a fixed point in the interior of the closed figure.

A, B, C, D, E … are all points that are at the same distance (equidistant) from the point O (in the interior of the closed figure). When we join all the points, we get the boundary of a closed figure.

Centre of a Circle

The fixed point O inside the closed figure is called the centre of the circle.

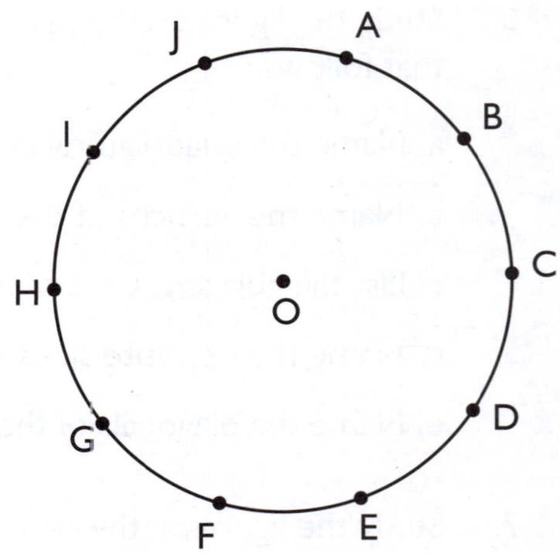

Radius of a Circle

The distance between the fixed point O and any point on the boundary of the closed figure is called the radius of the circle. Since all the points on the boundary are equidistant from the fixed point, the radius of a circle is fixed.

$$\overline{OA} = \overline{OB} = \overline{OC} = \overline{OD} = \overline{OE} = r$$

The radius of a circle is generally denoted by the letter "r". The length of the radius is different for circles of different sizes. The plural of radius is radii.

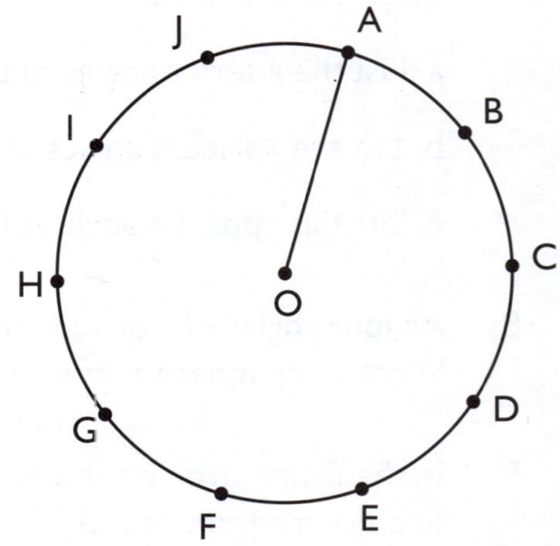

Diameter of a Circle

A line segment joining any two points on the boundary of the circle and passing through the centre of the circle is called the diameter of the circle.

The diameter of a circle is twice the radius.

In the circle with centre O given here, AF and ID are the diameters.

The diameter of a circle is generally denoted by the letter "d".

$$d = 2r$$

$$\text{diameter} = 2 \times \text{radius}$$

A circle can have any number of diameters.

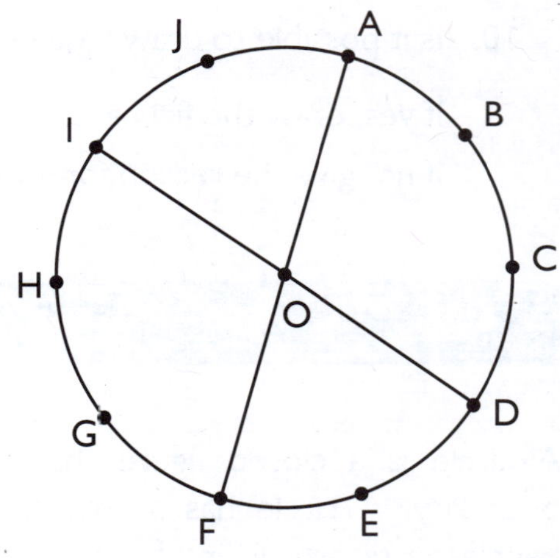

Circumference of a Circle

The length of the boundary of a circle is called its circumference.

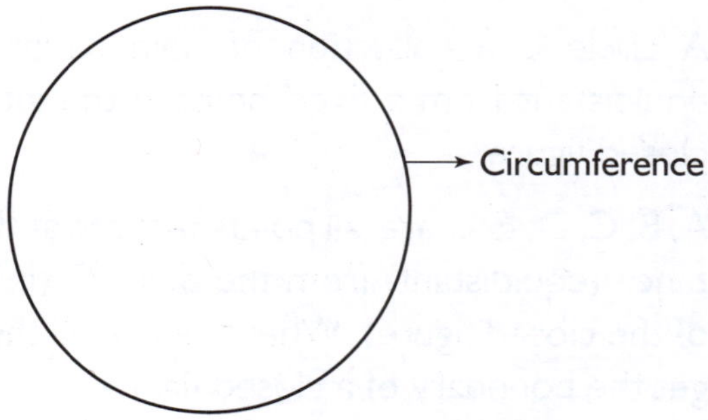

Chord of a Circle

A line segment joining any two points on the boundary of the circle is called the chord of a circle. The chord of a circle divides the circle into two parts.

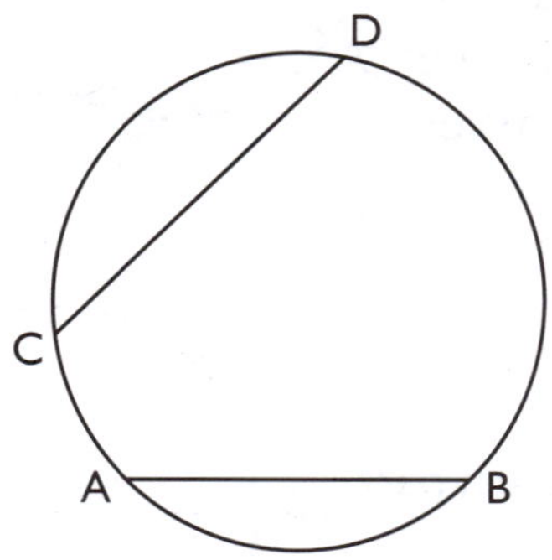

AB and CD are the chords of the circle.

The diameter is the longest chord of a circle.

Arc of a Circle

An arc of a circle is a segment of the circumference of the circle. The arc is denoted by "⌒".

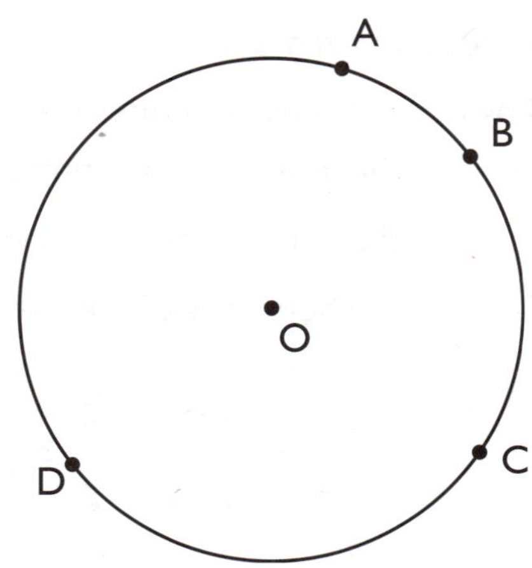

$\overset{\frown}{ABC}$ and $\overset{\frown}{ADC}$ are two arcs of the circle with centre O.

Given two points on a circle, the minor arc is the shortest arc linking them. The major arc is the longest. So in the circle with centre O, $\overset{\frown}{ABC}$ is the minor arc while $\overset{\frown}{ADC}$ is the major arc.

Concentric Circles

Circles having the same centre but different radii are called concentric circles.

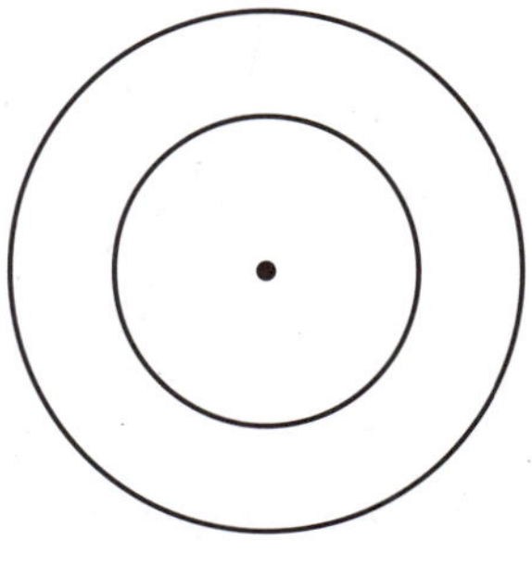

Segment of a Circle

A segment is a part of a circle enclosed by a chord and an arc of the circle. The chord of a circle divides the circle into two parts.

The region enclosed by the minor arc and the chord is called the minor segment and the region enclosed within the major arc and the chord is called the major segment.

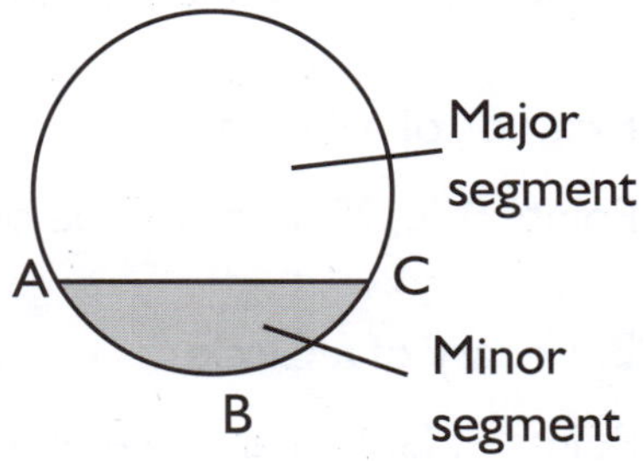

Sector of a Circle

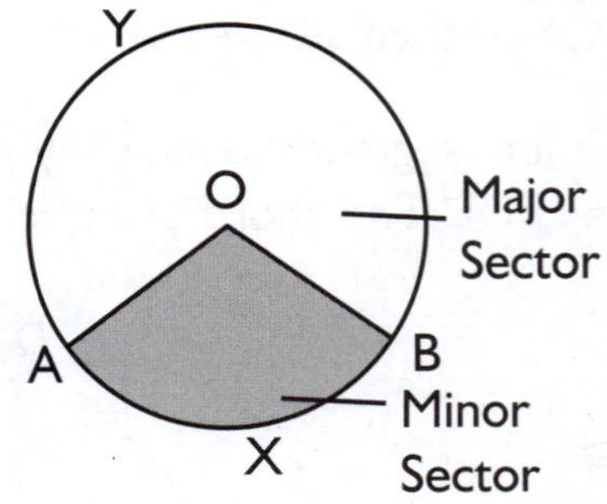

The region enclosed by an arc and a pair of radii of a circle is called a sector of the circle.

The region bounded by the minor arc $\overset{\frown}{AXB}$ and the radii OA and OB is called the minor sector. The region bounded by the major arc $\overset{\frown}{AYB}$ and the radii OA and OB is called the major sector.

Semicircle

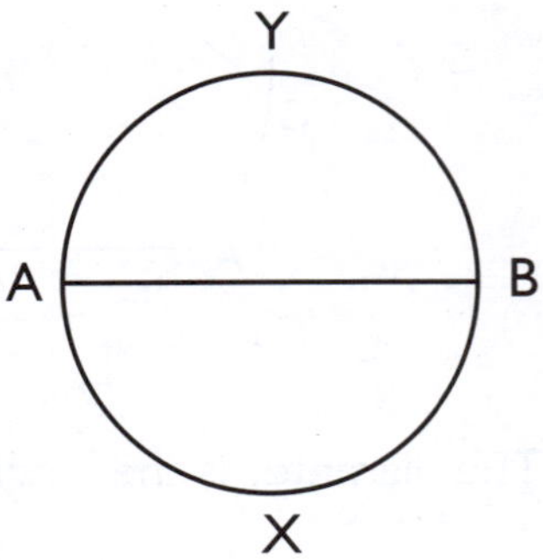

The diameter of a circle divides it into two equal parts. Each part is called a semicircle.

AXB and AYB represent two semicircles.

Interior and Exterior of a Circle

Any circle in a plane divides the plane into three parts:

1. the interior of the circle.
2. the exterior of the circle.
3. the boundary of the circle or the circumference of the circle.

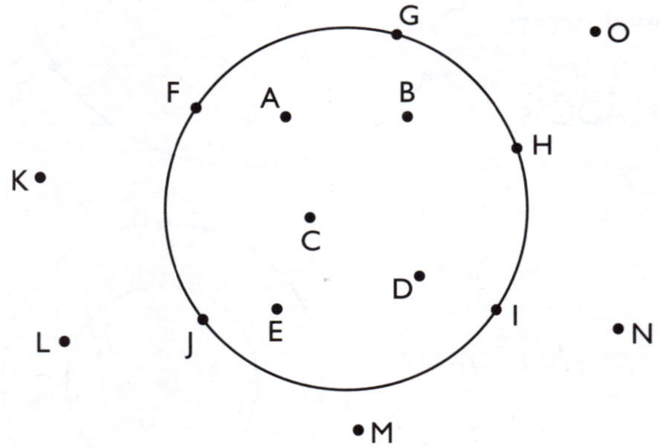

Question: What did the square say to the circle?

Answer: Been "around" long?

Interior of a Circle

Points A, B, C, D and E lie inside the circle.

Exterior of a Circle

Points K, L, M, N and O lie outside the circle.

Boundary of a Circle

Points F, G, H, I and J lie on the boundary of the circle.

Alert!

1. The diameter is the longest chord of a circle.
2. The diameter is twice the radius.

   $d = 2r$
3. In a circle there is a minor segment and a major segment.
4. In a circle there is a minor sector and a major sector.
5. A circle can be divided into two equal semicircles.

Practice Exercise 7.4

1. Make a point A on the paper. Keeping the point A as the centre, draw two circles with radii 2 and 4 cm. What kind of circles do you get?

2. Draw a circle having a radius of 3 cm. Draw two longest chords in the circle such that they are perpendicular to each other. What will be their point of intersection known as?

3. Draw a circle having a radius of 2 cm and mark the centre. Draw the diameter and find its length.

4. Draw a circle having a radius of 3 cm. Draw a chord XY such that the circle is divided into a major segment and a minor segment. In which segment does the centre of the circle lie?

5. Draw a circle having a radius of 4 cm. Divide it into two equal halves. What is the dividing line known as?

Higher Order Thinking Skills

HOTS

1. Distinguish between a line, a line segment and a ray using one figure.
2. How many times can two distinct non-parallel lines lying in the same plane intersect each other?
3. How many lines can be drawn from a given point in a plane?

Highlights

- A point shows position. It has no length, no breadth and no thickness.
- A line can be extended on both sides endlessly. A line has no definite length, no thickness and no breadth.
- A line segment is part of a line having two end points. It has a fixed length, but no breadth and thickness.
- A ray has one end point and can be extended endlessly on the other end.
- Infinite number of lines can pass through a single point.
- One and only one line can be drawn passing through two given points.
- When two rays have a common initial point, an angle is formed.
- A polygon bounded by three line segments is called a triangle.
- A perpendicular drawn from the vertex of a triangle to its opposite side is called the altitude.
- A line joining the midpoint of a side of a triangle to its opposite vertex is called the median of the triangle.
- A triangle has three altitudes and three medians.
- A polygon bounded by four line segments is called a quadrilateral. It has four vertices, four sides, four angles and two diagonals.
- The sum of the angles of a quadrilateral is 360°.
- A collection of points that are equidistant from a fixed point is called a circle. The fixed point is called the centre of the circle and the constant distance is called the radius of the circle.
- The diameter of a circle is twice the radius.
- Half of a circle is called a semicircle.
- The perimeter of a circle is called its circumference.
- Circles having the same centre but different radii are called concentric circles.
- The chord of a circle is a line joining any two points on the circumference of the circle.
- The diameter is the longest chord of a circle.
- The area bounded by an arc and a chord of a circle is called a segment.
- The area bounded by two radii of a circle is called a sector.

Paper Folding!!

Objective: To study the different parts of a circle.

Material required: A bangle, chart paper, a pair of scissors, pencil and coloured sketch pens

Procedure:

1. Draw four circles on a piece of chart paper with the help of a bangle.
2. Cut out the four circles.
3. Take one circle and fold it in half. Then open it. Mark the crease, which is the diameter, with a black sketch pen. Shade the two semicircles in different colours. Also outline the arcs in black. Since we have two semicircles, the two arcs will be equal.

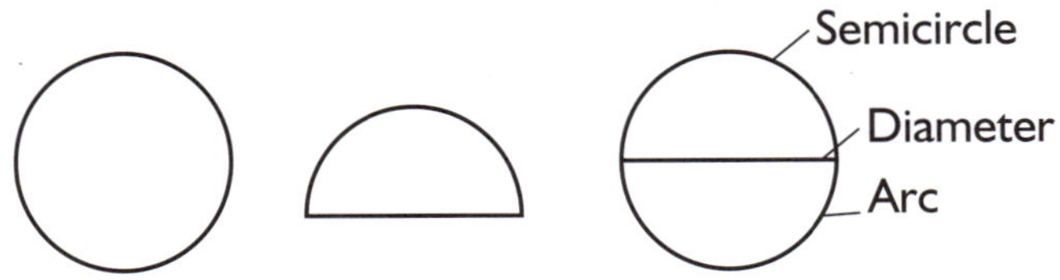

4. Now, take another circle and fold it in half and then half again. On opening the circle, we get four creases, which are also the radii of the circle. Mark the radii and the centre of the circle with a black sketch pen.

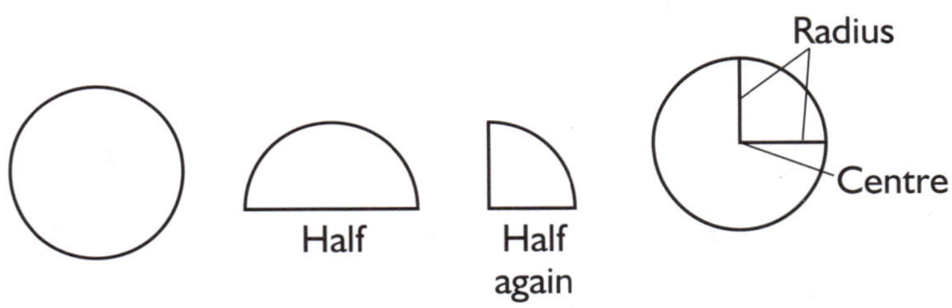

5. Next, take the third circle. Fold it in half three times. Open the folded parts. The creases will make the sector of the circle. Shade a sector in a colour of your choice.

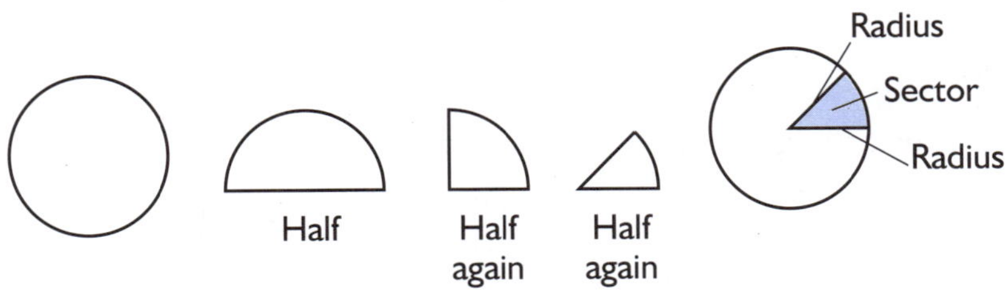

6. Now, take the last circle. Fold it in half and then half again. Turn one of the folds as shown. Then open it out. This crease will make a chord. Mark the chord and colour the segment.

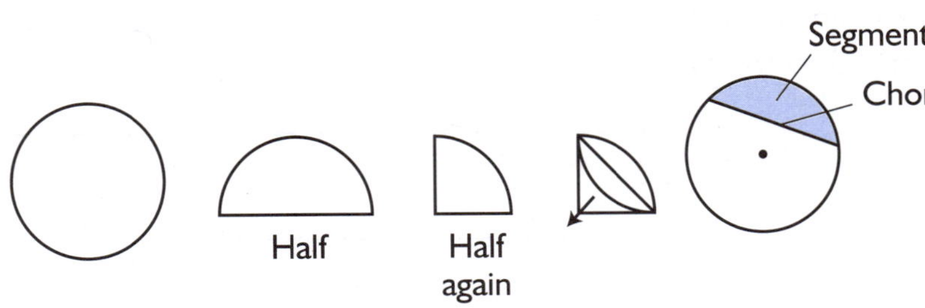

Now stick these four circles in your notebook.

CHAPTER 8

Elementary Shapes

In this chapter, we will study the following in detail:

1. lines
2. angles
3. triangles
4. quadrilaterals
5. polygons.

Lines

We have already studied lines, line segments and rays. We will now study pairs of lines in detail.

Pair of Lines

There can be four kinds of pairs of lines:

1. intersecting lines
2. parallel lines
3. perpendicular lines
4. skew lines.

Intersecting Lines

If two lines, AB and CD, meet at a point, they are called intersecting lines. The meeting point is called the point of intersection.

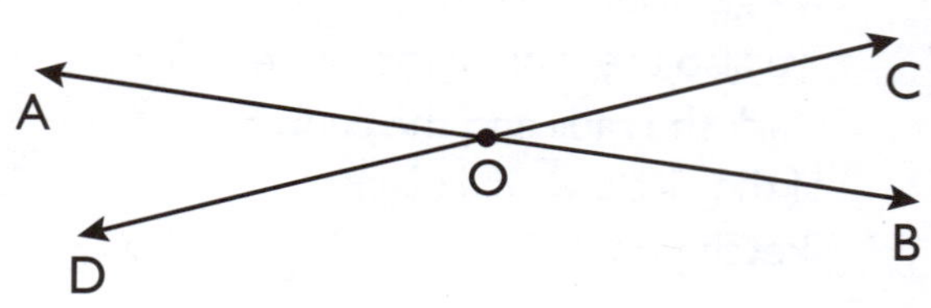

Alert!

Two lines can intersect at one point only.

Parallel Lines

If two lines never meet each other, they are called parallel lines. The distance between parallel lines is always the same. They are equidistant from each other. Parallel lines are represented by the symbol II.

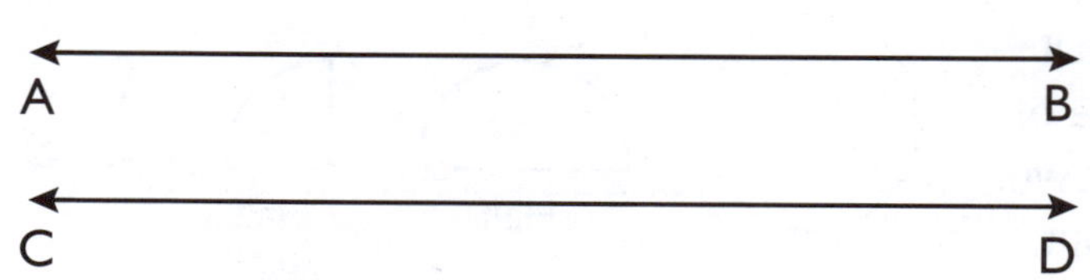

If $\overrightarrow{AB}$ is parallel to $\overrightarrow{CD}$, we write this as $\overrightarrow{AB} \parallel \overrightarrow{CD}$.

Perpendicular Lines

If a pair of lines intersect each other and form an angle of 90° or a right angle, the lines are said to be perpendicular to each other. Perpendicular lines are represented by the symbol $\perp$.

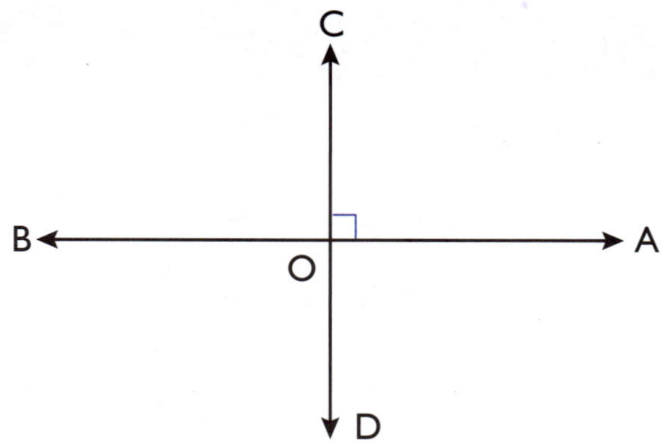

If, $\overleftrightarrow{AB}$ is perpendicular to $\overleftrightarrow{CD}$, we write this as $\overleftrightarrow{AB} \perp \overleftrightarrow{CD}$.

Skew Lines

Two lines in two different planes that are neither parallel nor intersecting are called skew lines. Here, lines ℓ and m are skew lines.

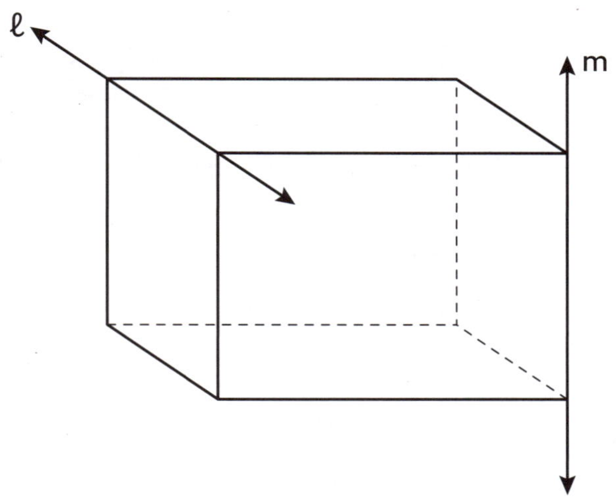

Concurrent Lines

Two or more lines that pass through the same point are called concurrent lines and the point of intersection is called the point of concurrency.

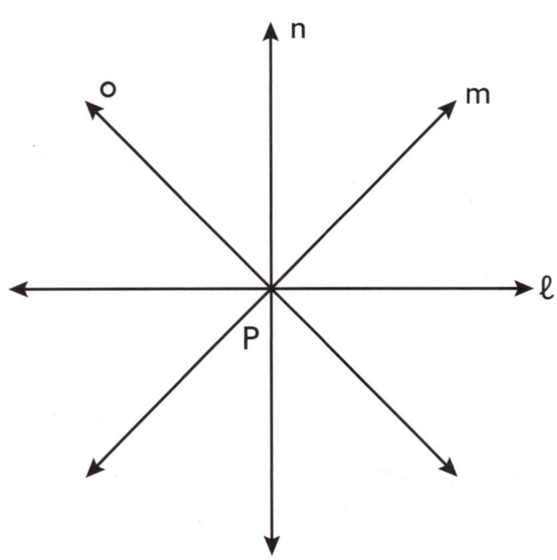

Lines ℓ, m, n, o are concurrent. The point of concurrency is denoted by P.

Angles

An angle is found when two lines converge at a point.

Types of Angles

Look at the hands of the clock in these four figures.

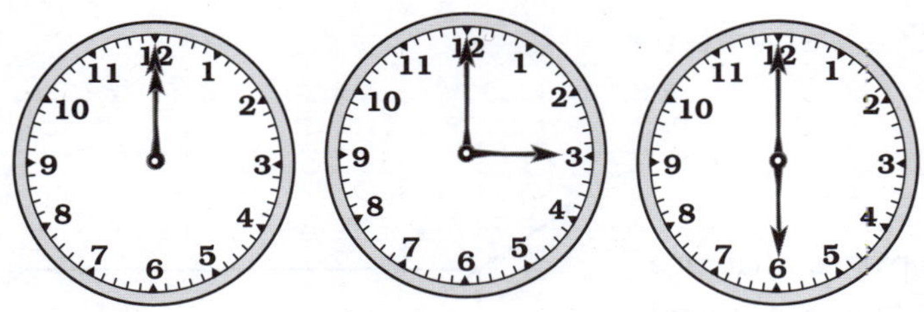

Suppose we begin at 12 midnight and thereafter look at the clock after every three hours, that is, at 3 am, 6 am, 9 am and then 12 noon.

The angles traced by the hour hand at these timings are:

12 midnight	0°
3 am	90°
6 am	180°
9 am	270°
12 noon	360°

Question: Why is the obtuse angle ugly?

Answer: Because it is not "a cute" angle.

These angles are known by special names.

1. **Zero angle:** An angle whose measure is 0° is called a zero angle. Line AB and line AC are two arms that form a zero angle.

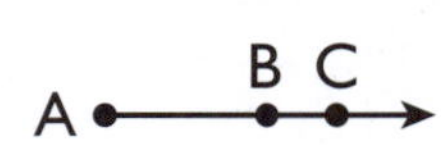

2. **Right angle:** An angle whose measure is 90° is called a right angle.

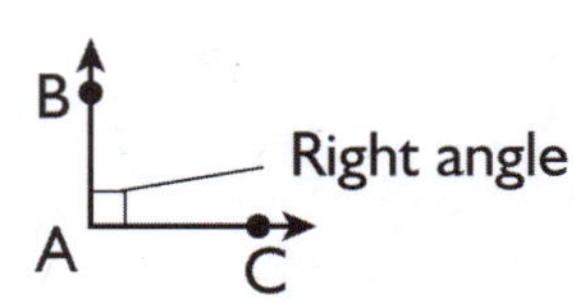

3. **Straight angle:** An angle whose measure is 180° is called a straight angle. Here angle ABC is a straight angle.

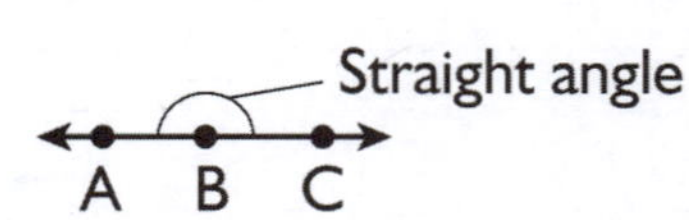

4. **Complete angle:** An angle whose measure is 360° is called a complete angle.

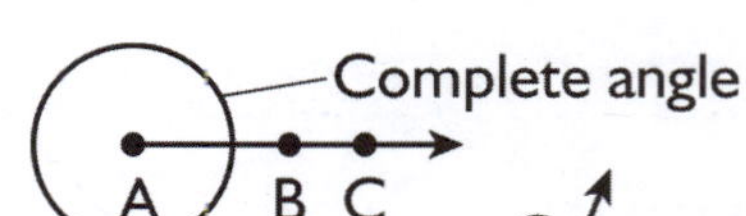

5. **Acute angle:** An angle that measures more than 0° but less than 90° is called an acute angle.

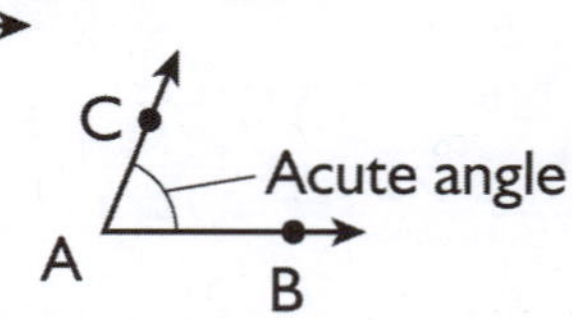

6. **Obtuse angle:** An angle that measures more than 90° but less than 180° is called an obtuse angle.

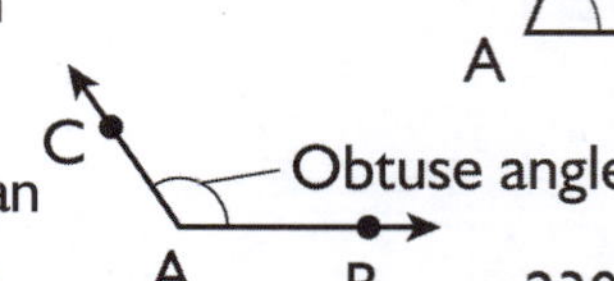

7. **Reflex angle:** An angle that measures more than 180° but less than 360° is called a reflex angle.

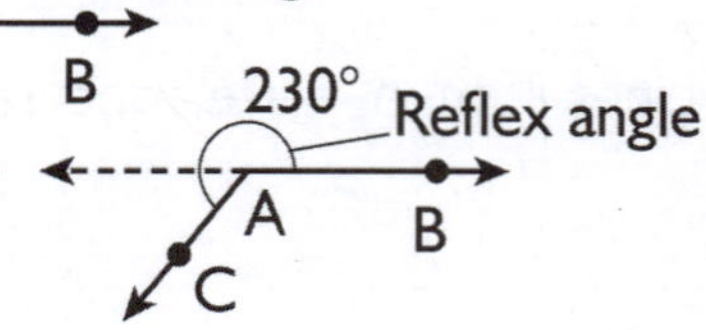

Triangles

We know that a triangle is a closed figure with three sides. The sum of the angles of a triangle is 180°. We will now study about different types of triangles. The symbol used to denote a triangle is △.

Types of Triangles

Triangles can be classified in two ways:

1. by their sides
2. by their angles.

Classification of Triangles by their Sides

Equilateral triangle

If all three sides of a triangle are equal, it is called an equilateral triangle.

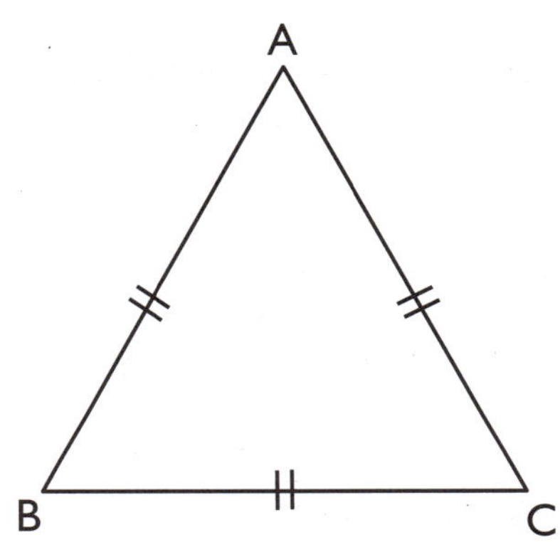

In triangle ABC, sides AB, BC and CA are equal in length, i.e., AB = BC = CA.

∴ △ABC is an equilateral triangle.

Isosceles triangle

If any two sides of a triangle are equal, it is called an isosceles triangle.

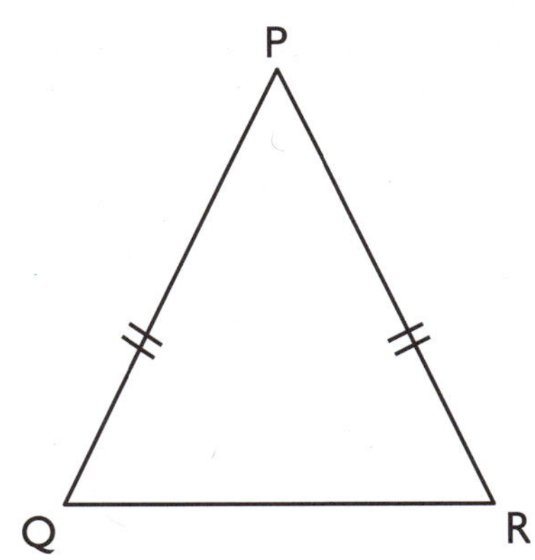

In △PQR, sides PQ and PR are equal in length, i.e., PQ = PR.

∴ △PQR is an isosceles triangle.

Scalene triangle

If no two sides of a triangle are of equal length or all sides of a triangle are of different lengths, the triangle is called a scalene triangle.

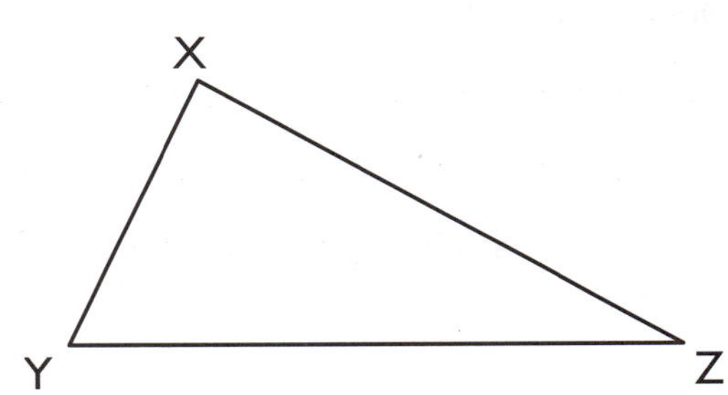

In △XYZ, XY ≠ YZ ≠ XZ. All three sides are of unequal length.

∴ △XYZ is a scalene triangle.

Classification of Triangles by their Angles

Acute-angled triangle

A triangle in which all the angles are acute or less than 90° is called an acute-angled triangle or an acute triangle.

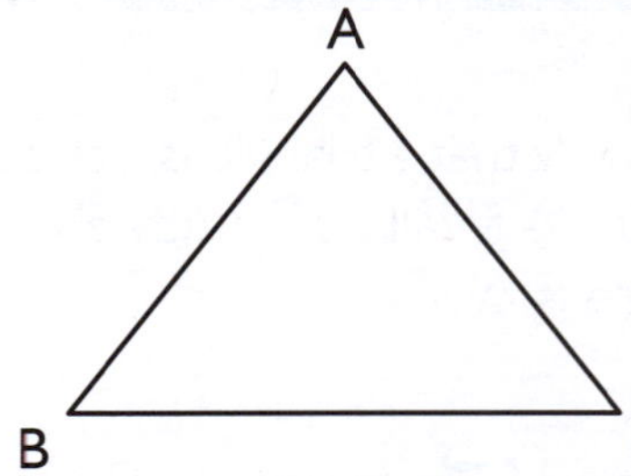

In △ABC, all angles (∠A, ∠B and ∠C) are acute angles.

Right-angled triangle

A triangle in which one of the angles is 90°, is called a right-angled triangle or a right triangle.

In △PQR, ∠PQR is 90°.

The side opposite the right angle is called the hypotenuse. PR is the hypotenuse.

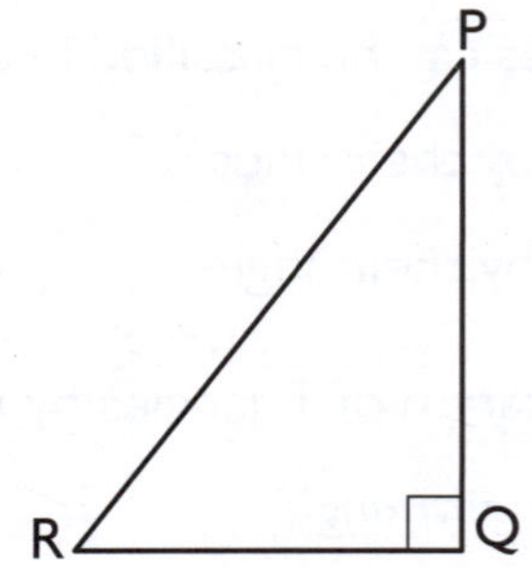

Alert!

It is easy to remember the spelling of hypotenuse. Remember it is HYPO-TEN-USE.

Obtuse-angled triangle

A triangle in which one of the angles is obtuse or greater than 90° and less than 180° is called an obtuse-angled triangle or an obtuse triangle.

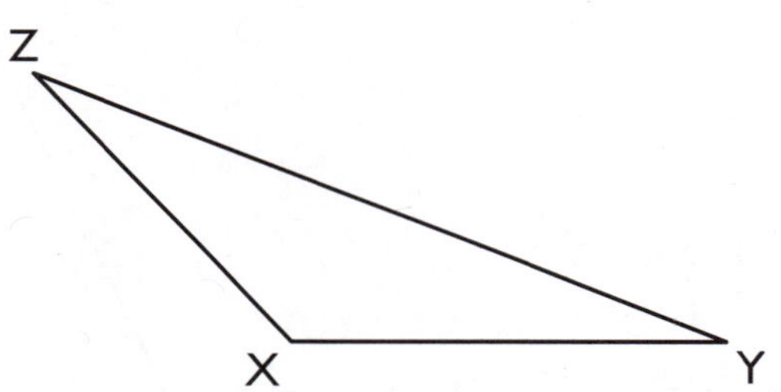

In △XYZ, ∠ZXY is obtuse.

Equiangular triangle

In a triangle, if all the angles are equal, it is called an equiangular triangle.

It is the same as an equilateral triangle in which all three sides are equal.

If a triangle has all sides equal, all its angles will also be equal and vice versa.

Alert!

Each angle of an equiangular triangle is 60°.

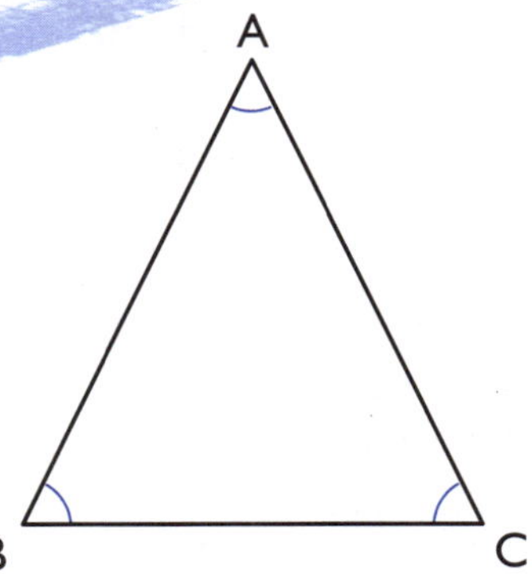

In $\triangle ABC$, all the angles are equal, i.e., $\angle A = \angle B = \angle C = 60°$.

Practice Exercise 8.1

1. Classify the following pairs of lines as

   a. intersecting   b. parallel   c. perpendicular

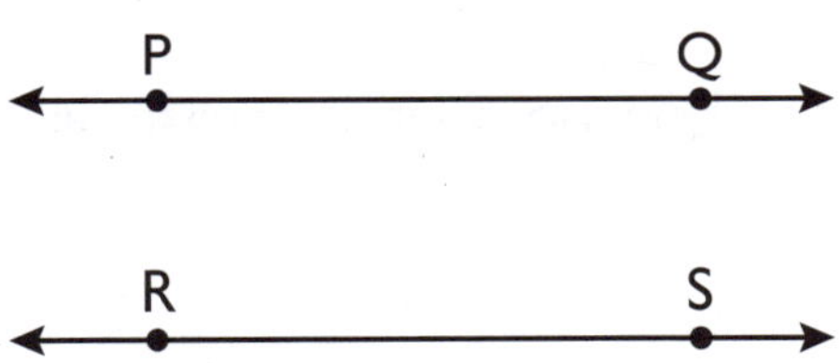

(i)

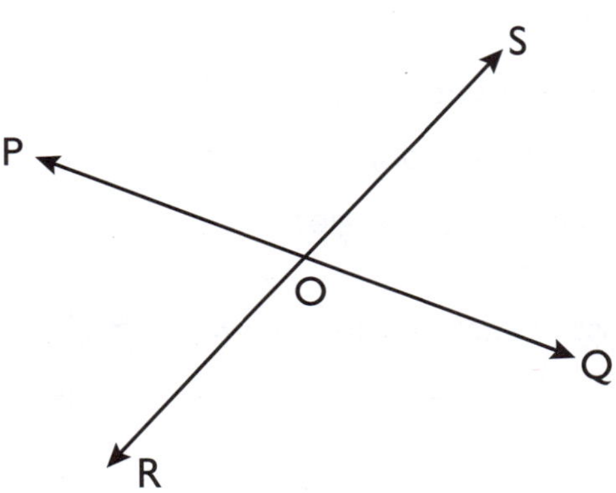

(ii)

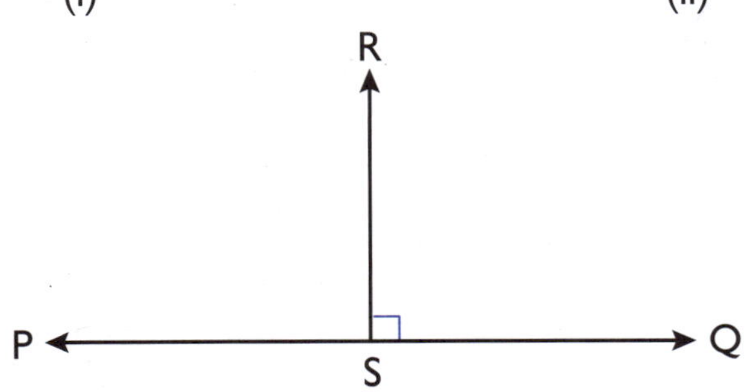

(iii)

2. What are concurrent lines? Draw a figure to depict them and mark the point of concurrency.

3. Complete the table given below by classifying the angles in the appropriate category.

a. 40° e. 120° i. 165° m. 75°

b. 90° f. 60° j. 30° n. 170°

c. 135° g. 180° k. 315° o. 330°

d. 215° h. 270° ℓ. 45° p. 360°

acute angle	
right angle	
obtuse angle	
straight angle	
reflex angle	
complete angle	

4. Find the measure of the angles formed between the minute hand and the hour hand of a clock at the following times:

a. 3 am b. 6 am c. 9 am d. 12 noon e. 3 pm

5. A man is facing east. In which direction will he be looking in each of these cases if he turns to the left by

a. one right angle
b. two right angles
c. three right angles
d. four right angles
e. one straight angle

6. Classify each of the following triangles as scalene, isosceles or equilateral.

a.

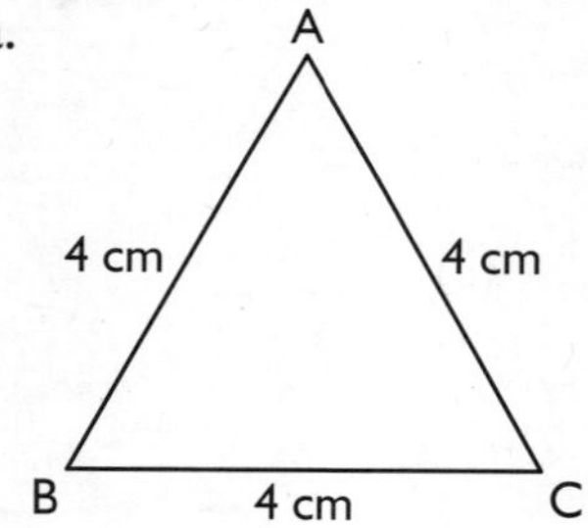

b.

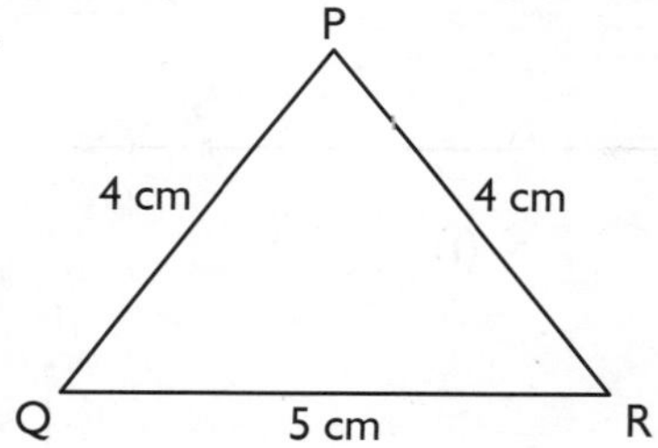

c.

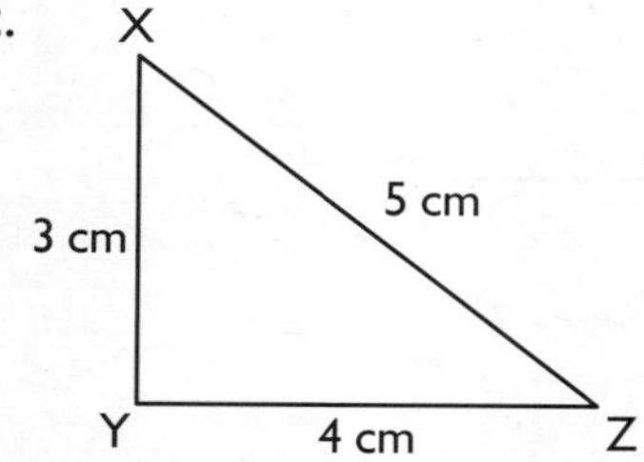

d.

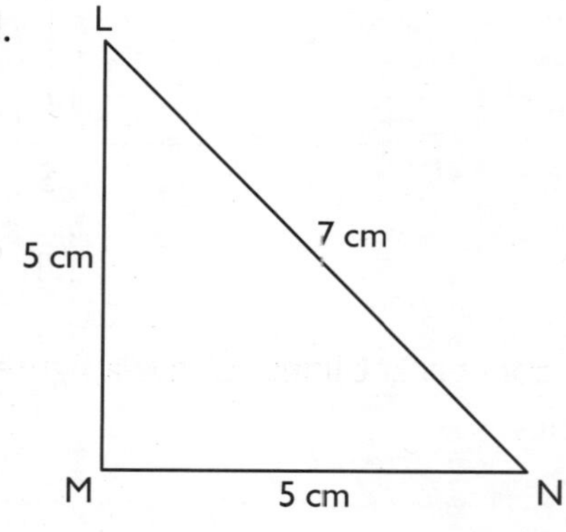

e.

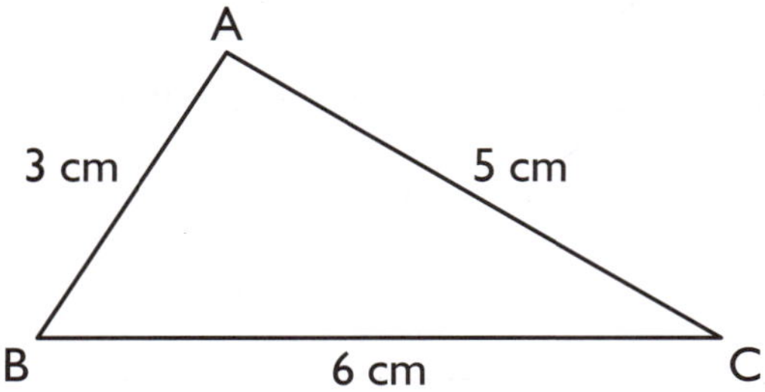

7. Check whether the three angles given will make a triangle. If so, classify them as acute, obtuse or right triangles.

a. 30°, 30°, 120°
b. 30°, 135°, 15°
c. 60°, 30°, 90°
d. 65°, 65°, 65°
e. 120°, 3°, 30°
f. 45°, 45°, 90°
g. 60°, 65°, 55°
h. 60°, 60°, 60°
i. 20°, 30°, 40°
j. 120°, 60°, 0°

8. The measures of the sides of some triangles are given below. Classify each triangle as scalene, isosceles or equilateral.

a. 7 cm, 6 cm, 5 cm
b. 6 cm, 6 cm, 6 cm
c. 4 cm, 3 cm, 4 cm
d. 2 cm, 3 cm, 4 cm
e. 5 cm, 6 cm, 6 cm

9. One of the equal angles of an isosceles triangle is 50°. Find its third angle.

10. Two angles of a triangle are 70° and 45°. Find the third angle.

Quadrilaterals

A quadrilateral is a closed figure bounded by four sides. It can be called a four-sided polygon. The sum of the angles of a quadrilateral is 360°. We will learn about the types of quadrilaterals and their properties in this section.

Types of Quadrilaterals

Quadrilaterals are classified according to their sides.

Quadrilaterals can be of several types. These are parallelogram, rectangle, rhombus, square, trapezium and kite. Some types are also included in the definition of other types. For example a square, rhombus and rectangle are also parallelograms.

Parallelogram

A quadrilateral in which the pairs of opposite sides are parallel is called a parallelogram.

In the parallelogram ABCD,

a. the opposite sides are parallel.

AB || DC and AD || BC

b. the opposite sides are equal.

AB = DC and AD = BC

c. the opposite angles are equal.

$\angle A = \angle C$ and $\angle B = \angle D$

d. the diagonals bisect each other.

AO = OC and BO = OD

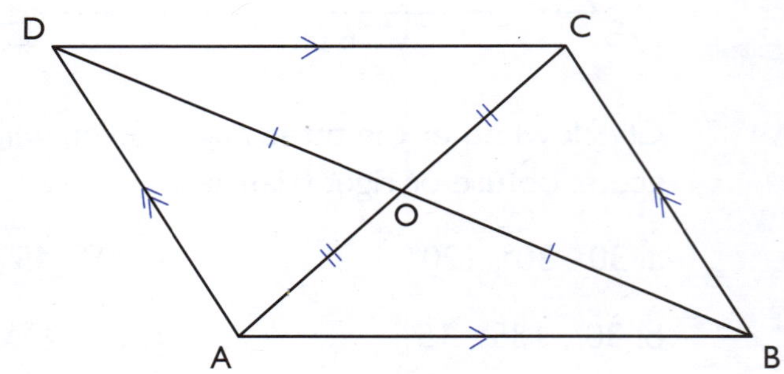

e. the diagonal divides the parallelogram into two equal triangles.

The diagonal AC divides the parallelogram into two triangles, ABC and ACD.

The diagonal BD divides the parallelogram into two triangles, ABD and BCD.

Alert!

The diagonals of a parallelogram are not equal.

Rectangle

A quadrilateral in which each angle is a right angle, is called a rectangle.

In the rectangle ABCD,

a. the opposite sides are parallel.

AB || DC and AD || BC

b. the opposite sides are equal.

AB = DC and AD = BC

c. all angles are equal and measure 90°.

$\angle A = \angle B = \angle C = \angle D = 90°$

d. the diagonals are equal.

AC = BD.

e. the diagonals bisect each other.

AO = OC = OB = OD

(since AC = BD)

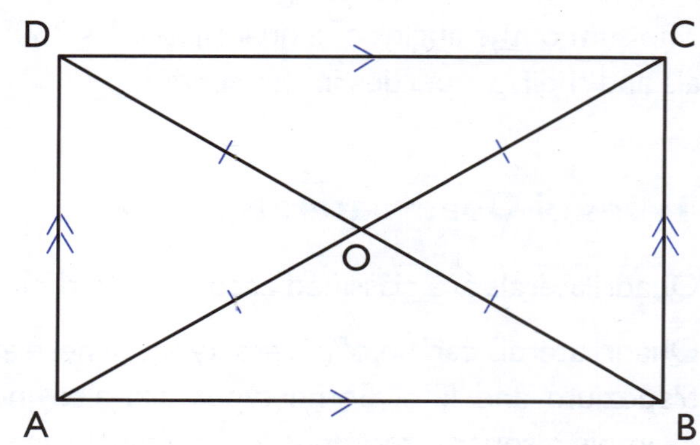

Alert!

Every rectangle is a parallelogram but every parallelogram is not a rectangle.

Rhombus

A quadrilateral in which all four sides are equal, is called a rhombus.

In the rhombus ABCD,

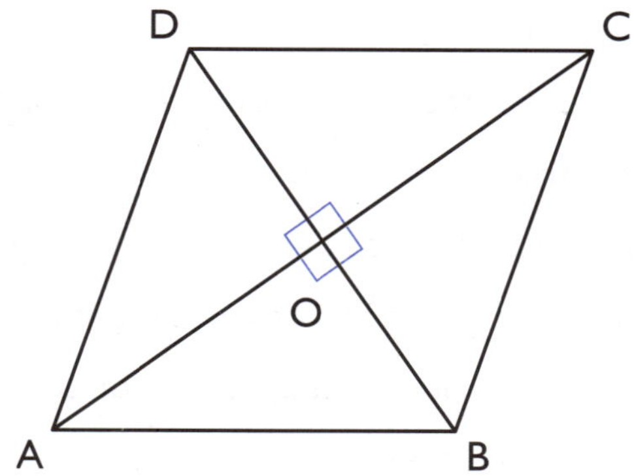

a. all sides are equal.

 AB = BC = CD = DA

b. the opposite sides are parallel.

 AB || DC and AD || BC

c. the opposite angles are equal.

 $\angle$A = $\angle$C and $\angle$B = $\angle$D

d. the diagonals bisect each other.

 AO = OC and OB = OD

e. the diagonals are perpendicular to each other.

 $\angle$AOB = $\angle$BOC = $\angle$COD = $\angle$AOD = 90°

Alert!

Every rhombus is a parallelogram but every parallelogram is not a rhombus.

Square

A quadrilateral in which all sides are equal and every angle is a right angle is called a square.
In the square ABCD,

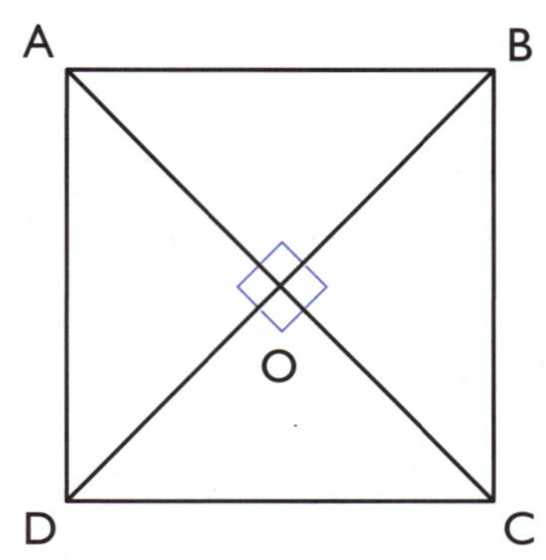

a. all sides are equal.

 AB = BC = CD = DA

b. opposite sides are parallel.

 AB || DC and AD || BC

c. all angles are equal and measure 90°.

d. the diagonals bisect each other.

 AO = OC = OB = OD

e. the diagonals are perpendicular to each other.

f. the diagonals are equal.

AC = BD

Alert!

A square is the only quadrilateral which has all sides and all angles equal.

Trapezium

A quadrilateral in which one pair of opposite sides is parallel is called a trapezium.

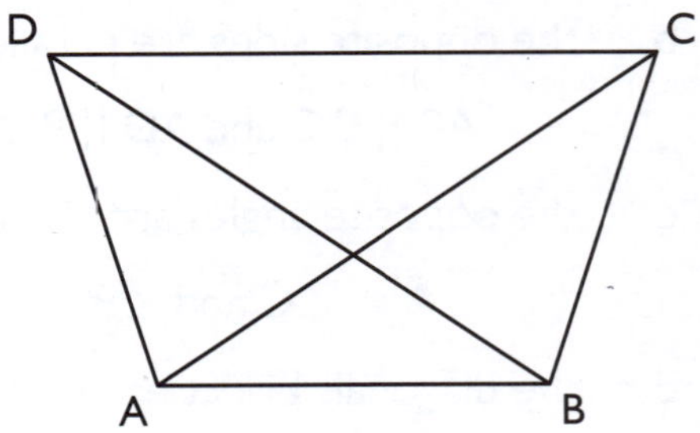

In the trapezium ABCD,

a. a pair of opposite sides is parallel.

b. the opposite sides are not equal.

c. the opposite angles are not equal.

d. the diagonals are not equal.

A quadrilateral in which a pair of opposite sides is parallel and the other two sides (non-parallel sides) are equal is called an isosceles trapezium.

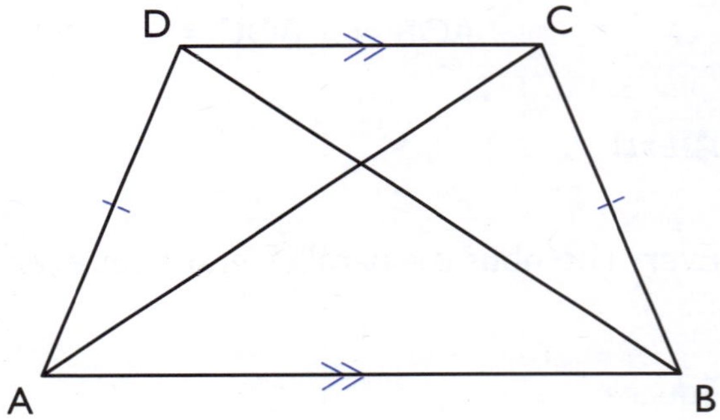

In the isosceles trapezium ABCD,

a. a pair of opposite sides is parallel.

AB || DC

b. non-parallel sides are equal.

AD = BC

c. the diagonals are equal.

AC = BD

d. $\angle A = \angle B$ and $\angle D = \angle C$.

Kite

A quadrilateral in which two pairs of adjacent sides are equal is called a kite.

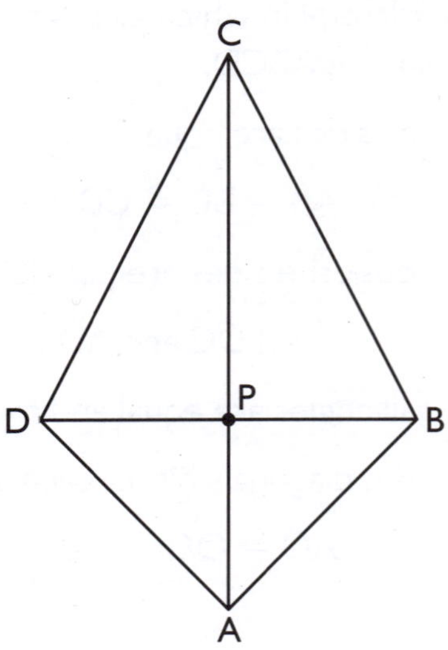

In the kite ABCD,

a. two pairs of adjacent sides are equal.

AB = AD and BC = CD

b. Diagonals intersect each other at right angles.

$\angle CPD = \angle CPB = \angle APD = \angle APB = 90°$

Polygons

We have learnt about polygons in the previous chapter. Polygons are simple closed figures made up of line segments only. Polygon are named depending on the number of line segments that make up the polygon.

The minimum number of line segments needed to make a polygon are 3.

If all the sides and angles of a polygon are equal, then the polygon is called a regular polygon, otherwise it is called an irregular polygon.

The names of polygons according to the number of sides they have are:

triangle	→	3 sides	tri means 3
quadrilateral	→	4 sides	quad means 4
pentagon	→	5 sides	penta means 5
hexagon	→	6 sides	hexa means 6
heptagon	→	7 sides	hepta means 7
octagon	→	8 sides	octa means 8
nonagon	→	9 sides	nona means 9
decagon	→	10 sides	deca means 10

Practice Exercise 8.2

1. Indicate whether the following statements are true or false.

   a. Every square is a rectangle.

   b. Every rhombus is a parallelogram.

   c. Every parallelogram is a trapezium.

   d. Every parallelogram is a rectangle.

   e. Every rhombus is a square.

   f. Every square is a rhombus.

   g. A nonagon has nine sides.

   h. A heptagon has seven sides.

i. A triangle with each angle equal to 60° is a regular polygon.

j. A quadrilateral with angles 120°, 60°, 90° and 90° is a regular polygon.

2. In the figure given below, $\overline{AB} \parallel \overline{CD}$ and $\overline{BC} = \overline{AD}$. What kind of quadrilateral is ABCD? If AB = 8 cm and BC = 6 cm, what is the length of CD and AD? If $\angle A = 120°$ and $\angle B = 60°$, write the measure of $\angle C$ and $\angle D$.

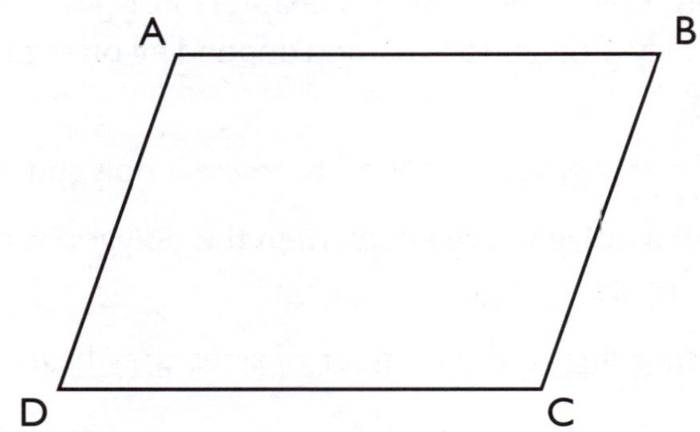

3. PQRS is a quadrilateral in which PQ = QR = RS = SP, PR = SQ. All angles, $\angle P$, $\angle Q$, $\angle R$ and $\angle S$ are equal and the diagonals bisect each other at right angles. Name the quadrilateral.

4. ABCD is a kite. Draw the figure and name the equal sides. Draw the diagonals AC and BD and let them meet at O. Is $\angle AOD = \angle AOB$? What is the measure of $\angle AOD$ and $\angle AOB$?

5. ABCD is a quadrilateral. $\overline{AB} = \overline{CD}$ and $\overline{AD} = \overline{BC}$. All interior angles are equal to 90°. $\overline{AC} = \overline{BD}$. Name the quadrilateral.

6. Distinguish between the following:

a. a square and a rectangle.

b. a square and a rhombus.

c. a trapezium and an isosceles trapezium.

7. Write the names of the polygons with the following number of sides:

a. six b. eight c. ten d. twelve e. four

8. A pentagon has sides measuring 5 cm, 6 cm, 7 cm, 5 cm and 10 cm. Is it a regular polygon? Give reasons.

9. In the parallelogram PQRS, $\angle P$ is double of $\angle Q$. Find all the angles of the parallelogram.

10. In the given figure, name the different polygons labelled as

a. ABC
b. PQRS
c. MQRN
d. AMSC
e. MQCS

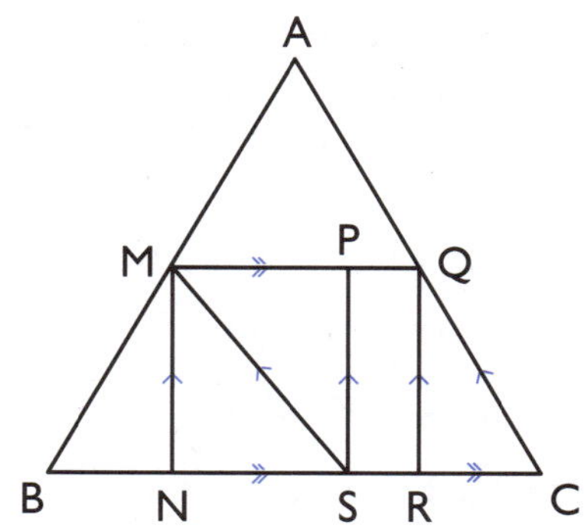

Solids or Three-dimensional Shapes

So far we have learnt about two-dimensional (2-D) figures and shapes. They can be drawn easily on the plane of a blackboard, book or notebook. These figures have length and breadth but no height and therefore are two-dimensional. The region which they enclose within their boundary is called their area.

Now, we shall study about three-dimensional (3-D) shapes. The three dimensions are length, breadth and height. In daily life, we see and use three-dimensional figures. A circle drawn on a piece of paper is two dimensional while a sphere is three dimensional.

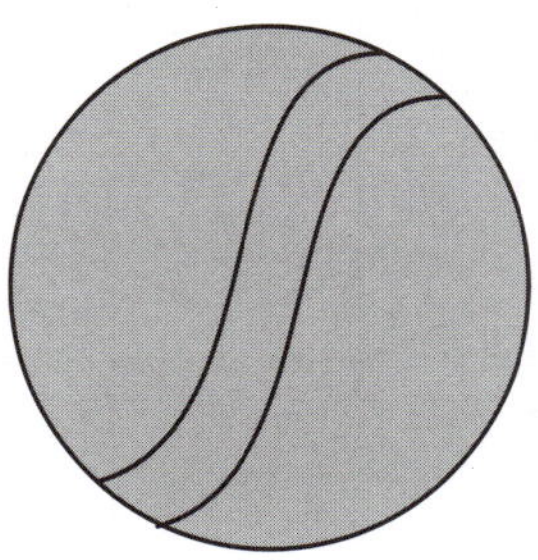

A tennis ball is also round but it is a solid three-dimensional figure. The shape is called a sphere.

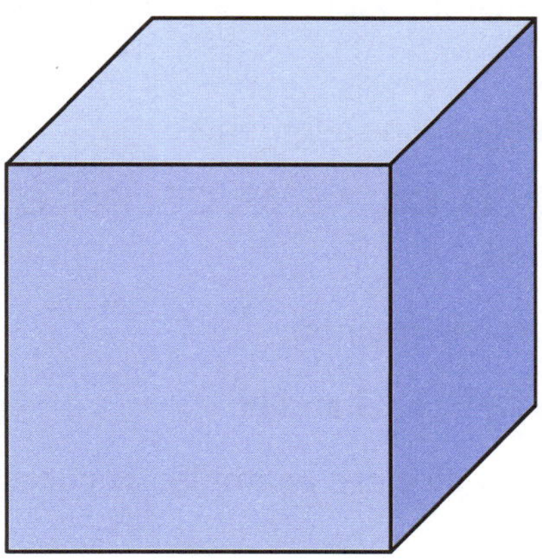

A cube (3-D)

Types of 3-D Figures

Cuboid

A three-dimensional shape that has length, breadth and height, all of which are different, is called a cuboid.

A cuboid has 6 faces (rectangular):

ABGF, BCHG, EHCD, AFED, ABCD and EFGH.

A cuboid has 12 edges (lines segments):

AB, BC, CD, AD, AF, FE, ED, FG, GH, EH, BG and CH.

A cuboid has 8 vertices (points):

A, B, C, D, E, F, G and H.

You can spot a cuboid when you use a geometry box, a lunchbox or a matchbox.

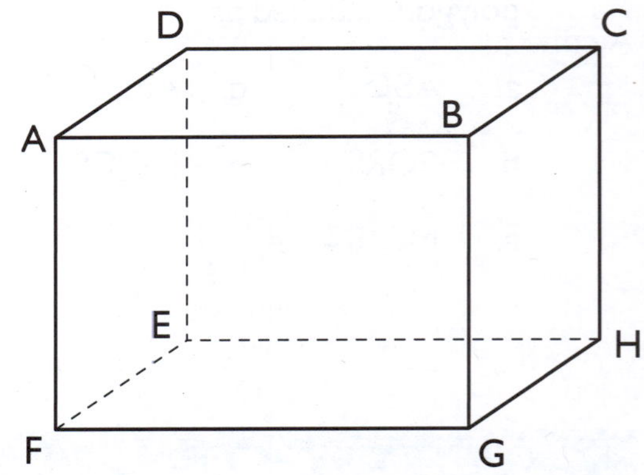

Cube

A three-dimensional shape that has length, breadth and height, all of which are the same or equal in length, is called a cube.

A cube has 6 faces (square):

EFGH, ADHE, ADCB, BCGF, ABFE and DCGH.

A cube has 12 edges (line segments):

AB, BC, CD, DA, AE, BF, CG, DH, EF, FG, GH and HE.

A cube has 8 vertices (points):

A, B, C, D, E, F, G and H.

A sugar cube and a dice are examples of cubes.

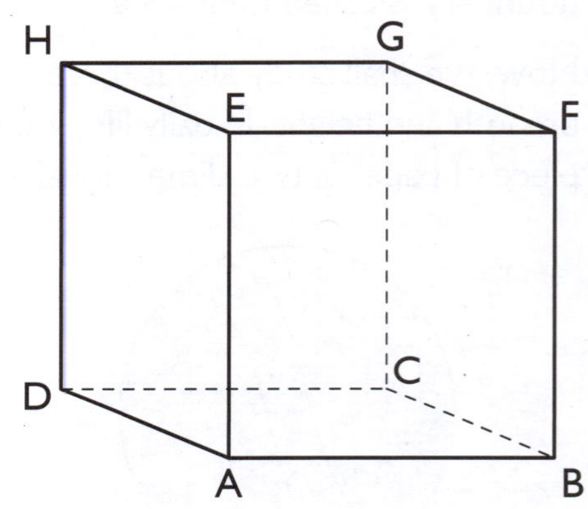

Cylinder

A cylinder has two flat circular surfaces and a curved surface. It has two circular edges and no vertex.

A tubelight, an unsharpened pencil, a can of soft drink are examples of cylinders.

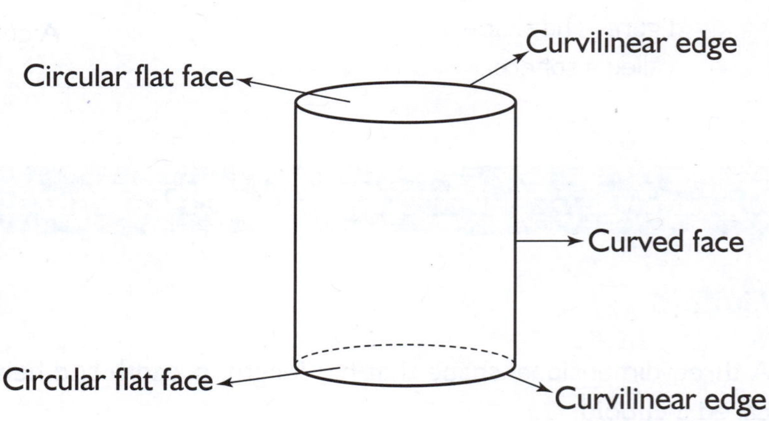

Cone

A cone has one curved face, one flat circular face, one vertex and one edge.

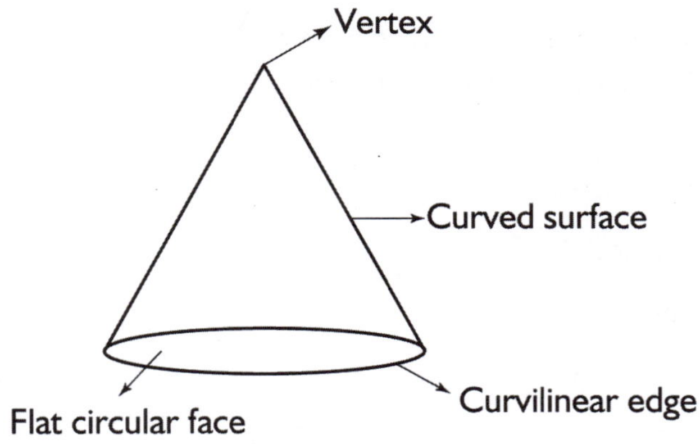

An ice-cream cone, a funnel and a party hat are common examples of a cone.

Sphere

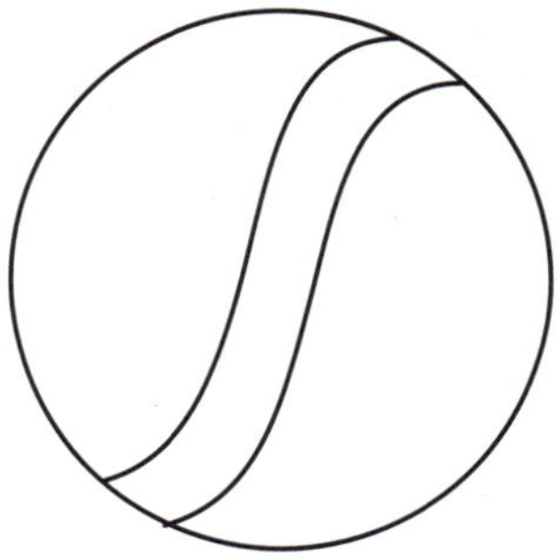

A sphere has one curved surface, no vertex and no edge.

A football, cricket ball, tennis ball and a marble are all examples of spheres.

Triangular Prism

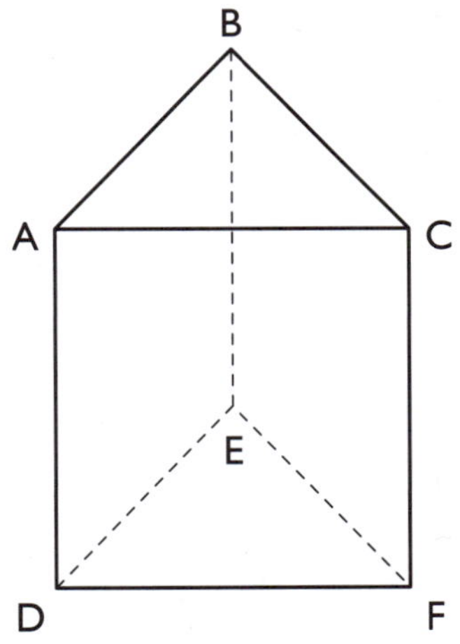

A triangular prism is a geometric solid whose bases are congruent triangles lying in parallel planes and whose sides are parallelograms.

A triangular prism has 5 faces: ABC and DEF (triangular), ABED, BCEF and ACFD (rectangular).

It has 9 edges: AB, BC, AC, AD, CF, BE, DE, EF and DF.

It has 6 vertices: A, B, C, D, E and F.

Alert!

Cubes and cuboids are also prisms. They are called square prisms and rectangular prisms, respectively.

Pyramid

A pyramid is a solid object with a polygon as its base. The sides are triangles that meet at the apex (top).

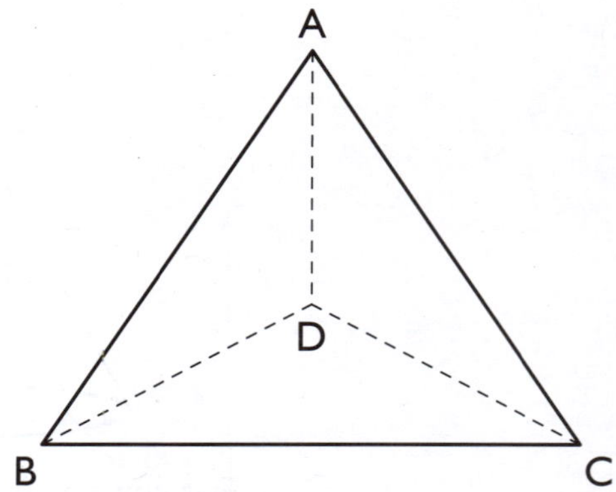

A triangular pyramid, which has a triangular base and all its three lateral surfaces are equilateral triangles, is called a tetrahedron.

A triangular pyramid has 4 faces:

ABD, ADC, BDC and ABC.

A triangular pyramid has 6 edges:

AB, AD, AC, BD, BC and CD.

A triangular pyramid has 4 vertices:

A, B, C and D.

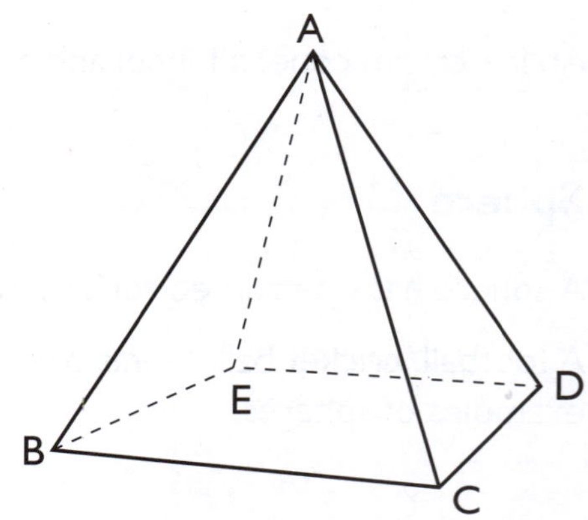

A pyramid with a square base is called a square pyramid.

It has 5 faces, 8 edges and 5 vertices.

Highlights

- Two lines can intersect at one and only one point.
- Two lines in a plane that are equidistant from each other are called parallel lines.
- Perpendicular lines intersect each other at 90° or at right angles.
- Three or more lines that intersect at the same point are called concurrent lines.
- An angle that measures between 0° and 90° is called an acute angle.
- An angle that measures between 90° and 180° is called an obtuse angle.
- An angle that measures between 180° and 360° is called a reflex angle.
- If a triangle has all sides equal, then it is an equilateral triangle.
- If a triangle has two equal sides, then it is an isosceles triangle.
- If a triangle has no sides equal, then it is a scalene triangle.
- Every triangle has atleast two acute angles, the third angle can be an acute, obtuse or right angle.
- The sum of the three angles of a triangle is 180°.
- Quadrilaterals can be of several types like parallelogram, rhombus, square, rectangle, trapezium and kite.
- A polygon is a closed figure with three or more line segments as sides.

Higher Order Thinking Skills

HOTS

1. In a polygon of "n" sides, the sum of all interior angles is $(n - 2) \times 180°$. What is the minimum value of "n"?
2. By how many degrees does the minute hand revolve in 25 minutes?
3. What is a tetrahedron? When is it called a regular tetrahedron?

Making Nets!!

Objective: To make a solid shape by cutting out paper and folding it.
The drawing of an unfolded shape is called a net of the solid.

Material required: Paper, chart paper and a pair of scissors

Procedure:

1. To make the net of a cube.

   Take the paper and draw 6 squares of the same size on it as shown in the figure. Paste this on the chart paper. Cut out the shape carefully and then fold it to make a cube. Remember to cut the net as one piece only.

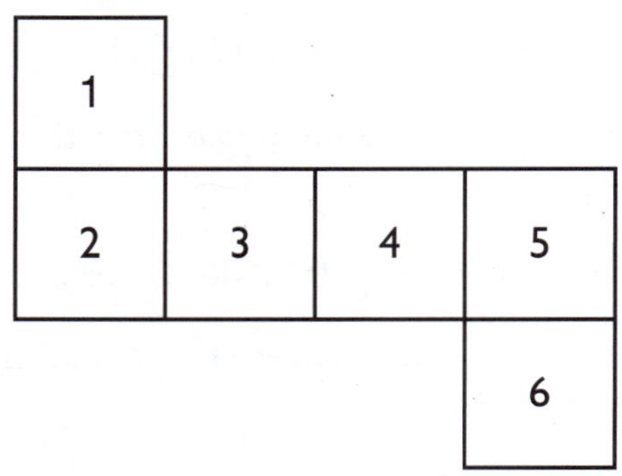

2. To make a net for a cuboid.

   On the paper draw four rectangles of equal length and breadth and two squares of equal sides, their sides being equal to the breadth of the rectangle. Paste them on the chart paper as shown below. Cut out the shape carefully as one piece and fold it to form a cuboid.

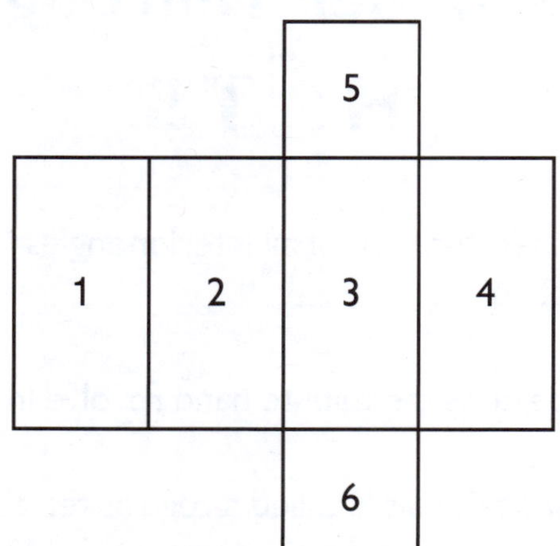

1. Identify the following as a point, a line or a plane:

   a. location of cities in a map
   b. a stretched wire between two poles
   c. floor of a room
   d. a sheet of a note book
   e. the edge of a dice

2. 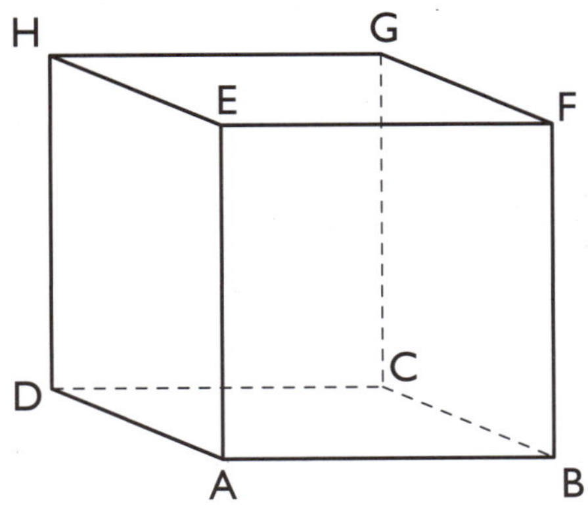

   In the above figure, identify and write the following:

   a. the points marked
   b. all the line segments
   c. the planes formed

3. Define and draw the following:

   a. a right angle
   b. an acute angle
   c. an obtuse angle
   d. a reflex angle
   e. a straight angle

4. Draw a triangle ABC and name the following:

   a. the three vertices
   b. the three sides
   c. the three angles

   Also draw the three medians of this triangle and name them.

5. Indicate whether the following statements are true or false.

   a. Every parallelogram is a trapezium but every trapezium is not a parallelogram.
   b. The diagonals of a parallelogram are equal.

Rewind

c. Every rhombus is a parallelogram but every parallelogram is not a rhombus.

d. The diagonals of a rhombus bisect each other at right angles.

e. A square is the only regular quadrilateral.

6. Name the polygon that has

a. 3 sides b. 6 sides c. 9 sides d. 5 sides e. 10 sides

7. Draw the following solid shapes:

a. cylinder b. regular pyramind c. prism

d. sphere e. square pyramind

8. Write the shapes of the following:

a. a geometry box
b. a football
c. a coin
d. a piece of chalk
e. a road roller
f. an oil funnel
g. an ice cream scoop
h. an ice cream cone
i. a marble
j. a duster

9. Find the measure of the third angle and name the triangle if the two angles of a triangle are

a. 100°, 20° b. 60°, 60° c. 90°, 35° d. 90°, 45° e. 80°, 40°

10. In the given figure, if $\overline{UV} \| \overline{WX}$ and $\overline{UX} \| \overline{VW}$, then what kind of quadrilateral is UVWX? If $\overline{UV}$ = 8 cm and $\overline{VW}$ = 6.5 cm, what is the length of $\overline{WX}$ and $\overline{XU}$? If $\angle U = 130°$ and $\angle X = 50°$, what is the measure of $\angle V$ and $\angle W$?

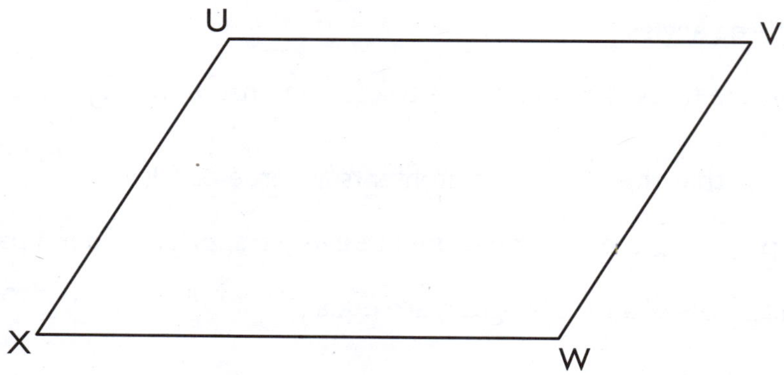

Geometrical Constructions

CHAPTER 9

We will now learn to draw, compare and construct geometrical figures. To draw or construct any geometrical figure, we need geometrical instruments. The most commonly used geometrical instruments are:

1. A ruler

2. A divider

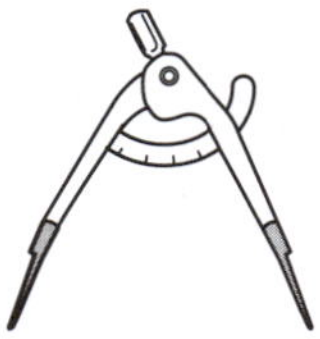

3. A compass

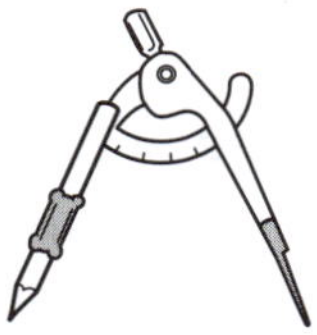

4. A protractor

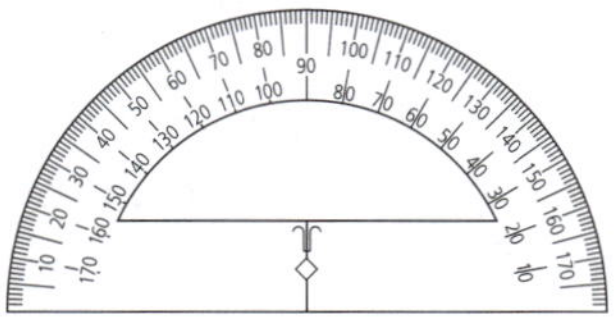

5. A pair of set squares

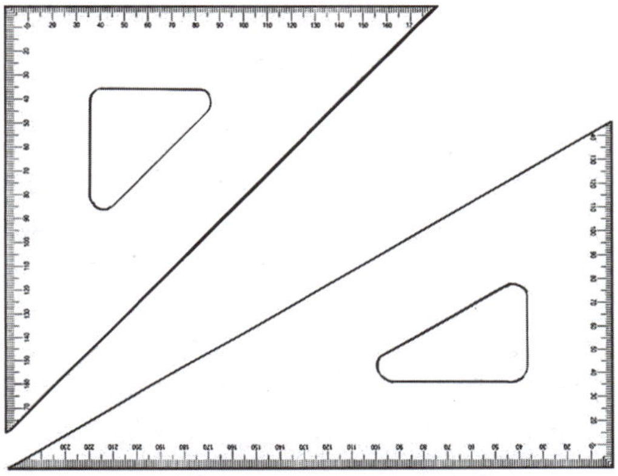

We will learn to draw and construct the following.

1. Line segments
2. Circles
3. Angles

Line Segments

In this section we will learn to:

1. Compare line segments.
2. Measure line segments.
3. Construct line segments.
4. Construct a perpendicular bisector of a line segment.
5. Draw a perpendicular at a point on the given line.
6. Draw a perpendicular to a given line from a point lying outside the line.

Comparison of Line Segments

Comparison of line segments means to find out which line segment is shorter and which is longer. This can be done in 3 ways.

a. By observation. b. By tracing.

c. By using a divider. d. By using a ruler.

By Observation

This is done by looking at the two line segments and noting which is shorter or longer. This is not an accurate method, for if the difference between the line segments is very small we cannot get the correct answer.

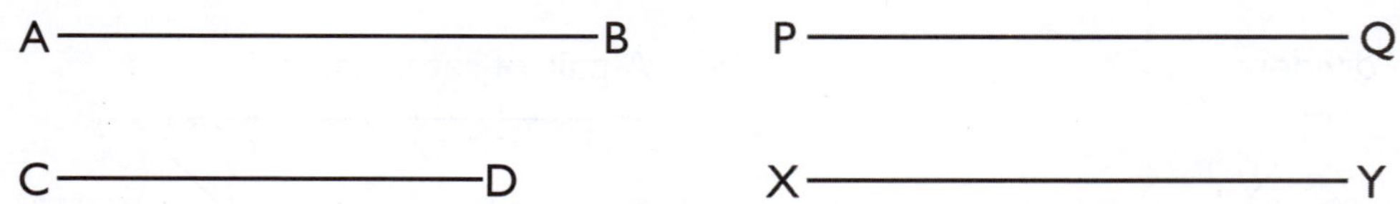

(i) (ii)

In figure (i) we can easily observe and say that $\overline{AB} > \overline{CD}$, but in figure (ii) the difference is very small, so by observing we cannot say which line segment is greater, $\overline{PQ}$ or $\overline{XY}$.

By Tracing

We can compare line segments by the tracing method. Trace one of the line segments say, $\overline{AB}$ on a tracing paper and place it along $\overline{CD}$ in such a way that point A of the traced segment $\overline{AB}$ coincides with point C of the line segment $\overline{CD}$. By doing so we can observe the following.

B lies between C and D

$\overline{AB} < \overline{CD}$

B lies on D

$\overline{AB} = \overline{CD}$

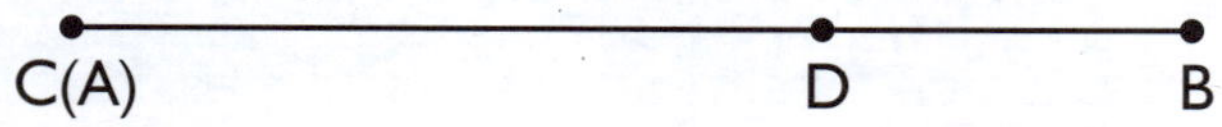

B lies beyond D

$\overline{AB} > \overline{CD}$

By Using a Divider

To compare the given line segments, we place the needle of one hand of the divider at the point A and open its other arm carefully so that the needle of the other arm falls on B.

Now, lift the divider carefully so that the opening of the two arms remains unchanged. Place one of the needles at point C of the line segment $\overline{CD}$ and the other arm is free to fall at any point on $\overline{CD}$.

If the other end falls exactly at D then $\overline{CD} = \overline{AB}$.

If the other end falls between C and D then $\overline{CD} < \overline{AB}$.

If the other end falls beyond D then $\overline{CD} > \overline{AB}$.

We can also place the divider on a ruler and measure the length's of $\overline{AB}$ and $\overline{CD}$ and compare them.

By Using a Ruler

To compare the given line segment we can measure their lengths using a ruler.

Measurement of Line Segments

To measure line segments, we use a ruler that has centimetre marks on one edge and inches marks on the other edge.

To measure the line segment $\overline{AB}$ with the help of a ruler, we place the ruler along $\overline{AB}$ in such a way that the 0 mark on the ruler coincides with point A and mark 6 coincides with point B of the line segment AB.

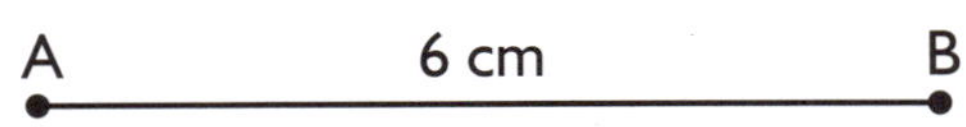

We can also use a divider. Open the divider and put one point on A and the other on B. Now, carefully put one point on the 0 of the ruler and the other point will fall on the 6 mark. This will give the length of the line segment $\overline{AB}$.

Construction of a Line Segment

We can draw a line segment of a given length in two ways.

1. By using a ruler.
2. By using a compass.

To construct a line segment of length 6.5 cm, we can use any of the two methods.

1. By Using a Ruler

Step 1 Make a point in your notebook and label it as A.

A•

Step 2 Place the ruler in such a way that the zero (0) mark on the ruler coincides with A.

Step 3 Now, move the sharp edge of the pencil along the edge of the ruler till it reaches the point 6.5 cm of the ruler.

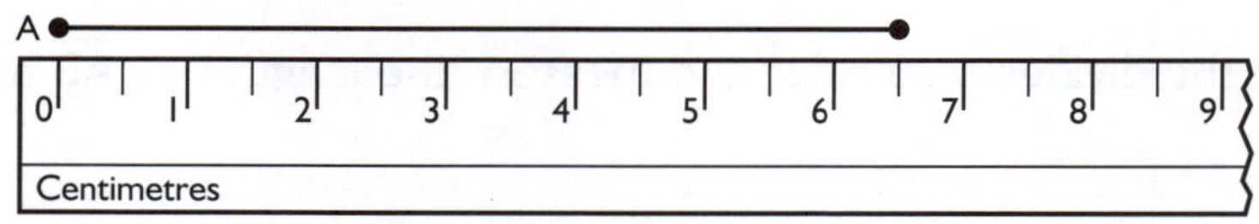

Step 4 Mark the second end as B. $\overline{AB}$ is the required line segment.

2. By Using a Compass

Step 1 Draw a line ℓ and mark a point A on it.

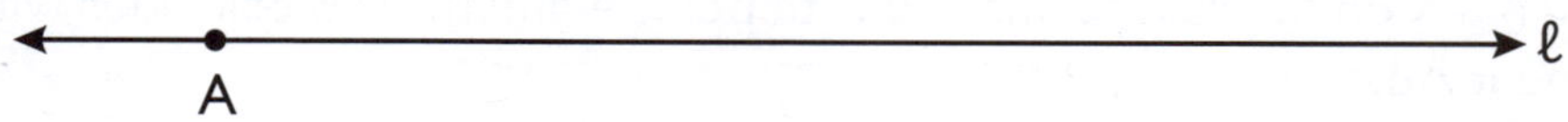

Step 2 Open the arms of the compass so that the end points of the two open arms equal to 6.5 cm.

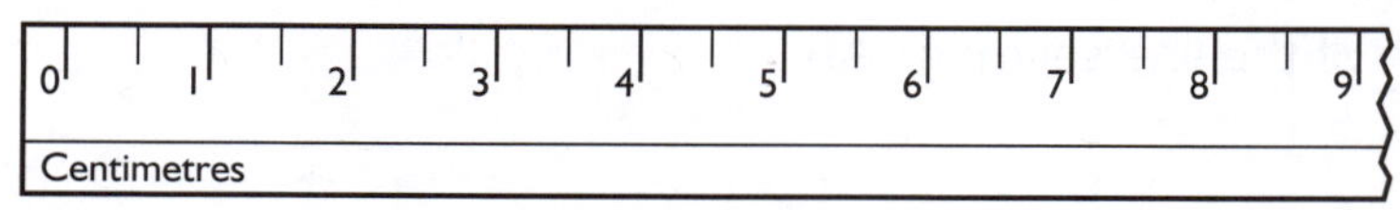

Step 3 Without disturbing the opening of the compass, place its needle at point A and draw an arc to cut the line ℓ at the point B.

Step 4 AB is the required line segment of length 6.5 cm.

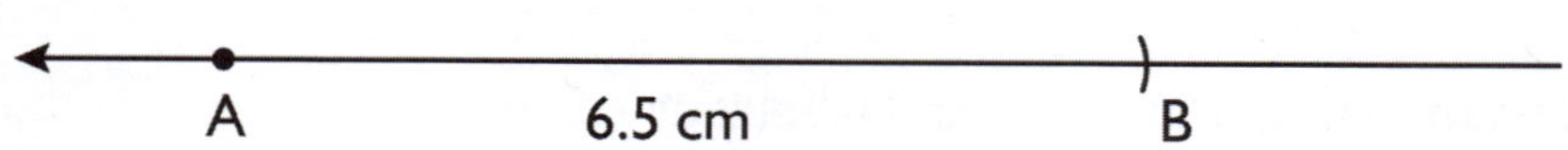

To Draw a Line Segment Equal to a Given Line Segment

Construction:

Draw a line segment ($\overline{AB}$) equal to $\overline{PQ}$.

Given:

A line segment $\overline{PQ}$.

Step 1 Draw a line (ℓ). Mark a point A on it.

Step 2 Take the compass and measure $\overline{PQ}$.

Step 3 Without disturbing the opening, place the needle of compass at point A on line ℓ and draw an arc, which cuts the line at the point B.

Step 4 AB is the required line segment, which is equal to the length of PQ, i.e., $\overline{AB} = \overline{PQ}$

To Draw a Line Segment whose Length is the Sum of the Lengths of Two Given Line Segments

Construction:

Draw a line segment $\overline{AD}$ equal to the sum of $\overline{AB}$ and $\overline{CD}$.

Given:

Two line segments $\overline{AB}$ and $\overline{CD}$.

Step 1 Draw a line 'ℓ' and mark a point A on it.

Step 2 Take the compass and measure AB.

Step 3 Without disturbing the opening, place its needle at A and draw an arc cutting line ℓ at B.

Step 4 Again adjust the compass and measure the line segment CD.

Step 5 Without disturbing the opening, place the pointer at C on the line ℓ and draw an arc cutting the line ℓ at D.

Step 6. $\overline{AD}$ is the required line segment whose length is equal to the sum of the lengths of line segments $\overline{AB}$ and $\overline{CD}$.

$$\overline{AD} = \overline{AB} + \overline{CD}$$

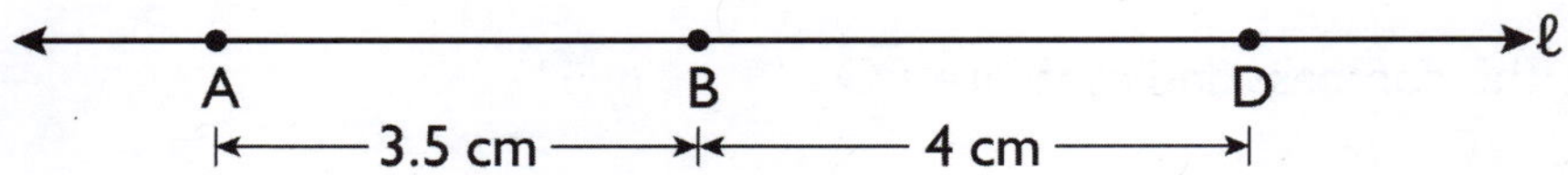

AC = AB + CD
= 3.5 cm + 4 cm
= 7.5 cm

Construction of a Perpendicular Bisector of a Line Segment

A line that is perpendicular to a given line segment and divides it into two equal halves is called the perpendicular bisector of the given line segment.

Construction:

Draw the perpendicular of a line segment AB = 6.5 cm using a ruler and a compass.

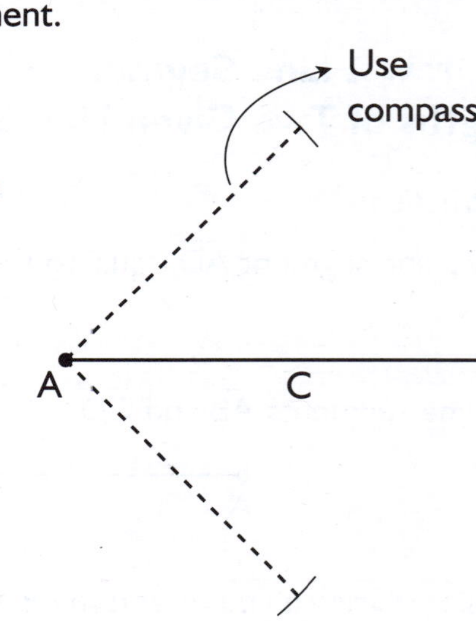

Step 1 Draw a line segment AB of length 6.5 cm.

Step 2 Taking A as the centre and with any radius more than half of AB, draw an arc on either side of AB.

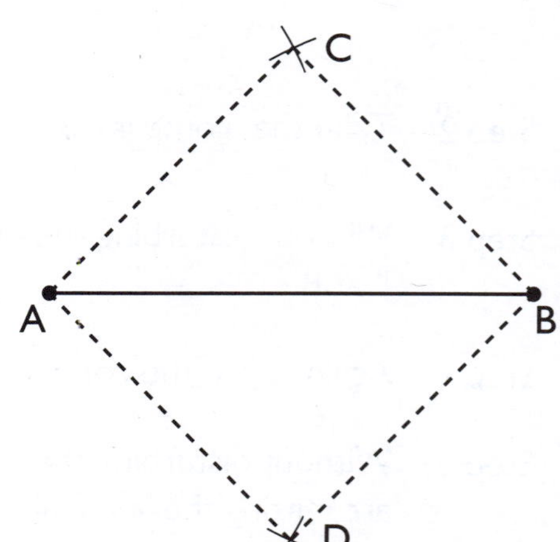

Step 3 Similarly, taking B as the centre and with any radius more than half of AB, draw another arc on either side of AB intersecting the previous arcs at C and D.

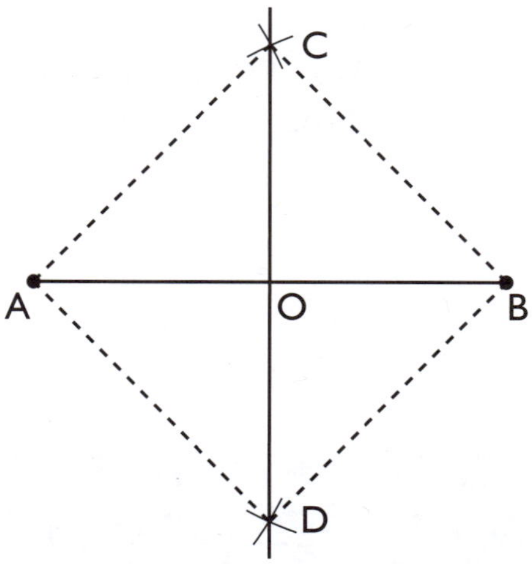

Step 4 Join C and D crossing AB at 0. Hence, CD is the required perpendicular bisector of AB.

Drawing a Perpendicular at a Point on the Line

Construction:

Draw a perpendicular at a point on the line segment AB = 6.5 cm using a ruler and a compass.

Given:

A line segment AB of length 6.5 cm and a point P lying on it.

To construct:

A line passing through P that is perpendicular to AB.

Step 1 Draw a line segment $\overline{AB}$ of length 6.5 cm and mark a point P on it.

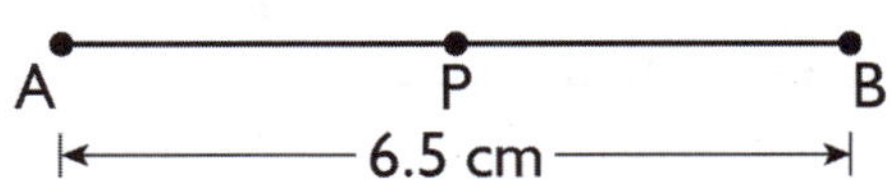

Step 2 Taking P as the centre and with any convenient radius, draw an arc cutting $\overline{AB}$ at X and Y.

Step 3 Taking X and Y as the centres and with any suitable radius draw arcs cutting each other at Q.

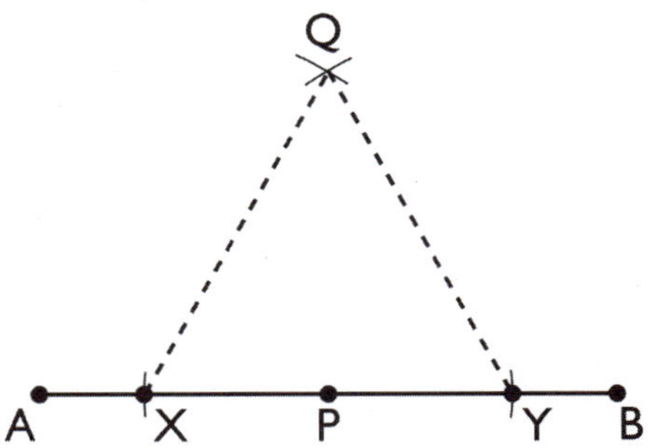

Step 4 Join P and Q.
Then PQ is perpendicular to AB passing through the point P.

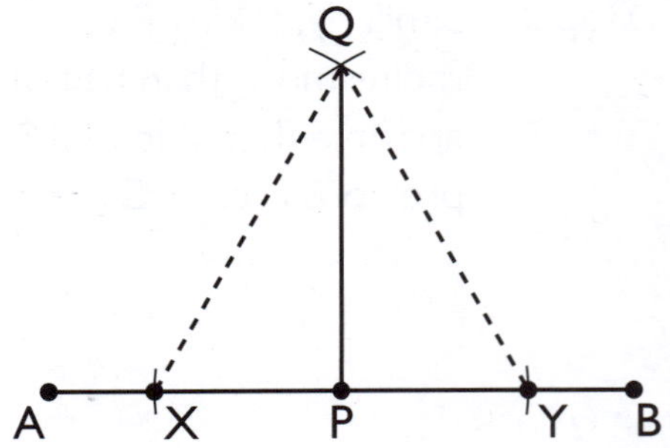

Drawing a Perpendicular to a Given Line from a Point Lying Outside the Line

Construction:

Draw a perpendicular at a point outside the line segment AB. The length of line AB is 6.5 cm.

Given:

A line segment AB of length 6.5 cm and point X lying outside the line.

To construct:

A line passing through X that is perpendicular to AB.

Step 1 Draw a line segment $\overline{AB}$ of length 6.5 cm and mark point X outside the line segment AB.

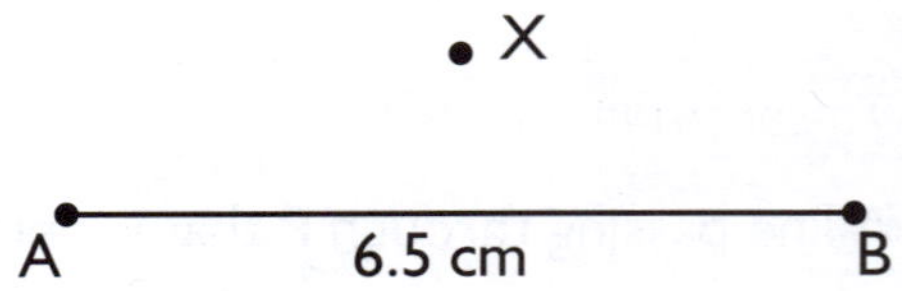

Step 2 Taking X as the centre and with any suitable radius, draw an arc cutting AB at P and Q.

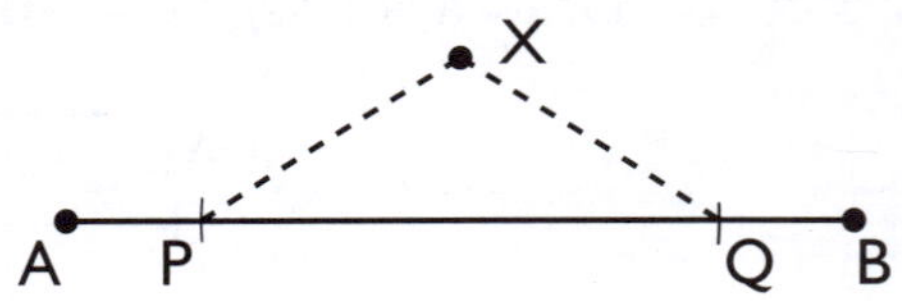

Step 3 Taking P and Q as centres and with a radius of more than half of PQ, draw arcs below AB intersecting each other at Y.

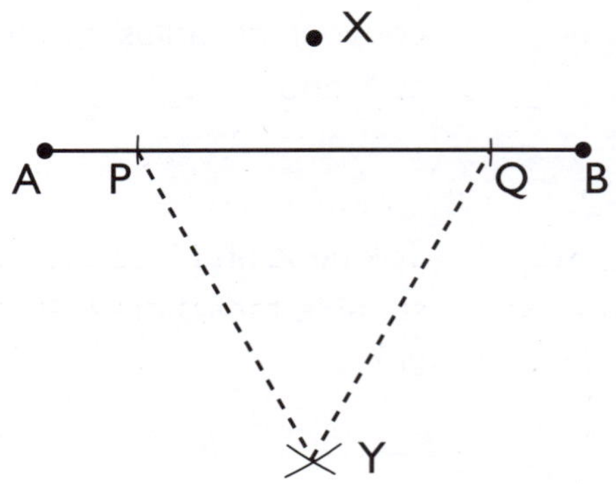

Step 4 Join X and Y.

XY is the required perpendicular to the line segment $\overline{AB}$ from point X lying outside the line segment AB.

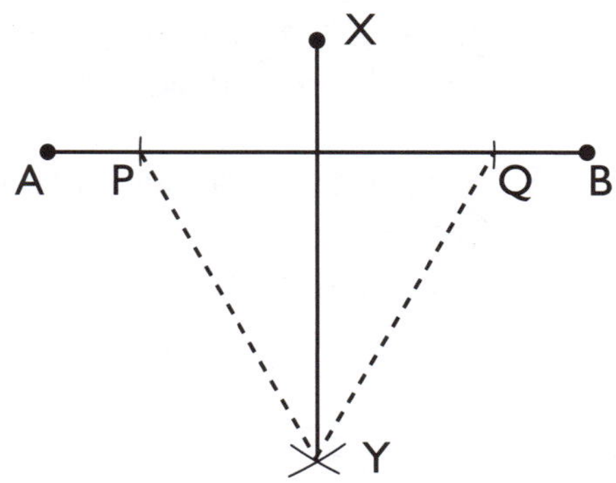

Construction of a Circle

A circle is the path covered by a point that moves in such a way that its distance from a fixed point always remains constant. The fixed point is called the centre and the constant distance is called the radius of the circle. Hence, a circle can be drawn if its centre and radius are known.

Construction:

Draw a circle with a radius of 4 cm.

Step 1 Mark a point 0 on a sheet of paper.

Step 2 Take a compass and measure 4 cm using a ruler.

Step 3 Without changing the opening of the compass, keep the needle at mark 0 and draw a complete arc holding the compass at its knob. After completing one complete round, we get the desired circle.

Practice Exercise 9.1

1. Using a ruler and a compass, draw line segments of the following lengths.

   a. 5.5 cm b. 7.2 cm c. 4.8 cm d. 6.4 cm e. 3.6 cm

2. Draw two line segments AB = 2.5 cm and CD = 4.4 cm. Construct the line segments of the following lengths.

   a. AB + CD b. CD − AB c. 2AB d. $\frac{1}{2}$CD e. 3AB − CD

3. Draw a line segment of length 4.5 cm. Mark a point P on it. Construct a perpendicular to the line segment passing through the point P.

4. Draw a line segment of length 6.6 cm and construct its perpendicular bisector.

5. Draw a line segment of length 5.5 cm. Draw a perpendicular to the line from point P lying outside the line.

6. Measure the following line segments using a divider and then list them in ascending order.

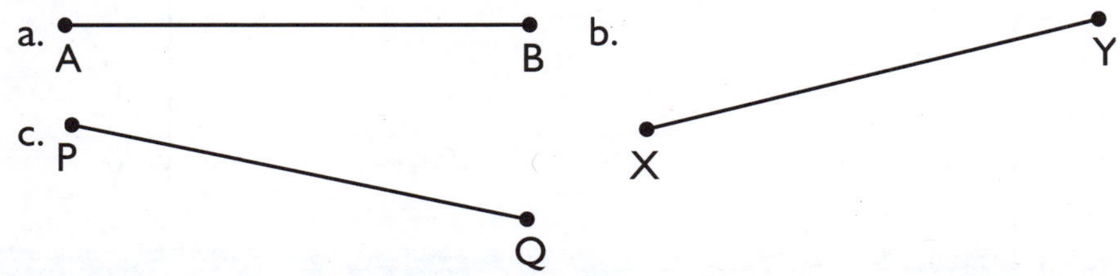

7. Draw a circle of radius 4.5 cm with centre at 0. Mark three points P, Q and R such that P is on the circle, Q is in the interior of the circle and R is in the exterior of the circle.

8. Draw three circles with the same centre and radii of 3 cm, 3.5 cm and 4 cm, respectively. What are these circles called?

9. Draw a line segment AB = 5 cm. Find its perpendicular bisector, which will give the midpoint of AB. Mark it as O. With O as the centre and OA or OB as the radii, draw a circle. What is the line segment AOB called in relation to the circle?

10. Draw a circle with centre A and radius 3.5 cm. Mark a point B on the circumference. Now with B as the centre and radius 3.5 cm, draw another circle. Does it pass through A? Join the centres A and B and find its perpendicular bisector.

Angles

In this section we will learn:

1. To measure an angle.
2. To compare angles.
3. To construct angles.
4. To bisect an angle.

Measuring an Angle

We measure an angle with the help of a protractor. The protractor looks like a D. The angles are marked from 0° to 180°, both in the clockwise direction as well as in the anti-clockwise direction. Zero is the midpoint at the base line of the protractor.

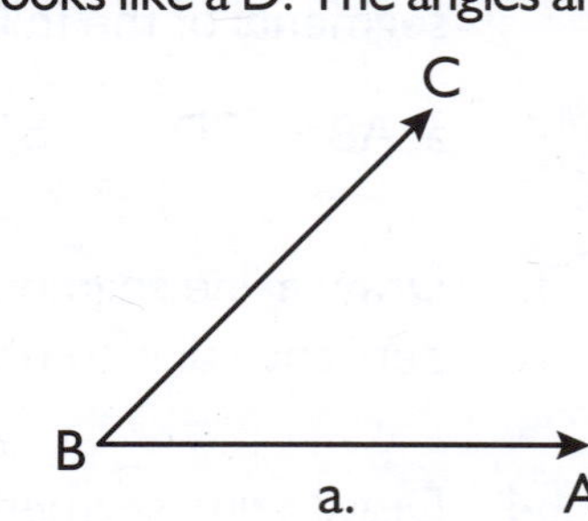

a.

Suppose we have to measure ∠ABC and ∠PQR.

To measure ∠ABC in Fig. (a), we place the 0 of the protractor on B and the base line of the protractor needs to coincide with BA. BA is on the right of 0. We start measuring from 0° and move in the anti-clockwise direction or start counting from 0° on the right side of B. We stop when the mark on the protractor coincides with the arm BC. The angle coincides with the mark. Note ∠ABC.

Similarly, to measure ∠PQR, place the protractor in such a way that the midpoint 0 on the baseline coincides with Q and the baseline overlaps PQ. Start measuring from 0° and move in the clockwise direction or start on the left side of Q. We stop when the mark on the protractor coincides with the arm QR. It coincides with the mark so ∠PQR is determined.

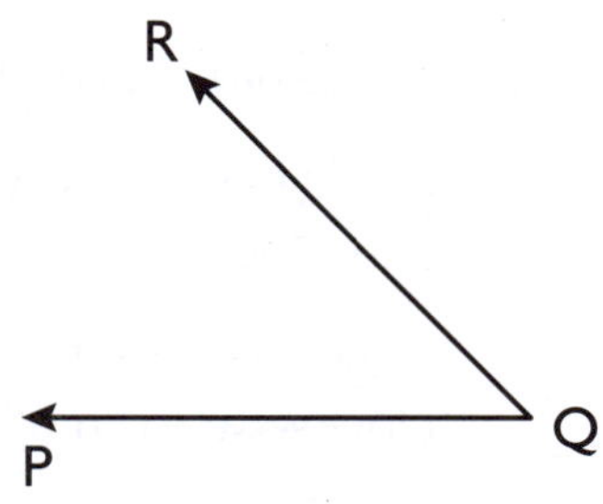

b.

Comparison of Angles

The magnitude of an angle depends upon the opening between the two rays that form the angle. If two angles have different openings between their arms then we say they have different magnitudes. The magnitude of two angles can be compared in the following ways.

1. By observation.
2. By measuring.
3. By tracing.

Construction of Angles

Angles can be drawn or constructed using the following instruments:

1. A protractor.
2. A ruler and a compass.

To Draw an Angle Using a Protractor

Just as we measure an angle using a protractor or "D", we can also draw an angle.

Let us draw an angle ABC of 45° with the help of a protractor.

Step 1 We draw a ray $\overrightarrow{AB}$.

Step 2 Now, place the protractor in such a way that the 0 mark on the baseline coincides with A. We place the baseline on $\overrightarrow{AB}$.

Step 3 Since point B is on the right side of the mark 0, start counting in the anticlockwise direction from the 0 mark.

Step 4 When you come at 45°, mark the point as C.

Step 5 Remove the protractor and join A and C. ∠CAB = 45°.

Alert!

1. Be careful while measuring the angle—always begin from the 0° mark.
2. If you have the ray on the right of the 0 mark, then start from 0° on the right or anti-clockwise from 0°.
3. If the ray is on the left of the 0 mark on the baseline, start from 0° on the left or clockwise from 0°.

Construction of an Angle Using a Ruler and a Compass

Construction:

To draw an angle equal to a given angle.

Given:

An angle ABC.

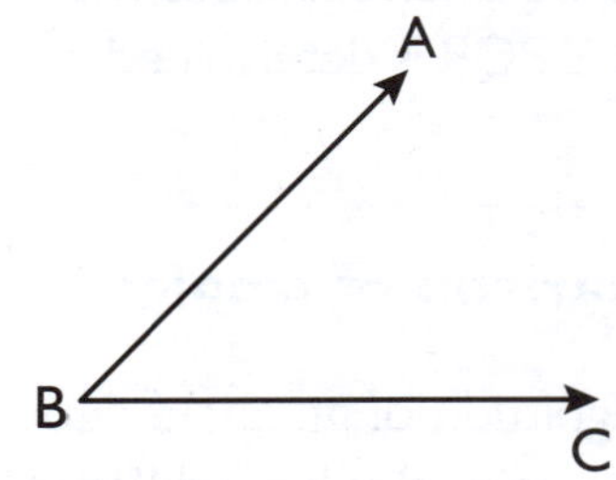

To construct:

Step 1 Taking B as the centre and any convenient radius, draw an arc cutting the arms of ∠ABC at points D and E.

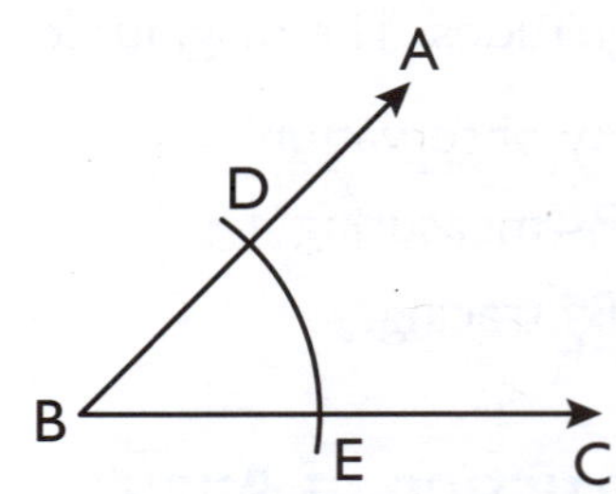

Step 2 Draw a ray $\overrightarrow{QR}$ with Q as centre and the same radius as before, draw an arc cutting QR at S.

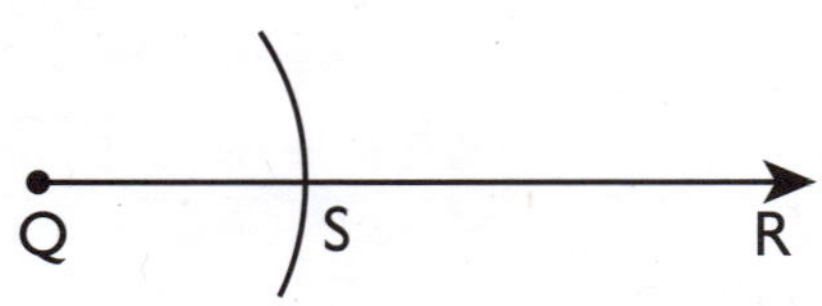

Step 3 Taking S as the centre and radius equal to DE, draw an arc intersecting the previous arc at T.

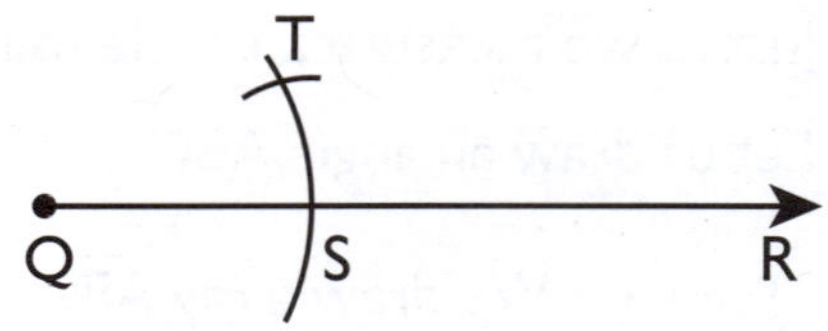

Step 4 Join QT and extend it to form ray $\overrightarrow{QP}$.

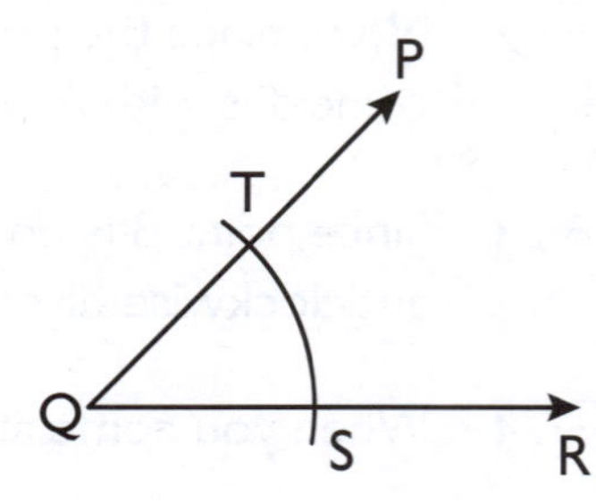

Step 5 PQR is the required angle.

Step 6 Verify by measuring angles ∠ABC and ∠PQR using a protractor. They should be equal in magnitude.

To Bisect a Given Angle

Construction:

Given:

An angle ABC.

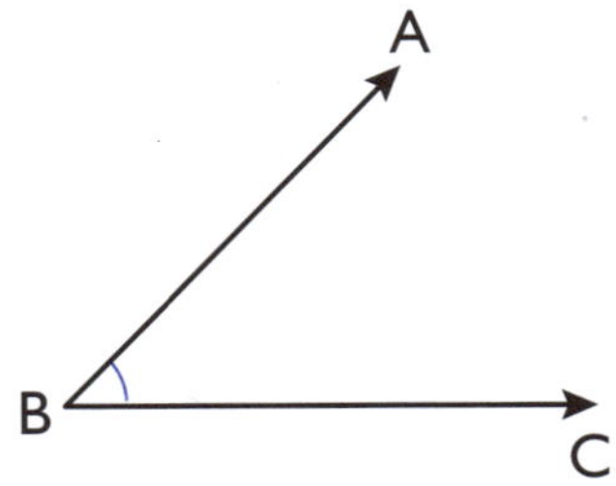

Question: Why did the girl sleep with a ruler?

Answer: She wanted to see how long she would sleep!

To construct the bisector of $\angle ABC$.

Step 1 Taking B as the centre and with any suitable radius, draw an arc cutting the arms $\overrightarrow{BC}$ and $\overrightarrow{BA}$ of $\angle ABC$ at D and E, respectively.

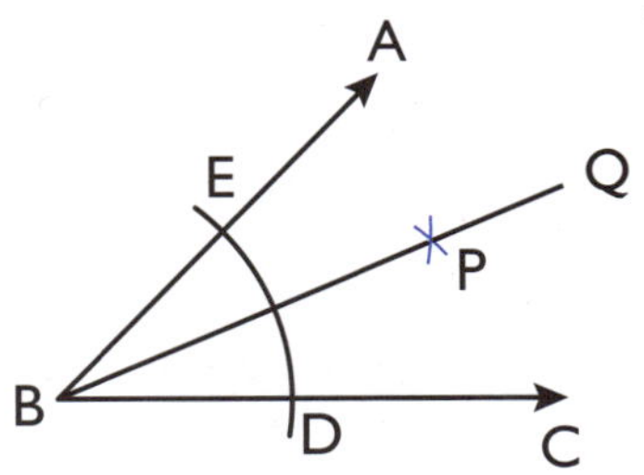

Step 2 Taking D as the centre and any radius more than half of DE, draw an arc between the two arms AB and BC.

Step 3 Similarly, taking E as the centre and with the same radius (as in Step 2) draw an arc intersecting the previous arc at P. Join BP and extend it to get $\overrightarrow{BQ}$.

Thus, ray $\overrightarrow{BQ}$ is the required bisector of $\angle ABC$ or $\angle CBA$.

Construction of Angles

Example 1: To construct an angle of 60°.

Step 1 Draw any ray $\overrightarrow{AB}$.

Step 2 Taking A as centre and with any suitable radius, draw an arc PQ that cuts AB at P.

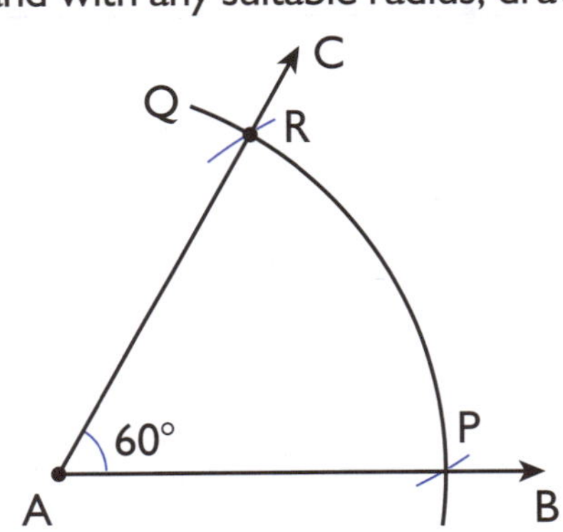

Step 3 Taking P as centre and radius equal to AP, draw an arc cutting the previous arc PQ at R.

Step 4 Join $\overrightarrow{AR}$ and extend it to get $\overrightarrow{AC}$.

Step 5 ∠BAC is the required angle equal to 60°.

Example 2: To construct an angle of 120°.

Step 1 Draw a ray $\overrightarrow{AB}$.

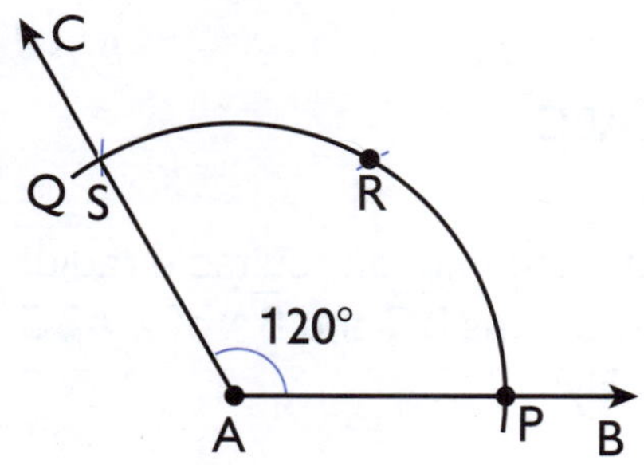

Step 2 Taking A as the centre and with any suitable radius, draw an arc PQ intersecting AB at P.

Step 3 Taking P as the centre and radius equal to AP, draw an arc intersecting PQ at R.

Step 4 Taking R as the centre and with the same radius, cut an arc PQ at another point S.

Step 5 Join $\overrightarrow{AS}$ and extend it to get $\overrightarrow{AC}$.

Step 6 ∠BAC is the required angle equal to 120°.

Example 3: To construct an angle of 90°.

Step 1 Draw a ray $\overrightarrow{AB}$ and mark a point C on it.

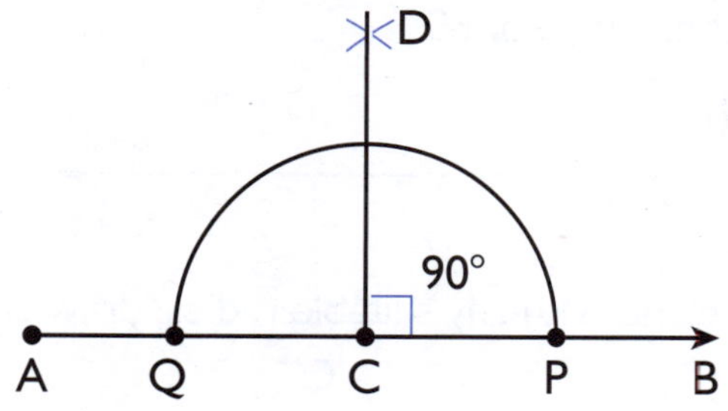

Step 2 Taking C as the centre and with any suitable radius, draw an arc PQ intersecting AB at P and Q.

Step 3 Taking P and Q as the centres and with any convenient radius, draw arcs intersecting each other at D.

Step 4 Join C and D to get the ray $\overrightarrow{CD}$.

Step 5 $\angle ACD = \angle DCB = 90°$, the required angle.

Example 4: To construct an angle of 30°.

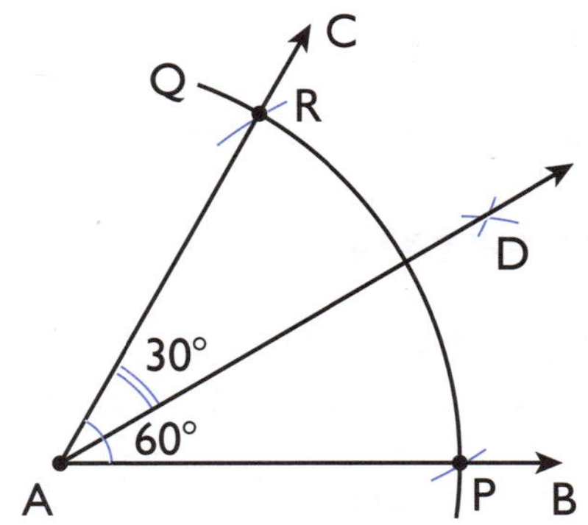

Step 1 Draw an angle of 60°. (Construction given earlier.)

Step 2 Bisect the angle.

Step 3 The bisector of the angle is called the angular bisector.

Step 4 Angular bisector of 60° divides it into two equal angles of 30° each.

Example 5: To construct an angle of 45°.

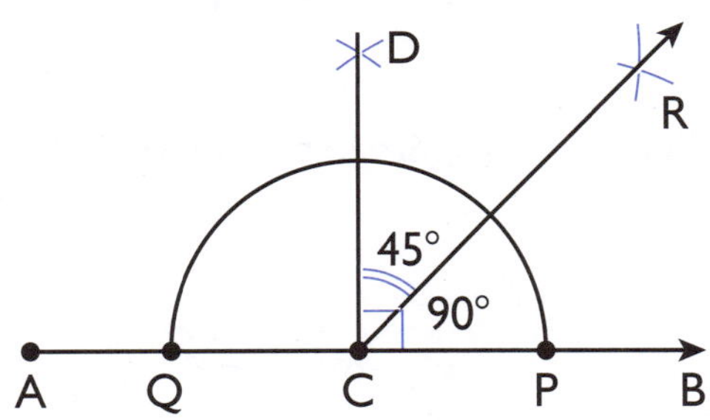

Step 1 Draw an angle of 90°.

Step 2 Bisect the angle.

Step 3 The bisector of the angle is called the angular bisector.

Step 4 Angular bisector of 90° divides it into two equal parts of 45° each.

Practice Exercise 9.2

1. Use a protractor and draw the following angles.

   a. 75° b. 100° c. 140°

2. Draw an angle of 135° with the help of a protractor and bisect it using a compass.

3. Draw an angle $\angle ABC = 70°$ with the help of a protractor. Now, draw $\angle PQR = \angle ABC$ using a ruler and a compass.

4. Using a ruler and a compass, construct an angle of 60°. Bisect the angle and then construct an angle of 30°.

5. Using a ruler and a compass, construct an angle of 120°.

6. Construct an angle of 45° using a ruler and a compass. Also bisect the angle.

7. Draw $\angle PQR = 65°$. Using a protractor, bisect the angle. Take a point K on the angular bisector and draw perpendiculars on the arms PQ and QR.

8. Draw $\angle AOB = 100°$ and construct $\angle XYZ$ such that $\angle XYZ = \frac{1}{4} \angle AOB$.

Higher Order Thinking Skills

HOTS

1. Classify the triangles in the given figure in two ways: (i) by their sides, (ii) by their angles.

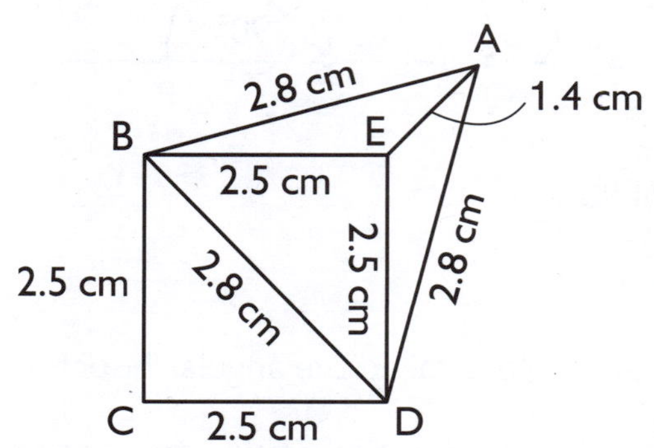

2. Draw $\angle ABC$ of measure 80° with the help of a protactor. Now, with a ruler and compass, construct $\angle DEF = \angle ABC$.

3. Construct three circles with centre "O" and radii of 2 cm, 3 cm and 4 cm, respectively. What are such circles called? Mark a point P in the interior of all the circles. Mark a point R lying in the exterior region of all the circles.

Highlights

- A geometry box consists of the following instruments that are useful for geometrical constructions.

  a. a ruler b. a protractor c. a pair of set squares

  d. a compass e. a divider

- Many constructions can be made with the help of a ruler and compass.
- A circle can be constructed if its radius is known.
- Circles with the same centre but different radii are called concentric circles.
- A perpendicular bisector divides a line segment into two equal parts and meets the segment at right angles.
- Angles measuring 60°, 120°, 90°, 30°, 45° and 15° can be constructed with the help of a ruler and compass. These angles are all multiplies of 15°.
- The simplest angle to be constructed with the aid of a ruler and compass is that of 60°.
- An angle bisector divides an angle into two equal parts.

Hexagon in a Circle!

Objective: To construct a regular hexagon inside a circle

Material required: Ruler, compass, pencil, coloured sketch pens

Procedure:

Draw a circle with centre O and any suitable radius. With the *given* radius and with the pointer at any point on the circumference of the circle, draw an arc to cut the circle in point A. Keeping the radius constant and with the pointer at A, draw an arc to cut off the circle at B. Similarly draw arcs to cut the circle at C, D, E and F. Join AB, BC, CD, DE, EF and FA. We get a regular hexagon ABCDEF. Measure the sides of the hexagon. They will be of equal lengths. Each angle at the vertex will be of 120°. Join A, B, C, D, E and F to the centre of the circle "O". There will be six radii, three diameters and six chords. Measure the angle at the centre. Each angle will be of 60°.

Once the hexagon is constructed, the six equal parts of the hexagon can be coloured with different colours to make it look beautiful. You can also make different designs on each segment.

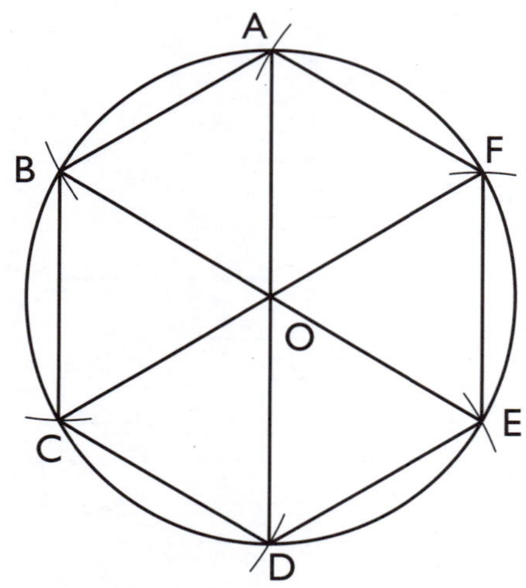

Symmetry

CHAPTER 10

What is Symmetry?

We see symmetry around us in nature and in our environment. When we look at ourselves in the mirror, we see that our eyes and ears are symmetrical about a vertical line.

In nature, we see symmetry in the shapes of flowers, leaves, butterflies, etc.

Many man-made structures also display symmetry. For example, the Taj Mahal, Indian Gate, Howrah Bridge are examples of symmetrical constructions.

Many letters of the English alphabet are symmetrical about a horizontal or vertical line.

A B D O

Many geometrical figures are symmetrical as well.

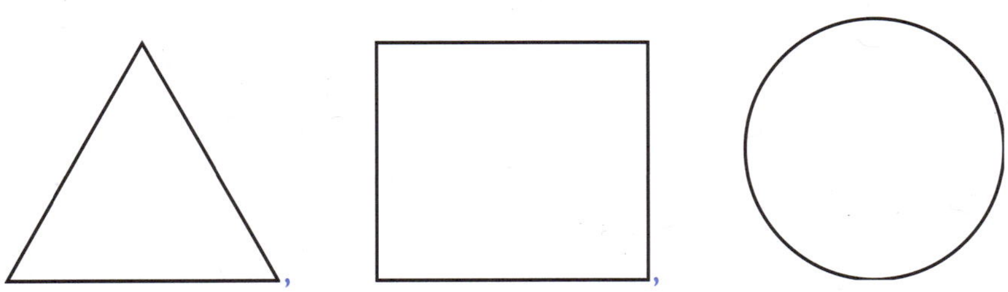

Symmetry is the quality of being made up of exactly similar parts facing each other or around as axis. This axis or line that divides a figure into two identical halves is called the axis of symmetry.

Examples of non-symmetrical figures are stones, rocks, etc.

Symmetry in the Letters of the English Alphabet

Here are some examples where the line of symmetry is horizontal.

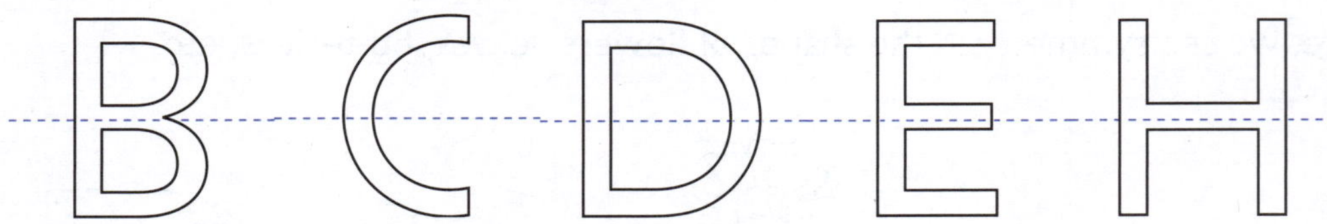

Here are few examples where the line of symmetry is vertical.

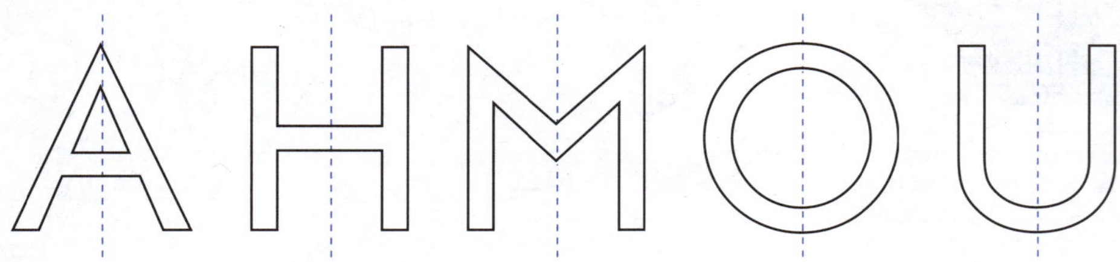

There are some letters in the English alphabet that are not symmetrical about any line.

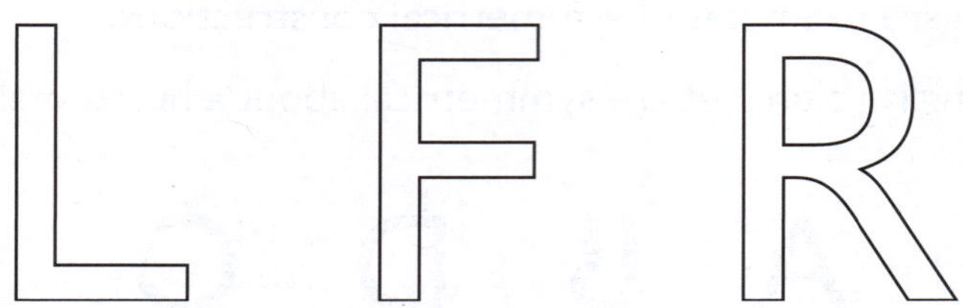

Symmetry in Geometrical Shapes

Many geometrical shapes are also symmetrical.

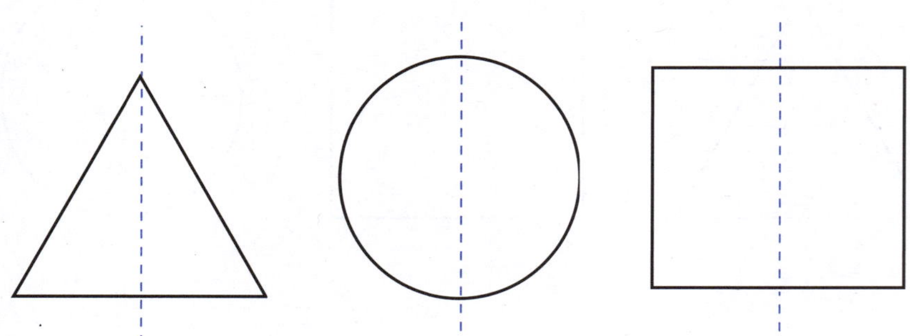

Isosceles Triangle   Circle   Square

There are some geometrical shapes that do not have any line of symmetry like the scalene triangle or any irregular polygon.

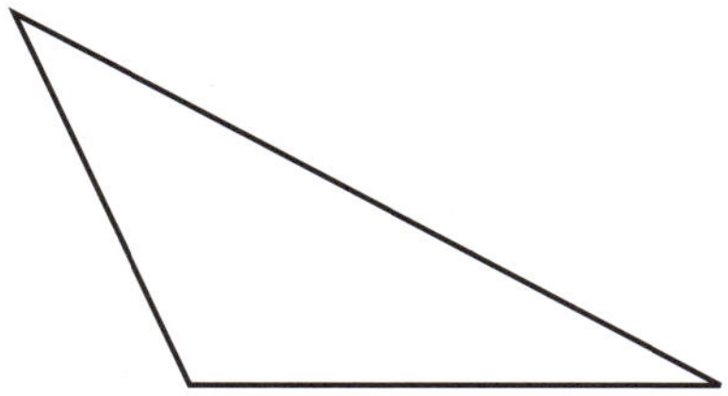

Scalene Triangle

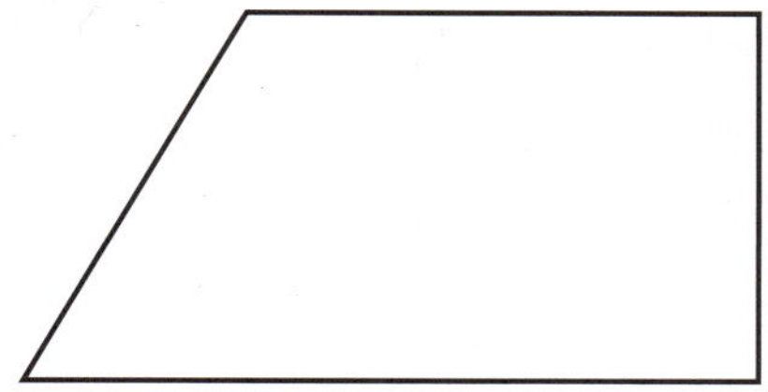

Irregular Polygon

Shapes and Figures with More than One Line of Symmetry

Here are some examples of letters of English alphabet with more than one line of symmetry.

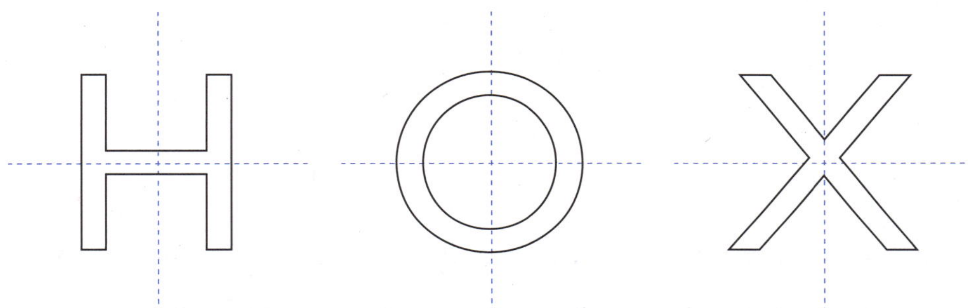

Each of these letters are symmetric about two lines.

Similarly, some geometrical shapes have two or more lines of symmetry.

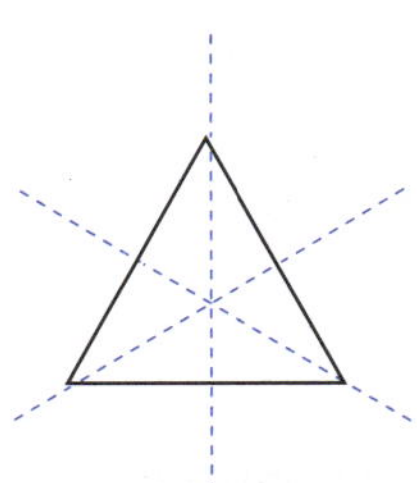

An equilateral triangle has three lines of symmetry.

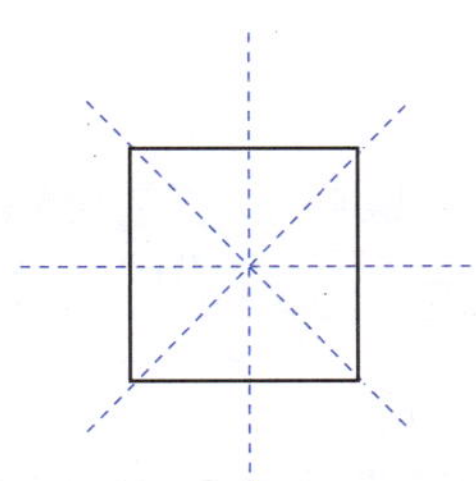

A square has four lines of symmetry.

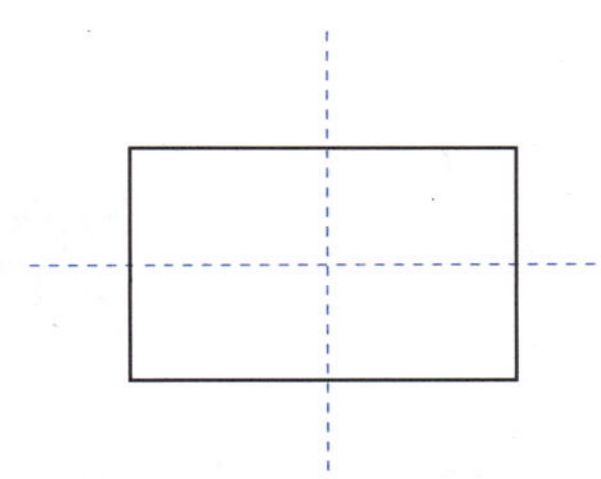

A rectangle has two lines of symmetry.

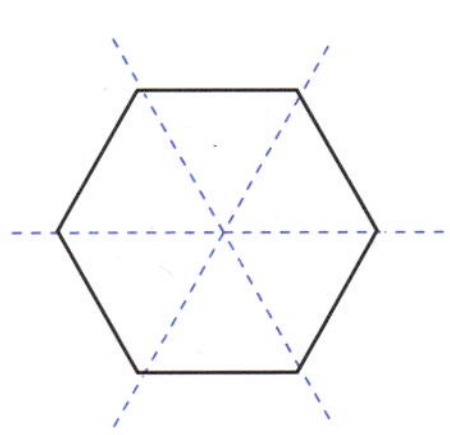

A regular hexagon has three lines of symmetry.

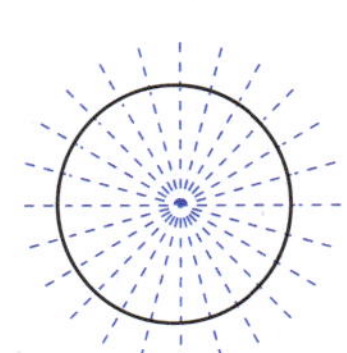

A circle has infinite lines of symmetry.

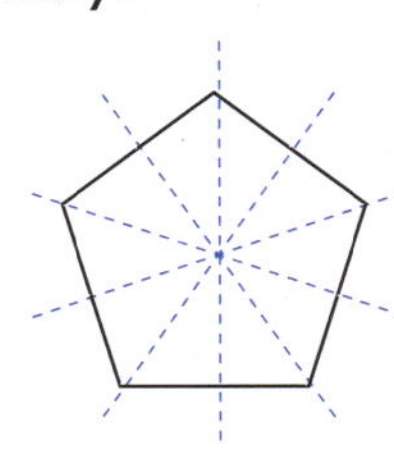

A pentagon has five lines of symmetry.

Mirror or Reflection Symmetry

We know that we can see our reflection in a mirror. The object and its reflection are symmetrical and the mirror forms the axis of symmetry.

There is lateral inversion in a mirror. If we put up our right arm, the reflection will show that the left arm is up.

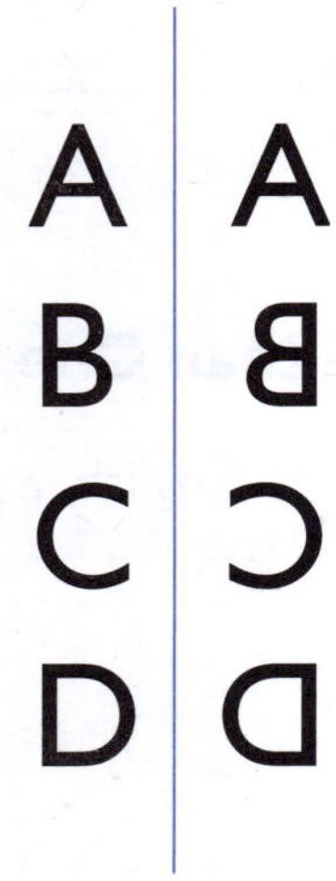

Alert!

With respect to a reflection of an object in a mirror, keep in mind the following facts:

1. The length of the image remains the same as the length of the object.
2. The distance of the image from the mirror is equal to the distance of the object from the mirror.
3. The reflection of an object in a mirror looks laterally inverted.

Practice Exercise 10.1

1. Identify each of the following figures as symmetrical or non-symmetrical.

a. 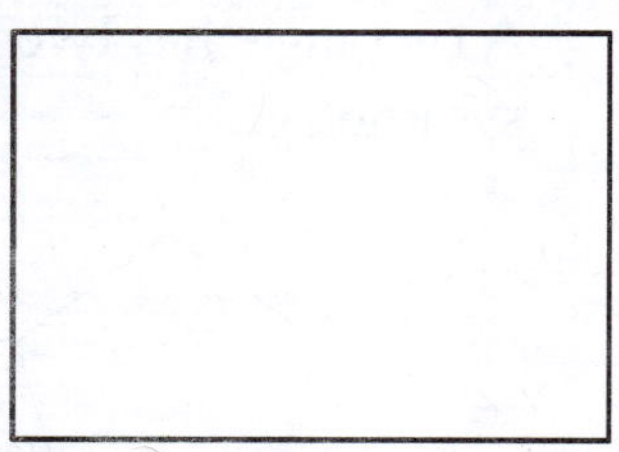

b. 

c. 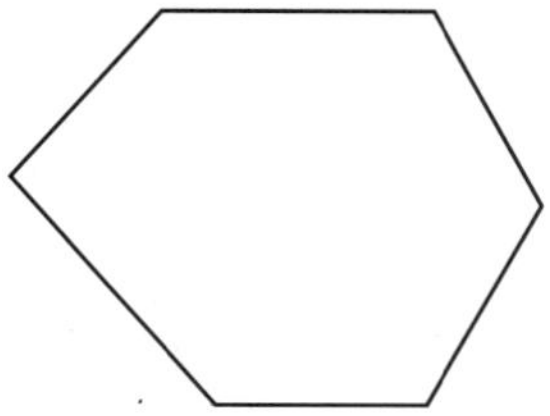

d. 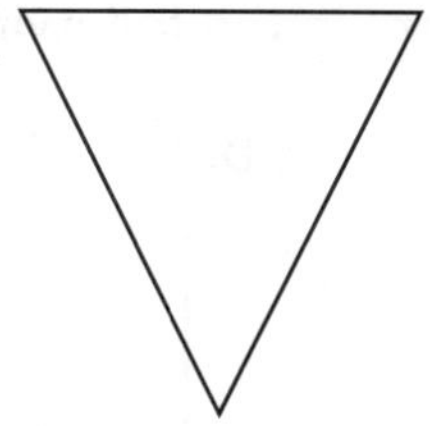

e. 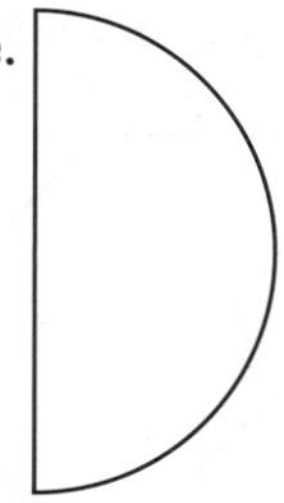

2. Draw the lines of symmetry for the following letters of the English alphabet.

a. 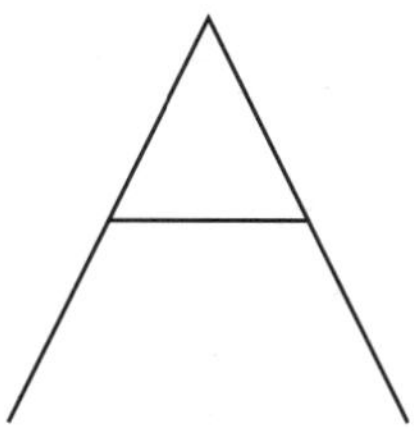

b. 

c. 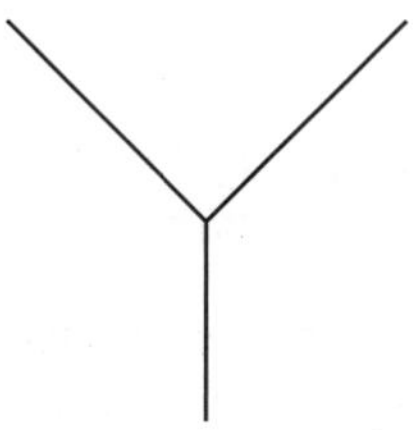

d. 

3. In the following figures, the dotted line is the line of symmetry. Copy and complete each figure so that the figure is symmetrical.

a. 

b. 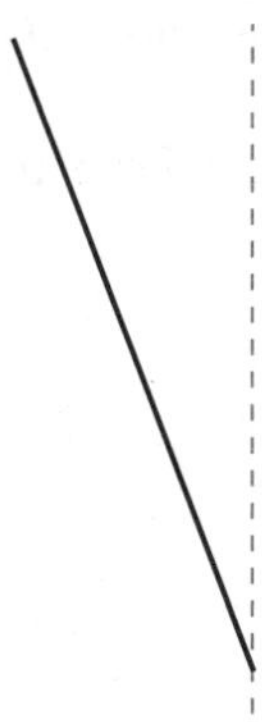

c. 

d. 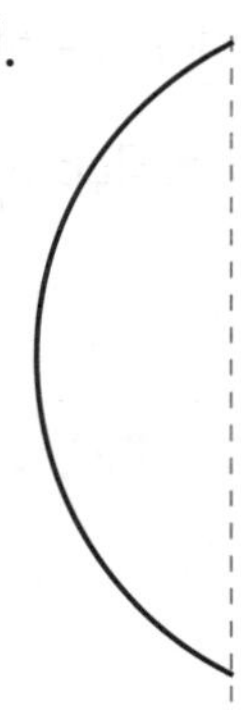

e. 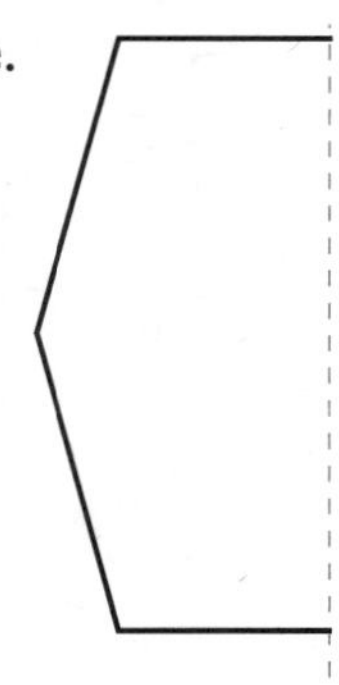

4. How many lines of symmetry do the following figures have?

a. Circle.

b. Pentagon.

c. Equilateral triangle.

d. Parallelogram.

e. Scalene triangle.

5. Draw the lines of symmetry in the following figures.

a.

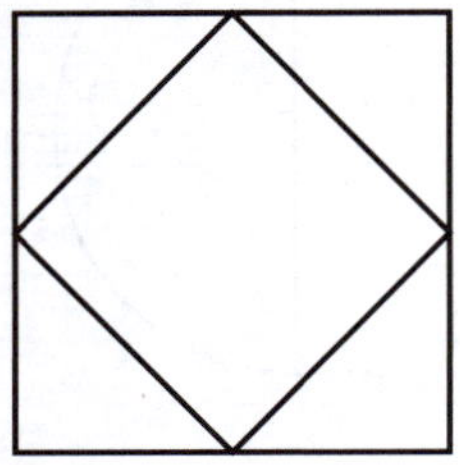

b.

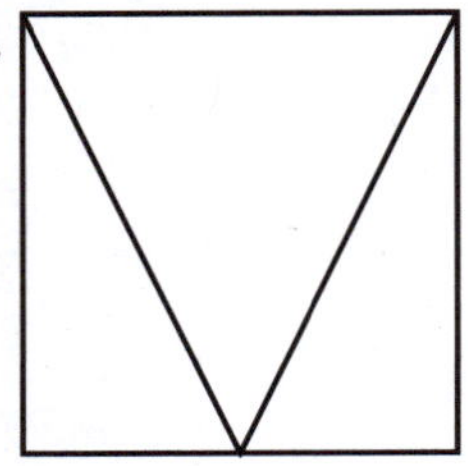

c.

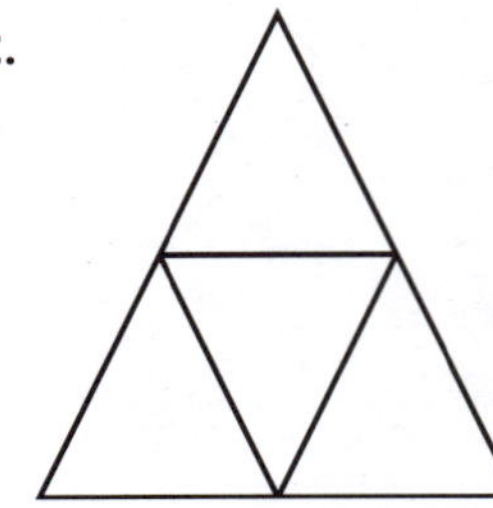

d.

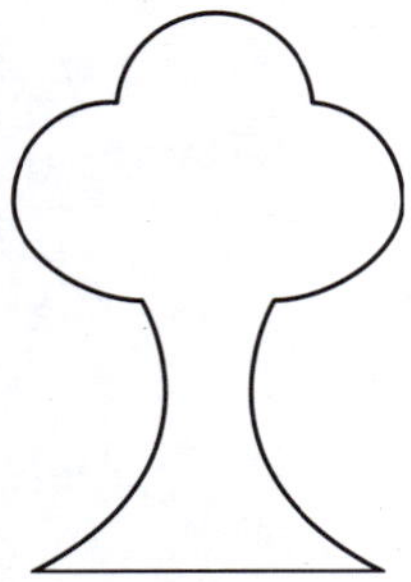

e.

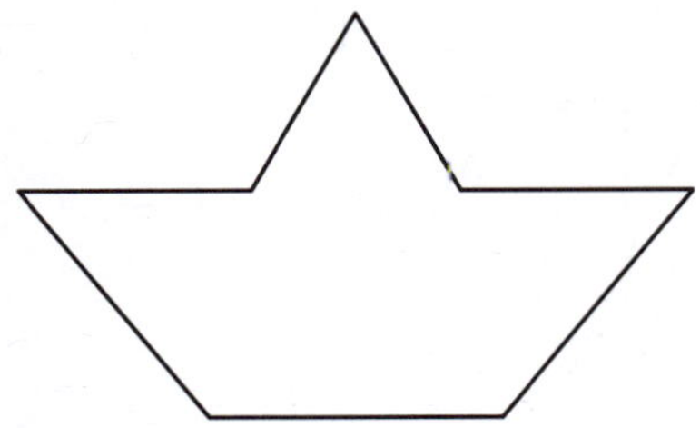

Highlights

- A figure is said to be symmetrical when an imaginary line seems to divide it into two identical parts, such that if they are superimposed on each other, they coincide.
- The line that divides a figure into two identical parts is called the line or axis of symmetry.
- A symmetrical figure can have more than one line of symmetry.
- In a mirror reflection, the image formed has a lateral symmetry.

Higher Order Thinking Skills

HOTS

1. Take a sheet of paper and fold it into two halves. Punch a hole. Open the sheet. Are the two holes symmetrical about the fold? What is the fold of the paper called?

2. Draw three objects from your day to day life that have no line of symmetry.

3. What is the another name that you can give to the line of symmetry of
   a. an isosceles triangle b. circle c. parallelogram.

Maths Lab Activity

Objective: To observe symmetry in man-made structures and in nature.

Material required: Collect 5 pictures of monuments depicting symmetry, 5 flowers and 5 leaves

Procedure:

1. Collect 5 pictures of buildings or monuments that are symmetrical .
2. Collect 5 varieties of flowers that are symmetrical. Dry them and paste in you note book. Learn the names of the flowers.
3. Collect 5 varieties of leaves that are symmetrical. Paste them in your notebook. Learn the names of the plants.

This is symmetry in man-made structures and in nature.

Here is a hexagon. Can you make it a cube by adding only 3 extra lines?

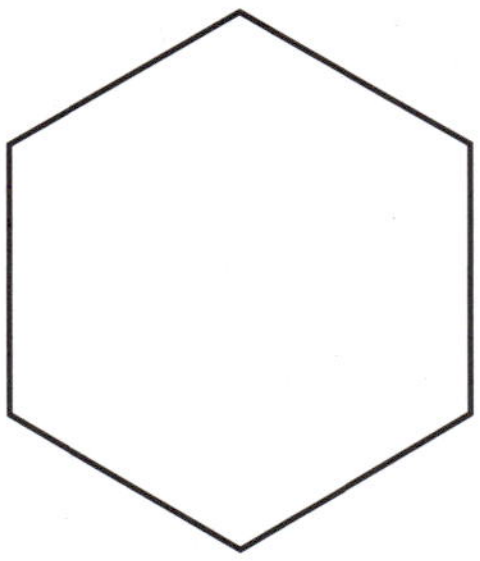

Answer for Brainteaser on page 185

CHAPTERS 9–10

Rewind

1. Draw the following triangles.

   a. A triangle with no axis of symmetry.

   b. A triangle with one axis of symmetry.

   c. A triangle with three axes of symmetry.

2. Write two letters of the English alphabet having:

   a. No axis of symmetry.

   b. One axis of symmetry.

   c. More than one axes of symmetry.

3. Draw a circle with centre O and radius 3.4 cm. Draw a diameter AB and another diameter CD. Join AC, CB, BD and DA. What kind of quadrilateral is ABCD?

4. Given two line segments AB = 6.4 cm and CD = 2.8 cm, construct a line segment whose length is equal to

   a. AB + CD   b. AB − CD   c. 3CD

5. Draw a circle with centre O and radius 4 cm. Draw a chord PQ of length 3.2 cm. Draw the perpendicular bisector of PQ. Does it pass through the centre?

6. Draw an angle PQR of measure 85° using a protractor. Construct the bisector of the angle using a compass and ruler.

7. Using a divider and a ruler, draw a line segment AB = 7 cm. Using a compass and a ruler find the perpendicular bisector of AB. Name it P. At the point P, draw an angle of 60° using a ruler and a compass only. Name the adjacent angles. If one angle is 60° (as constructed), what will be the measure of the other angle?

8. a. Construct an angle of 75° using a ruler and a compass only.

   b. Construct an angle of 135° using a ruler and a compass only.

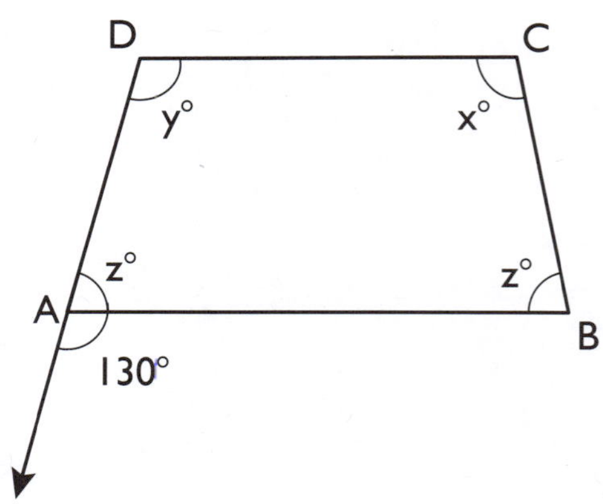

9. In the figure ABCD, AB || CD.

   Find the values of x, y and z.

10. Draw a line segment XY of length 5.5 cm using a ruler and divider. Draw a perpendicular to the line from point P lying outside the line.

Test Yourself

Unit II

1. Study the figure and list the following:

   a. All vertices of the polygon.

   b. All sides of the polygon.

   c. All angles of the polygon.

   d. All diagonals of the polygon.

   e. The name of the polygon.

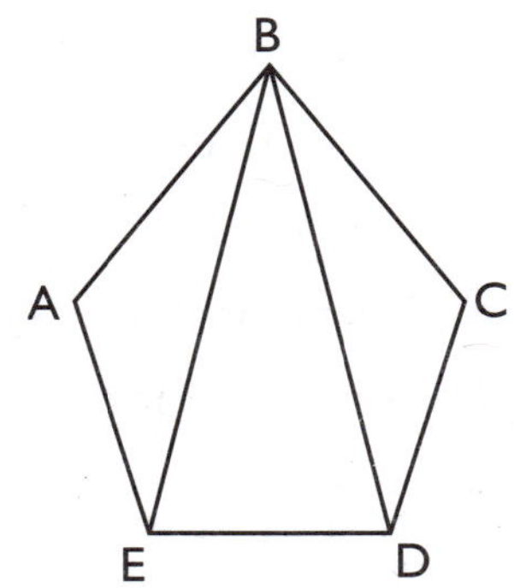

2. Study the circle with centre O and answer the following:

   a. List the two diameters.

   b. Name any two chords.

   c. Name two radii.

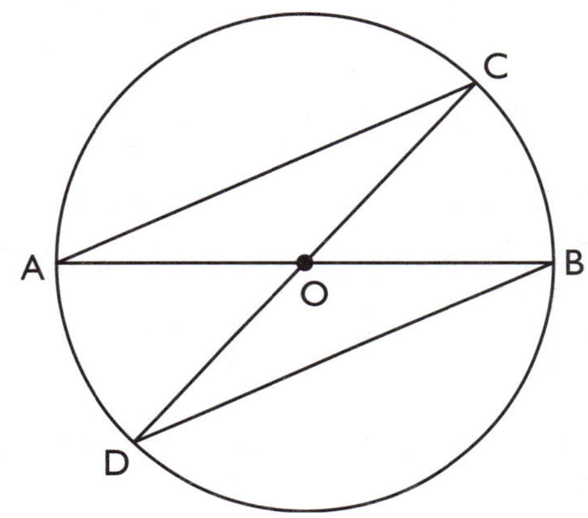

3. Fill in the blanks.

   a. A triangle has ______ sides, ______ vertices and ______ angles.

   b. A median of a triangle is the ______ that joins a vertex to the ______ of the opposite side.

   c. An altitude of a triangle is the ______ drawn from a vertex to the opposite side.

4. Draw a quadrilateral ABCD and name the following.

   a. The four vertices. b. The four sides. c. The four angles.

   d. Two pairs of opposite sides. e. Two pairs of opposite angles.

5. Indicate whether the following statements are true or false.

   a. A point has a length and width.

   b. From one point we can draw only one line.

   c. The maximum number of points of intersection of three lines is 3.

d. An infinite number of lines can be drawn through a given point.

e. Two interseting planes intersect at a point only.

6. Classify the following angles as acute, obtuse, right, reflex, straight and complete angles.

a. 48°	b. 114°	c. 170°	d. 180°	e. 210°
f. 360°	g. 65°	h. 140°	i. 270°	j. 89°
k. 90°	l. 8°	m. 181°	n. 359°	o. 60°

7. The sum of three angles of a triangle is 180°. Which of the following will form a triangle? Name the triangle (if formed).

a. 60°, 45°, 60°   b. 75°, 25°, 80°   c. 110°, 30°, 40°

d. 90°, 45°, 45°   e. 60°, 60°, 60°

8. In a triangle DEF, mark the following:

a. The points P, Q, R in the interior of $\triangle$DEF.

b. The points X, Y, Z in the exterior of $\triangle$DEF.

c. The points A, B and C on $\triangle$DEF.

9. Write one difference between the following pairs.

a. Square and rectangle.   b. Square and rhombus.

c. Rectangle and parallelogram.

10. Draw neat diagrams to show the following shapes.

a. Cube   b. Cuboid   c. Cone   d. Cylinder   e. Sphere

11. Copy and draw the reflection of the points, line and triangle in the mirror line 'ℓ' shown below.

a.

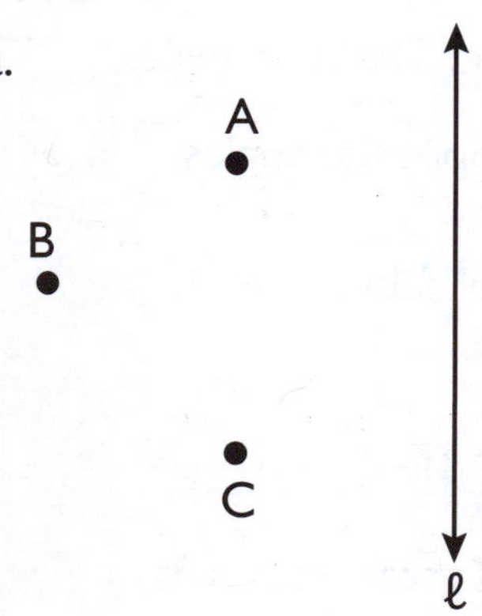

b.

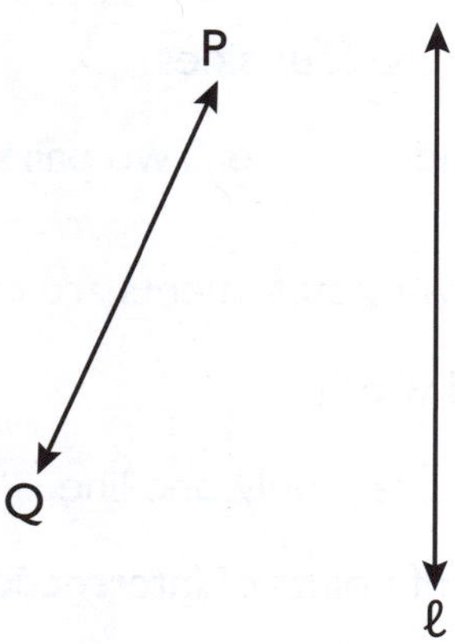

c.

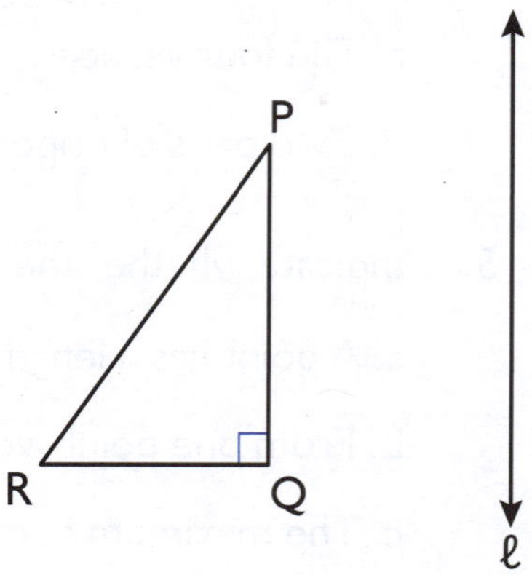

12. Which of the digits from 0 to 9 have lines of symmetry? Draw them.

13. Draw five letters of the English alphabet that have one line of symmetry.

14. Draw the following geometrical shapes and draw *a* line of symmetry in each of them.

    a. Square b. Rectangle c. Hexagon d. Circle e. Kite

15. Using a ruler and a compass, draw a line segment AB = 5.5 cm. Construct the prependicular bisector of the line.

16. Using a ruler and a compass, draw a line segment CD = 6 cm. With centre C and radius 3 cm, draw a circle. With centre D and radius 3.5 cm, draw another circle. Where the two circles intersect, mark the points as P and Q.

17. Using your protractor, draw an angle of 112°. Bisect this angle using only a compass.

18. Using a ruler and a compass, construct a square of side 4 cm.

19. Using a rule and compass, construct a rectangle whose sides are 5 cm and 3 cm

20. Using a ruler and compass, construct the following angles.

    a. 120° b. 60° c. 45°

Answer for Brainteaser on page 181

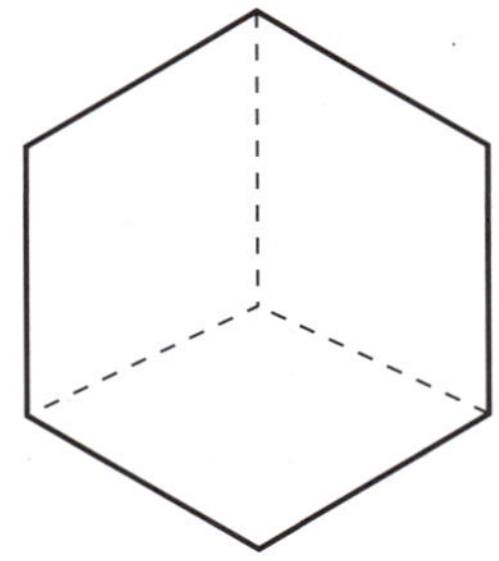

CHAPTER 11

Introduction to Algebra

Algebra is a branch of mathematics that involves the use of letters of the alphabet as numbers. These letters are called literal numbers. So we know two types of numbers: (i) based on digits, (ii) based on letters.

Literal numbers are used for unknown quantities and are also called variables.

Example 1: Radha has ₹60 in her piggy bank and Sadhana gives her ₹x. The total amount of money that Radha now has is ₹100. How much money did Sadhana give Radha?

Let the money that Sadhana gave Radha be ₹x. So, Radha has in her piggy bank:

$$₹60 + ₹x = ₹100$$

or $$60 + x = 100$$

$$x = 100 - 60$$

$$\therefore \quad x = ₹40$$

Example 2: The perimeter of a square is 120 m. Find the side of the square.

Let the side of the square be ℓ.

Perimeter of the square $= 4\ell$

$$4\ell = 120$$

$$\ell = \frac{120}{4} = 30 \text{ m}$$

The side of the square is 30 m. Here, the unknown quantity is the side of the square, which we denoted by the alphabet ℓ.

Thus, day-to-day problems can be solved with the help of algebra.

The basic operations of addition, subtraction, multiplication, division and powers of simple arithmetic can be applied to literal numbers.

Fundamental Operations of Literal Numbers

1. Addition

Let x and y be two literal numbers, then their sum is written as $x + y$.

Also, $$x + y = y + x$$

2. Subtraction

Let x and y be two literal numbers, then their difference is written as $x - y$ or $y - x$.

But, $$x - y \neq y - x$$

3. Multiplication

Let x and y be two literal numbers, then their multiplication or product is written as $x \cdot y$ or $x \times y$.

Also, $x \cdot y = y \cdot x$

4. Division

Let x and y be two literal numbers, then their division is written as $x \div y$, or $\frac{x}{y}$, where $y \neq 0$.

Also, $\frac{x}{y} \neq \frac{y}{x}$

5. Power

If x is multiplied by itself 7 times, then it is written as $x \times x \times x \times x \times x \times x \times x = x^7$.

$$x^7 \neq 7x$$

x^7 means x multiplied by itself 7 times. 7x means x multiplied by the number 7.

Algebraic Expressions

An algebraic expression is made up of numerals, literal numerals (letters) and the signs of operations. Each expression can have one or more terms.

Example 1: $7x + y$ — This has two terms, 7x and y. It has a plus sign in between.

Example 2: $3x^2 + 2x - 5$ — This has three terms $3x^2$, 2x and 5. Between $3x^2$ and 2x there is a plus sign and in front of 5 there is a minus sign. Hence (-5) is taken as a term.

Example 3: $7xy + 2xz + 5yz$ — Here there are three terms, each connected to the other with a plus sign.

Different terms connected with the signs of operation form an algebraic expression.

1. 7x is made up of 7 multiplied by x. 7 is a numerical factor and x is a literal factor. So, two factors multiplied together give an algebraic expression. It consists of only one term.
2. $4xy + 7y + 8x + 5$. This is an algebraic expression that consists of four terms.

   4xy, 7y, 8x and 5

   4xy is 4 multiplied by x multiplied by y

   7y is 7 multiplied by y

8x is 8 multiplied by x

and 5 is a constant.

Coefficients

A numerical or constant quality placed before the variable and multiplying the variable in an algebraic expression is called the coefficient.

Example 1: In 8x, 8 is the coefficient of x.

x is the coefficient of 8.

Example 2: In $4x^2y$, $4x^2$ is the coefficient of y.

4y is the coefficient of x^2.

Factors

Each quantity in a term is called a factor.

In $4x^2$, 4, x, x are the factors.

In 8xy, 8, x, y are the factors.

Now, here is an example to give a complete understanding of all the quantities in an algebraic expression.

$$5x^2y + 10xy^2 + 2xy + 8$$

Number of terms = 4

Factors of each term.

$$5x^2y = 5 \times x \times x \times y$$

$$10xy^2 = 10 \times x \times y \times y$$

$$2xy = 2 \times x \times y$$

$$8 = 8$$

Coefficients of:

x^2 in $5x^2y$ is 5y

y in $5x^2y$ is $5x^2$

Like and Unlike Terms

Two or more terms having the same algebraic factors are called like terms and two or more terms having different algebraic factors are called unlike terms.

11xy, 7xy, −xy, 3xy are like terms because in each term, there is x and y.

25x and 25y are not like terms. The factor 25 is the same but the literal numbers are different.

Like terms	Unlike terms
$7x^2$, $10x^2$, $5x^2$	$5x^2$, $10y^2$
ab, 2ab, 7ab	a^2b, ab^2, ab
xyz, 10xyz, 15xyz	2xy, 2yz

Kinds of Algebraic Expressions

The number of terms in a given algebraic expression determines its kind.

An algebraic expression containing only one term is called a monomial (*mono* means one).

An algebraic expression containing two terms is called a binomial (*bi* means two).

An algebraic expression containing three terms is called trinomial (*tri* means three).

An algebraic expression containing many terms is called a polynomial (*poly* means many).

Table No. 11.1

Kind	Number of Terms	Example
Monomial	One	$7x$, $2y$, $-4a$
Binomial	Two	$7x + 5y$, $a + 2b$, $7m^2 + 10n^2$
Trinomial	Three	$ax^2 + bx + c$, $4x + 3y - 7z$
Polynomial	Many	$x^3 + 3x^2 + 3x + 1$

Alert!

1. $4 + y$ means 4 added to y.
2. $4 \times y$ means 4 multiplied by y.
3. $3p^2$ means $3 \times p \times p$.
4. In $x - y$, coefficient of y is (-1).

Question: Why was the maths book very upset?

Answer: Because it had too many problems.

Practice Exercise 11.1

1. Write the following as algebraic expressions.

   a. Seven times y.

   b. 6 plus x.

   c. x^2 plus 2x minus 6.

   d. x plus y is equal to 2.

e. 10 times x plus 4 times y.

f. a is 7 more than b.

g. a is 9 less than c.

h. One-fourth of a number x minus 8.

i. The square of t plus 10.

j. a plus b minus c multiplied by d.

2. Write the following algebraic expressions in words.

a. $x + 7$ b. $2x - 3$ c. $\frac{y + 1}{3}$

d. $\frac{a + b - c}{d}$ e. $(10a + b)c$

3. Write the numerical coefficients of the following algebraic expressions.

a. $10x^2$ b. $7xy$ c. x d. $2a^2b^2$ e. $9mn$

4. Write the coefficient of x in the following algebraic expressions.

a. $25xy$ b. $7y^2 + 3x$ c. $p^2 + q^2 + 2px$

d. $-10x + y$ e. $9xy + 19xy^2$

5. Write the number of terms in each algebraic expression and then identify them as monimial, binomial, trinomial or polynomial.

a. $p^2 + 2pq + q^2$ b. $x^2 - y^2$ c. $8m$

d. $a^2 + b^2 + c^2 + 2ab + 2bc + 2ca$ e. $p \times q \times r$

6. Separate the like terms from the unlike terms.

a. $x^2, x^2y, 3x^2, 7yx^2, zyx$

b. $10pq, 10q, 10p, 10, 7pq$

c. $m, -n, m^2, n^2, 14m, 14m^2n^2$

d. $pqr, 15pqr, -7qr, 8pq, 9pr$

e. $a^2, b^2, c^2, a^2 + b^2 + c^2, 7b^2, -c^2, 10a^2$

7. Complete the table.

Algebraic Expression	Number of Terms	Kind of Algebraic Expression	Factors of each Term
a. $x^2 + y^2$			
b. $ax + by + cz$			
c. $8pqr$			
d. $a^2 + b^2 + c^2 + d^2$			
e. $m^2 - 2mn + n^2$			

8. Pick the like terms and add them.

   a. pq, 7pq, −10pq, pqr b. x^2, $4x^2$, $7x^2y$ c. a, 15a, 20abc, $12a^2$

   d. 5xyz, $10x^2yz$, $15xy^2z$, $25xyz^2$, 30xyz e. m^2, $3m^2$, $-7m^2$, $8m^2$, $5n^2$

9. Write the following statements as algebraic expressions.

   a. One pencil costs ₹5 and a pen costs ₹10. Write the total cost if Rajeev buys x pencils and y pens.
   b. Sana is 2 years older than her sister Sania. Write Sana's age if Sania is p years old.
   c. Sameer thinks of a number, adds 27 to it and then divides it by 10.
   d. Surabhi is h cm tall. Her friend Shamli is 5 cm shorter than Surabhi. Write Shamli's age.
   e. Aman is x years old now. Write his age 7 years from now and 7 years ago. Also write the expression for his mother's age who will be 3 times older than Aman after 7 years.

10. Find the value of the given algebraic expressions.

   a. $a + b + c$ if $a = 5$, $b = 7$, $c = 9$
   b. $pq + qr + rp$ if $p = 2$, $q = 5$, $r = 3$
   c. $m^2 - n^2$ if $m = 5$, $n = 4$
   d. $4a^2 - 12ab + 9b^2$ if $a = 1$, $b = 2$
   e. $x^3 + y^3 + z^3 + 3xyz$ if $x = 1$, $y = 0$, $z = -1$

Higher Order Thinking Skills

HOTS

1. Aruna went to the market with ₹p. She bought an item A for ₹a and item B for ₹b. Express the amount left with her.

2. How many minutes are equal to 5 seconds? Solve using algebra.

3. The number of bacteria in a culture is *x* today. It becomes double of itself after one week. What will be its number after three weeks?

Highlights

- Algebra is a branch of mathematics that involves letters of the alphabet and numbers.
- The letters of the alphabet used in algebraic expressions are called literal numbers.
- Quantities that can change are called variables.
- Quantities that are fixed are called constants.
- Variables are denoted by literal numbers, that is, by letters of the alphabet.
- Constants are denoted by numbers.
- The basic operations of arithmetic are followed in algebra.

  Sum $x + y$

  Difference $x - y$

  Product $x \times y$

  Division $\frac{x}{y}$

- An algebraic expression consists of literal numerals and numbers.
- Types of algebraic expressions

monomial	one term
bionomial	two terms
trinomial	three terms
polynomial	many terms

Understanding Algebra

Objective: To understand algebraic equations.

Material required: Small placards of 5 cm × 5 cm. Each placard in the pools is labelled as follows:

Pool 1	numbers	1 to 9
Pool 2	letters	x, y, z
Pool 3	letters	a, b, c
Pool 4	operations	+, −, ×, ÷

Procedure:

1. Each student has to pick up one placard from each of the pools. The students have four placards each.
2. With the placards, how many equations can you form? Make a list of them.
3. Repeat the activity with a new set of placards from the pools.

CHAPTER 12

Algebraic Equations

What is an Equation?

Equation comes from the word "equal to".

1. When Rita and Gita sit on a see-saw and at one point balance each other's weight, we say that their weights are balanced or equal.

In the first figure, the see-saw is not balanced, whereas in the figure on the right, the see-saw is balanced and is straight.

2. A shopkeeper uses a balance to weigh vegetables. He places some onions on the pan on one side and weights on the other side. If he has to weigh 1 kg of onions, he uses the weight accordingly and keeps increasing or decreasing the number of onions till the weight is balanced.

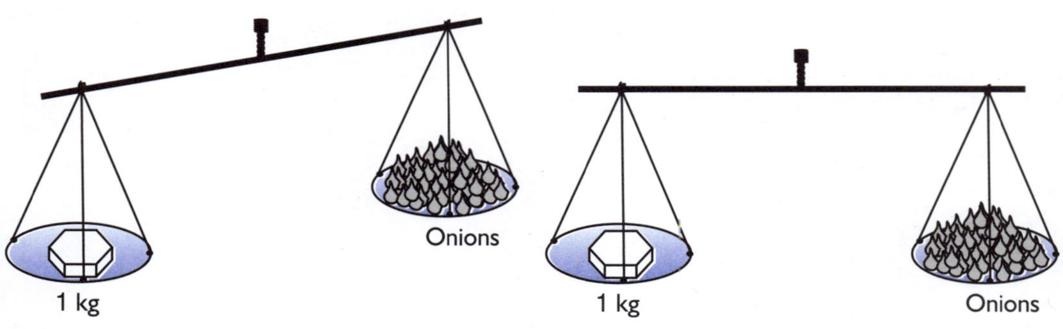

$$2x = 10$$

The equation is a very basic idea in algebra. An equation is like a mathematical sentence in which the amounts on both sides are equal.

We have 2x on the left hand side, 10 on the right hand side of the "equal to" sign. Now we have to find the value of x so that the left hand side is also 10. Can you guess the answer? Yes, it is 5.

Thus, when an algebraic expression is made equal to another algebraic expression, it is called an equation.

The algebraic equation, in such a case is called a linear equation or a simple equation.

Examples of simple equations are:

a. $x + 10 = 25$ b. $y - 25 = 30$ c. $2x + 3 = 11$

d. $\frac{y + 7}{2} = 14$ e. $8p + 2 = 4p + 14$

How to Solve a Linear Equation

Linear equations can be solved by three methods:

1. Trial and error method
2. Systematic method
3. Direct method

Trial and Error Method

To solve an equation, we know that the left-hand side (LHS) should be equal to the right-hand side (RHS). We put different values in the variable so that the LHS is equal to the RHS. As soon as the two sides are equal, we stop the trial. The particular value that makes LHS = RHS is called the solution or root of the equation.

Example 1: $x + 5 = 10$

		LHS		RHS	
	Given	$x + 5$	=	10	
Let	$x = 1$	$1 + 5$	=	6	
	$x = 2$	$2 + 5$	=	7	
	$x = 3$	$3 + 5$	=	8	
	$x = 4$	$4 + 5$	=	9	
	$\boxed{x = 5}$	$5 + 5$	=	10	← We stop here.

The solution of the equation is $x = 5$.

Example 2: $2x - 3 = 5$

		LHS		RHS
	Given	$2x - 3$	=	5
Let	$x = 1$	$2 \times 1 - 3$	=	-1

$x = 2$	$2 \times 2 - 3$	=	1		
$x = 3$	$2 \times 3 - 3$	=	3		
$\boxed{x = 4}$	$2 \times 4 - 3$	=	5	$\leftarrow$	We stop here.

The solution of the equation is $x = 4$.

Example 3: $4y + 8 = 32$

		LHS		RHS		
	Given	$4y + 8$	=	32		
Let	$y = 1$	$4 \times 1 + 8$	=	12		
	$y = 2$	$4 \times 2 + 8$	=	16		
	$y = 3$	$4 \times 3 + 8$	=	20		
	$y = 4$	$4 \times 4 + 8$	=	24		
	$y = 5$	$4 \times 5 + 8$	=	28		
	$\boxed{y = 6}$	$4 \times 6 + 8$	=	32	$\leftarrow$	We stop here.

The solution of the equation is $y = 6$.

Example 4: $\frac{y + 3}{6} = 2$

		LHS		RHS		
	Given	$\frac{y + 3}{6}$	=	2		
Let	$y = 1$	$\frac{1 + 3}{6}$	=	$\frac{4}{6}$		
	$y = 2$	$\frac{2 + 3}{6}$	=	$\frac{5}{6}$		
	$y = 3$	$\frac{3 + 3}{6}$	=	$\frac{6}{6} = 1$		
	$y = 4$	$\frac{4 + 3}{6}$	=	$\frac{7}{6}$		
	$y = 5$	$\frac{5 + 3}{6}$	=	$\frac{8}{6}$		
	$y = 6$	$\frac{6 + 3}{6}$	=	$\frac{9}{6}$		
	$y = 7$	$\frac{7 + 3}{6}$	=	$\frac{10}{6}$		
	$y = 8$	$\frac{8 + 3}{6}$	=	$\frac{11}{6}$		
	$\boxed{y = 9}$	$\frac{9 + 3}{6}$	=	$\frac{12}{6} = 2$	$\leftarrow$	We stop here.

The solution of the given equation is $y = 9$.

Example 5: $\frac{3p}{5} - 1 = 2$

		LHS		RHS
	Given	$\frac{3p}{5} - 1$	=	2
Let	p = 1	$\frac{3 \times 1}{5} - 1$	=	$\frac{3}{5} - 1$
	p = 2	$\frac{3 \times 2}{5} - 1$	=	$\frac{6}{5} - 1$
	p = 3	$\frac{3 \times 3}{5} - 1$	=	$\frac{9}{5} - 1$
	p = 4	$\frac{3 \times 4}{5} - 1$	=	$\frac{12}{5} - 1$
	p = 5	$\frac{3 \times 5}{5} - 1$	=	$\frac{15}{5} - 1 = 3 - 1 = 2$ ← We stop here.

The solution of the equation is p = 5.

The trial and error method is lengthy and tedious.

Systematic Method

In this method, we apply the basic operations of addition, subtraction, multiplication or division on both sides of the equation so that the balance is maintained.

Example 1: $x + 5 = 10$

Subtract 5 from both sides

$x + 5 - 5 = 10 - 5$

$x + 0 = 10 - 5$

$x + 0 = 5$

x = 5 is the solution.

Example 2: $2x - 3 = 5$

Add 3 on both the sides

$2x - 3 + 3 = 5 + 3$

$2x + 0 = 5 + 3$

$2x + 0 = 8$

$2x = 8$

Divide by 2 on both the sides.

$\frac{\cancel{2}x}{\cancel{2}} = \frac{8}{2}$

x = 4 is the solution.

Example 3: $4y + 8 = 32$

Subtract 8 from both the sides.

$$4y + 8 - 8 = 32 - 8$$
$$4y + 0 = 32 - 8$$
$$4y + 0 = 24$$
$$4y = 24$$

Divide both the sides by 4.

$\frac{\cancel{4}y}{\cancel{4}} = \frac{24}{4} = 6$ is the solution.

$$y = 6$$

Example 4: $\frac{y + 3}{6} = 2$

Multiply both the sides by 6.

$$\frac{(y + 3)}{\cancel{6}} \times \cancel{6} = 2 \times 6$$
$$y + 3 = 12$$

Subtract 3 from both the sides.

$$y + 3 - 3 = 12 - 3$$
$$y + 0 = 12 - 3$$
$$y + 0 = 9$$

$y = 9$ is the solution.

Example 5: $\frac{3p}{5} - 1 = 2$

Add one on both the sides.

$$\frac{3p}{5} - 1 + 1 = 2 + 1$$
$$\frac{3p}{5} + 0 = 2 + 1$$
$$\frac{3p}{5} + 0 = 3$$
$$\frac{3p}{5} = 3$$

Multiply both sides by 5.

$$\frac{3p}{\cancel{5}} \times \cancel{5} = 3 \times 5$$
$$3p = 15$$

Divide both sides by 3.

$\frac{\not{3}p}{\not{3}} = \frac{15}{3} = 5$ is the solution.

$p = 5$

Direct Method

In this method, we just shift the numerical value from one side to the other and change the sign, that is,

$+$	becomes	$-$
$-$	becomes	$+$
$\times$	becomes	$\div$
$\div$	becomes	$\times$

This is the simplest way to solve an equation.

Example 1: $x + 5 = 10$

$x = 10 - 5$

$x = 5$

5 is transposed from the LHS to the RHS and the sign is changed from $+$ to $-$.

Example 2: $2x - 3 = 5$

$2x = 5 + 3$

3 is transposed from LHS to RHS and the sign is changed from $-$ to $+$.

$\frac{2x}{2} = \frac{8}{2}$

Divided by 2. $x = \frac{8}{2}$

$x = 4$

Example 3: $4y + 8 = 32$

$4y = 32 - 8$ (+8 changes to −8)

$4y = 24$

$y = \frac{24}{4}$

$y = 6$ (×4 is changed to ÷4)

Example 4: $\frac{y + 3}{6} = \frac{2}{1}$

Multiply by 6 on both the sides.

$y + 3 = 2 \times 6$

$y + 3 = 12$

$y = 12 - 3$

$y = 9$

Example 5: $\frac{3p}{5} - 1 = 2$

$$\frac{3p}{5} = 2 + 1$$

$$\frac{3p}{5} = 3$$

$$3p = 5 \times 3$$

$$3p = 15$$

$$p = \frac{15}{3} = 3$$

The same five examples have been shown by three different methods. You can decide which is the simplest one and use it!

Alert!

1. An equation should always have an "equal to" sign between two expressions.
2. When a term is transposed from one side to the other, the sign of the term changes.

Practice Exercise 12.1

1. Classify the following as algebraic expressions or algebraic equations.

   a. $2x + 3$ b. $3x + 7 = 0$ c. $4m - 3$ d. $8p = 16$ e. 20 m

2. Write the following statements as algebraic equations.

   a. 5 multiplied by x plus three is equal to 23

   b. 10 subtracted from 7x is equal to 95

   c. 4 times a number is equal to 100

   d. One-fifth of a number plus twenty-one is equal to forty-one

   e. The diameter of a circle is twice its radius

3. Solve the following equations by the trial and error method.

   a. $y + 9 = 12$ b. $x - 4 = 2$ c. $5y = 25$

   d. $\frac{3y + 1}{2} = 5$ e. $7x - 3 = 18$

4. Solve the following equations by the systematic method.

a. $2m + 9 = 15$ b. $2k - 20 = 0$ c. $5x - 4 = 31$

d. $\frac{3x + 2}{5} = 1$ e. $8p = 0$

5. Use the direct method to solve the following linear equations.

a. $3x + 12 = 18$ b. $\frac{20y}{5} = 40$ c. $7a - 10 = 4$

d. $3(x - 10) = 9$ e. $\frac{y}{6} = \frac{1}{3}$

6. Solve the following equations.

a. $2x - 7 = x + 5$ b. $3(x - 5) = 2(x + 1)$ c. $0 = 5x - 15$

d. $10 = 3x - 5$ e. $3(x - 2) = 15$

7. A number is increased by 5 and the resulting number is 15. Find the number.
8. The cost of a dozen pens is ₹120. Find the cost of one pen.
9. The sum of three consecutive natural numbers is 45. Find the numbers.
10. Nidhi is four times as old as her daughter Rupali. If the sum of their ages is 55 years, find the ages of Nidhi and Rupali.
11. For a class picnic, the students collected ₹480 for transport. If each student paid ₹8. Find the number of students in the class.
12. In an isosceles triangle two sides are equal. The unequal side is 7 cm. The sum of the three sides is 25 cm. Find the length of the equal sides.

Higher Order Thinking Skills

HOTS

1. Suma is a twice as old as her brother. In 6 years time, the sum of their ages will be 39. What are their ages now?
2. Five times the price of a pen is ₹52 more than three times its price. Find the price of a pen.
3. Can you find the solution to the equation $10 + 10 = 10x - 10$? Give reason for your answer.

Highlights

- A linear equation is an algebraic expression equal to another algebraic expression or a constant.
- An equation has a left hand side (LHS) and a right hand side (RHS) and they are equal.
- A variable that satisfies a given equation is called the solution or root of the equation.
- If we add, subtract, multiply or divide the same number on either side of an equation, the solution (answer) remains unchanged.
- When we transpose a number from one side to the other, we change the sign of the number.

  $+$ becomes $-$

  $-$ becomes $+$

  $\times$ becomes $\div$

  $\div$ becomes $\times$
- A linear equation is also called a simple equation.
- Equations can be solved by the trial and error method, systematic method or the direct method.

Identify two numbers whose product is 48. When the larger number is divided by the smaller number, we get a quotient of 3?

Answer: We can try and find the answer using algebra.

Let us suppose the two number are a and b.

Given: $a \times b = 48$

Given: $\frac{a}{b} = 3$ or $a = 3b$.

So, the greater number is three times the smaller number.

Now, solving the equation for b:

$$a \times b = 48 \text{ or } 3b \times b = 48$$

$$\text{or } b^2 = \frac{48}{3} \quad b^2 = 16, b = 4.$$

$\therefore\ b = 4$.

We know that $a = 3b$

So, $a = 3 \times 4 = 12$

The numbers are 12 and 4.

What's My Equation?

Objective: To understand the concept of balancing an equation.

Material required: Paper and pen

Procedure:

A list of equations is provided. Simplify each equation to its simplest form.

a. 125 less than my number is 500. What is my number?

b. My number is $\frac{1}{2}$ of 54 minus 6.

c. Multiply my number by 3 and you have 240.

d. Nine times my number is the same as 2×27.

e. John is 7 years older than his brother. If their combined age is 31, what are their ages?

f. Twice a number subtracted by 3 is 18.

g. A number x plus 22.2 is equal to 38.6.

h. Thrice a number plus 4 is 32.

i. Two times five added to three times eight gives a number.

j. The length of a rectangular paper is twice its breadth.

Complete the table with the operation corresponding to the word given. The first one is done for you.

	Word	Operation
1.	less than	subtraction
2.	of	
3.	multiply	
4.	times	
5.	combined	
6.	sum	
7.	difference	
8.	product	
9.	total	
10.	more than	

CHAPTERS 11–12

Rewind

1. Fill in the blanks:

   a. The coefficient of "a" in 7ab is ____________.

   b. Three times x increased by five is ____________.

   c. a^2b and ab^2 are ____________ terms.

   d. 6x and (−6x) are ____________ terms.

   e. The coefficient of x is ____________.

2. Identify the following expressions as monomial, binomial or trinomial terms.

   a. $4pqr$ b. $4p + 4r$ c. $4p^2 + 8pq + 4q^2$

   d. $-20x^2$ e. $x^2 + y^2$

3. Write algebraic equations for the following statements.

   a. The product of 3 and 5 added to ten is equal to twenty-five.

   b. Half of x plus 7 is equal to 21.

   c. "p" divided by 4 and decreased by 2 is equal to 6.

   d. Three times the sum of x and y is 27.

   e. The square of a number x is equal to forty-nine.

4. Balance the equations choosing the correct value from the options given in brackets.

   a. $x + 3 = 12$ (3, 4, 9, 7)

   b. $y - 4 = 7$ (3, 11, 5, 2)

   c. $8x = 72$ (8, 1, 9, 6)

   d. $2a + 5 = 15$ (3, 6, 5, 4)

   e. $b - 25 = 10$ (15, 0, 35, 25)

5. Solve the following equations.

   a. $3x - 4 = 14$ b. $7(m + 5) = 42$ c. $\frac{y}{3} - 9 = 8$

   d. $\frac{x - 3}{5} = 4$ e. $3(p + 2) - 2(p + 5) = 8$

Rewind

CHAPTERS 11–12

6. If a number is multiplied by 18 and 12 is added to it, we get 120. Find the number.

7. Ajit is 8 years younger than his brother, Akhil. If the sum of their ages is 32, find their ages.

8. Five times the price of a book is ₹150 more than three times its price. Find the price of the book.

9. The sum of three consective odd numbers is 135. Find the numbers.

10. The length of a rectangular field is 3 times its breadth. If the perimeter of the rectangle is 56 m, find its length and breadth.

CHAPTER 13 Ratio and Proportion

We can compare two things by subtraction or by division.

Who is taller and by how much?

Reena is taller than Seema by 25 cm. How did we arrive at the answer? We subtracted Seema's height from Reena's. Another way of comparing their heights is by division.

$$\frac{\text{Seema's height}}{\text{Reena's height}} = \frac{100\text{ cm}}{125\text{ cm}} = \frac{4}{5}$$

Seema is $\frac{4}{5}$th Reena's height.

Example: Anuj has 5 kites and Tanuj has 10 kites.

Who has more kites?

How many more kites does Tanuj have than Anuj?

$$10 - 5 = 5\text{ kites}$$

We can also compare the information by saying that Tanuj has twice the number of kites that Anuj has or Anuj has half the number of kites that Tanuj has.

$$\frac{\text{Number of kites that Anuj has}}{\text{Number of kites that Tanuj has}} = \frac{5}{10} = \frac{1}{2}$$

This comparison is by division.

Ratio is the comparison of two like things by division.

It is written as a fraction.

Hence, if two things are to be compared, the units should be the same.

Ratio is a pure number. It has no units!

Example 1: Rohit is 3 years old. His brother Mohit is 6 years old. Compare their ages.

$$\frac{\text{Rohit's age}}{\text{Mohit's age}} = \frac{3\text{ years}}{6\text{ years}} = \frac{3}{6} = \frac{1}{2}$$

The ratio of Rohit's age to Mohit's age is 1:2

1:2 is read as "one is to two".

$$\frac{\text{Mohit's age}}{\text{Rohit's age}} = \frac{6\text{ years}}{3\text{ years}} = \frac{6}{3} = 2$$

The ratio of Mohit's age to Rohit's age is 2:1

2:1 is read as "two is to one".

The ratio $\frac{1}{2}$ is not equal to $\frac{2}{1}$.

Example 2: The time taken by Gopi to reach school is 1 hour and the time taken by Gunjan to reach school is 40 minutes. Compare the time taken by the two students to reach school.

$$\frac{\text{Time taken by Gopi to reach school}}{\text{Time taken by Gunjan to reach school}} = \frac{1 \text{ hr}}{40 \text{ minutes}}$$

$$= \frac{60 \text{ minutes}}{40 \text{ minutes}} = \frac{60}{40} = \frac{6}{4} = \frac{3}{2}.$$

Gopi : Gunjan = 3:2

$$\frac{\text{Time taken by Gunjan to reach school}}{\text{Time taken by Gopi to reach school}} = \frac{40 \text{ minutes}}{1 \text{hr}}$$

$$= \frac{40 \text{ minutes}}{60 \text{ minutes}} = \frac{40}{60} = \frac{4}{6} = \frac{2}{3}$$

Gunjan : Gopi = 2:3

The ratio 3:2 is not equal to 2:3.

It is important to note here that the units should be the same. Hence 1 hour has been converted to 60 minutes in this example.

Any ratio can be written in the form of a fraction $\frac{p}{q}$.

p: the numerator is called the antecedent.

q: the denominator is called the consequent.

Comparison Of Two Ratios

1. Two ratios can be compared by making the consequents (the denominators) the same.
2. To make the consequents the same, find the LCM of the denominators.
3. Then, the ratio with the greater antecedent (the numerator) is greater.

Example: Compare ratios 5:12 and 3:20

$5:12 = \frac{5}{12}$ and $3:20 = \frac{3}{20}$

The LCM of 12 and 20 is 60.

$$\frac{5}{12} = \frac{25}{60} \quad \text{and} \quad \frac{3}{20} = \frac{9}{60}$$

$$\frac{25}{60} > \frac{9}{60}$$

Therefore 5:12 > 3:20.

Practice Exercise 13.1

1. Express the following ratios as fractions and reduce them to the lowest form.

   a. 12:36 b. 27:81 c. 44:77 d. 15:95 e. 14:91

2. Write the given ratios in the simplest form.

   a. 15 cm to 35 cm b. ₹10 to ₹28 c. 40 kg to 160 kg

   d. 80 seconds to 16 seconds e. 30 chocolates to 50 chocolates

3. Write the following ratios in the simplest form.

   a. 1hr 15 min : 45 min

   b. ₹2.50 : ₹4.50

   c. 150 p : ₹2

   d. 3 months : 1 year 3 months

   e. 1 dozen : 1 score

4. Identify the larger ratio in the following pairs.

   a. 4:7, 15:28 b. 6:22, 9:11 c. 3:10, 2:15

   d. 7:9, 5:81 e. 5:32, 7:144

5. Write the following ratios in descending order.

   a. 1:2, 2:3, 3:4 b. 7:9, 9:11, 2:3 c. 5:7, 6:13, 3:14

   d. 3:10, 7:20, 11:30 e. 3:8, 5:24, 7:48

6. The ratio of the number of girls to boys in a class is 6:11. If the total number of students in the class is 51, find the number of girls in the class.

7. A box contains some lollypops and chocolates. They are in the ratio of 7:9. If the total number of items in the box is 480, find the number of each variety.

8. Given that a teacher earns ₹45,000 a month and that her monthly expenditure is ₹30,000, answer the following questions.

   a. What is the ratio of her expenditure to her income?

   b. What is the ratio of her savings to her income?

   c. What is the ratio of her savings to her expenditure?

9. A survey was done to find the number of families who read two popular newspapers—*The Times of India* (*TOI*) and *Hindustan Times* (*HT*)—in a residential colony. Six hundred families were surveyed. The survey revealed that 350 families read *TOI* while 250 families read *HT*. Find the ratio of:

   a. The readers of *HT* to the readers of *TOI*.

   b. The readers of *HT* to the total number of families surveyed.

   c. The readers of *TOI* to the total number of families surveyed.

   d. Which is the larger ratio–the ratio in answer b, or the ratio in answer c?

10. Divide ₹720 among A, B and C in the ratio 5:4:9.

Proportion

When two ratios are equal, they are said to be in proportion.

Hence, proportion is the equality of two ratios.

If two ratios, a:b and c:d are equal, we can write them as a:b = c:d or

$$\frac{a}{b} = \frac{c}{d}$$

The symbol used for proportion is ::

Hence a:b = c:d is written as
a:b :: c:d

Here, a is the first term, b is the second term, c is the third term and d is the fourth term.

The first and the fourth terms are called the extremes because they are at the ends.

The second and the third terms are called the means because they are in the middle.

$$\frac{a}{b} = \frac{c}{d}$$

$$ad = bc$$

Product of the extremes = Product of the means

If four terms are in proportion, the product of the extremes = product of the means.

Continued Proportion

If the second term and the third term are the same, then the proportion is called continued proportion.

$$a:b :: b:c$$

$$\frac{a}{b} = \frac{b}{c} \quad b^2 = ac$$

$b^2 = ac$ is called the mean proportion.

Also, since the second term and third term are the same, the fourth term is called the third proportion.

So, in a continued proportion:

1. second term = third term.
2. $b^2 = ac$ is called the mean proportion.
3. The fourth term c is called the third proportion.

Example 1: Find x, where 3:x :: 4:12.

$$3:x = 4:12$$

$$\frac{3}{x} = \frac{4}{12}$$

$$4x = 3 \times 12$$

$$x = \frac{3 \times \cancel{12}^{3}}{\cancel{4}} = 9$$

$$x = 9.$$

Example 2: If 10, 20 and c are in continued proportion, find the third proportion or c.

$$10:20 :: 20:c$$

or $$\frac{10}{20} = \frac{20}{c}$$

$$10c = 20 \times 20$$

or $$c = \frac{20 \times 20}{10} = 40$$

The third proportion = 40.

Example 3: Find the mean proportion of the following numbers: 5, 20.

5:x : : x:20 or $\frac{5}{x} = \frac{x}{20}$ or $x^2 = 100$ $\boxed{x = 10}$

Example 4: The cost of one dozen pencils is ₹60. How much will 75 pencils cost?

Let the cost of 75 pencils be ₹x.

Pencils	Cost (in ₹)
12	60
75	x

There are two ways to solve this problem.

To write this as a ratio:	This can also be solved as:
$12:60 :: 75:x$	$12:75 :: 60:x$
or $12:60 = 75:x$	or $12:75 = 60:x$
or $\frac{12}{60} = \frac{75}{x}$	or $\frac{12}{75} = \frac{60}{x}$
or $12x = 60 \times 75$	or $12x = 75 \times 60$
$x = \frac{\overset{5}{\cancel{60}} \times 75}{\cancel{12}}$	$x = \frac{75 \times \overset{5}{\cancel{60}}}{\cancel{12}}$
$x = ₹375$	$x = ₹375$

Example 5: Rohit drives his car at a constant speed of 50 km/hr. How long does he take to reach his office from home if the distance is 35 km?

Rohit covers 50 km in 1 hour (60 mins)

Rohit cover 35 km in x min

Distance	Time
50 km	1 hr = 60 min
35 km	x

To write this as a ratio:	This can also be solved as:
$50:35 :: 60:x$	$50:60 :: 35:x$
or $50:35 = 60:x$	or $50:60 = 35:x$
or $\frac{50}{35} = \frac{60}{x}$	or $\frac{50}{60} = \frac{35}{x}$
or $50x = 60 \times 35$	or $50x = 35 \times 60$
or $x = \frac{6\cancel{0} \times \overset{7}{\cancel{35}}}{5\cancel{0}}$	or $x = \frac{\overset{7}{\cancel{35}} \times 6\cancel{0}}{5\cancel{0}}$
$x = 42$ min	$x = 42$ min

Practice Exercise 13.2

1. Fill in the blanks so that the four terms are in proportion.

   a. ______ :4 :: 32:16
   b. ______ 5 :: 15:25
   c. 18: ______ :: 10:5
   d. 30: ______ :: 24:12
   e. 7:15 :: ______ :30
   f. 9:12 :: ______ :8
   g. 8:20 :: 16: ______
   h. 5:7 :: 35: ______
   i. ______ :36 :: 4:12
   j. 7:105 :: ______ :15

2. Which of the following ratios are in proportion?

   a. 4, 7, 5, 9 b. 5, 25, 6, 30 c. 21, 7, 81, 9 d. 15, 40, 3, 8 e. 8, 15, 5, 9

3. Write the given three numbers in continued proportion.

   a. 3, 9, 27 b. 12, 36, 108 c. 2, 8, 32 d. 10, 15, 20 e. 4, 6, 9

4. Find the mean proportion of the following.

   a. 9, 81 b. 5, 45 c. 4, 16 d. 4, 100 e. 12, 48

5. Find the value of x in the following questions given that the three number are in continued proportion.

   a. x, 8 and 64 b. 25, x and 4 c. 36, x, 49
   d. 6, 18, x e. 4, 20 and x

6. A gardener plants 16 trees in 4 hours. How many trees will he plant in 6 hours?

7. In a hostel canteen, 10 kg of sugar is sanctioned for 21 students in a week. How much sugar will be required for 441 students?

8. The cost of 15 watches is ₹75,000. What will be the cost of 28 watches?

9. A car travels 165 km in 3 hours. How long will it take to travel 330 km, if it is moving at a constant speed?

10. A carpenter makes 54 tables in 18 days. In how many days can he make 24 tables working at the same rate?

Unitary Method

Unitary comes from the word "unit." In the unitary method, we find the value of a single unit (or one unit) and then find the value of the desired quantity.

All questions that have been solved using the proportion method can also be solved using the unitary method. Here we use the intermediate step of finding the value of a single item and then proceeding ahead.

Example 1: The cost of 5 kg of apples is ₹300. Find the cost of 8 kg of apples.

Cost of 5 kg of apples = ₹300

The cost of 1 kg apples = ₹$\frac{300}{5}$ = ₹60

We divide to get the cost of 1 unit, that is 1 kg.

The cost of 1 kg apples = ₹60

∴ The cost of 8 kg apples = 60×8 = ₹480

We multiply the unit cost with the quantity whose price we need to find out.

Example 2: The cost of 8 pens is ₹80. What will be the cost of 13 pens?

Cost of 8 pens = ₹80

∴ The cost of 1 pen = ₹$\frac{80}{8}$ = ₹10

Cost of 13 pens = ₹10 $\times 13$ = ₹130

Example 3: Anita can read 12 pages of a book in 3 minutes. How many pages will she complete in 2 hours?

In 3 minutes she reads 12 pages of a book.

∴ in 1 minute she reads $\frac{12}{3} = 4$ pages

∴ in 2 hrs (2×60 minutes) she will read

= 120 minutes $\quad 4 \times 120 = 480$ pages

Practice Exercise 13.3

1. If 15 litre of petrol is consumed by a car in covering a distance of 250 km, how many kilometers will it go with 40 litres of petrol?
2. A basket of 25 kg of oranges costs ₹400. How much will 18 kg of oranges cost?
3. Class VI-A collected ₹3,500 from 50 students for an excursion. In Class VI-B there are 44 students. How much money will the class contribute for the same excursion if the same amount of money is collected from each student?

4. Ann earns ₹45,000 in 30 days. How much will be earned in a week?

5. Two dozen eggs cost ₹180. Find the cost of 30 eggs.

6. 15 litres of juice can fill 100 small glasses. How many litres of juice will be required to fill 350 glasses?

7. Rita brought 15 stamps for ₹225 from the post office. How many stamps can she buy for ₹470?

8. Jagat pays ₹9,600 as rent for a quarter of a year. What will the rent be for a year?

9. A factory produces jute bags. In one year it can produce 2,700 bags. How many bags can it produce in 30 months?

10. Forty-five cartons are required to pack 9,000 mathematics books to be sent to a school. If 1,200 more books are required, how many more cartons will be needed?

Higher Order Thinking Skills

HOTS

1. The scale of a map is 1:30,00,000. What is the actual distance between two cities A and B, if they are shown 4 cm apart on the map?

2. If 16 loaves of bread, each weighing 400 g cost ₹200, find the cost of 20 loaves of bread each weighing 500 g.

3. If 30 men can weave 450 m of cloth in a day, how many metres of cloth can be woven by 12 men in a day?

As I was going to St. Ives,
I met a man with seven wives,
Every wife had seven sacks,
Every sack had seven cats,
Every cat had seven kits,
Kits, cats, sacks and wives,
How many were going to St. Ives?

Answer for Brainteaser on page 216

Highlights

- The ratio of a number p to another number q ($q \neq 0$) is a fraction $\frac{p}{q}$ and is written as p:q.
- The ratio of two numbers is expressed in its simplest form.
- A ratio has no units.
- A ratio is the comparison between two similar quantities.
- When two ratios are equal, they are said to be in proportion.

  If a:b = c:d, then we say that the two ratios are in proportion.
- The symbol for proportion is a:b :: c:d.
- The first and fourth terms of a proportion are called extremes, the second and third terms are called means.
- If a, b, c, d are in proportion, then a:b :: c:d

  or a:b = c:d

  or $\frac{a}{b} = \frac{c}{d}$

  or ad = bc

  that is, the product of the extremes = the product of the means
- If a, b, c are in continued proportions, then a:b :: b:c and $ac = b^2$.
- In continued proportion, the second term is called the mean proportion as the second and third terms are the same. The fourth terms is called the third proportion.
- The unitary method is the method of finding the value of a single item. The values of the desired quantity can then be found out.

Maths Lab Activity

How Do You Spend Your Day?

Objective: To understand the concept of ratio.

Material required: A sheet of paper and coloured sketch pens

Procedure:

1. Write the number of hours you spend engaged in different activities during the day using different coloured sketch pens.

sleeping	eating
playing	on the computer
at school	other activities
watching TV	on the telephone

2. Now, find the ratio of the time spent on each activity to the total time in one day.
3. You can also find the ratios between any two different activites.

Answer for Brainteaser on page 214

Only one person.....I was going to St. Ives!

Rewind

1. Find the ratio of:

   a. 25 to 100   b. 60 paise to ₹6   c. 35 minutes to 1 hr

   d. 200 ml to 1 ℓ   e. 40 cm to 1 metre

2. The number of boys and girls in a school are 2100 and 1800, respectively. Express the ratio of the number of boys to that of girls in the simplest form.

3. The ratio of milk and chocolate powder in a chocolate cookie is 5:2. Find the weight of each in a chocolate cookie whose weight is 700 grams.

4. A sum of ₹10,500 is to be divided between three friends Humpty, Dumpty and Grumpy in the ratio 3:5:7. Find the share of each.

5. Ashima's monthly salary is ₹56,000. She saves ₹8,000 per month. Find the ratio of:

   (i) her savings to her earnings.

   (ii) her earning to her expenditure.

   (iii) her savings to her expenditure.

6. Find the value of x in the following.

   a. 11: 33 :: x:45   b. 85:51 :: x:57   c. 29:x :: 11:55

   d. x:124 :: 12:48   e. 18:14 :: 90:x

7. a. Find the third proportion of the following.

   (i) 15, 45   (ii) 10, 20   (iii) 14, 42

   b. Find the mean proportion between the following.

   (i) 16 and 25   (ii) 25 and 144   (iii) 64 and 81

8. If 2 dozen bananas cost ₹45, find the cost of 5 dozen bananas.

9. 10 labourers can repair a road in 25 days. In how many days will 50 labourers repair it?

10. If 15 litres of petrol is consumed by a car in covering a distance of 250 km, how many kilometres it will cover with 45 litres of petrol?

CHAPTER 14

Perimeter and Area

Perimeter

The perimeter of any closed figure is the sum of all its bounding sides or the sum of the lengths of its bounding sides.

Example:

Radha wants to make a triangular lawn outside her house. She asks the gardener to put bricks around the triangle. The number of bricks used will depend on the total length of the boundary. How will the gardener measure the boundary?

The boundary or perimeter = AB + BC + CA

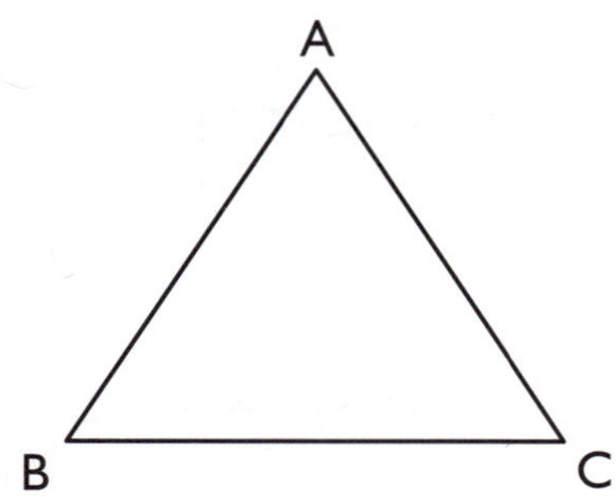

Thus, the perimeter of any closed figure is the sum of its sides.

We can find the perimeter of any closed rectilinear figure like a rectangle, square, triangle, hexagon, etc.

Formulae Used to Calculate the Perimeter of Closed Figures

1. Perimeter of a Triangle

The sides of a $\triangle$ABC are a, b and c.

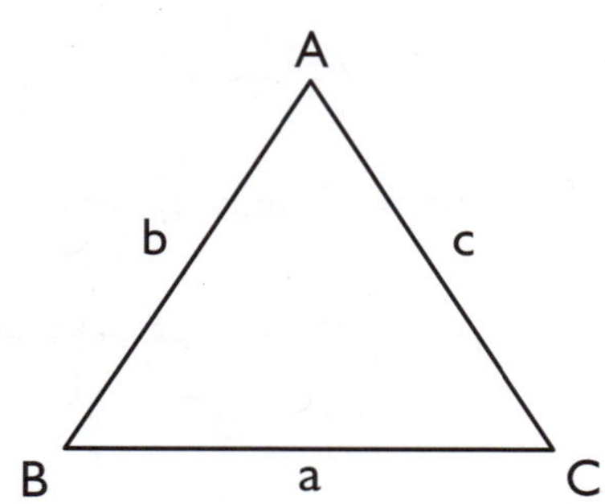

Perimeter $= AB + BC + CA$

$= c + a + b$
$= a + b + c$ units

Perimeter of a triangle $= (a + b + c)$ units

2. Perimeter of a Square

The sides of a square are equal. Let each side be of length ℓ.

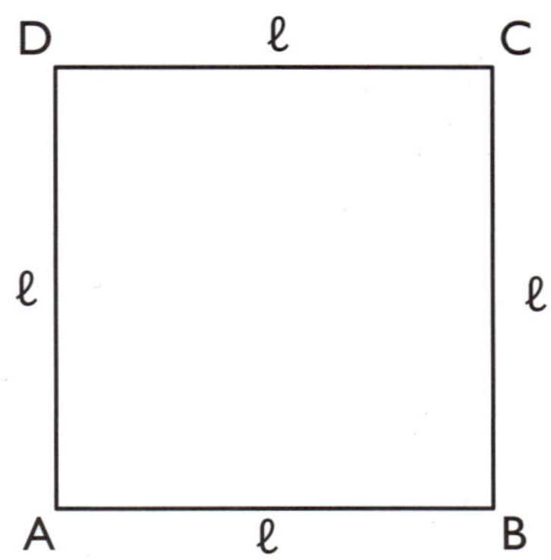

The perimeter of the square ABCD $= AB + BC + CD + DA$
$= \ell + \ell + \ell + \ell$
$= 4\ell$ units

∴ Perimeter of a square is 4ℓ units.

3. Perimeter of a Rectangle

The opposite sides of a rectangle are equal.

Let the adjacent sides be denoted by ℓ and b.

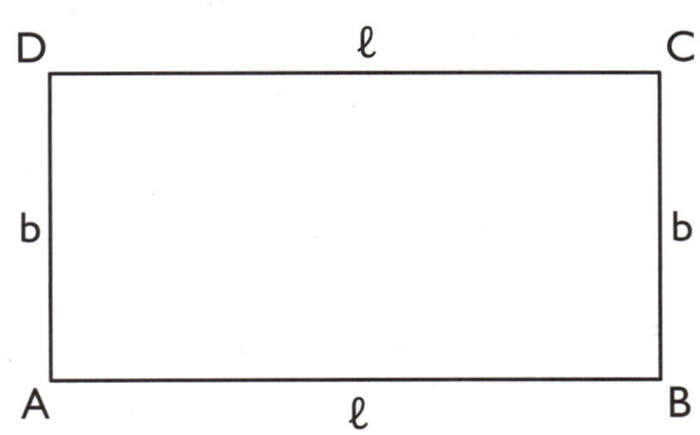

The perimeter of the rectangle ABCD $= AB + BC + CD + DA$
$= \ell + b + \ell + b$
$= 2\ell + 2b$
$= 2(\ell + b)$ units.

∴ Perimeter of a rectangle is $2(\ell + b)$ units.

4. Perimeter of a Regular Polygon

A *regular* polygon is a polygon whose sides are all equal.

Example:

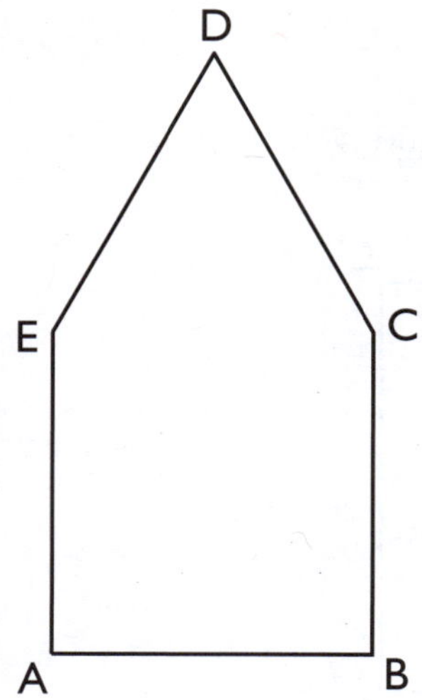

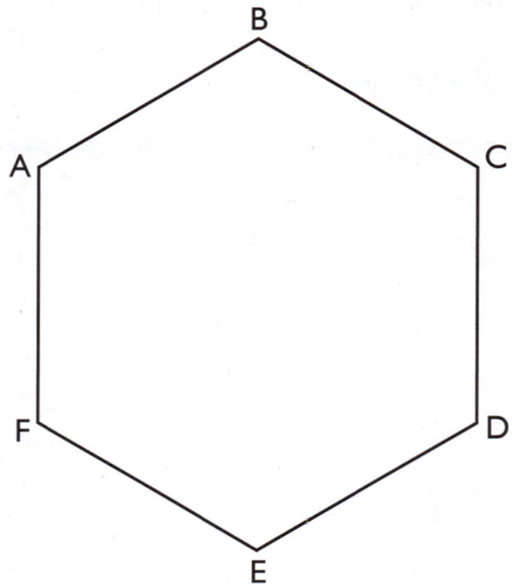

Perimeter of a pentagon = AB + BC + CD + DE + EA

Perimeter of a hexagon = AB + BC + CD + DE + EF + FA

$\therefore$ Perimeter of a regular polygon = Number of sides $\times$ Length of the sides

The perimeter of figures having different sizes can be the same. For example, we consider the three rectangles shown below.

The rectangles have different lengths and breadths, however, the perimeters are the same.

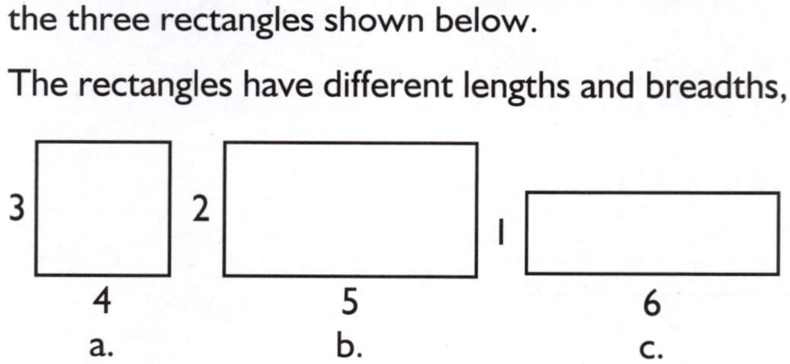

a. $p = 2(\ell + b) = p = 2(4 + 3) = 14$

b. $p = 2(\ell + b) = p = 2(5 + 2) = 14$

c. $p = 2(\ell + b) = p = 2(6 + 1) = 14$

Example 1: Find the perimeter of a rectangular plot of land whose length is 1 km and breadth is 300 m.

Length is 1 km = 1,000 m

Breadth is 300 m

Perimeter of the rectangular plot $= 2[\ell + b]$

$= 2[1000 \text{ m} + 300 \text{ m}]$

$= 2[1,300] \text{ m}$

$= 2,600 \text{ m}$

$= 2 \text{ km } 600 \text{ m}$

Example 2: Find the perimeter of a regular octagonal field whose side is 40 m.

A regular octagon has 8 sides.

Perimeter of a regular octagon = 8 × length of side

= 8 × 40 m

= 320 m

Example 3: A triangular park has sides 60 m, 50 m and 40 m. How much wire will be required to put a fence round the park? What will be the cost of fencing, if the wire costs ₹25 per metre?

Perimeter of the triangle = Sum of its sides

= a + b + c

= 60 m + 50 m + 40 m

= 150 m

∴ The length of wire required is = 150 m

Cost of fencing = ₹25 × 150 m

= ₹3,750

Example 4: The perimeter of square park is 1,250 m. What is the length of each side?

Perimeter of a square is = 4 × sides

$$1250 \text{ m} = 4 \times \ell$$

$$\therefore \quad \ell = \frac{1250}{4} = 312.5 \text{ m}$$

Example 5: Tarun and Arun go jogging in the morning. They both jog the same distance. Tarun goes around a pentagonal park of side 30 m. Arun jogs around a rectangular park of breadth 15 m. What is the length of the park that Arun jogs around?

Perimeter of a regular pentagon = 5 × length of a side

= 5 × 30 m

= 150 m

Tarun jogs a distance of 150 m.

Arun also jogs the same distance but around a rectangular park.

Perimeter of a rectangle = $2(\ell + b)$

$$150 \text{ m} = 2[\ell + 15]$$

$$150 \text{ m} = 2\ell + 30$$

$$150 - 30 = 2\ell$$

$$120 = 2\ell$$

$$60 \text{ m} = \frac{120}{2} = \ell$$

So, the length of the park that Arun jogs around is 60 m.

Practice Exercise 14.1

1. Find the perimeter of the following figures. (All lengths are in cm.)

a. 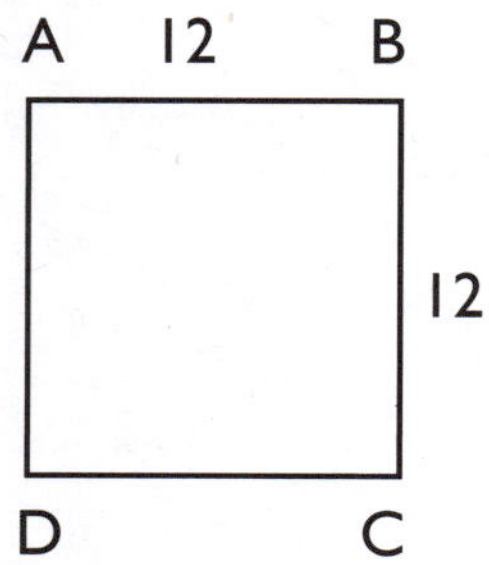

b. 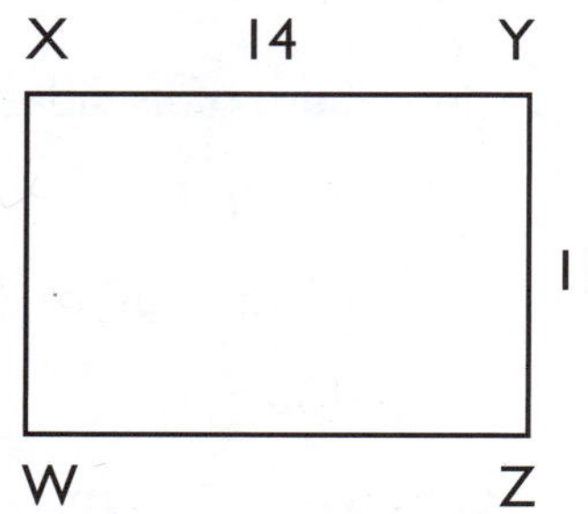

c. 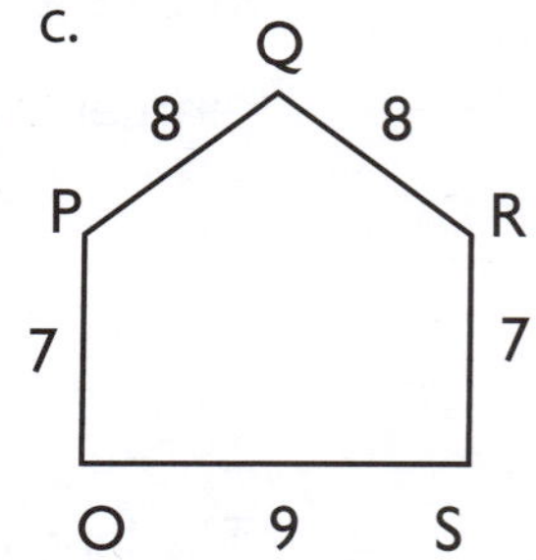

2. Find the perimeter of the following triangles.

   a. A triangle with sides 13 cm, 9 cm and 5 cm.

   b. An equilateral triangle with side 7 cm.

   c. An isosceles triangle with two equal sides of 9 cm each and the third side of 6 cm.

3. Find the sides of the following figures whose perimeters are given.

   a. The side of a regular pentagon whose perimeter is 60 cm.

   b. The side of a regular septagon whose perimeter is 63 cm.

   c. The side of a regular decagon whose perimeter is 200 cm.

4. A rectangular painting of 28 cm length and 12 cm breadth has to be framed. What will be the cost of framing it, if the wood strip costs ₹15 per cm?

5. Anita takes her pet dog for a walk around a square park. The side of the square park is 25 m. How many metres does she cover in 4 rounds of the park?

6. Raj takes 4 rounds of a rectangular park of length 60 m and breadth 15 m and Rani takes 3 rounds of a square park whose side is 35 m. Who covers more distance and by how much?

7. How many trees can be planted at a distance of 8 m each around a rectangular field whose length is 150 m and breadth 90 m?

8. A park is in the form of a regular hexagon of side 35 m. Find the cost of fencing it at the rate of ₹3.50 per metre.

9. The cost of making a boundary line with paint around a square field is ₹1,250 at the rate of ₹25 per metre. Find the length of the side of the field.

10. After walking 3 times along the boundary of a triangular park with equal sides, Manpreet finds that he has walked 2,250 m. Find the length of each side of the park.

Area of a Plane Figure

The space enclosed within the boundary of any figure is called the area.

Example:

ABCD is a rectangle. The boundary ABCD is the perimeter of the rectangle.

The shaded region within the boundary is the area of the rectangle.

We can easily calculate the area of a rectangle using graph paper.

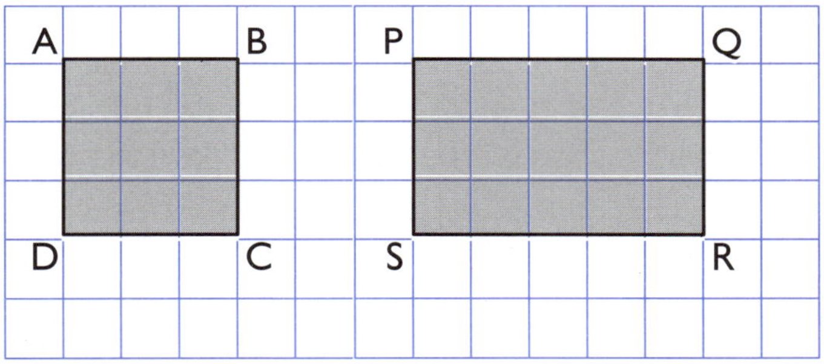

Let us find the area of the figures given above.

1. Area of ABCD = 3 squares length wise × 3 squares breadth wise
   = 9 sq cm (each length is in cm)
2. Area of PQRS = 5 squares length wise × 3 squares breadth wise
   = 15 sq cm

Thus, area of a rectangle = $\ell \times b$ square (sq) units

A square has length = breadth

that is $\ell = b$.

Area of a square $= \ell \times \ell$ sq units

$= \ell^2$ sq units

$=$ side $\times$ side sq units

Example 1: Find the area of a handkerchief each side of which is 11 cm.

Area of a square = side × side

= length × length

= 11 cm × 11 cm

= 121 cm^2 or 121 sq cm

Example 2: Find the area of rectangular park whose length is 20 m and breadth 15 m.

Area of a rectangle $= \ell \times b$

= 20 m × 15 m

= 300 m^2 or 300 sq m.

Example 3: Find the cost of painting the ceiling of a room at the rate of ₹15 per m^2 if the length is 15 m and the breadth 12 m.

Area of the ceiling $= \ell \times b$

= 15 m × 12 m

= 180 m^2 or 180 sq m.

Cost of painting is ₹15 per m^2.

$\therefore$ Total cost = 180 × 15 = ₹2,700.

Example 4: A rectangular courtyard has to be paved with marble. The length of the courtyard is 25 m and its width is 18 m. The size of each marble slab is 9 sq m. How many marble slabs will be required to pave the courtyard?

Area of the rectangular courtyard $= \ell \times b$

= 25 m × 18 m

Area of a marble slab = 9 m^2

Number of marble slabs required $= \dfrac{\text{Area of the courtyard}}{\text{Area of each marble slab}}$

$= \dfrac{25 \times \cancel{18}^{\,2}}{\cancel{9}} = 50$ marble slabs

Example 5: Arjun has a colourful sheet of paper of size 22 cm in length and 16 cm in breadth. He has to paste photographs of all his classmates on it. The size of each photograph is 4 cm × 2 cm. How many photographs can he paste on one sheet? How many students are there in Arjun's class?

Area of the sheet of paper = 22 cm × 16 cm

Area of a photograph = 4 cm × 2 cm

Number of photographs on one sheet $= \dfrac{\text{Area of sheet of paper}}{\text{Area of each photograph}}$

$$= \frac{\overset{11}{\cancel{22}} \times \overset{4}{\cancel{16}}}{\cancel{4} \times \cancel{2}} = 44 \text{ photographs}$$

Number of students in Arjun's class = Total number of Arjun's classmates + Arjun

$= 44 + 1$

$= 45$

Practice Exercise 14.2

1. The measure of the side of three squares are given here. Find the area of each square.

   a. 15 m b. 1 m 10 cm c. 7.5 cm

2. Find the area of a rectangular grassland whose length is 27 m and breadth 15 m.
3. Find the cost of a plot of land that is 45 m long and 33 m broad given that the cost of land is ₹6,500 per square metre.
4. 500 square tiles of side 25 cm are laid across the hall of a room. What is the area of the hall in sq m?
5. A rectangle is 81 m long and 36 m broad. Find the side of a square whose area is equal to the area of this rectangle.
6. A room has a floor area of 15 m by 10 m. A square carpet of side 7 m is laid on the floor. How much of the floor area is not carpeted?
7. In a rectangular park having a length of 45 m and width of 18 m, four corners of 3^2 m are demarcated for planting trees. Find the area of the park that can be used by the children for playing.

AB = DC = 45 m AD = BC = 18 m

8. The perimeter of a square lawn is 100 m. Find the area of the square lawn. What will be cost of planting grass in the lawn at the rate of ₹13 per sq m?

9. Mr Gupta and Mr Mathur want to buy a plot of land each. The property dealer has a square plot and a rectangular plot of the same perimeter. The rectangular plot is 80 m long and 30 m broad, which Mr Gupta wants to buy. Does Mr Mathur get the larger plot or the smaller one, and what is the difference in size?

10. A rectangular field is 75 m long and its breadth is 15 m less than its length. Find the cost of fencing it at the rate of ₹4 per metre. Also find the cost of turfing it at the rate of ₹7 per sq m.

Conversion of units:

Units of length	Units of area
1 cm = 10 mm	$1 \text{ cm}^2 = (10 \times 10) \text{ mm}^2 = 100 \text{ mm}^2$
1 m = 100 cm	$1 \text{ m}^2 = (100 \times 100) \text{ cm}^2 = 10{,}000 \text{ cm}^2$
1 dm = 10 cm	$1 \text{ dm}^2 = (10 \times 10) \text{ cm}^2 = 100 \text{ cm}^2$
1 dam = 10 m	$1 \text{ dam}^2 = (10 \times 10) \text{ m}^2 = 100 \text{ m}^2$
1 km = 10 hm	$1 \text{ km}^2 = (10 \times 10) \text{ hm}^2 = 100 \text{ hm}^2$
1 km = 1000 m	$1 \text{ km}^2 = (1000 \times 1000) \text{ m}^2 = 1000000 \text{ m}^2$

Larger units of area

1 are = 100 m^2 and 1 hectare = 10,000 m^2

100 ares = 1 hectare 100 hectares = 1 sq. km

Higher Order Thinking Skills

HOTS

1. How many times will a boy have to run round a square park whose length is 60 metres to cover a distance of 6 km?

2. A rectangle is 16 m by 9 m. Find the side of a square whose area equals the area of the rectangle. By how much does the perimeter of the rectangle exceed the perimeter of the square?

3. What happens to the area of a rectangle if its length is halved and its breadth is doubled?

Highlights

- The total length of the boundary of a closed figure is called its perimeter.

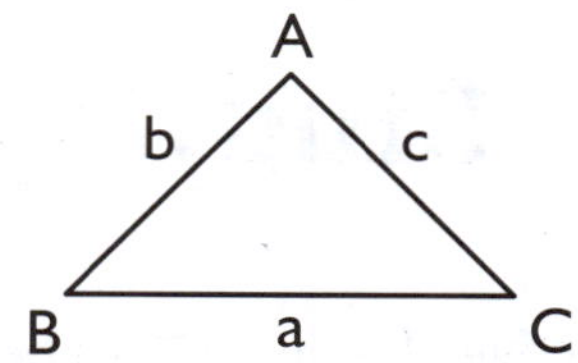

- The perimeter of a triangle is the sum of its sides.
  P = a + b + c units.

- The perimeter of a rectangle is p = 2[ℓ + b] units.

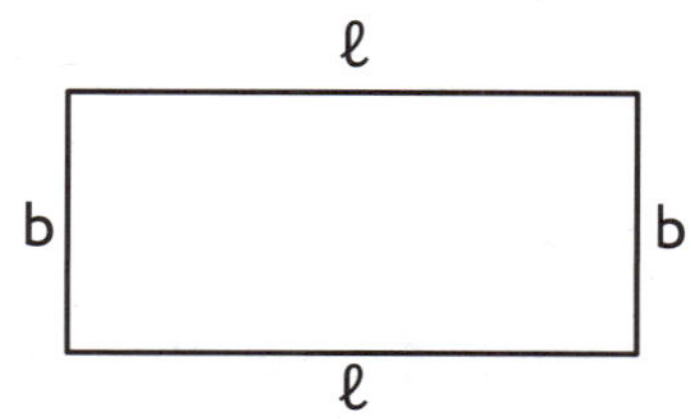

- The perimeter of a square is p = 4ℓ units (side).

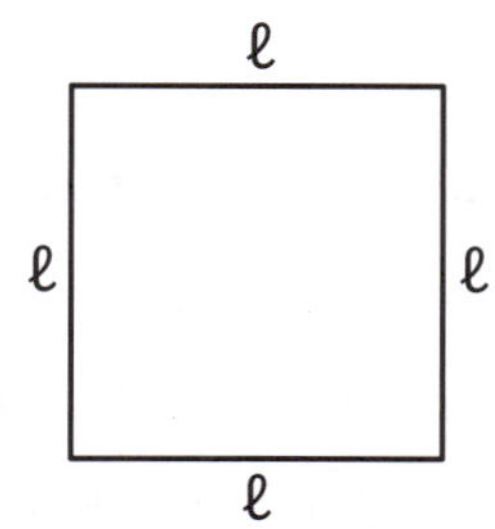

- The measure of the space enclosed within a closed figure is called its area.
- Area of a rectangle = ℓ × b sq units.
- Area of a square = ℓ × ℓ = ℓ^2 sq units.

Drawing an envelope trick!! You can draw an envelope shape on a paper without lifting your pen even once and without repeating a line. Try it. Looks difficult but it is easy!

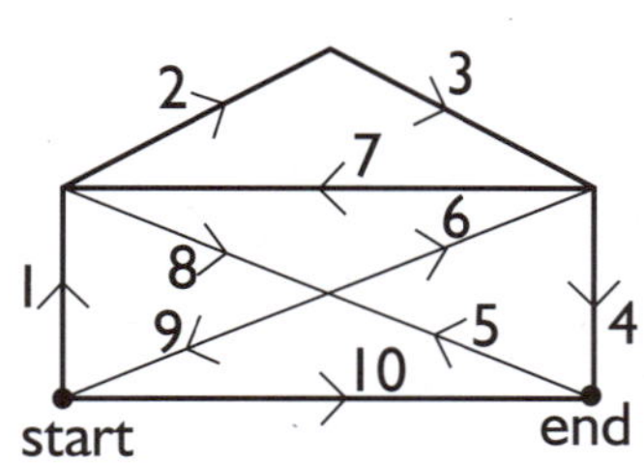

Studying the Perimeter and Area

Objective: To distinguish between the perimeter and area of a rectangle/square.

Material required: Coloured ribbon or wool, a pair of scissors, graph paper and glue

Procedure:

1. Cut a length of ribbon (say 20 cm).
2. Draw a rectangle of length 6 cm $\times$ 4 cm on the graph paper.
3. Cut the 20 cm ribbon into four pieces. Two pieces of 6 cm each and two pieces of 4 cm each.
4. Paste them on the rectangle.
5. The region enclosed within the rectangle is the area, i.e., $6 \times 4 = 24$ cm^2.
6. The length of the 20 cm ribbon is the perimeter of the rectangle.
7. You may now cut another 20 cm piece of ribbon.
8. Now, divide it into 4 equal parts of 5 cm each.
9. Put them around a square of side 5 cm drawn on the graph paper.
10. The area of the square is 5×5 cm^2 = 25 cm^2.
11. The perimeter of the square is also 20 cm.

This shows that the perimeter may be the same but the areas can be different.

Data Handling

CHAPTER 15

Data

Data is the collection of information in the form of numerical figures.

Example 1: Newspapers carry details of the runs scored by batsmen during cricket series.

Example 2: A class teacher keeps an account of marks scored by students through the term and tallies them as the final results at the end of the term.

These figures are called data.

There are two types of data:

1. Primary
2. Secondary

Primary data is the data collected by an individual personally.

Example 1: The sports teacher, Mr Singh, surveyed a class to find out the number of students interested in the various games offered in the school.

Badminton	Football	Cricket	Swimming	Tennis
10	13	15	10	12

Example 2: At an ice cream parlour, the sales manager, Mr Gupta, wanted to know the various flavours of ice cream popular with school kids. He collected the data by asking 100 school kids to fill a form.

Vanilla	Strawberry	Chocolate	Butter Scotch	Pineapple
20	15	35	25	5

Secondary data is collected from newspaper, magazines, television, internet and other sources.

Organisation of Data

When data is collected for a larger group, it becomes difficult to write the entire data in a single column. So we make use of a new term called frequency.

Let us first understand the term frequency.

Frequency

The number of times a particular value occurs in a data is called frequency.

Tally Marks

These are vertical lines used as a symbol for counting the number of times a particular value occurs. They are written in group of 5 with four vertical lines and one diagonal cutting across them.

Example: |||| implies 4

𝍸 implies 5

Data once collected should be arranged in a proper order so that we can get information at a glance.

Example 1: In discussing the marks scored by Rohan in school, the data can be presented in two ways. In the first we can say that in English, Hindi, Sanskrit, mathematics, social studies, computer studies and science he scored 35, 45, 95, 62, 38, 45 and 72. In the second, we can present the same information in a tabular form.

English	35
Hindi	45
Sanskrit	95
Mathematics	62
Social Studies	38
Computer Science	45
Science	77

So, it is clear that while the first presentation of data looks random and confusing, in the second, the presentation of facts is neat and easy to understand.

Example 2: A group of 50 students were asked to name their favourite TV show. The choice included *Ramayan*, *Jai Hanuman*, *Tom and Jerry*, *Vikram aur Vetal* and *Bingo*.

This information was written as tally marks and then from the data collected the frequency was read. This table is called *the* frequency table.

TV show	Tally marks	Frequency
Ramayan	𝍸 𝍸	10
Jai Hanuman	𝍸 𝍸 |||	13
Tom and Jerry	𝍸 |||	8
Vikram aur Vetal	𝍸 𝍸 ||	12
Bingo	𝍸 ||	7

Example 3: A cricket match was organised between the four sections of Class VI. The runs scored by the players were as follows:

10, 15, 10, 10, 10, 15, 20, 25, 30, 15, 25, 10, 25, 45, 40, 35,
25, 15, 29, 10, 20, 10, 20, 30, 30, 50, 15, 15, 20, 10, 50, 30,
45, 15, 10, 40, 10, 20, 10, 0, 15, 10, 40, 30, 20, 50

A frequency table can now be prepared with the help of tally marks using this information.

Runs	Tally marks	Frequency
0			1
10	𝍸 𝍸		11
15	𝍸 |||	8
20	𝍸		6
25						4
30	𝍸	5
35			1
40					3
45				2
50					3

Alert!

What is important here is that as you cancel a number in the data, put a tally for it against the appropriate number in the table. At the end, count the respective tally marks and write the frequency.

Practice Exercise 15.1

1. Define the following.

   a. data b. frequency

   How many types of data are there? Name them.

2. Complete the given frequency table.

Marks	Tally marks	Frequency
2	|||	
4	~~||||~~ |	
6	~~||||~~ |||	
8	~~||||~~ ||	
10	||||	

   What is the total frequency?

3. In the given frequency table, the frequency of temperatures during a month is given. Draw the tally marks.

Temperature in °C	Tally marks	Number of days
32		4
34		7
36		10
38		6
40		3

   a. What was the maximum temperature during the month?

   b. What temperature persisted for the maximum number of days?

4. The heights (in cm) of the students in a particular class are listed below. Make a frequency table for the same.

130	126	128	120	122	130	122	120	124	122
126	120	124	122	126	120	128	130	122	124
120	130	122	126	122	120	130	126	130	128

5. Roopa throws a dice and notes down the number on the top face. She repeats this experiment a number of times and wants to prepare a frequency table using tally marks. Help her to do so.

2	6	2	1	3	4	6	2	3	5	4	2	5	3	2	5
1	1	3	6	4	2	4	6	6	4	2	1	4	2	3	1
6	4	4	5	5	3	2	5	1	3	1	6	2	6	4	2

6. The games teacher was asked to give grades to the Class VI students. He sent them in a jumbled manner. The class teacher requested the class monitor to make a frequency table and help her. The grades are:

A	B	C	D	B	C	D	A	B	B
B	C	A	D	D	C	B	C	D	A
C	A	B	D	A	B	A	A	B	B
D	D	D	A	B	C	D	A	C	C

Show how the class monitor was able to assist his teacher.

7. The result of a mathematics unit test were as follows:

70, 80, 90, 80, 80, 60, 80, 70, 90, 60, 100, 60, 70, 60, 80,

70, 80, 70, 90, 60, 80, 70, 60, 50, 50, 80, 80, 50, 60, 80

Prepare a frequency table and answer the questions.

a. What are the maximum marks obtained?

b. What are the least marks obtained?

c. What mark was obtained by the maximum number of students?

d. How many students appeared for the test?

e. How many students got an A+ (90 and above)?

8. A survey was done at the toll gate of an expressway and the symbols of a few cars were noted. They are listed below:

Maruti S		Honda H		Santro И		VW W		Mercedes 		
S,	S,	H,	H,	И,	И,	W	S,	S	H	H,
И,	И,	И,	S			S,	S	И,	И,	W
W	S,	И,	И	И	H,	H,	S			

Present the information with the help of *a* frequency table and answer the following questions.

a. Which make of car crosses the toll gate the maximum number of times?

b. Which make of car is seldom seen?

c. Which make of car is second in number in crossing the toll gate?

9. A village school started at the beginning of the new century. The number of students enrolled in Class VI are given in the frequency distribution table below.

Year	2000–2001	2001–2002	2002–2003	2003–2004	2004–2005	2005–2006	2006–2007	2007–2008	2008–2009	2009–2010
Number of students	60	70	80	90	100	110	100	90	110	120

a. In which year were the maximum number of students enrolled?

b. In which two academic years were the same number of students enrolled?

10. The following frequency table gives the number of hours spent per week by children in playing sports.

Number of hours	Tally marks	Frequency
12	|||	3
13	卌 ||	7
14	卌 |||	8
15	卌 卌	10
16	卌 ||||	9
17	卌 |	6
18	||	2

a. What is the maximum number of hours spent per week on sports?

b. What is the minimum number of hours spent per week on sports?

c. How many students spend less than 15 hours per week on sports?

Representation of Data

Numerical data can be represented in the form of pictures so that at a glance one can figure out the answers. There are many ways to do so, but we will learn two ways.

a. Pictograph b. Bar graph

Pictograph

In a pictograph, we use symbols or pictures to represent data. A scale is fixed by a symbol or picture to represent the given frequency in the data.

Example: Mr Brown has an ice cream parlour. The sale of ice cream per day is represented weekly on a colourful board. The ice cream cone represents the sale.

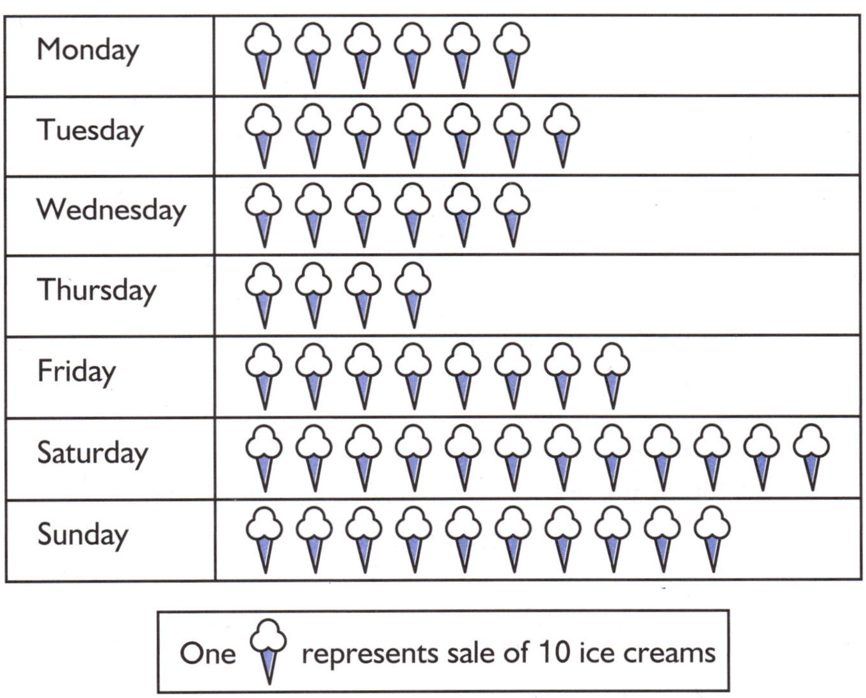

1. On which day of the week did Mr Brown sell the maximum ice creams?
   Saturday ($12 \times 10 = 120$ cones).
2. On which day of the week did Mr Brown sell the least number of ice creams?
   Thursday ($4 \times 10 = 40$ cones).

Bar Graph

A bar graph is a chart with rectangular bars of uniform width and the lengths proportional to the frequency of the specific quantity in the data.

A bar graph can be drawn vertically or horizontally. The bars should have equal spacing between them.

Alert!

1. A bar graph can be drawn on graph paper for accuracy.
2. The width of the bars must be uniform in all cases.
3. Bars can be vertical or horizontal.

Example 1: The bar graph given below shows the marks that Anubhav scored in the first term examination. Read the graph and answer the questions.

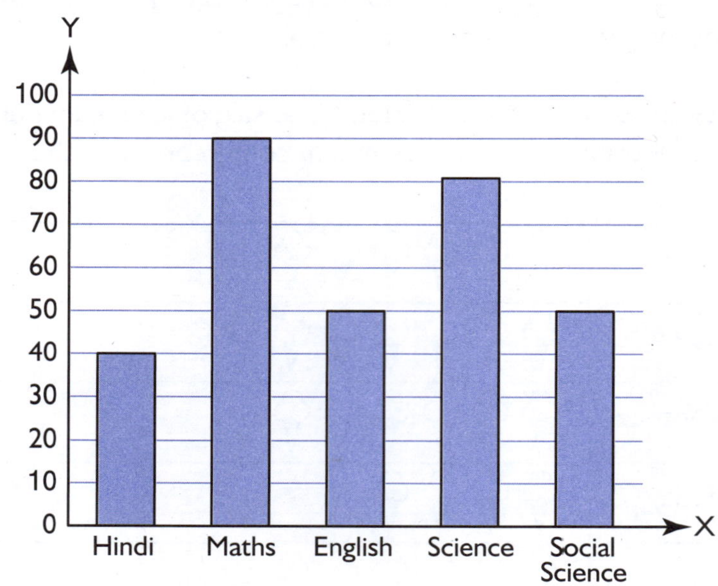

1. In which subject did Anubhav score the minimum marks?
2. In which two subjects did Anubhav score the same marks?
3. In which subject did Anubhav score the maximum marks?
4. How many marks did Anubhav score in science?
5. What is the difference between his marks in Hindi and in mathematics?

Answers:

1. Hindi
2. English and social studies
3. Maths
4. 80 marks
5. 50 marks

Alert!

The horizontal axis (line) is called the x-axis.

The vertical axis (line) is called the y-axis.

Their point of intersection is called the origin and marked as 0.

Example 2: A shoe company does a survey to find the shoe size that is most commonly used.

Size	4	5	6	7	8	9	10
Number of students	100	250	400	600	300	150	50

Depict the information on a bar graph.

Step 1 Draw the x-axis and y-axis on the graph paper and name them. Also name O.

Step 2 Write the scale on the y-axis. 1 cm represent 50 cm.

Step 3 Draw a vertical bar of width 1 cm to represent the size of the shoe.

Step 4 Leave a uniform space (say 1 cm) and draw the next bar.

Step 5 The length of the bars should be according to the data given.

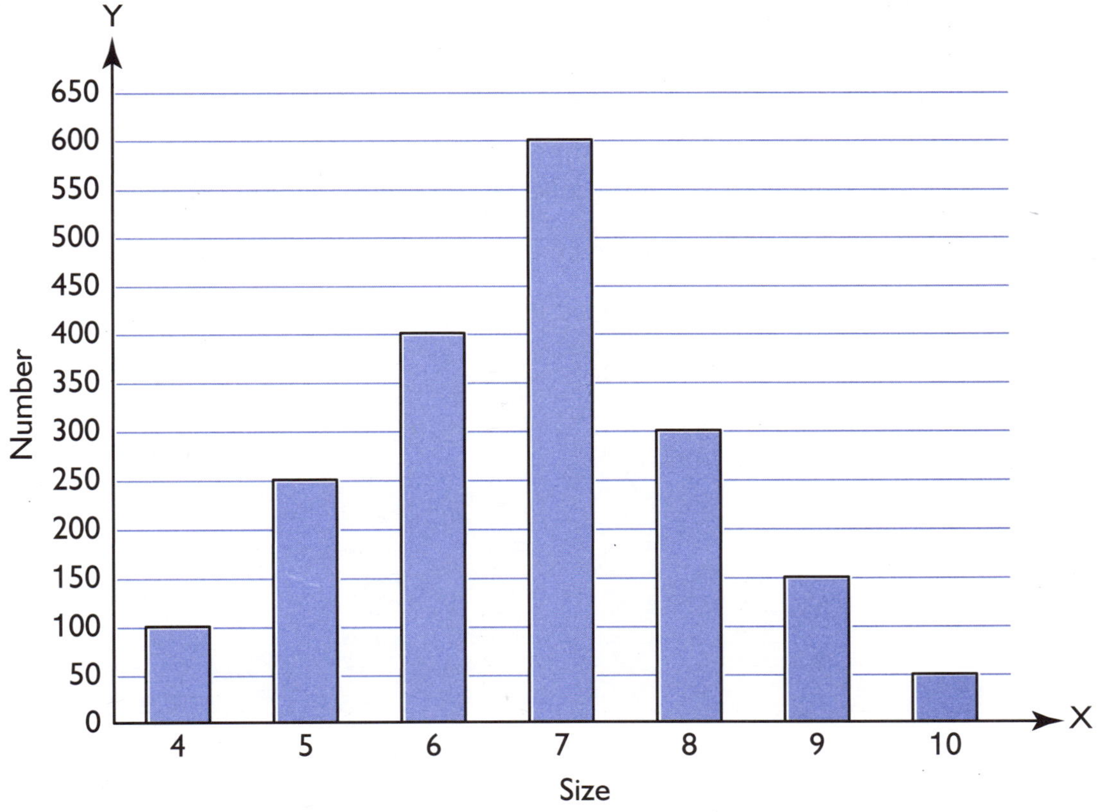

Practice Exercise 15.2

1. The pictograph given below shows how many letters were collected from a post box on each day of a certain week.

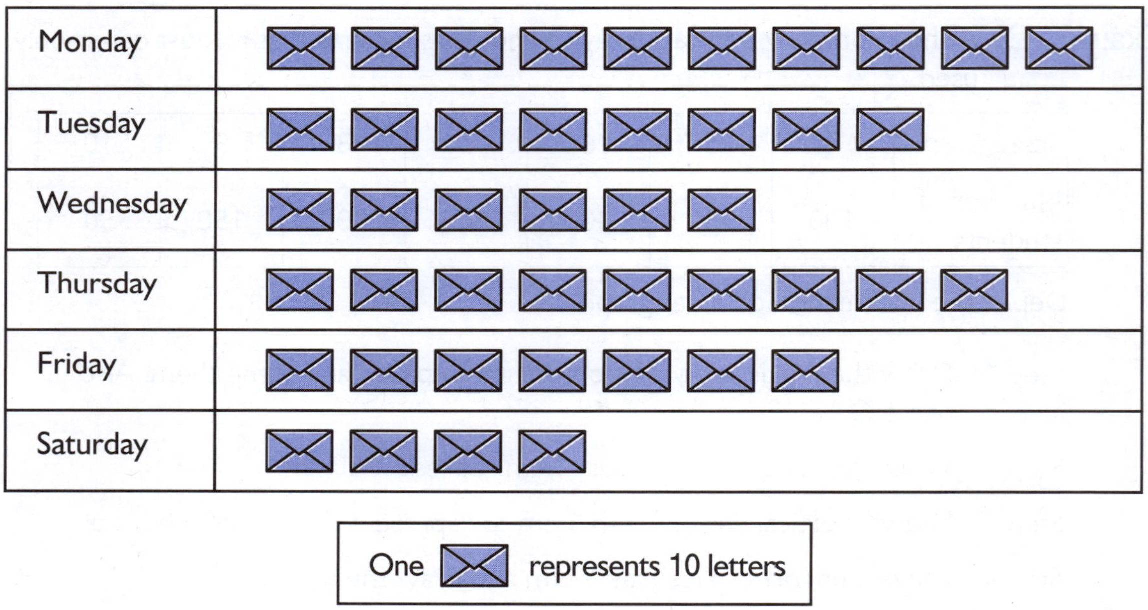

From the pictograph, answer the following questions.

a. On which day were the minimum number of letters collected?

b. How many more letters were collected on Thursday than on Wednesday?

c. How many fewer letters were collected on Friday than on Tuesday?

d. On which day were the maximum number of letters collected?

e. What was the total number of letters collected over the week?

2. The pictograph given below shows how many trees were planted by schools during a tree plantation drive.

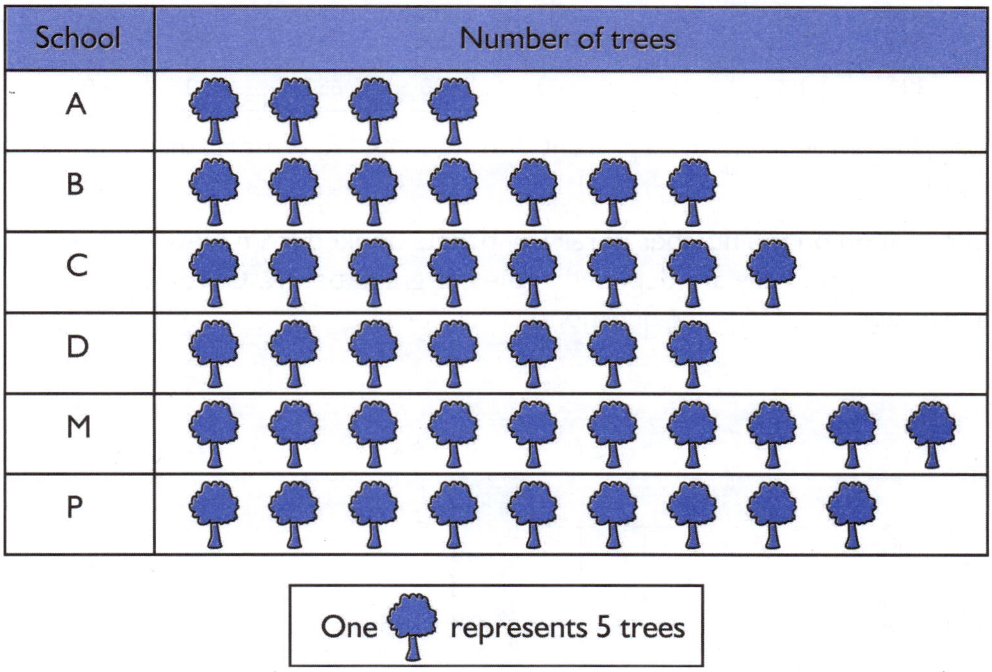

From the pictograph, answer the following questions.

a. Which school planted the maximum number of trees? How many trees did they plant?

b. Which school planted the least number of trees?

c. Which two schools planted the same number of trees?

d. What is the difference in the number of trees planted by school C and school P?

e. Planet earth is richer by how many trees after their tree planting campaign?

3. The following table shows the number of 'i10' Santro cars sold in the first six months of 2010. Represent this information through a pictograph. Use the symbol [i10] to represent 100 cars.

Jan.	Feb.	Mar.	Apr.	May	June
300	400	200	500	600	400

4. A school offers training in several sports to its students. A tabular representation of the games and the students who opt for them is given below. Represent the information as a pictograph.

Use the symbol [☺] to represent 25 students.

Cricket	Football	Tennis	Basketball	Volleyball	Hockey
225	200	150	100	50	75

5. The number of students enrolled in the primary section of a school in the last decade are as follows:

2000–2001	2001–2002	2002–2003	2003–2004	2004–2005	2005–2006	2006–2007	2007–2008	2008–2009	2009–2010
200	300	400	450	600	500	650	550	600	750

Use the symbol  to represent 50 students. Represent the information on a pictograph.

6. Information on the number of railway tickets booked from New Delhi to various cities on a given day are depicted in the bar graph below. Observe the bar graph and answer the following questions.

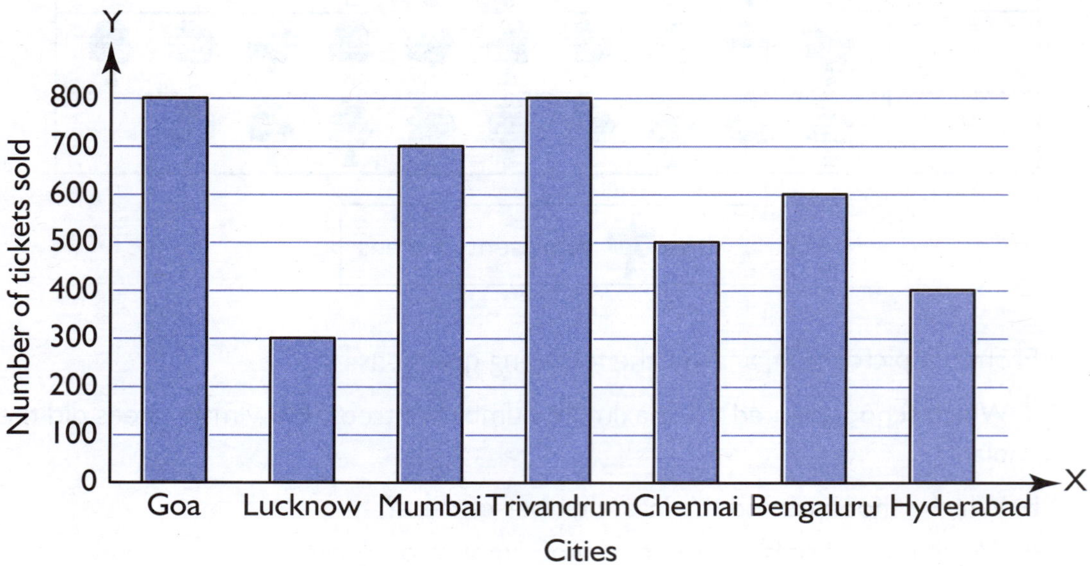

a. What does the x-axis represent? What does the y-axis represent?

b. For which two cities were the sale of tickets maximum?

c. For which city was the sale of tickets the minimum?

d. How many tickets were sold for Mumbai?

e. Find the difference in the number of tickets sold for Bengaluru and Chennai.

f. Find the sum of tickets sold for Chennai and Hyderabad.

g. Find the toal number of tickets sold.

7. Read the bar graph given below and answer the following questions.

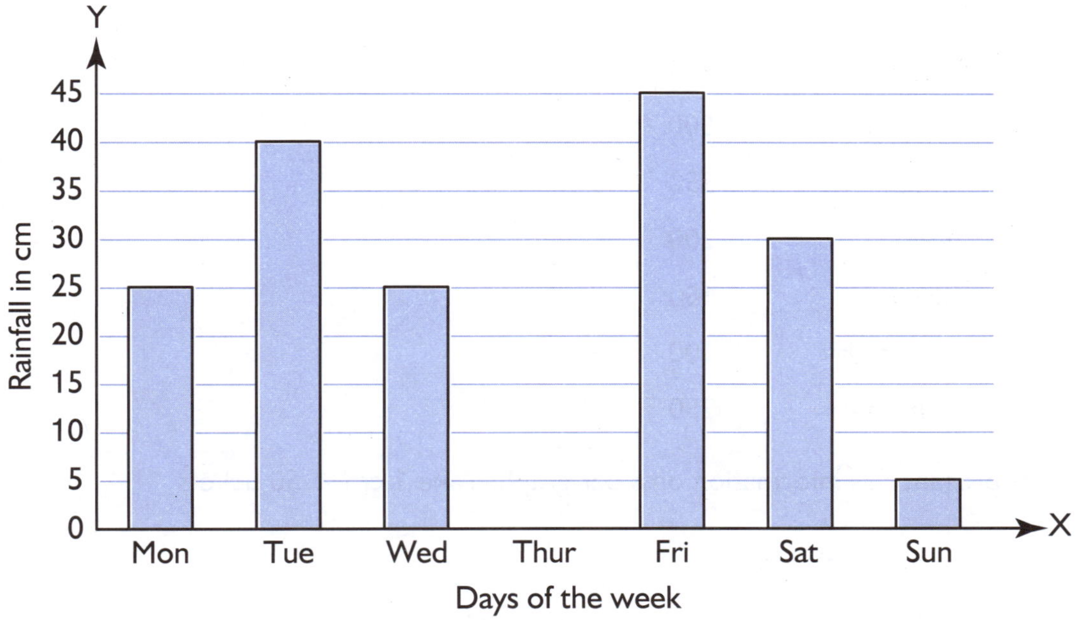

a. What information does the bar graph represent?

b. On which day was the rainfall maximum?

c. On which day was there no rain?

d. Which two days had the same amount of rainfall and what was the amount of rainfall?

e. How many cm of rainfall was there on Tuesday?

f. What is the difference in the amount of rainfall on Saturday and Sunday?

g. Find the total amount of rain during the week.

8. The number of merit certificates given to students from class III to VIII are as follows:

Classes	Merit certificates
3	50
4	60
5	70
6	150
7	90
8	80

Represent the information on a bar graph by taking a suitable scale. Represent each class by a different colour bar.

How many students in total received a merit card?

9. The following are the number of tickets sold for a popular *Harry Potter* film at a multiplex.

Friday	400
Saturday	500
Sunday	350
Monday	200
Tuesday	150
Wednesday	100
Thursday	250

Represent this information on a bar graph. Take 1 cm = 50 tickets.

Answer the following.

a. On which day were the least tickets sold?

b. On which day was the houseful board put?

c. How many tickets were sold in all during the week?

10. The school transport office conducted a survey to find out the mode of transport used by Class 6 students to come to school. Represent the information on a bar graph.

School bus	100
Private bus	60
Car	40
Cycle	20
Walking	20
Scooter	10

Scale 1 cm = 10 students

Answer the following questions.

a. How many students do physical exercise on the way to school?

b. Which is the most commonly used mode of transport?

c. How many students are there in Class 6 of this school?

Highlights

- Collection of information in terms of numbers is called data.
- The collection, recording and presentation of data help us to draw inferences from them.
- Tally marks make the data easy to count and understand.
- The representation of data in the form of pictures is called a pictograph.
- A bar graph is a representation of data using rectangular bars of uniform width and drawn at equal distances. The length of the bars gives the required information.
- Bar graph and pictographs are drawn to a specified scale.

Question: In one year there are several months that have 30 days and several months that have 31 days. How many months have 28 days?

Answer for Brainteaser on page 244

Maths Lab Activity

Goals

Objective: To learn tabulation of information.

Material required: Graph paper, pencil, ruler, coloured pens

Procedure:

1. Write the names of football teams A, B, C, D, E, F, G, H in a tabular form in different colours.
2. Each team has scored certain number of goals in the entire season. They are as follows:

Teams	Goals Scored
Team A	25
Team B	12
Team C	17
Team D	22
Team E	20
Team F	11
Team G	7
Team H	30

3. Write the names of the top four teams that have qualified for the quarter final.
4. Draw a pictograph to show the total goals scored by these 8 countries on a graph paper. Use a football as a symbol for goal.

Mathematics can be a lot of fun! Enjoy this activity.

Answer for Brainteaser on page 243

All the months have 28 days.

Rewind

CHAPTERS 14–15

1. Find the perimeter of the following figures.

   a. A square whose side is 11 cm.

   b. A rectangle whose dimensions are — $\ell = 12$ cm, b = 9 cm.

   c. A triangle whose sides are 8 cm, 6 cm and 5 cm.

2. The area of a rectangle is 108 cm^2. If its breadth is 9 cm, find its length.

3. What will happen to the area of a square if its side is:

   a. doubled b. tripled c. halved

4. Two plots of land have the same perimeter. One is a square with a side of 60 m, while the other is a rectangle whose breadth is 12 m. Which plot of land has the greater area and by how much?

5. The floor of a school auditorium is fully carpeted. There are 40 carpets in the auditorium, each measuring 25 m × 12.5 m. What is the total area of the floor?

6. Two rooms of floor sizes 15 m × 12 m and 10 m × 8 m are to be tiled with square tiles of side 50 cm. How many tiles will be needed in all?

7. Find the area of the shaded portion in the two figures given below.

a.

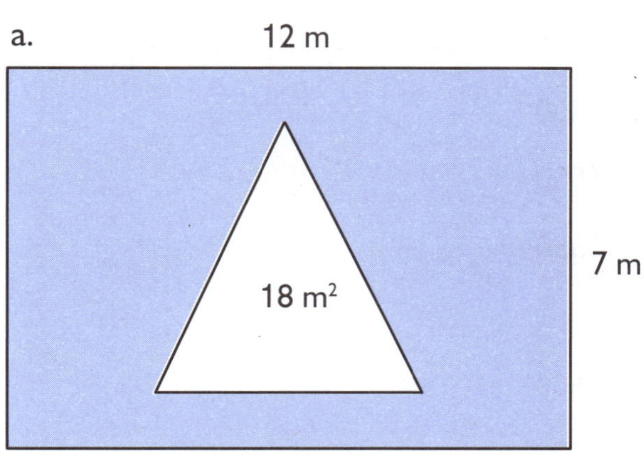

b.

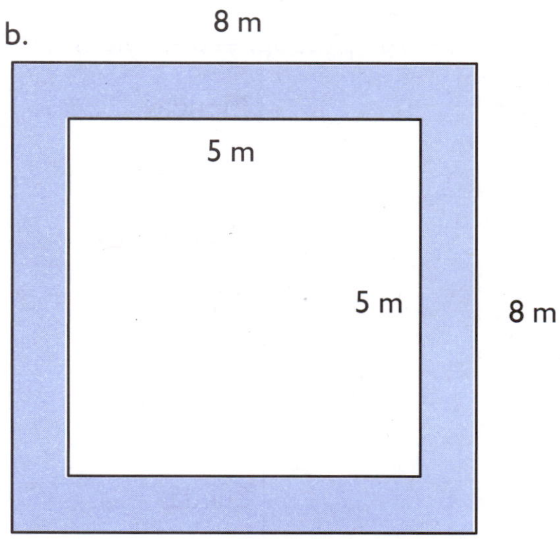

8. Calculate the area and perimeter of the following figures.

a.

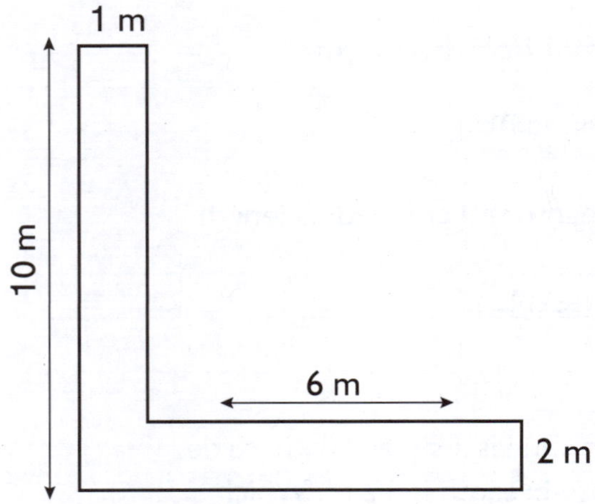

b.

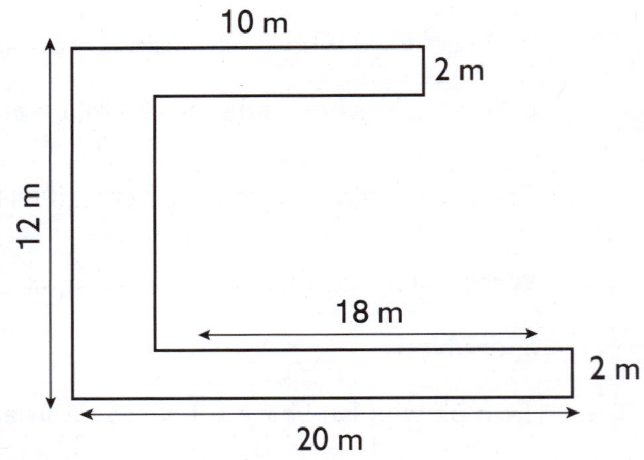

9. The number of students in five different sections of Class VI are given below.

Express the data with the help of a bar graph.

Section	A	B	C	D	E
Number of students	35	50	55	40	45

10. A shopkeeper sold the following number of packets of dry fruits during a week.

Monday	400
Tuesday	500
Wednesday	350
Thursday	—
Friday	600
Saturday	700
Sunday	650

Use 1 box to represent 100 packets of dry fruits and $\frac{1}{2}$ box to represent 50 packets of dry fruits. Draw a pictograph.

Test Yourself

Unit III

1. Write the following, using numbers, literal numbers and signs of operations.

   a. There are 35 students in a class. If another "x" number of students join the class, what will be the total strength of the class?

   b. If the cost of a book is x and a geometry box is ₹y, what is the total cost of four books and one geometry box?

   c. Quotient of p divided by q added to the product of p and q.

2. If $x = 3$, $y = 2$ and $z = 0$, find the value of:

   a. $x - y - z$ b. $x(y + z)$ c. $z(x + y)$

   d. $2x + 3y - z$ e. $x \cdot y + y \cdot z + z \cdot x$

3. Write the coefficient of "y" in the following expressions:

   a. $-8xy$ b. $2x - 5y$ c. $8 + x - 2y$

   d. mxy e. $18xyz$

4. Classify the following as monomial, binomial or trinomial terms.

   a. $7ab$ b. $m + m + m + m + m$

   c. $\dfrac{a + a + a}{b + b}$ d. $a \cdot a + 2a \cdot b + b \cdot b$

   e. $(p + p + p)(q + q + q + q)(r + r)$

5. Verify the following:

   a. The solution of $4x - 7 = 25$ if $x = 8$

   b. The solution of $7 + 3x = 16$ if $x = 3$

   c. The solution of $\dfrac{x}{4} = 2$ if $x = 8$

6. Solve the following equations and verify the answer by substitution.

   a. $3z + 12 = 15$ b. $5 - \dfrac{x}{3} = 2$ c. $\dfrac{20y}{3} = 40$

   d. $28 = 4 + 3(x + 5)$ e. $16 + (m - 6)4 = 0$

7. Mrs Mehta is 24 years older than her son. If the sum of their ages is 98 years, find their ages.

8. If 5 balloons are given to each child at a birthday party, how many balloons are needed for "n" number of children? If a total of 155 balloons are distributed at the party, find the number of children at the party.

9. Express the following ratios in their simplest form.

a. ₹8.30 : ₹24.90 b. 3 weeks : 30 days c. 48 min : 3 hrs 20 min

d. 3 kg 750 gm : 5 kg e. 36 cm : 3 m 60 cm

10. Out of the 250 persons working in a factory, 175 are men and the rest are women. Find the ratio of:

a. The number of men to that of women.

b. The number of men to that of the total number of people in the factory.

c. The number of women to that of the total number of people in the factory.

11. Find the value of x, if the following terms are in continued proportion.

a. 25, x, 64 b. 48, 36, x c. x, 160, 256

12. A machine manufactures 48 parts in 8 hours. How many parts will it manufacture in 48 hours?

13. Find the perimeters of the following figures.

a.

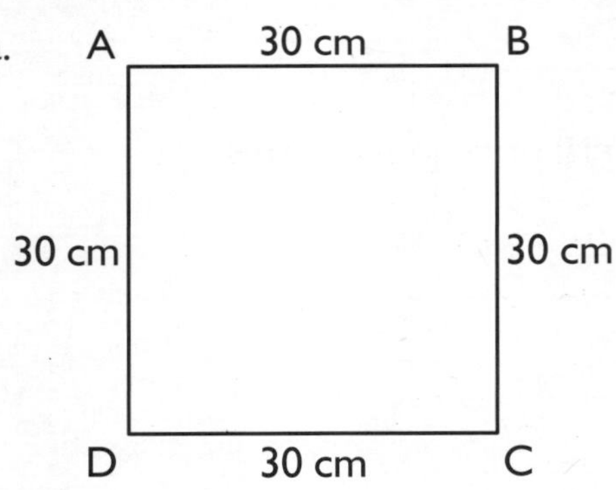

b.

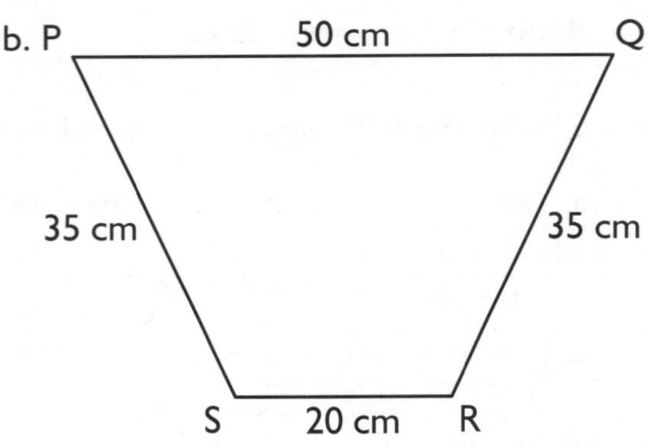

c.

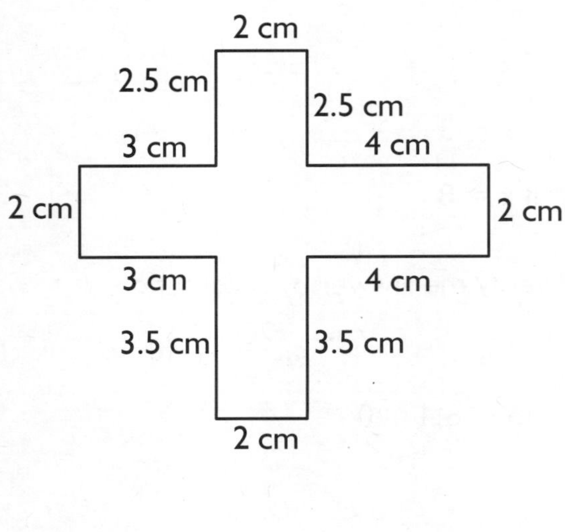

14. The length of a wire is 108 m. If the wire is used to make a regular pentagon and a regular hexagon, find the difference of the lengths of the sides of the two figures.

15. A rectangle is 16 m by 9 m in size. Find the side of the square whose area is the same as the area of the rectangle. By how much does the perimeter of the rectangle exceed the perimeter of the square?

16. A room is 9.5 m long and 7.4 m wide. If the floor of the room is to be covered with rectangular tiles of size 20 cm by 10 cm, find the cost of tiling the room at the rate of ₹5 per tile.

17. During the rainy season, students of a class made a count of the umbrellas brought to class from Monday to Friday. The count was Monday, 15, Tuesday, 25, Wednesday, 20, Thursday, 10 and Friday, 5. Represent this data in the form of a pictograph.

    Use 1 umbrella  to represent 5 umbrellas.

18. Study the bar graph and answer the following questions.

    a. What information does the graph represent?

    b. How many clubs are organised in the school?

    c. What does the y-axis represent?

    d. Which club has the least number of participants?

    e. Which club is the most popular among the students?

    f. How many students are there in the mathematics club?

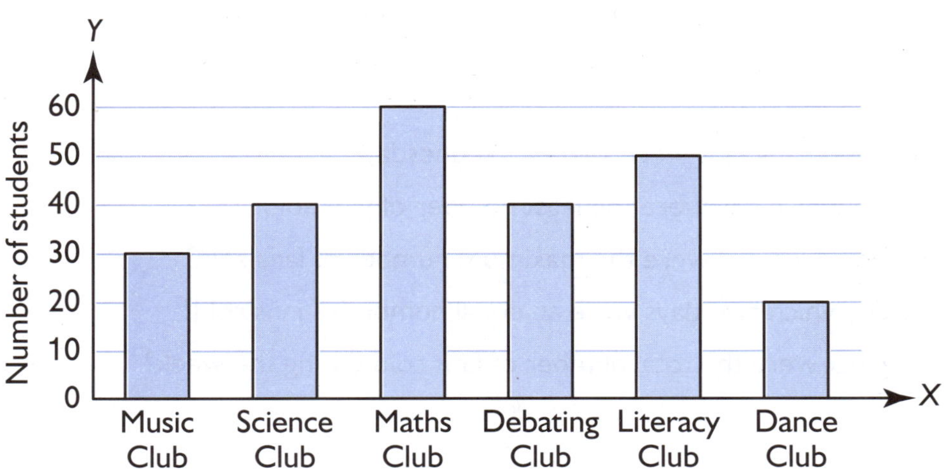

19. The speed at which different animals run is given below. Express the data with the help of a bar graph.

Lion	90 km/hr
Deer	80 km/hr
Horse	55 km/hr
Dog	50 km/hr
Elephant	30 km/hr
Hare	35 km/hr
Tortoise	10 km/hr

20. Read the pictograph given below and answer the following questions.

Sale of fans on different days of a week

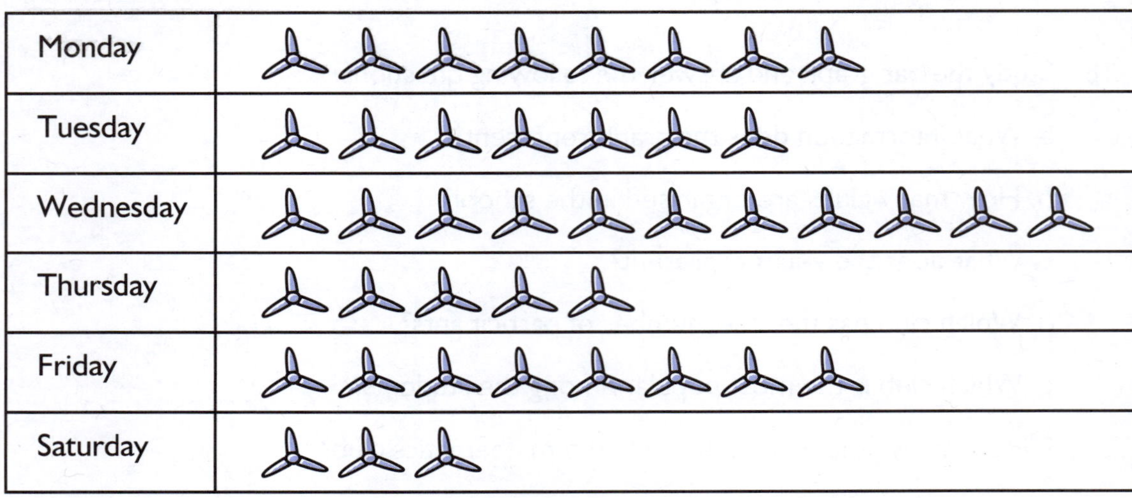

Each symbol  represents 5 fans

a. How many fans were sold on Wednesday?

b. On which day were the least number of fans sold?

c. On which day were the maximum number of fans sold?

d. On which two days were an equal number of fans sold?

e. What were the total number of fans sold during the week?

Model Sample Test Paper

Self Appraisal | Maxmium marks: 80

Time: 3 hours

Section A | $(10 \times 1 = 10)$

1. Write the place value and face value of the underlined digit in the number 7$\underline{8}$,12,345.
2. Find the value of

   $2 \times 6{,}843 + 3 \times 6{,}843 + 5 \times 6{,}843$.
3. Reduced $\frac{975}{1{,}475}$ to the lowest term.
4. In the given figure, name:

   (i) The two points.

   (ii) The line segment.

5. Name the quadrilateral in which two pairs of adjacent sides are equal and where the diagonals intersect each other at right angles.
6. Draw the axes of symmetry for the following figure.

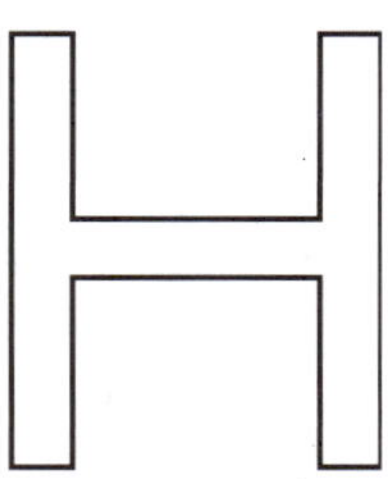

7. Write the following as algebraic expressions.

   (i) p subtracted from 3 times 9.

   (ii) c divided by 4 and the result increased by 7.
8. Find the mean proportional between 36 and 49.
9. Name the specific quadrilaterals that have only two lines of symmetry.
10. What is the difference between a cube and a cuboid?

Section B (5 × 2 = 10)

11. The LCM of a pair of numbers is 108. If the product of the numbers is 1,944, what is the HCF of the numbers?
12. Solve the following:

    $[-15 - (-37)] + [-18 - (-101) + 81]$
13. The sum of two numbers is 100. If one of them is 63,856, find the other number.
14. Draw an angle of 70° with a protractor. Bisect it with the help of a compass.
15. Write a statement for each of the given equations.

    (i) $x - 9 = 18$ (ii) $9y = 108$

Section C (10 × 3 = 30)

16. Leo walks 365 m every day. Find the distance covered by him in 140 days. Estimate the product to the nearest thousand.
17. The population of a town is 4,50,772. One out of every 7 is reported to be educated. In all, how many educated persons are there in the village? How many uneducated persons are there?
18. What should be added to the sum of (−26) and 31 to make it equal to the sum of (−35) and (−11)?
19. Arrange the following fractions in ascending order and find the difference between the greatest and the smallest fractions.

    $3\frac{3}{5}, 2\frac{4}{7}, \frac{19}{6}, \frac{18}{8}$
20. Shipra bought books for ₹529.65 and a notebook for ₹212.80. If she gave the shopkeeper ₹1,000, how much money will he return?
21. Name the following parts of the given circle.

    a. Radius

    b. Diameter

    c. Chord

    d. Semicircle

    e. Minor arc

    f. Centre

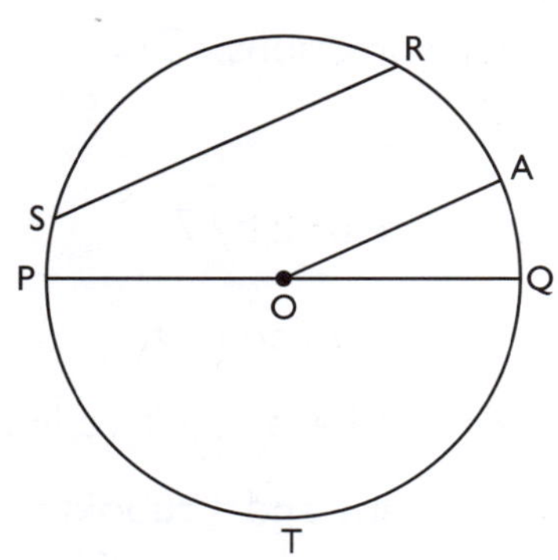

22. Find the values of the given expressions given that:

$p = 1.5$, $q = 2.5$ and $r = 4$.

a. $6p + q + r$

b. $5q - r - p$

c. $3r - p + q$

23. The number of classrooms on the ground floor of a public school is 10 less than twice the number of rooms on the first floor. If the number of rooms on the first floor is y, write the expression for the number of rooms on the ground floor of the school. If the total number of rooms in the school is 50, find the number of rooms on the two floors.

24. Determine the cost of fencing a rectangular park 300 m long and 200 m broad at the rate of ₹9 per metre.

25. The following pictograph gives details of the number of absentees during a week in a school with 330 students.

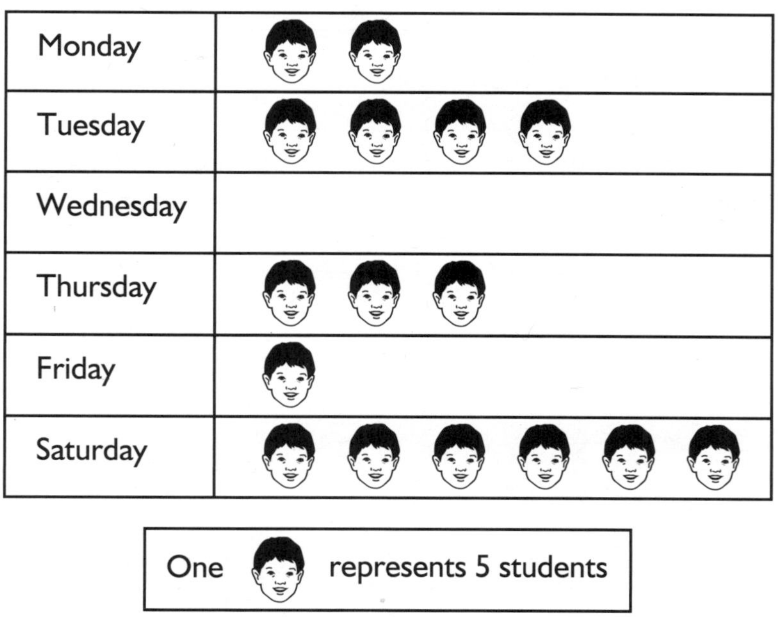

a. On what day were there maximum numbers of absentees?

b. On what day were all the students present?

c. What was the total number of absentees during the week?

Section D

$(5 \times 6 = 30)$

26. Simplify

a. $11 + \{ 20 + 2 \text{ of } 6 + (30 + 50 - 27 \div 9)\}$

b. $30 - [20 - 4 \times 3 - 2 (-\overline{2 + 3})]$

27. The ratio of the number of women in a village to the total population of the village is 5:11. If there are 4,000 women in the village, then what is the total population of the village? What is the population of men in the village?

28. A park is rectangular in shape. Its length is 500 m and breadth is 300 m. Five square flower beds of size 50 sq. m are dug in the park. find the remaining area of the park. Also find the cost of turfing this area at the cost of ₹3 per sq. m.

29. The number of cycles produced by a factory in a week is given below.

Mon	Tue	Wed	Thurs	Fri	Sat
80	900	1,200	700	1,400	600

Draw a bar graph to represent this information.

30. Draw a line segment AB of length 5 cm. At A, construct an angle of measure 60°. At B construct an angle of measure 90°. Suppose their arms meet at C, find the measure of $\angle C$.

Answers

Practice Exercise 1.1

1.a. 24,789 b. 13,579 c. 23,468
2.a. 97,531 b. 98,742 c. 86,432
3.a. 24,782 b. 52,790 c. 98,701
4.a. 98,699 b. 24,780 c. 52,788
5. 22,199, 24,789, 56,482, 62,345, 98,912
6. 54,321, 45,123, 31,245, 23,451, 12,345
7.a. 90,000 + 6,000 + 700 + 20 + 0
b. 80,000 + 1,000 + 900 + 40 + 5
c. 60,000 + 5,000 + 400 + 80 + 3
8.a. 87,542 b. 15,639 c. 69,327
9.a. Place value 8,000; face value 8
b. Place value 90; face value 9
c. Place value 70,000; face value 7
10.a. 9; nine b. 10; ten c. 100; hundred
d. 9,999; nine thousand nine hundred and ninety-nine
e. 10,000; ten thousand, f. 20,118
g. twenty thousand one hundred and eighteen

Practice Exercise 1.2

1.a. 3,000 b. 4,000 c. 8,000 d. 8,000
e. 6,000
2.a. 90,000 b. 1,70,000 c. 6,90,000 d. 70,000
e. 2,40,00
3.a. 2,00,000 b. 4,00,000 c. 8,00,000
d. 36,00,000 e. 46,00,000

4.a. Estimated sum = 2,220	Actual sum = 2,213
b. Estimated sum = 5,400	Actual sum = 5,391
c. Estimated sum = 14,000	Actual sum = 13,872
d. Estimated sum = 1,40,000	Actual sum = 1,42,052
e. Estimated sum = 11,00,000	Actual sum = 10,37,352
5.a. Estimated diff. = 30	Actual diff. = 35
b. Estimated diff. = 500	Actual diff. = 498
c. Estimated diff. = 2,000	Actual diff. = 2,408
d. Estimated diff. = 30,000	Actual diff. = 31,790
e. Estimated diff. = 7,00,000	Actual diff. = 7,09,500

6.a. 2,100 b. 2,00,000 c. 21,000 d. 50,000
e. 1,80,000
7.a. 2 b. 50 c. 10 d. 600 e. 200
8. Yes, she will be able to pay off her loan.
9. 100 10. 24

Practice Exercise 1.3

1.a. XLV b. LXIX c. XCIX d. LXXX
e. LXXV
2.a. 72 b. 49 c. 249 d. 1654 e. 98
3.a. Meaningless b. Meaningless c. Meaningless
d. Meaningful, 44 e. Meaningful, 264
4.a. $<$ b. $<$ c. $<$ d. $<$ e. $>$
5.a. 150; CL b. 649; DCXLIX c. 134; CXXXIV d. 45; XLV e. 559; DLIX

Practice Exercise 2.1

1.a. 12 b. 175 2.a. 73 b. 5
3.a. 2 b. 0 4.a. 2 b. 18
5.a. 76 b. 9 6.a. 8 b. 5
7.a. 1 b. 33 8.a. 54 b. 61
9.a. 119 b. 26 10.a. 0 b. 567

Practice Exercise 2.2

1.a. 1, 5, 7 and 35 b. 1, 2, 4, 8, 16, 32 and 64
c. 1, 2, 3, 4, 5, 6, 8, 10, 12, 15, 20, 24, 30, 40, 60 and 120 d. 1, 17 e. 1, 3, 9, 27, 81, 243, 729
2.a. 7, 14, 21, 28, 35 b. 11, 22, 33, 44, 55 c. 13, 26, 39, 52, 65 d. 20, 40, 60, 80, 100 e. 25, 50, 75, 100, 125
3.a. 2 b. 31, 37, 41, 43, 47 c. 71, 73, 79, 83, 89, 97
d. 101, 103, 107, 109, 113, 127, 131, 137, 139, 149
e. 51, 52, 54, 55, 56, 57, 58, 60, 62, 63, 64, 65, 66, 68, 69.
4. Co-prime: 15, 17; 49, 51 Twin primes: 5,7; 11,13; 41, 43
5. 90, 91, 92, 93, 94, 95, 96
6.a. 29 + 3 b. 53 + 3 c. 61 + 2 d. 47 + 83
e. 37 + 43
7.a. 35 b. 143 c. 57 d. 34 e. 161
8. 23 and 92 are not co-prime numbers as 23 is a factor of 92.
9.b. 225 d. 51,015 e. 16,215
10.a. T c. T d. T g. T

Practice Exercise 2.3

1. a, c, d 2. a, c, e 3. a, b, e
4. a, b, c, d 5. a, c, e 6. a, b, c, d

Answers

7. a, c, e   8. a, b, e   9. a, c, d
10. a, c, e

Practice Exercise 2.4

1.a. 7×7 b. $2 \times 2 \times 2 \times 3 \times 3 \times 3$ c. $2 \times 2 \times 2 \times 3 \times 13$ d. $2 \times 2 \times 2 \times 2 \times 2 \times 2 \times 2 \times 2 \times 2 \times 2$ e. $2 \times 2 \times 2 \times 2 \times 2 \times 2 \times 5 \times 5 \times 5$
2.a. $2 \times 2 \times 2 \times 2 \times 2$ b. $3 \times 3 \times 5$ c. $3 \times 3 \times 3 \times 3$ d. $2 \times 2 \times 3 \times 11$ e. $3 \times 3 \times 7 \times 7$
3.a. 27 b. 9 c. 50 d. 256 e. 90
4.a. 12 b. 115 c. 81 d. 10 e. 747
5. 6   6. 16   7. 15
8. 31   9. 64   10. 150 cm

Practice Exercise 2.5

1.a. 198 b. 936 c. 4,620 d. 13,860 e. 864
2.a. 192 b. 1,920 c. 720 d. 315 e. 684
3.a. HCF = 3, LCM = 189, Product = 567
b. HCF = 13, LCM = 52, Product = 676
c. HCF = 25, LCM = 5,625, Product = 1,40,625
d. HCF = 10, LCM = 4,200, Product = 42,000
e. HCF = 27, LCM = 810, Product = 21,870
4. 10, co-primes   5. LCM = 690
6. HCF = 2   7. 845   8. 8 am   9. 1440
10. 9,99,720

Rewind (Chapters 1–2)

1.a. P = 24,688   S = 24,690
b. P = 9,99,999   S = 10,00,001
2.a. 80,00,000 + 4,00,000 + 50,000 + 3,000 + 700 + 60 +5 b. 5,00,00,000 + 10,000 + 800 + 9
3.a. 22,19,939   Indian system
2,219,939   International system
Place value: 20 lakh, 2 millions
b. 9,89,12,85,375   Indian system
9,891,285,375   International system
Place value: 9 crore, 90 million
4.a. 92,000 b. 19,000
5.a. > b. >   6.a. 24 b. 9
7.a. HCF = 90, LCM = 1,350, Product = 121500
b. HCF = 10, LCM = 4,200, Product = 4,20,000
8. 17   9. 36 m   10. 5,460

Practice Exercise 3.1

1.a. Commutative b. Associative c. Additive Identity d. Distributive e. Commutative f. Identity element g. Distributive h. Commutative i. Commutative j. Distributive
2. a. 12,700 b. 1,23,400 c. 6,25,000 d. 4,26,000 e. 32,500
3.a. 224 b. 320 c. 375 d. 6,72,500 e. 86,000
4.a. 70,620 b. 87,414 c. 23,276 d. 1,12,448 e. 67,80,678
5. 165. Both scored the same marks. Commutative
6. 5,500. Distributive property.
7. Educated 7,725; uneducated 77,250
8. 9,99,900, 9,99,000, 900
9. 20,000
10.a. $41 + 42 + 43 + 44 + 45 + 46 + 47 + 48 + 49 + 50 = 455$
$51 + 52 + 53 + 54 + 55 + 56 + 57 + 58 + 59 + 60 = 555$
b. $(1 \times 2) + (2 \times 3) + (3 \times 4) + (4 \times 5) + (5 \times 6) = \frac{5 \times 6 \times 7}{3}$
$(1 \times 2) + (2 \times 3) + (3 \times 4) + (4 \times 5) + (5 \times 6) + (6 \times 7) = \frac{6 \times 7 \times 8}{3}$
c. $1 + 3 + 5 + 7 + 9 = 25 = 5 \times 5$
$1 + 3 + 5 + 7 + 9 + 11 = 36 = 6 \times 6$
d. $1 + 5 + 10 + 10 + 5 + 1$
$1 + 6 + 15 + 20 + 15 + 6 + 1$

Practice Exercise 4.1

1.a. −234 b. Decrease in marks c. 70 km west d. 10°C above 0°C e. 5 years ago
2.a. +500 b. −20 c. −10 d. +600 e. −5
3.a. +10 b. (−200) c. (−120) d. +21 e. 0
4.a. 10 b. 20 c. 2 d. 20 e. −100
5.a. 10 units to the left of 0 b. 12 units to the right of 0 c. 4 units to the left of 0 d. 0 e. 8 units to the right of 0
6.a. < b. > c. < d. < e. >
7.a. −2, −1, 0, 1 b. 1, 2, 3, 4 c. −3, −2, −1, 0, 1, 2, 3 d. −6, −5 e. 0
8.a. −7, −4, −3, 0, 2 b. −4, −2, 1, 3, 9 c. −27, −17, −7, 7, 17 d. −9, −7, 6, 8, 10 e. −101, −29, −11, 24, 50
9.a. 14, 11, 0, −7, −8 b. 15, 8, −5, −6, −12 c. 6, 1, 0, −3, −4 d. 8, 7, 3, −8, −9 e. 20, 10, −50, −150, −200
10.a. 6 b. −5 c. −6 d. 8 e. −9

Practice Exercise 4.2

1.a. −2 b. 4 c. 0 d. 0 e. 0
2.a. 257 b. (−255) c. 0 d. 90 e. (−88)

3.a. (−1) b. 41 c. (−43) d. 89 e. (−91)
4.a. 63 b. 86 c. 36 d. (−77) e. 34
5.a. (−18) b. (−14) c. 45 d. 45 e. (−111)
6.a. 54 b. 144 c. (−260) d. (−336) e. 92
7.a. 8 b. 12 c. (−11) d. (−201) e. 42
8.a. −252 b. (−20) c. 45 d. (−1) e. (−1)
9. 0 10. 4

Rewind (Chapter 3–4)

1. 27,200 2. 31,17,000
3.a. 90,00,000 b. 1,50,00,000
4.a. b. c.

5.a. 1,300 b. 2,000
6. 29 7. −1,301 8. 0 9. 108
10. −78

Practice Exercise 5.1

1.a. $\frac{3}{8}$ b. $\frac{2}{6}$ c. $\frac{5}{8}$ d. $\frac{1}{4}$ e. $\frac{3}{6}$
2.a. $\frac{2}{5}$ b. $\frac{3}{7}$ c. $\frac{5}{12}$ d. $\frac{7}{11}$ e. $\frac{6}{12}$
3.a. N = 7, D = 8 b. N = 11, D = 13 c. N = 5, D = 17 d. N = 31, D = 60 e. N = 19, D = 39
4.a. $\frac{3}{13}$ b. $\frac{2}{5}$ c. $\frac{1}{3}$ d. $\frac{7}{9}$ e. $\frac{5}{8}$
5.a. $\frac{9}{42}$ b. $\frac{8}{15}$ c. $\frac{17}{25}$ d. $\frac{7}{20}$ e. $\frac{3}{16}$
6. a, d
7.a. $2\frac{1}{3}$ b. $2\frac{1}{5}$ c. $4\frac{1}{6}$ d. $2\frac{2}{7}$ e. $3\frac{7}{8}$
8.a. $\frac{11}{5}$ b. $\frac{8}{7}$ c. $\frac{37}{11}$ d. $\frac{19}{2}$ e. $\frac{7}{3}$
9. a, b, e

Practice Exercise 5.2

1. b) c) d)
2. To write five equivalent fractions.
3.a. $\frac{8}{9}$ b. $\frac{13}{43}$ c. $\frac{4}{7}$ d. $\frac{11}{25}$ e. $\frac{5}{6}$
4.a. 16 b. 75 c. 104 d. 44 e. 6, 18, 24, 18
5.a. $<$ b. $<$ c. $=$ d. $<$ e. $>$
6.a. $\frac{1}{6}, \frac{5}{12}, \frac{2}{3}$ b. $\frac{5}{18}, \frac{7}{12}, \frac{11}{8}$ c. $\frac{3}{5}, \frac{7}{10}, \frac{5}{6}$ d. $\frac{3}{12}, \frac{5}{12}, \frac{7}{12}$ e. $\frac{2}{15}, \frac{4}{15}, \frac{7}{15}, \frac{11}{15}$
7.a. $\frac{5}{3}, \frac{2}{3}, \frac{1}{3}$ b. $\frac{5}{6}, \frac{7}{12}, \frac{1}{4}$ c. $\frac{3}{7}, \frac{3}{11}, \frac{3}{13}$ d. $\frac{7}{8}, \frac{1}{4}, \frac{1}{16}$
e. $\frac{11}{12}, \frac{5}{6}, \frac{2}{3}, \frac{4}{9}$
8. In science theory 9. Saturday
10. Section A

Practice Exercise 5.3

1.a. $\frac{2}{3}$ b. $\frac{9}{11}$ c. $\frac{13}{14}$ d. $7\frac{11}{24}$ e. $15\frac{1}{12}$
2.a. $\frac{4}{15}$ b. $\frac{2}{25}$ c. $2\frac{1}{3}$ d. $2\frac{8}{15}$ e. $3\frac{1}{9}$
3.a. $\frac{3}{5}$ b. $\frac{13}{21}$ c. $4\frac{4}{5}$ d. $1\frac{191}{200}$ e. $5\frac{21}{35}$
4. $\frac{1}{5}$ 5. Seema, $\frac{2}{35}$ km 6. $1\frac{2}{5}$ litres
7. $13\frac{1}{2}$ kg 8. $23\frac{1}{2}$ m 9. $1\frac{11}{12}$ hours
10. $\frac{29}{30}, \frac{1}{30}$

Test Yourself Unit 1

1.a. 63,979; 63,981
b. 84,999; 85,001
c. 86,540; 86,542
2.a. 67,200 b. 79,000 c. 7,60,000
3.a. LXXV b. DCLXXXIX c. MDCXCIX
4. 99,936
5.a. Not divisible b. Divisible c. Not divisible
6. 30 litres 7.a. 30 b. 5 c. 21
8. 1,254 9. ₹1,05,26,15,200
10. 19,210
11.a. −99, −26, −4, 0, 5 b. 90, 15, 0, −18, −75
c. −71, −23, 23, 27, 45
12.a. −126 b. 122 c. 20
13.

X	−5	−4	−3	−2	−1	0	1	2	3	4	5	6
−4	20	16	12	8	4	0	−4	−8	−12	−16	−20	−24
−3	15	12	9	6	3	0	−3	−6	−9	−12	−15	−18
−2	10	8	6	4	2	0	−2	−4	−6	−8	−10	−12
−1	5	4	3	2	1	0	−1	−2	−3	−4	−5	−6
0	0	0	0	0	0	0	0	0	0	0	0	0
1	−5	−4	−3	−2	−1	0	1	2	3	4	5	6
2	−10	−8	−6	−4	−2	0	2	4	6	8	10	12
3	−15	−12	−9	−6	−3	0	3	6	9	12	15	18
4	−20	−16	−12	−8	−4	0	4	8	12	16	20	24

14. $3\frac{1}{8}$ 15. $4\frac{1}{6}$ 16. $4\frac{3}{4}$

Answers

17.a. $\frac{2}{3}, \frac{11}{15}, \frac{3}{4}, \frac{28}{30}$ b. $\frac{1}{4}, \frac{2}{6}, \frac{5}{8}, \frac{11}{12}$ c. $\frac{5}{8}, \frac{2}{3}, \frac{3}{4}, \frac{8}{9}$

18. 9 19. 96 20. $1\frac{13}{33}$ m

Practice Exercise 6.1

1.a. 0.6 b. 0.09 c. 0.52 d. 0.057 e. 0.245
2.a. 0.15 b. 0.7 c. 0.045 d. 8.008 e. 222.02
3.a. 0.3 b. 0.11 c. 203.6 d. 147.03 e. 5000.05
4.a. 10,100 b. 10,100,1000 c. 81,10,100 d. 6,100,1000 e. 66,10,100,1000
5.a. $5 \times 1 + \frac{8}{10} + \frac{3}{100}$
b. $6 \times 10 + 2 \times 1 + \frac{3}{10} + \frac{7}{100}$
c. $1 \times 100 + 2 \times 10 + 5 \times 1 + \frac{4}{10}$
d. $1 \times 10 + 2 \times 1 + \frac{5}{10} + \frac{4}{100} + \frac{3}{1000}$
e. $3 \times 100 + 2 \times 10 + 6 \times 1 + \frac{5}{10} + \frac{4}{100} + \frac{3}{1000}$
6.a. 0.888 b. 3.123 c. 51.023 d. 111.111 e. 989.509
7.a. 2.4, 2.5, 2.6 b. 7.126, 7.127, 7.128 c. 16.1, 16.2, 16.3 d. 20.04, 20.05, 20.06 e. 152.4, 152.5, 152.6
8.a. 0.50, 0.500, 0.5000 b. 3.60, 3.600, 3.6000 c. 20.70, 20.700, 20.7000 d. 62.350, 62.3500, 62.35000 e. 146.90, 146.900, 146.9000
9.a. 0.5 b. 0.60 c. 0.85 d. 0.16 e. 0.058
10. To draw

Practice Excerice 6.2

1.a. $<$ b. $>$ c. $=$ d. $>$ e. $<$
2.a. 1.200, 2.150 b. 0.800, 10.810 c. 6.350, 6.530, 6.500 d. 9.01, 9.001, 9.100 e. 49.900, 4.990
3.a. 0.05, 0.15, 5.005, 5.115 b. 7.19, 7.39, 17.309, 17.390 c. 10.0, 10.01, 10.1, 10.105 d. 0.555, 5.55, 55.5, 5550 e. 1.427, 14.2, 14.25, 14.27
4.a. 42.3, 42.0, 4.23, 4.2, 0.423 b. 1.91, 1.21, 0.21, 0.19, 0.03 c. 666.5, 66.5, 55.6, 6.56, 0.665 d. 89.2, 89.1, 89.03, 89.02, 89.01 e. 1,991, 199.1, 19.91, 1.991
5.a. $\frac{19}{10} = 1\frac{9}{10}$ b. $\frac{27}{100}$ c. $\frac{3333}{10} = 333\frac{3}{10}$
d. $\frac{87003}{1000} = 87\frac{3}{1000}$ e. $\frac{4125}{1000} = 4\frac{1}{8}$
6.a. 0 1.7 b. 15.7 c. 2.57 d. 24.68 e. 2.219
7.a. 0.8 b. 2.25 c. 0.072 d. 0.418 e. 0.86
8.a. 9.6 b. 2.06 c. 13.375 d. 70.25 e. 7.16
9. Any three decimal less than in each part.
10. Any three decimals more than in each part.

Practice Exercise 6.3

1.a. 73.08 b. 108.999 c. 56.758 d. 112.005 e. 37.905
2.a. 17.21 b. 190.001 c. 126.395 d. 760.768 e. 3.568
3.a. 12.83 b. 15.869 c. 12.241 d. 106.863 e. 113.299
4. 38.45 5. 74.33 6. 2.7482
7. ₹205.85 8. Delhi, 20.9°C 9. 5.8 cm
10. 73.75 l

Rewind (Chapter 5–6)

1.a. $\frac{3}{5}$ b. $\frac{5}{9}$ c. $\frac{13}{7}$ d. $\frac{15}{4}$ e. $\frac{7}{11}$
2.a. $\frac{9}{15}$ b. $\frac{15}{55}$ c. $\frac{18}{48}$ d. $\frac{84}{108}$ e. $\frac{16}{52}$
3.a. $\frac{61}{36}$ b. $14\frac{5}{6}$ c. $\frac{3}{14}$ d. $\frac{173}{28}$ e. $3\frac{3}{4}$
4.a. 0.02 b. 0.006 c. 4.9 d. 0.16 e. 0.31
5.a. $\frac{5}{10}$ b. $\frac{9}{10}$ c. $\frac{35}{100}$ d. $\frac{3}{100}$ e. $\frac{97}{100}$
6.a. 29.858 b. 1.898 c. 52.1
7. ₹52.5 8. $3\frac{1}{5}$ litres
9. $\frac{19}{35}, \frac{4}{7}, \frac{3}{5}, \frac{2}{35}$ 10. 24.25 km

Practice Exercise 7.1

1.a. A, B, C b. $\overline{AB}, \overline{BC}, \overline{AC}$ c. $\overrightarrow{BA}, \overrightarrow{BC}$ d. $\overleftrightarrow{AC}$
2.a. R b. $\overrightarrow{OP}, \overrightarrow{OQ}$
3.a. $\overleftrightarrow{LM}$ b. $\overrightarrow{NL}, \overrightarrow{NM}, \overrightarrow{NS}, \overrightarrow{NT}$ c. $\overline{LN}, \overline{NM}$
d. L, N, M
4.a. X, Y, O, P and Q b. M, S, T, R and N c. A, B, C and D
6.a. One b. Infinite
7.a. Linear AB; Curved APB
b. Linear AB, BC, CD, DA; Curved DXB, DYB
c. Linear AB, BC, CD, AD, PQ, QR, RS, SP, CP, BS, AR, DQ
d. Linear AB, BC, CD, DA; Curved SP, PQ, QR, RS;
10.a. Line segment b. Ray c. Line d. Line segment e. Ray

Answers

Practice Exercise 7.2

1.a. Vertex O, arms $\overrightarrow{OP}$, $\overrightarrow{OQ}$ b. Vertex S, arms $\overrightarrow{SR}$, $\overrightarrow{ST}$ c. Vertex B, arms $\overrightarrow{BA}$, $\overrightarrow{BC}$
2.a. angles RSQ, PSQ b. angles EBD, CBD angles DBC, ABC, angles c. angles AOB, COB, angles AOX, AOB, COX, COB
3.a. X, Y, Z b. XY, YZ and ZX c. angles XYZ, YZX, ZXY
5. Yes. P is the common vertex.
6. Angles PMB, PMA, BMN, AMN, DNM, CNM, DNQ and CNQ
7.a. Midpoint b. Centroid c. Perpendicular d. acute e. right f. 180°
8.a. ℓ and m, m and n, ℓ and n b. p and q, p and r, ℓ and p, n and p, ℓ and q, m and q, n and q, ℓ and r, m and r, n and r. c. r and ℓ d. m, p and r e. Triangles ACD, ABD, DFG and AEG
9. 120° 10. 60°

Practice Exercise 7.3

1.a. Sides AB, BC, CD and DA; Vertices A, B, C and D. Angles ABC, BCD, CDA and DAB
b. Sides PQ, QR, RS, SP; Vertices P, Q, R, S; Angles PQR, QRS, RSP, SPQ
c. Sides LP, PN, NM, ML; Vertices L, P, N, M; Angles LPN, PNM, NML, MLP.
3.a. A, B, C, D b. O, L, M, N c. P, Q, R, S
4. 80°
6.a. ABCD, ADCB b. A, B, C, D c. AB, BC; BC, CD; CD, DA; DA, AB d. AB, DC; AD, BC e. AC and BD
7.a. Angles SPQ, PQR, QRS, RSP b. Angles P and Q, Q and S, R and S, R and P c. ∠RPQ and ∠RSP; ∠RQS and ∠SRP
8. 90° 9. 135°
10. No, the sum of the angles is greater than 360°

Practice Exercise 7.4

1. Concentric circles 2. Centre of the circle
3. Diameter 4 cm 4. In the major segment
5. Diameter

Practice Exercise 8.1

1.a. (ii) b. (i) c. (iii)
3. Acute angle (a) (f) (j) (l) (m)
Right (b)
Obtuse (c) (e) (i) (n)
Straight (g)
Reflex (d) (h) (k) (o)
Complete (p)
4.a. 90° b. 180° c. 270° d. 360° e. 90°
5.a. N b. W c. S d. E e. W
6.a. Equilateral b. Isosceles c. Scalene d. Isosceles e. Scalene
7.a. Yes, Obtuse b. Yes, Obtuse c. Yes, Right d. No e. No f. Yes, Right g. Yes, Acute h. No i. No j. No
8.a. Scalene b. Equilateral c. Isosceles d. Scalene e. Isosceles
9. 80° 10. 65°

Practice Exercise 8.2

1.a. True b. True c. False d. False e. False f. True g. True h. True i. True j. False
2. Parallelogram. CD = 8 cm, AD = 6 cm, ∠C = 120°, ∠B = 60°
3. Square 4. AB = AD, BC = CD, Yes 90°
5. Rectangle 6.a. In a square all sides are equal where as in a rectangle, opposite sides are equal b. In a square all interior angles are equal to 90° c. In an isosceles trapezium, the non-parallel sides are equal.
7.a. hexagon b. octagon c. decagon d. dodecagon e. quadrilateral
8. No. The sides are not equal 9. ∠P = ∠R = 120°, ∠Q = ∠S = 60°
10.a. Triangle b. Parallelogram c. Parallelogram d. Trapezium e. Parallelogram

Rewind (Chapter 7–8)

1.a. Point b. a line c. Plane d. Plane e. Line
2.a. A, B, C, D, E, F, G, H b. AB, BC, CD, DA, EF, FG, GH, HE, BF, CG, AE, DH, c. ABCD, BCGF, ADHE, EFGH, ABFE and CDHG
3. Definitions 4. Construction
5.a. T b. F c. T d. T e. T
6.a. Triangle b. Hexagon c. Nonagon d. Pentagon e. Decagon.
8.a. Cuboid b. Spherical c. Circular d. Cylinder e. Cylinder f. Conical g. Cylinder h. Cone i. Sperical j. Cuboid
9.a. 60°, obtuse b. 60°, acute c. 55°, right d. 45°, right e. 60°, acute

Answers

10. Parallelogram, WX = 8 cm, XV = 6.5 cm
∠V = 50° ∠W = 130°

Practice Exercise 10.1

1. Symmetrical a, d, e; Non-symmetrical b, c
4.a. Infinite b. Five c. Three d. Two e. None

Rewind (Chapter 9–10)

7. 120° 9. x = 130°, y = 130°, z = 50°

Test Yourself Unit II

1.a. A, B, C, D, E b. AB, BC, CD, DE, AE c. ∠A, ∠B, ∠C, ∠D, ∠E d. BE, BD e. Pentagon
2.a. AB, CD b. AC, BD c. OA, OB, OC, OD
3.a. three, three, three b. line, midpoint
c. perpendicular
5.a. F b. F c. T d. T e. F
6. i) acute ii) obtuse iii) obtuse iv) Straight
v) reflex vi) complete vii) acute viii) obtuse
ix) reflex x) acute xi) right xii) acute
xiii) reflex xiv) reflex xv) acute
7.b. acute angled c. obtuse angled d. right angled e. Equiangular

Practice Exercise 11.1

1.a. 7y b. 6 + x c. $x^2 + 2x - 6$ d. x + y = 2
e. 10x + 4y f. a = b + 7 g. a = c − 9
h. $\frac{1}{4}x - 8$ i. $t^2 + 10$ j. (a + b − c)d
2.a. x plus 7 b. 2x minus 3 c. y plus 1 divided by 3 d. a plus b minus c divided by d e. 10 times a plus b multiplied by c
3.a. 10 b. 7 c. 1 d. 2 e. 9
4.a. 25y b. 3 c. 2p d. −10 e. $9y + 19y^2$
5.a. 3-Trinomial b. 2-Binomial c. 1-monomial
d. 6-polynomial e. 1-monomial
6. Like Terms:
a. x^2y, $7yx^2$; x^2, $3x^2$ b. 10pq, 7pq c. m, 14m
d. pqr, 15pqr e. a^2, $10a^2$; c^2, $-c^2$

7.	Number of terms	Kind of algebraic Experession	Factors of each term
a.	2	Binomial	
b.	3	Trinomial	
c.	1	Monomial	
d.	4	Polynomial	
e.	3	Trinomial	

8.a. −2pq b. $5x^2$ c. 16a d. 35xyz e. $5m^2$
9.a. 5x + 10y b. p + 2 c. (x + 27) ÷ 10
d. h − 5 e. x + 7, x − 7, 3(x + 7)
10.a. 21 b. 31 c. 9 d. 16 e. 0

Practice Exercise 12.1

1.a. Expression b. Equation c. Expression
d. Equation e. Expression
2.a. 5x + 3 = 23 b. 7x − 10 = 95 c. 4x = 100 d. $\frac{1}{5}x + 21 = 41$ e. d = 2r
3.a. 3 b. 6 c. 5 d. 3 e. 3
4. a. 3 b. 10 c. 7 d. 1 e. 0
5. a. 2 b. 10 c. 2 d. 13 e. 2
6.a. 12 b. 17 c. 3 d. 5 e. 7
7. 10 8. ₹10 9. 14, 15, 16
10. 44, 11 11. 60 12. 9 cm

Rewind (Chapter 11–12)

1.a. 7b b. 3x + 5 c. Unlike d. Like e. 1
2.a. Monomial b. Binomial c. Trinomial
d. Monomial e. Binomial
3.a. 5z + 10 = 25 b. $\frac{x}{2} + 7 = 21$ c. $\frac{p}{4} - 2 = 6$
d. 3(x + y) = 27 e. $x^2 = 49$
4.a. 9 b. 11 c. 9 d. 5 e. 35
5.a. 6 b. 1 c. 51 d. 23 e. 12
6. 6 7. 12, 20 8. ₹75
9. 43, 45, 47 10. length = 21 m, breadth = 7 m

Practice Exercise 13.1

1.a. $\frac{1}{3}$ b. $\frac{1}{3}$ c. $\frac{4}{7}$ d. $\frac{3}{19}$ e. $\frac{2}{13}$
2.a. 3:7 b. 5:14 c. 1:4 d. 5:1 e. 3:5
3.a. 5:3 b. 5:9 c. 3:4 d. 1:5 e. 3:5
4.a. 4:7 b. 9:11 c. 3:10 d. 7:9 e. 5:32
5.a. 3:4, 2:3, 1:2 b. 9:11, 7:9, 2:3 c. 5:7, 6:13, 3:14 d. 11:30, 7:20, 3:10 e. 3:8, 5:24, 7:48
6. 18 7. Lollypops 210, Chocolates 270
8.a. 2:3 b. 1:3 c.1:2
9.a. 5:7 b. 5:12 c.7:12, 7:12 10. 200, 160, 360

Practice Exercise 13.2

1.a. 8 b. 3 c. 9 d. 15 e. 14 f. 6 g. 40
h. 49 i. 12 j. 1
2. b, d
3.a. 3:9 :: 9:27 b. 12:36 :: 36:108 c. 2:8 ::8:32
d.10:15 :: 15:20 e. 4:6 :: 6:9

Answers

4.a. 27 b. 15 c. 8 d. 20 e. 24
5.a. 1 b. 10 c. 42 d. 54 e. 100
6. 24 7. 210 kg 8. ₹1,40,000
9. 6 hrs 10. 8 days

Practice Exercise 13.3

1. $666\frac{2}{3}$ km 2. ₹288 3. ₹3080
4. ₹10,500 5. ₹225 6. 52.5 litres
7. 31 8. 38,400 9. 6,750 bags
10. 6 Cartons

Rewind Chapter 13

1.a. 1:4 b. 1:10 c. 7:12 d. 1:5 e. 2:5
2. 7:6 3. Milk 500 gm, Chocolate 200 gms
4. ₹2,100, ₹3,500, ₹4,900
5.a. 1:7 b. 7:6 c. 1:6
6.a. 15 b. 95 c. 145 d. 31 e. 70
7.a. i) 135 ii) 40 iii) 126 b. i) 20 ii) 60 iii) 72
8. ₹112.50 9. 5 days 10. 750 km

Practice Exercise 14.1

1.a. 48 b. 50 c. 39 2.a. 27 cm b. 21 cm
c. 24 cm 3.a. 12 cm b. 9 cm c. 20 cm
4. ₹1200 5. 400 m 6. Raj, 90 m
7. 60 trees 8. ₹735 9. 12.5 m
10. 250 m

Practice Exercise 14.2

1.a. 225 sq m b. 1.21 sq m c. 56.25 sq cm
2. 405 sq m 3. ₹96,52,500
4. 31.25 sq m 5. 54 m 6. 101 sq m
7. 774 sq m 8. 625 sq m, ₹8,125
9. Mr. Mathur gets the larger plot, 625 sq m more
10. ₹1,080, ₹31,500

Practice Exercise 15.1

2. 28
3. IIII, 𝍸 II, 𝍸 𝍸, 𝍸 I, III, 40°C, 36°C
7.a. 100 b. 50 c. 80 d. 30 e. 4
8.a. И b. Ⓨ c. S
9.a. 2009–2010 b. 2005–2006, 2008–2009
c. 60
10.a. 15 hours b. 18 hours c. 18

Practice Exercise 15.2

1.a. Saturday b. 30 c. 10 d. Monday e. 440
2.a. M, 50 b. A c. B, D d. 5, e. 225
6.3. Lucknow 6.4. 700 6.5. 100
6.6. 900 6.7. 4100
7. i) Rainfall during a week ii) Friday iii) Thursday
iv) Monday and Wednesday 25 cm v) 40 cm
vi) 25 cm vii) 170 cm
8. 500
9. i) Wednesday ii) Saturday iii) 1950
10.a. 40 b. School Bus c. 250

Rewind (Chapter 14–15)

1.a. 44 cm b. 42 cm c. 19 cm
2. 12 cm
3.a. Increases 4 times b. Increase 9 times
c. Reduced by one-fourth
4. Square plot, 2304 m^2 5. 12,500 m^2
6. 1040 tiles 7.a. 66 cm^2 b. 39 m^2
8.a. Area 22 m^2, Perimeter 34 m b. Area 76 m^2,
Perimeter 80 m

Test Yourself Unit III

1.a. $35 + x$ b. $4x + y$ c. $\frac{p}{q} + p \times q$
2.a. 1 b. 6 c. 0 d. 12 e. 6
3.a. $-8x$ b. -5 c. -2 d. mx e. 18xz
4.a. monomial b. monomial c. monomial
d. trinomial e. monomial
5.a. True b. True c. True
6.a. 1 b. 9 c. 6 d. 3 e. 2
7. 37 years, 61 years 8. 5n, 31
9.a. 1:3 b. 7:10 c. 6:25 d. 3:4 e. 1:10
10.a. 7:3 b. 7:10 c. 3:10
11.a. 40 b. 27 c. 100
12. 288
13.a. 120 cm b. 140 cm c. 34 cm
14. 3.6 m 15. 12 m, 2m 16. ₹17,575
18.a. Representation of students in various S.U.P.W clubs b. six c. Number of students d. Dance club e. Maths club f. 60
20.a. Mon 40, Tue 35, Wed 55, b. Sat
c. Wednesday d. Monday, Friday e. 210

Model Sample Test Paper

1. Place value 8,00,000 Face Value 8
2. 68,430 3. 39:59

Answers

4. i. P and Q ii. $\overline{PQ}$
5. Rhombus
7. i. $27 - p$ ii. $\frac{c}{4} + 7$
8. 42
9. Rectangle and Parallelogram
10. Cube has all sides equal whereas cuboid has l, b, and h different.
11. 18 12. 186 13. 36.144
15. i. 9 subtracted from x is equal to 18
    ii. Nine times 'y' is equal to 108
16. 51,000
17. Educated 64,396 Uneducated 3,86,376
18. -51
19. $\frac{18}{8}, 2\frac{4}{7}, \frac{19}{6}, \frac{18}{5}$; Difference $\frac{27}{20}$
20. ₹257.55
21.a. OA, OQ, OP b. PQ c. SR d. PTQ, PRQ e. SR f. O
22.a. 15.5 b. 7 c. 13
23. $2y - 10$, G.F. 30, F.F. 20
24. ₹9,000
25.a. Saturday b. Wednesday c. 80
26.a. 120 b. 124
27. 8,800, 4,800 28. 1,37,500 sq m ₹4,12,500

Assessment of Mathematical Skills				
	Exceptional	**Good**	**Average**	**Needs Improvement**
Notation and Terminology	Uses appropriate mathematical terminology and notation	Uses near correct mathematical terminology and notation	Partial or scattered usage of mathematical terms and notation	Shows incorrect or no understanding of terms and notations of mathematical concepts
Problem Solving/ Strategising	Is able to efficiently analyse a problem and arrive at an efficient solution	Is able to draw on prior knowledge and arrive at an appropriate solution	Shows some evidence of using concepts learnt resulting in only a partially correct solution	Is unable to apply concepts learnt. Faces difficulties in arriving at a solution.
Methodology, Formulation and Steps	Uses clear effective steps and reasonings to demonstrate the solution	Uses appropriate steps to arrive at the solution	Is able to use steps at times but falters at others	Is unable to identify steps and formulae needed for arriving at the solution, and hence arrives at incorrect solutions.
Calculation and Final Result	Is able to calculate and arrive at the final answer with accuracy and precision	Is able to calculate and arrive at the final answer with a fair level of accuracy	Resists advanced computations and tends to perform incomplete or erroneous calculations	Is prone to calculation errors. Limited understanding of units.

Assessment of Mathematical Skills				
	Exceptional	**Good**	**Average**	**Needs Improvement**
Geometry	Has a clear and visual understanding of the relationship between geometrical figures	Has a fairly good understanding of the relationship between various geometrical figures and is able to visualise concepts with minimum assistance	Is able to understand simple geometrical concepts, but falters while visualising concepts or tackling advanced concepts	Has a high level of difficulty in understanding and recalling geometrical concepts and needs assistance at visualising the solution
Mensuration	Has a clear and visual understanding of mensuration concepts and is able to translate real-world problems to math	Has a good understanding of mensuration concepts and is able to visualise and solve problems with minimum errors	Is able to understand simple mensuration concepts but falters while visualising or solving real-world problems.	Has a high level of difficulty in understanding and visualising 3-D-shapes. Needs assistance in attempting a solution
Algebra	Has a clear understanding of algebraic patterns and formulae and is able to formulate approaches to a problem	Has a good understanding of algebraic patterns and formulae and is able to formulate appropriate solution	Is able to solve simple algebraic problems but has trouble identifying complicated patterns	Has a high level of difficulty in identifying and remembering patterns and needs assistance in attempting a solution